Contents

Preface v
Letter From the Directors vii
Introduction iv

Section One: *Learning*
Learning 2 Peter 1 1
Learning 2 Peter 2 21
Learning 2 Peter 3 41
Learning Jude 57

Section Two: *Applying*
Applying: Lesson 1: *Determined to Increase* 87
Applying: Lesson 2: *Determined to Pay Attention* 99
Applying: Lesson 3: *Determined to Do Right* 109
Applying: Lesson 4: *Determined to Be Right* 121
Applying: Lesson 5: *Determined to Stand* 133

Section Three: *Building*
Building: Lesson 1: *Pay Attention to What True Faith Makes You!* 145
Building: Lesson 2: *Pay Attention to Those Who Try to Fake You!* 159
Building: Lesson 3: *Pay Attention to Where True Faith Takes You!* 175
Building: Lesson 4: *Pay Attention to the Words That Save You!* 191
Building: Lesson 5: *Pay Attention to What He Expects of You!* 207

Section Four: *Special Study*
Are We Looking for a New Heavens and a New Earth? 223
Romans 8 and Eschatology 237
Dual Fulfillment Prophecies 241
What do We Know About Heaven? 245
Does a Physical "New Earth" Demand a Physical "New Body?" 255

Section Five: *Sermon Seeds* 263

About the Authors 291

Kaio Publications recognizes that the topic of new heavens and new earth is the cause of many discussions and even disagreements today. We encourage readers to engage in their own diligent study of God's Word to deepen their understanding. The articles and discussions in this book are the result of each author's diligent research and study into the subjects addressed. Each author's thoughts and conclusions are their own, having reached them after much study. We earnestly encourage readers to approach Scripture on any topic with reverence, maintaining an open mind and steadfast commitment to seeking God's truth. We publish these hoping they spark study, discussion, and unity—even if we reach differing conclusions.

Preface

Thank you for your interest in the Excel Still More Bible Workshop! Our hope is that this book will be of great use to you and your study as well as a great blessing to your ministry. The E.S.M. Bible Workshop is designed to take us into a deeper study of God's Word. The method is simple: Learn, Apply, and Build. We believe that in using this pattern of study, we can grow stronger in the Lord by digging deep, applying it to our lives, and building a stronger faith by using tools that we find in the text.

In years past we have attended workshops such as the Workshop in the Word held in Durango, Colorado. The workshop was designed to teach the New Testament books in an exegetical fashion by digging deep into the text to get a better grasp of knowledge from that text. After several years, the workshop ended, and we yearned for that type of workshop again.

Ideas were exchanged, conversations were had, and the workshop started to form. A name for the workshop that continued to stand out was from the words of Paul in 1 Thessalonians 4:1,10: "Excel Still More." It was then that the workshop was born, and we knew this was something we had to do.

Our goal is to simply provide a great workshop and study tool to help us in our everyday study of the Bible. A deep study of the context reveals many things about the writer and his writing. We want to help in providing tools to grasp the context of each text, make application to our lives, and find faith builders that will help us grow stronger in the Lord and in our everyday walk.

As we began to collaborate, we knew exactly whom we wanted to partner with for this wonderful project: Denny Petrillo and Joe Wells. Through their many years of study, teaching, and hands-on work for the Kingdom, they bring much knowledge and ability to the table that make them amply capable to delve into the text with us.

We are very excited about this endeavor because we believe that it is something that will help us on our path to Heaven! Our efforts are completely geared toward providing material that will help us grow as disciples of Jesus and continue to transform our lives. We also know that as our lives are transformed by God and His Word, we will be better prepared to live and share that Word so He can change and transform those around us.

So, throughout your time in this study, grow! Grow in the Lord and excel still more in your knowledge, application, and faith because your soul depends on it, your family depends on it, and the Church depends on it. Grow because the world needs you to excel in finding those who are lost and guiding them to Jesus. Grow because your family needs you to excel in teaching them about Jesus and showing them how to live, walk, and be like Jesus—moving mountains to direct the hearts and minds of the lost to our risen Savior!

Each year we will strive to put out a wonderful, Bible-filled workshop that lays a strong foundation for growth in the knowledge of God's Word. We hope and pray this book will wind up on the shelves of people all over the world and help us all continue to learn His Word, apply it, and build a stronger faith!

Excel Still More!

Letter From the Directors

Dear friends,

Thank you so much for your interest in the *Excel Still More* Bible Workshop! We truly want this work to be something that lifts you up in your study, faith, and relationship with the Lord.

Our hope in this great study is simple: to help you learn the text, apply the text, and build a strong faith. Our faith and spirituality are our foundation in Christ that will drive us to reach our goal of Heaven, and through this work we intend to do all we can to help you achieve this goal. As Christians we want to grow in the grace and knowledge of our Lord Jesus Christ, and we pray this book and workshop will be tools to help us all do that.

Our intent for this work is to provide an easy-to-use book with reliable resources, so you can gain profitable knowledge from the text. We are so thankful for all of the authors of this book. Their efforts and work in the Lord's Kingdom have blessed so many, and we are thankful for their contributions to the work of the Excel Still More Bible Workshop!

Our prayers are with you as you embark on this study of 2 Peter and Jude. Grow as you learn, apply, and build to become a spiritual champion, fighting the good fight of faith for the Lord as a servant warrior to the King. Excel Still More, friends, and the Lord will bless you more abundantly than you ever thought possible!

Excel Still More Bible Workshop Directors

Introduction

The *Excel Still More* Bible Workshop is directed toward a deep study of a particular book or topic of the Bible. Our platform is a simple three-step pattern.

1. **Learn the text.**
2. **Apply the text.**
3. **Build off of the text.**

With these three objectives in mind, which we call the "L.A.B. Technique," we will be studying the book of 2 Peter and Jude in an exegetical, applicable, and buildable fashion. It is our goal to always be honest with the text in every way, by looking not only at what the writer had to say but also why he said it, who it was said to, and what it meant to them. By studying the text with an open and honest heart, we can be very open minded in the way that we study the text.

Paul wrote, *"Be diligent to present yourself approved to God as a workman who does not need to be ashamed, accurately handling the word of truth"* (2 Tim. 2:15).

We surely want to be accurate in our understanding of what the Holy Spirit has divinely given to us, so we can accurately handle that wonderful truth in our daily lives. This great truth that has come from God is what guides us as ministers, preachers, elders, deacons, fathers, husbands, mothers, wives, teachers, and followers of Jesus. To have salvation we must know the truth, to grow in our faith we must have the truth, and to lead the Church and our families, we must live the truth.

Jesus said, *"If you continue in My word, then you are truly disciples of Mine; and you will know the truth, and the truth will make you free"* (Jn. 8:31-32).

The truth is what we are interested in, it is what we are searching for, and it is what we want to live our lives by. The truth of God given through the Holy Spirit and written by the pen of man is the revelation of God's grace to mankind, revealing His plan of salvation given through His Son. God has revealed His Word and His way to us, blessing our lives beyond all measure by telling us of His creation, His power, His plan, His love, His truth, and His grace. Without the revelation of God given to all of humanity, we would not have any knowledge of God or His Son. How blessed we are that we have a God who loves us so much that not only did He send His Son, but He also gave us His Word to tell us about Him.

God has given us His Word. It tells us just how important the truth is, but it also emphasizes how vital it is that we grow in that truth. This is precisely where this workshop comes into play. We know the truth is important, and we know just how important it is for that truth to transform our lives in every way. However, it is up to us to put forth the effort to grow in His truth. It is an effort that should not be taken lightly. It is our hope that this workshop is yet another tool to add to your arsenal to fight against all that Satan throws at you as you build a stronger faith through the wonderful study!

Paul wrote, *"Finally then, brethren, we request and exhort you in the Lord Jesus, that as you received from us instruction as to how you ought to walk and please God (just as you actually do walk), that you excel still more"* (1Thess. 4:1).

To *"excel still more"* is to achieve that which is set in front of you. In our case Heaven has been set in front of us, and it is up to us to walk in a manner worthy of Heaven. When I excel, I grow; when I excel still more, I grow and grow and grow! What does this mean? It means that I never stop growing! I never stop growing in the truth of God's Word!

John wrote, *"But whoever keeps His word, in him the love of God has truly been perfected. By this we know that we are in Him: the one who says he abides in Him ought himself to walk in the same manner as He walked"* (1 Jn. 2:5-6).

I am to walk in truth as Jesus walked in truth, and the only way to begin to do that is to know the truth. Jesus Himself said that the truth would be that which would sanctify us (John 17:17). It is by that wonderful truth that we have become the sanctified (Acts 26:18; Heb. 10:10). Those who are sanctified are those who have been set apart, and those who are set apart are those who have been *"rescued from the domain of darkness and transferred to the Kingdom of His beloved Son"* (Col. 1:13).

We who are the set apart are to be set apart in every aspect of our lives—set apart in how we love, how we act, how we study, how we live, how we lead, how we follow, and by our knowledge of God's wonderful Word. For this task of growing in our knowledge of His truth, we at the *Excel Still More Bible Workshop* have developed a method of study that we hope will be of great value to you as you study the Word of God. This method is very simple and is the pattern of this book.

Each chapter will be separated into three sections.

Section #1: Learn—This section will cover the exegesis of the chapter. It is designed to go through the text in a verse-by-verse fashion, identifying key words, phrases, and verses. Every word in each verse is important because it gives you the meaning of what is being said. It is a well-known fact that the context of a verse is everything. Looking at the context allows us to define words of importance. This requires examining the original language in which the Scriptures were written. Those languages consist of Hebrew, Aramaic, and Kione Greek. Denny Petrillo will be leading us in the exegesis of 2 Peter and Jude.

Section #2: Apply— his section will take all that we have learned in the exegesis and make application to our everyday lives. While the exegesis of the passage is of the upmost importance, the application is crucial as well. A person may know the Bible from front to back and have every word memorized, but if he isn't able to apply what he has learned, he has fallen short of what really matters. To apply the text is to grow from the text. It means that I realize the right way to live, love, and submit myself—now I want to do it. Paul wrote in Roman 12:2, "And do not be conformed to this world, but be transformed by the renewing of your mind, so that you may prove what the will of God is, that which is good and acceptable and perfect." The transformation of the heart is due to the realization that I must change. The Word is what tells me that I need to change and how I need to change. Therefore, the application portion is vitally important to the learning of each passage. Joe Wells will be directing our thoughts on exactly how we can apply each passage to our lives.

Section #3: Build—This section will introduce "faith builders." By this point we have studied the passage exegetically and made application of the text to our lives. Now we will be looking for different ways to build our faith from the text itself. We need a firm understanding of just how important it is to not only build faith but to build our own faith. I can't get to Heaven on someone else's faith, just like I can't earn a master's degree through someone else's study and hard work. I must have my own faith to get there. When I have my own faith, which is rooted in the Word of God, I can then share it! I share it with my wife, my children, the brethren, and the world. A strong faith can do all things because the faithful trust in God. Garrett Bernethy will be directing our thoughts in the building sessions.

Learning the text, applying the text, and building from the text (L.A.B) is vital to our daily walk. Incorporating these three methods of learning can and will give you the strength to handle all situations in life. It will better prepare you as a preacher, elder, or deacon in the Church. It will better prepare you as a father or mother, husband, or wife, as you strive to take your family to Heaven. It will provide you with the right tools to parent your children in the discipline and instruction of the Lord. Why? Because you will have the Word of the Lord in your "mind," you will live the Word in your "actions," you will be faithful to the Word in your "direction." Mind, action, and direction all pointed one way—toward the Lord.

The challenge of this book is simple: *Excel Still More* in all that you do. Excel for the Lord, excel in His Word, excel in His ways, and excel in His work. When you excel, so does your marriage, your family, your children, and the Church. By excelling still more in the Lord, you will bring about change that causes transformation to a world that usually does nothing but conform. So be the one who excels in all you do and be the effective change to a world that needs you!

Learning
2 Peter 1

DENNY PETRILLO

INTRODUCTORY NOTES

A. Authorship

1. As with the first epistle, Peter identifies himself as the author of the letter in the first verse. As usual, there are those who question this statement: "Even though the writer of this letter identifies himself in the Greek as *Symeōn Petros*, there are problems in determining his real identity" (Arichea and Hatton, 63). For centuries, conservative scholars have scrambled to provide evidence for Petrine authorship of this epistle. However, the burden of proof is on those rejecting the clear claim of verse 1, *not on the person accepting the claim of verse 1*.

2. It is admitted that there is a lack of attestation from early Christian writers. However, this does not provide a death blow to Petrine authorship. Consider the words of Blum: "Although it is true that 2 Peter is not mentioned by name by writers in the second century, several things may account for this. For one thing, the brevity of 2 Peter, its remote destination, and the persecution of its recipients could have led to the lack of any second-century reference to it. Also, we need to remember that much of the literature of the early church has not survived. For example, many, if not most, of the writings of Origen (c. 185–c. 254) are not extant. The odds against writings of the second century surviving were very high. Again, there is, as already has been said, some evidence of traces of 2 Peter in second-century writers" (259).

3. Logic does not support the claim that the book is a pseudograph: "If epistolary pseudepigraphy was rejected by Christians, then who would have written this letter? Hardly a good man! If it had been a false teacher, what was his motivation? After all, the book does not seem to have any distinctive views that would require presentation under an assumed name" (Blum 261).

4. "Second Peter was acknowledged as Scripture by Origen (c. 240) who said, 'Peter…has left one acknowledged epistle, and, it may be, a second also; for it is doubted.' Eusebius placed it among the disputed books rather than among the spurious writings. By the time of Cyril of Jerusalem (c. 315–86), 2 Peter was considered canonical; and Cyril's acceptance of it as well as its acceptance by Athanasius, Augustine, and Jerome settled the issue for the early church.

These leaders acknowledged 2 Peter to be Scripture because the evidence, both internal and external, showed its solid worth" (Blum 261).

5. Internal evidence is strong for the letter to have been written by the apostle. In addition to the claim of 1:1, he groups himself with the other apostles (1:1), claims to be an eyewitness to the Transfiguration (1:17-18), and groups himself among the prophets (1:18-21). Equally, he claims this is his second letter (3:1).

6. Arguments for a pseudonymous letter have serious issues (Blum 255-61). Logic is that the text should be accepted according to its claim: it is from the apostle Peter.

B. Date & Place of Writing

1. 1. Peter implies that a majority of Paul's writings (if not all of them) were composed when he penned this letter (3:15-16). That would require the book to come after 60 A.D.
2. He seems to be aware that his death is near (1:15).
3. Many favor Rome as the place of writing. However, it is known that Peter did a lot of traveling, and so it is conceivable that the letter was penned from one of those locations.
4. As a result, I believe Peter wrote the epistle probably around 64-68 A.D.

C. Destination

1. In 3:1 Peter says, "This is now, beloved, the second letter I am writing to you…." If this is a reference to 1 Peter, then this second letter is also addressed to Christians who are scattered throughout "Pontus, Galatia, Cappadocia, Asia and Bithynia" (1 Pet. 1:1).
2. These are all churches found in Asia Minor, with a majority of the locations found in modern-day Turkey. Silvanus probably visited these areas in the order Peter lists them when he carried to them the letter (cf. 1 Pet. 5:12).

D. Recipients

1. These early Christians were facing serious challenges to their relationship with Christ. Foremost of those challenges was an intense persecution that brought untold misery and suffering (1 Pet. 1:6-7; 2:18-20; 3:1, 13-17; 4:1-4, 12-19; 5:10).
2. If we believe the same group is now receiving this epistle, then they have persisted in their faith for several more years (depending on the dates for both epistles. No more time, however, then 6 years).
3. These Christians are now dealing with challenges from false teachers (chap. 2) and those who doubt the promise of the Second Coming.

Learning 2 Peter 1

E. Purpose/Occasion of Writing

1. The list of key words below gives us a clear view of the major areas of discussion and concern in this epistle. In addition, biblical exegetes recognize the importance of purpose statements in inspired writings. Fortunately, Peter supplies us with such a purpose statement in 3:1-2: "This is now, beloved, the second letter I am writing to you in which I am stirring up your sincere mind by way of reminder, that you should remember the words spoken beforehand by the holy prophets and the commandment of the Lord and Savior spoken by your apostles."

    a. *A reminder that they have all the information they need to live faithfully (1:3).* The false teachers, whom Peter will address in chapter 2, are continually trying to unsettle these Christians in both their faith in the Gospel and in their knowledge of the truth. Peter assures them that they have all they need. They have "the prophetic word made more sure" (1:19-21).

    b. *Encouragement to grow (1:5-9).* Christians are not designed to be static. Rather, they take measured steps to improve—both in conduct and knowledge (cf. 3:18).

    c. *Encouragement to escape corruption (1:4, 9).* God's people mirror His holiness (cf. 1 Pet. 1:18). They are not going to follow the false teachers who encourage sensuality (2:2), "indulge the flesh in its corrupt desires" (2:10) or allow their lusts to deny God's promises (3:3).

    d. *A warning about false teachers (2:1-22).* These powerful enemies of the truth wield considerable influence, to the extent that "many will follow" them (2:2). Peter warns the Christians that they are "forsaking the right way" (2:15).

    e. *A reminder that God knows how to rescue the godly and punish the disobedient (2:4-9).* Christians must never lose sight of the sovereignty of God. He has everything under control and will eventually bring all into Judgment.

    f. *A warning about false doctrine (3:1-15).* Peter devoted considerable time in chapter 2 discussing the men themselves who teach error. Here he concentrates on their insidious doctrine.

F. Themes and Theology

There are many great themes to identify, but here are a few:

1. *God is in control.* The name of "God" (θεός) is found 9 times in this short epistle. When we add the references to Jesus (9 times), the Lord (14 times) and Christ (8 times), we have an impressive 40 references to deity. That is an *average* of 13 references *per chapter!* It is easy to see that this is a book about God and His work. Despite the influence of the false teachers (2:1-22), God will bring them to judgment (2:9).

2. *The importance of knowledge.* False teachers have always had one major approach: get people to believe their information is faulty or insufficient. The false teachers in 2 Peter are no different. They "malign" the way of truth (2:2) and "exploit you with false words" (2:3). Peter assures them that God's "divine power has granted to us everything pertaining to life and godliness" (1:3), immediately disarming the need for the false teachers. He promises them that they have "the true knowledge of Him who called us" (1:3), and that His promises enable Christians to win the battle against sin (1:4). Note that "knowledge" occurs 14 times in the book!

3. *Understanding righteousness.* As noted in the key word list, the word for righteousness is found 12 times in this epistle. Noah (2:5) and Lot (2:7-8) serve as examples of righteousness. Their goal is to be a part of the new heavens and new earth, "where righteousness dwells" (3:13).

4. *Judgment Day.* There is a coming "day of God" (3:12), therefore they must "be found…spotless and blameless" (3:14)

5. *This evil world.* This world and the men who live in it are corrupt (φθορά—1:4; 2:12[2], 19). It is important for Christians to see them as God sees them. When they do, they will not give the corrupt men the respect and attention they crave.

6. *This power of lust.* The attitude that motivates the wicked of this world (i.e., the false teachers) is lust (ἐπιθυμία—1:4; 2:10, 18; 3:3). This lust is ultimately a challenge to the power of God.

7. *Christ is coming.* At the Parousia of Christ (παρουσία—1:16; 3:4, 12) there will be a final judgment (κρίσις) where God will deal with these wicked men (2:4, 9, 11; 3:7). Their end will be destruction (ἀπώλεια—2:1[2], 3, 7, 16).

8. *Follow Jesus.* If Christians continue to follow the Savior (1:1, 11; 2:20; 3:2, 18) they will be considered godly (εὐσέβεια—1:3, 6, 7; 2:9; 3:11) rather than ungodly (ἀσεβής—2:5, 6, 3:7)

G. Key Words and Phrases

1. *Knowledge* (γνῶσις) — 14 times (1:2, 3, 5, 6, 8, 16, 20; 2:12, 20, 21[2]; 3:3, 17, 18). {οἶδα — 3 times — 1:12, 14; 2:9}

2. *Lord* (κύριος) — 14 times (1:2, 8, 11, 14, 16; 2:9, 10, 20; 3:2, 8, 9, 10, 15, 18). Note: "our Lord"— 8 times (1:2, 8, 11, 14, 16; 2:20; 3:15, 18).

3. *Righteous/just* (δίκαιος) — 12 times (1:1, 13; 2:5, 7, 8[2], 9, 13[2], 15, 21; 3:13).

4. *Day* (ἡμέρα) — 12 times (1:19; 2:8[2], 9, 13, 3:3, 7, 8[2], 10, 12, 18).

5. *God* (θεός) — 9 times (1:1, 2, 3, 4, 17, 21; 2:4; 3:5, 12).

6. *Jesus* (Ἰησοῦς) — 9 times (1:1[2], 2, 8, 11, 14, 16; 2:20, 3:18).

7. *Glory* (δόξα/ εὐδοκέω) — 9 times (1:3, 17[3]; 2:10; 3:12, 13, 14, 18).

8. *Christ* (Χριστός) — 8 times (1:1[2], 8, 11, 14, 16; 2:20; 3:18).

9. *Love* (ἀγάπη) – 8 times (1:7, 17; 2:15; 3:1, 8, 14, 15, 17).

10. *Godly* (ἅγιος) — 8 times (1:3, 6, 7; 2:5, 6, 9; 3:7, 11).

11. *Judgment* (κρίσις) — 7 times (2:3, 4, 6, 9, 11; 3:1, 7).

12. Destruction words:

    a. *Destruction* (ἀπώλεια) --5 times (2:1[2], 3; 3:7, 16); ἀπόλλυμι—2 times (3:6, 9)

    b. *Corruption/Destruction* (φθείρω) – 5 times (1:4; 2:12[3], 19)

    c. *Destroy* (λύω) — 4 times (1:20; 3:10, 11, 12)

13. *Way/road* (ὁδός) — 6 times (1:11, 15; 2:2, 15[2], 21).

14. *Save/Savior* (σωτήρ) — 6 times (1:1, 11; 2:20; 3:2, 15, 18).
15. *Prophet* (προφήτης) — 6 times (1:19, 20, 21; 2:1, 16, 3:2).
16. *Promise* (ἐπαγγελία) — 5 times (1:4; 2:19; 3:4, 9, 13.
17. *Remember* (ὑπόμνησις) — 5 times (1:12, 13, 15; 3:1, 2).
18. *Diligent* (σπουδάζω) — 5 times (1:5, 10, 15; 3:12, 14).

H. Outlines

Various outlines from commentators:

1. Schreiner (282)
I. Greeting (1:1–2)
II. God's Grace the Foundation for a Life of Godliness (1:3-11)
   1. Divine Provision (1:3-4)
   2. Pursue a Godly Life Diligently (1:5-7)
   3. Godly Virtues Necessary for Entrance into the Kingdom (1:8-11)
III. Peter's Apostolic Reminder (1:12-21)
   1. The Function of the Reminder: To Stir Them for Action (1:12-15)
   2. The Truth of Jesus' Coming Is Based on Eyewitness Testimony (1:16-18)IV.
   3. The Truth of Jesus' Coming Is Based on the Prophetic Word (1:19-21)
IV. The Arrival, Character, and Judgment of False Teachers (2:1-22)
   1. The Impact of False Teachers (2:1-3)
   2. The Certain Judgment of the Ungodly and the Preservation of the Godly (2:4-10a)
   3. False Teachers Judged for Their Rebellion and Sensuality (2:10b-16)
   4. The Adverse Impact of the False Teachers on Others (2:17-22)
V. Reminder: The Day of the Lord Will Come (3:1-18)
   1. Scoffers Doubt the Coming Day (3:1-7)
   2. The Lord's Timing Is Different from Ours (3:8-10)
   3. Living Righteously because of the Future Day (3:11-18).

2. B. Blum (265-6)
I. Salutation and Blessing (1:1-4)
II. The Essential Christian Virtues (1:5-15)
   A. The Efforts for Christian Fruitfulness (1:5-9)
   B. The Confirmation of Election (1:10-11)
   C. The Need for Reminders (1:12-15)
III. Christ's Divine Majesty (1:16-21)
   A. Attested by Apostolic Eyewitnesses (1:16-18)
   B. Attested by Divinely Originated Prophecy (1:19-21)
IV. False Prophets and Teachers (2:1-22)
   A. Warning Against False Teachers (2:1-3)
   B. Three Examples of Previous Judgments (2:4-10a)
   C. The Insolence and Wantonness of the False Teachers (2:10b-16)

      D. The Impotence of Their Teaching (2:17-22)
  V. The Promise of the Lord's Coming (3:1-18)
      A. The Certainty of the Day of the Lord (3:1-10)
      B. The Ethical Implications of the Day of the Lord (3:11-16)
      C. The Need to Guard Against Error and to Grow in Grace (3:17-18)

3. Hite

1:1-11	**Remember** the importance of knowing God and Jesus our Lord and Savior.
1:12-16	PURPOSE STATEMENT
1:16-21	**Remember** where our message came from and trust in it.
2:1-22	**Remember** that God knows how to rescue the godly from temptation and keep the unrighteous under punishment for the day of the Lord.
3:1-2	PURPOSE RESTATED
3:3-13	**Remember** what God has done since the beginning of Creation and what He will do at the end.
3:14-18	**Remember** to be on your guard and are not carried away and fall.

4. My own outline

  I. Epistolary Salutation (1:1-2)
  II. A Reminder (ὑπομιμνήσκω) of Things They Already Know (1:3-21)
      A. The fruit of true knowledge (1:3-4)
          1) They become partakers of the divine nature (4)
          2) They escape the corrupt world (4)
      B. Growth according to true knowledge (1:5-11)
      C. The basis of true knowledge (1:12-21)
          1) The witness of the writer himself (12-15)
          2) The eyewitness account of the apostles (16-18)
          3) The established prophetic word (19-21)
  III. Instruction in Things They Need to Know and Understand (1:13–2:10)
      A. Warning based on 1:19—false prophets arose in the past and they will arise among you (2:1)
      B. What can be expected of false teachers (2:1-3a)
      C. What the false teachers fail to realize (that you need to know (2:3b-8)
          1) God has judgment awaiting the angels (4)
          2) God punished the ancient world, but saved Noah (5)
          3) God destroyed (κατακρίνω) Sodom and Gomorrah, but saved righteous Lot (6)
      D. On the basis of these examples, you should know
          1) God will save the godly
          2) God will punish the ungodly (2:9)
      E. Description of the ungodly (ἀσεβής) and their influence—based on their failure to recognize vv. 3-9
  IV. A Reminder (ὑπομιμνήσκω) of Things They Know Concerning the Parousia (3:1-18)
      A. A reiteration of the basis of true knowledge: God's Word (3:1-2; cf. 1:12-21)
      B. A restatement of what they need to know (γινώσκω): Mockers will come denying the

Parousia-judgment (3:3; cf. 1:19-21)
   1. They fail to recognize the power of God's Word
      a. In the flood (5-6)
      b. In the destiny of this present world and the ungodly (ἀσεβής)
   2. But you need to recognize:
      a. God is not bound by time (8)
      b. God's delay is out of a desire for repentance (9)
      c. God will come again and destroy the world (10-12)
      d. The godly/righteous (δικαιοσύνη) will have their reward (13)
C. Recognizing these facts you should learn (3:15-16):
   1. To rely on the promises of the Scriptures (15-16)
   2. To beware of those who would lead you astray (17)
   3. To grow…in knowledge (18a)
D. Benediction (18b)

SUMMARY

2 Peter is both a warning and an encouragement. The brethren there were in danger of falling away from Christ by following the insidious doctrines of the false teachers (chapter 2). The book describes Christians as those who, through the power of God, are able to escape the corruption that is in the world (1:4). It also describes how they are able to keep from becoming entangled again in that corruption (1:10). Peter teaches them that the way to avoid spiritual digression is a commitment to focused spiritual progress (1:5-8). In short, they (and us today) are either growing in our relationship with God or we are sliding backwards (3:18).

Peter says that the Lord Jesus has called us from a corrupt lifestyle by His own glorious example of moral excellence (1:3). Since we have been rescued from the mire of moral and spiritual corruption, we should "apply all diligence" toward spiritual progress. Growing is planned. It is intentional. If we are not growing, it is because we have not devised a method to bring about growth. This book can help develop that plan.

EXEGETICAL NOTES

Chapter Overview: In this chapter Peter has a major challenge before him. He is attempting to establish the Christians in two vital areas: (1) Their own spiritual strength (1:1-11) and (2) their confidence in the inspiration and authority of the Scriptures (1:12-21). No teacher would want to deal with any false doctrine or false teacher unless he first had the confidence that his readers were established in these two vial areas. Any attempt to instruct concerning a false doctrine when the readers are shaky and unstable (cf. James 1:6-9) could result in a shipwreck of their faith. Paul maintains the same basic idea in Ephesians 4:11-14 where, after saying they are mature and equipped, argues "As a result, we are no longer to be children, tossed here and there by waves, and carried about by every wind of doctrine, by the trickery of men, by craftiness in deceitful scheming…." 2 Peter's false teachers are also scheming and deceitful (2:1, 3, 18, 19), and Peter wants these Christians to be equipped spiritually to deal with them and their false doctrine. Having established the faith of the Christians (chapter 1), the writer is now ready to deal with the two major problems confronting them (false teachers—chapter 2; false doctrine—chapter 3).

1:1—The epistle begins with the author identifying himself as **Simeon [Simon]** Peter (cf. Matt. 16:16; Luke 5:8). This designation has created quite the stir in the scholarly realm and has provided biblical critics much to debate. As noted in the introduction, there are considerable numbers who object to the authenticity of this epistle. Some point to this verse as an obvious attempt of some second-century author to dupe readers into believing the apostle himself penned these words. Such an attempt would be nothing short of a lie and overt deception written by an imposter. When modern scholars accept this view of the epistle, it is a wonder why they even bother writing a commentary on it at all! Why devote such attention to a spurious work? "But if these three chapters are the Word of God, as the signature implies, then we are interested in every word" (Clark 3).

Peter next describes himself with two words connected with **and**. Both of these words—**servant** and **apostle** might seem like the bottom and top positions in Christianity. With Peter, these words are closely connected and reflect his view of serving Christ as an apostle. Peter was personally selected by Jesus (John 1:42) and was among the inner circle of apostles (Matt. 17:1—along with James and John). His position as an apostle was jeopardized by his threefold denial of Jesus (Matt. 26:69-75). However, the forgiving nature of Jesus restored Peter to this important role (John 21:15-19). In that restoration, Jesus charged Peter to "tend My sheep" (v. 17). Peter is fulfilling that charge with his words in this epistle. He draws upon his experience (1:16-18), inspiration (1:19-21), and authority (3:2) to help Jesus' sheep escape the corruption that is in the world (1:3) and to be prepared for the inevitable coming of Jesus (3:11-13).

The epistle is addressed to **those who have received a faith of the same kind as ours**. The word translated **received** (λαγχάνω) and means "to obtain something as a portion, receive, obtain (by lot, or by divine will)" (Bauer 581). The word captures the beauty of God's plan to provide salvation as a free gift (cf. Rom. 6:23). The word translated the **same kind** (ἰσότιμος) refers to something of equal honor or value. Peter and the other apostles did not receive something special or different than every other person who obeys the Gospel of Christ. "There is no distinction between believers. All alike are sinners who owe their presence in the heavenly city to the amnesty of the King. Isotimos can mean 'of equal value.' Here it probably means 'of equal standing' (Abbott-Smith

Learning 2 Peter 1

'equally privileged'). There is a political nuance to the word: there are no second-class citizens in God's kingdom" (Green 78). Hite notes: "This is the basis for the entire letter—the establishment of a faith that is equal to or like that of the apostles. Throughout the book he certifies that faith against the uncertainties of false teachers" (7).

The reception of this wonderful **faith** came **by the righteousness** of **Jesus**. Peter had discussed this word (δικαιοσύνη) frequently in the first epistle (2:24; 3:12, 14, 18; 4:18) and will continue the emphasis in this letter (2:5, 7-8, 21; 3:13). Peter is not using the word to describe the way in which God justifies man (as in the Roman epistle), but rather is following the way Jesus used the word (cf. Matt. 5:20; 6:1, 33). The word describes the quality of one's life to live according to divine standards. Jesus, who lived perfectly, can be said to be fully **righteous**. It is on the basis of His **righteousness** that believers can receive the same **faith**. Peter has not lost sight that it is through the work of Jesus that anyone has "entrance into the eternal kingdom of our Lord and Savior Jesus Christ" (v. 11). Thankfully, because of His **righteousness** we can "escape the defilements of the world by the knowledge of the Lord and Savior Jesus Christ" (2:20). The verse ends with the clause **by the righteousness of our God and Savior Jesus Christ.** Blum provides a fitting description of this phrase: "The phrase 'of our God and Savior Jesus Christ' raises a well-known problem. Is Peter speaking of one person or two? Is Jesus called God here? The grammar leaves little doubt that in these words Peter is calling Jesus Christ both God and Savior" (Blum 267).

1:2 —It is easy to see this verse, with the oft-repeated phrase "**grace and peace**" to be nothing more than a typical first century greeting. Such would be an unfortunate dismissal of the power of this verse. Peter recognizes that the Christian succeeds in this evil world through the **grace** (God's undeserved forgiveness) and **peace** (contentment based upon our reconciliation with God—cf. Rom. 5:1-4; Phil. 4:6). However, Peter does not stop there. These essential qualities are **multiplied to you.** It is not possible to receive "too much grace" and to be over-supplied with "peace." It is important for the readers to understand that God has an endless amount of these and that He is willing to give them generously (cf. Eph. 2:7). In a world filled with corruption (1:4), false teachers (2:1-22) and doubt (3:3-4), how does the Christian survive? Thankfully our God multiplies His **grace and peace.** An important theme in this epistle is given here. Peter says these gifts are multiplied in the **knowledge of God and of Jesus our Lord.** The word **knowledge** (ἐπίγνωσις) will prove to be one of the key concepts in this letter, occurring 14 times in just three chapters (see special study at end of 1:5). False teachers are trying to destroy what these Christians know. They are introducing "destructive heresies," including those who deny the very work of Jesus being described here (2:1). To combat error, Peter turns to **knowledge**. If these Christians can learn and hold steadfastly to the truth, they will survive the onslaught of error. Thus Peter concludes the epistle by returning to this theme: "You therefore, beloved, **knowing** this beforehand, be on your guard lest, being carried away by the error of unprincipled men, you fall from your own steadfastness, but grow in the grace and **knowledge** of our Lord and Savior Jesus Christ" (3:17-18).

1:3 —The knowledge mentioned in verse 2 is what enables them to **see** what God has done for them. Those blinded by the error of the world will not be able to behold this divine truth (cf. 1:9; 1 John 2:11). Peter says that Jesus' **divine power** was at work in providing the saving message—a message that gives **grace and peace.** In the parable of the sower, Satan works to steal away the seed (the Word of God) from men's hearts (Luke 8:12). He has been busy attacking God's Word since the Garden. He knows that it is the implanted Word that saves men's souls (James 1:21).

His power, in contrast to that of Jesus, is far weaker. Peter describes Jesus as having divine ("that which belongs to the nature or status of deity, divine," Bauer 446) **power** (δύναμις—"potential for functioning in some way, power, might, strength, force, capability," Bauer 262). It is without question that Satan would use all of his might to discredit or destroy the saving message of the Gospel. He has failed, and his failure is because of the **divine power** of Jesus. Peter says that Jesus **has granted to us everything pertaining to life and godliness**. The word **everything** (πᾶν) is correctly translated and intended to express totality and completeness. The word will not be used when it remains insufficient. Peter says that what has been **granted** to us is e**verything pertaining to life and godliness**. This is not intended to mean all the books of the Bible, for several have yet to be written. Rather, Christ (through the preaching of the apostles and prophets) have given humanity the crucial information needed to have life and godliness. This vital information was first given in oral form but later recorded in the pages of Scripture (cf. Eph. 3:1-5). This is why we today can also claim the promise of this verse! **Life** (ζωή) is thought by some scholars to be in reference to eternal life. If this is the meaning here, then Christ has provided mankind the necessary information to get to Heaven (v. 11; 3:13-14; cf. 2 Tim. 1:10). It is also possible that Peter is referring to our daily existence. How are we to live in the midst of an evil and immoral world? How can we live so that we escape the corruption that is in the world (v. 4)? While both of these are true, it is my opinion that Peter means the latter: our daily life. **Godliness** (εὐσέβεια) is a key word in 2 Peter, occurring eight times. It is a word that describes holy and righteous conduct, where one imitates the qualities of God (cf. 1 Tim. 1:5; 1 Pet. 1:13-19). Christ has not left us without spiritual direction. We can know how to live and live in a way that pleases God (Rom. 12:1-2; Eph. 5:17).

The intellectualism and pseudo-knowledge of the false teachers (2:1-3) is in clear contrast to the **true knowledge** provided by God through Jesus. His truth is what sanctifies (John 17:17) and sets men free from the bondage to sin (John 8:32). For one to follow *any other doctrine* besides the Gospel of Christ is to follow "destructive heresies" (2:1) and "doctrines of demons" (1 Tim. 4:1-3). We join with Paul in saying "I count all things to be loss in view of the surpassing value of knowing Christ Jesus my Lord" (Phil. 3:8). Equally, Jesus taught that our eternal life is tied to our knowing God (John 17:3; cf. 1 John 3:1-5; 2 Thess. 1:7-10). (Note: Has Peter switched from describing Jesus to referring to God—the **Him** mentioned here? Most scholars think so).

The amazing story of redemption, going back to mankind's first sin and continuing through each generation, is a reflection upon the nature and character of God. He could have given up on us. Rather, from the foundation of the world devised a plan to provide salvation to mankind through the sacrifice of Christ (Eph. 3:11; Rom. 3:21-26; Heb. 9:15). What kind of God would reach out to such a stubborn and rebellious people? Answer: a God who possess **glory and excellence** (for a discussion on these words, see Sermon Seed: "God—His Word and His Character).

1:4 —By these is in reference to God's "glory and excellence." Those amazing attributes have now **granted to us** (notice it is God's gift freely given—not earned or deserved). The word **granted** (δωρέομαι—same word as in v. 3) means "to present something as a gift or confer a benefit, probably with some suggestion of formality" (Bauer 266). What is it that God has generously given? Peter says it is God's **promises**. Two words describe those promises: (1) **precious** (τίμιος—"being of exceptional value…of great worth/value, precious," Bauer 1006). Part of what makes His promises **precious** is the great cost required—the death of Jesus. (2) **magnificent** (μέγας—"The superlative μέγιστος, at times used by contemporary authors, occurs only once in the NT, where it is used in the elative sense *very great, extraordinary* (Diod S 2, 32, 1) ἐπαγγέλματα 2 Pet. 1:4," Bauer 624). See Sermon Seeds for a discussion of **promises** made in this book.

> 2 Peter was written to assure the church of the surety of God's eschatological promises, which had come under attack by the heretics. The promises Peter has in mind are about Christ's coming (3:4) and the new heaven and new earth (3:13), as well as the believers' entrance into the eternal kingdom (1:11). The apostle strives to assure the church that delay in Christ's return and the coming judgment does not mean that God's promises will not be fulfilled (3:9). Whatever delay there may be is due to God's calculation of time and His mercy (3:8–9) (Gene Green 185).

These **promises** enable the Christian to **become partakers of the divine nature**. Our connection to God is established when we make His promises an active part in our lives. We do not offer lip-service to those promises but conduct ourselves in full conviction that those promises will soon become reality. When we do this, we have linked ourselves with God and are **partakers** of His **nature**.

> The divine virtue and transcendent goodness manifested in Jesus both constitute and validate the call to come and participate in the divine nature. We are promised a share in His moral excellence during this life, and of His glory hereafter. For, taken together, the triple agency of the promises, the power and the person of the Lord Jesus regenerate a man and make him a sharer in God's own nature, so that the family likeness begins to be seen in him (Michael Green 83).

When we are truly connected with God, and His promises are motivations for our lives, this enabled us to live victoriously. Peter describes us as **having escaped the corruption that is in the world by lust**. The whole world lies in the power of the evil one (1 John 5:19), which is why it is so **corrupt** (φθορά—depravity). However, those born of God (cf. 1 Pet. 1:3) have God who "keeps him and the evil one does not touch him" (1 John 5:18). "We participate in the divine nature only after we have escaped or turned our backs on (note the decisiveness of the aorist participle) that attitude (cf. James 1:21)" (Michael Green 83).

1:5—Peter begins this verse with **Now for this very reason also**. God has done His part. He has provided Christians "everything pertaining to life and godliness." He has given us motivation through "His precious and magnificent promises." It is our turn to use what God has given and to move forward. Christianity is not static, and one should never level off in the Christian walk. Peter will conclude the epistle with a command to "grow in the grace and knowledge of our Lord and Savior Jesus Christ" (3:18). Specifically, what should Christians be doing to insure proper growth? Verses 5-7 provide one of the clearest paths for Christian growth. Each one has to determine to grow. Each one must commit to a plan that will bring that growth. Peter says that each must **apply all diligence**. The word **apply** (παρεισφέρω) means "make every effort, do your best" (Bauer 774). The word **diligence** (σπουδή) means "earnest commitment in discharge of an obligation or experience of a relationship, eagerness, earnestness, diligence, willingness, zeal" (Bauer 939). Where has God made room for lazy Christians in His church? Where has God said, "Ok you can relax now until Judgment Day"? Where has God said, "You've arrived. There is no more room for growth"? Each must develop a plan, and Peter outlines a perfect (God-developed) plan that, when implemented, will guarantee that each is "neither useless nor unfruitful" (v. 8), and "will never stumble" (v. 10).

Peter begins with what every Christian has: **faith**. He said in verse 1 "to those who have received a faith of the same kind as ours." This faith, then, is the foundation required for Christian advancement. Sadly there are those who are weak in faith. That is, their trust, reliance, and confidence in God is shaky, uncertain, and unstable. When such is the case it is like building a Christian life on sand (cf. Matt. 7:24-27). It will not and cannot succeed. However, Peter is confident that their faith is strong. They possess confidence in God and His promises. When such a faith exists, the Christian is able to **supply** other essential attributes. See the Sermon Seed "Christian Graces" for a brief description of each of these. The word **supply** (ἐπιχορηγέω) means "to provide (at one's own expense), supply, furnish" (Bauer 387). Notice: "at one's own expense." God is not going to force growth, neither is He going to give it to one who gives half-hearted effort. Each must be willing to pay the price for growth!

With a solid foundation of **faith**, Peter now directs the Christian to add **moral excellence**. This word (ἀρετή) was used of God in verse 3 ("excellence"). Peter had said that we should "become partakers of the divine nature" (v. 4), and the repetition of this word is one way that we connect with the divine. God is **excellent** in every way, and His children should imitate that ("like Father, like son"). This concept naturally ties to what Peter spoke about in the first letter. There he proclaimed that God was "holy," and therefore we—as His children—should "be holy yourselves also in all your behavior; because it is written, 'you shall be holy for I am holy'" (1 Pet. 1:15-16). Translators have supplied the word **moral**, which is certainly the meaning here. Bauer defines the word as "uncommon character worthy of praise, excellence of character, exceptional civic virtue" (130). This word stands in direct contrast to the "corruption" and "lust" mentioned in verse 4.

Knowledge (γνῶσις) is the third characteristic listed by Peter. Already Peter has mentioned this word in verses 2 and 3. Knowledge is unquestionably a key concept in the book. The false teachers are bringing in "destructive heresies" (2:1) and were "reviling where they have no knowledge" (2:12). For the Christian to survive in a world filled with Satan's lies (John 8:44) and false teachers, he must have good information. He must have the truth (John 17:17). God has given "true knowledge" (vv. 3, 8), and that knowledge will empower them to win the war against sin. Some might be surprised that this word is listed third. After all, isn't **knowledge** the starting point for a Christian walk? First, this assumes that Peter intends for these eight traits to be a "stairstep" description of Christian growth. That is, one must begin with **faith**. Then, after securing a solid faith, focus on **moral excellence**. Once a Christian possesses this **moral excellence** he should advance to **knowledge**—and so on. Is this what Peter intends? "There seems to be no apparent underlying reason for the order in which these qualities are listed; the only thing significant is that the list begins with faith and ends with love (v. 7), thus giving the impression that these qualities are needed in order to live a truly Christian life" (Arichea and Hatton 78). "We must conclude that we are dealing with a conventional form, based on the notion that the virtues are interconnected so that in the virtuous life one develops out of another" (Bauckham 185). Therefore, it is best to conclude that Peter is presenting a list of characteristics, all of which the Christian continues to work on each and every day. *Second*, Peter is emphasizing how the Christian must continue to grow in **knowledge**. Information secured that led to one's initial faith is important for sure. But so is increasing in knowledge. We are all called to be workmen, handling accurately the Word of truth (2 Tim. 2:15). We can "be destroyed for lack of knowledge" (Hos. 4:6). Therefore, we must "grow…in knowledge" (3:18). The question then, is: "What—specifically—are we doing to grow in knowledge?"

1:6—Peter now adds a fourth attribute: **self-control**. This word (ἐγκράτεια) means "restraint of one's emotions, impulses, or desires, self-control" (Bauer 274). The world is filled with unbridled passion and lust. The false teachers were fueled by "sensuality" (2:2) and "counted it a pleasure to revel in the daytime…having eyes full of adultery and that never cease from sin" (2:13-14). The Christian is called to a higher standard of life and morality. Yet this higher standard can only be achieved by developing self-control. This type of control keeps one's eyes from looking on sin (Job 31:1) and the lips from speaking lies (Col. 3:9). It keeps the heart pure (Matt. 5:8) and the conscience clean (1 Tim. 1:5).

> The importance of "self-control," then, lies in recognition of it as a premier virtue for Jews as well as Greeks. Considered as "pure and stainless," it serves as the antidote for "desire" and "pleasure," which are "profane, impure and unholy" (Philo, Sp. Leg. 1.150). In this document it summarizes the strong bodily control which makes disciples able to stand at God's judgment and enter the kingdom of Jesus. Alternately, it contrasts the true disciple with the opponents who are credited with living a life of "freedom," presumably from law and rule as well as freedom from judgment (Neyrey 160).

> In contrast to this lifestyle of uncontrolled lust, Peter enjoined diligence in self-control. Christians who know who Jesus is, what He has done, and what He is yet to do control their desires instead of allowing their desires to control them. Only through such a lifestyle of self-control can they be "found in peace, without spot, and blameless in His sight" at the coming of the Lord (3:14). This seems to be the import of self-control in 2 Peter 1:6 (Owen 11).

Next, Peter says the Christian should have **perseverance**. This word (ὑπομονή) means "the capacity to hold out or bear up in the face of difficulty, patience, endurance, fortitude, steadfastness, perseverance" (Bauer 1039). Christianity, when lived according to the divine standards, is faced with daily challenges. Each one of those challenges stand as potential faith-destroyers. Satan, ever hard at work, is attempting to wear the Christian down to where he gives up. This is why it is essential that the Christian steels himself for the long haul and mentally prepares for today's struggles.

> In the Christian world the term appears thirty-two times in the NT, for example, in Pauline virtue lists (Rom. 5:3–4; 1 Tim. 6:11; 2 Tim. 3:10; Tit. 2:2), James (James 1:3, 12; 5:11; cf. 5:7–8, 10, which use a synonym), and in a list in Rev. 2:19 (plus six other times in Revelation). It indicates endurance, but in a spiritual battle rather than in a physical battle or an athletic contest. It is the virtue needed to stand firm in one's commitment to Jesus over the long haul in the face of persecution (thus its prominence in James and Revelation) or other hardships. In 2 Peter the need is to stand firm in their commitment in the face of the enticements of the teachers whom our author opposes (Davids 181).

The Christian is next admonished to add to his perseverance, **godliness**. This word (εὐσέβεια) was used in verse 3, where Peter affirmed that God has given us all of the information we need to be godly. The word is generally defined as "awesome respect accorded to God, devoutness, piety, godliness" (Bauer 412). However, there is no English word that captures the extent of this great NT word. As noted earlier, I believe Paul's words in 1 Timothy 1:5 captures the qualities of a godly person.

> Christ has given believers everything to be godly, and yet believers must pursue godliness. The term *godliness* refers to piety or, more simply, to living a life that is like God. Believers

should live in a holy and "godly" way since Jesus is going to return (2 Pet. 3:11). The word *godliness* is especially common in the Pastoral Epistles for living the kind of life that pleases God (1 Tim. 2:2; 3:16; 4:7-8; 6:3, 5-6, 11; 2 Tim 3:5; Tit. 1:1) (Schreiner 300).

1:7—Brotherly kindness is the seventh of eight qualities. This word (φιλαδελφία) employs the Greek word *phileo*, which generally lines up with the English word *like*. Christians are commanded to love (the next word), but they must also develop an affinity for each other. It is difficult to function in Christianity when the brothers and sisters don't like each other. In such a case, they tolerate each other and grudgingly work side by side in Christian worship and service. However, God desires much more than this. By focusing on what joins us together and what we share (cf. vv. 3-4), Christians should have a family love that is often seen between brothers and sisters.

> In the New Testament, and among Christians, the word came to mean affection between fellow-believers, including sympathetic concern for others and the care of those in need. Other ways to translate this term are "love and affection for your fellow Christians" or "concern for one another as brothers and sisters ought to have for each other" (Arichea and Hatton 80-81).

The list is completed with arguably the most important word in the NT: **love**. This is the common *agape* love (ἀγάπη) which is the highest kind of love. It is that which is demonstrated by God in His sending of Jesus (John 3:16). It represents a desire for the best for others, especially in their relationship with God. As a result, a person demonstrating this kind of love will "do no wrong to a neighbor" (Rom. 13:10). A person who shows *agape* love will be honest, faithful. and forgiving. Jesus taught that the two greatest commandments were to love God and love one's neighbor (Matt. 22:36-40).

1:8—Peter is now going to explain why each Christian must possess the qualities just listed. In this verse he will describe the advantages these qualities provide. In verse 9 he will describe the negative disadvantages faced by people lacking these qualities. See Sermon Seed: "Advantages and Disadvantages: The Importance of the Christian Graces." Peter begins by saying **if these qualities are yours and are increasing**. Two observations here. First, he says they **are yours**. The Christian hasn't 'dabbled' in these, demonstrating an occasional spurt of faith and self-control. Instead, they have claimed possession. He has determined that this is his life-course and will be the qualities which describe him and define him. Second, he says **and are increasing**. It is always a temptation to rest on our past accomplishments and become stagnant. When this happens one is actually regressing instead of progressing. Maintaining the status quo is not acceptable to God (see 3:18). Can a Christian increase in faith? In knowledge and perseverance? Can he show himself to be more kind and loving? Of course! Not only can he, but he must. Peter identifies the benefits of such growth. First, when they are increasing, they **render** (καθίστημι—to make or cause) you to not be **useless**. This word (ἀργός) describes one who is unproductive and therefore is of no value. A similar idea (although a different word) is used by Paul in 2 Timothy 2:21. There a man cleanses himself, thus making him "useful to the master." Secondly, one with these qualities will not be unfruitful. This word (ἄκαρπος) describes one who was expected to contribute but has failed to produce. It is akin to a fruit tree that produces no fruit. Of what value is such a tree, and of what value is such a person? We are commanded to bear fruit (John 15:1-5). We produce fruit when we lead others to Christ, when we strengthen the weak, and when we demonstrate the "fruit of the Spirit" (Gal.

Learning 2 Peter 1

5:22-23). Third, Peter identifies what is the reason one has avoided being **useless** and **unfruitful**: he has learned the **true knowledge of our Lord Jesus Christ**. God has described what He desires from His children. He has provided crucial information that enables each Christian to live in a way that pleases Him (Eph. 5:17). This is the fifth time Peter has referenced **knowledge**. Unlike the lies and falsehoods of the evil teachers, God—through Christ—has given us everything we need to know (v. 3). When one truly knows Jesus, they have no problem seeing Him as the **Lord** (ruler, master, controller) **Jesus** (Savior) **Christ** (the Messiah; God's anointed King).

1:9—A person **who lacks** the eight qualities noted in verses 5-7 are now described. First, they are **blind**. This common word (τυφλός) is frequently used to describe one who is unable to see with his eyes. However, the word also is used to describe one "being unable to understand, incapable of comprehending, blind, of mental and spiritual blindness in imagery" (Bauer 1021). Peter is here describing one who cannot "see" the importance of having these qualities and making sure he is growing in them. Second, this person is **short-sighted**. This word (μυωπάζω) describes one who has "tunnel vision" and is unable to see the big picture. He is focused on a few things, missing out on many other important things. How does a person fall into such spiritual blindness? Because he has **forgotten his purification from his former sins**. This is Peter's third observation about the person lacking the qualities of verses 5-7. "Here, as almost all commentators agree, the reference is to purification at baptism (Acts 22:16; 1 Cor. 6:11; Eph. 5:26; Tit. 3:5; Barn. 11:11).... The forgiveness received in baptism is a decisive break with the old sinful life and should therefore be the beginning of a virtuous life. The Christian who does not pursue virtue must have forgotten his baptism and is in danger of relapsing into his pre-Christian condition (2:22)" (Bauckham 189-90).

1:10—By using the word **therefore**, Peter is ready to wrap up this first section. He gives his second command (imperative), which is related to the first. In verse 5 Peter commanded that they "applying all diligence [σπουδή]" they "supply" their faith with seven other essential attributes. Peter returns to the word **diligence** (σπουδάζω), commanding them to "to be especially conscientious in discharging an obligation, be zealous/eager, take pains, make every effort, be conscientious" (Bauer 939). Such a warning must not be lost on them (or on us). Our salvation is not assured (despite those who promote the doctrine of "once saved, always saved.") If one does not apply **diligence**, he or she most certainly could **stumble**. What Peter commands is that they are **diligent** to **make certain** two crucial truths: 1) God's **calling**—which came through the Gospel (2 Thess. 2:14). 2) God's **choosing you**. God only chooses those who have answered the Gospel call. Their obedience to the Word of Christ has provided them transference from the kingdom of darkness into the "kingdom of His beloved Son" (Col. 1:13). The Calvinistic idea that God chose someone before his birth is foreign to the teachings of the NT and contradicts the nature of God. He is willing to save all (3:9; cf. 1 Tim. 2:4; Rom. 10:11), which is why the Great Commission is to take the saving message "into all the world" (Matt. 28:18-20; Mark 16:15-16). Peter further shows the possibility of apostasy by saying **as long as you practice these things, you will never stumble**. What happens if someone stops practicing these eight qualities? They will **stumble** and will not be granted "entrance into the eternal kingdom" (v. 11). Peter, however, is stating this in the positive. Practicing the eight qualities of verses 5-7 and growing them is not some impossible dream. God does not give us commands that are impossible to fulfill (cf. 1 John 5:3). Each Christian should, and must, have and develop these qualities.

1:11—At the conclusion of the first main section of chapter 1 (1:1-11), Peter says "for in this way the entrance into the eternal Kingdom of our Lord and Savior Jesus Christ will be abundantly supplied to you." The adverb *houtos*, translated **in this way**, maintains that if the readers will give diligence to confirm their "call and election" they will gain entrance into the eternal Kingdom. The word **supplied** (epichoregethesetai from ἐπιχορηγέω) is from the same Greek word in verse 5 where the Christian is encouraged to obtain or supplement the various qualities listed in verses 5-7. If the Christian will supply himself or herself with these qualities, then God will supply for him a place in the eternal kingdom of Christ. Some New Testament passages show one becomes a citizen of Christ's earthly kingdom at the time of conversion (Col. 1:13; Heb. 12:28; Rev. 1:6, 9). 2 Peter refers to the kingdom in a future sense. Here the readers will enter the eternal kingdom at the time of the second coming of Christ (cf. Matt. 25:34; Acts 14:22; 2 Tim. 4:18). The phrase **eternal kingdom** does not occur elsewhere in the New Testament and is rarely found in the Old Testament (Ps. 145:12; Dan. 4:3, 34; 7:14, 27). Peter's usage of **eternal** (aionios) and **kingdom** (basileia) demonstrates a transition to an eschatological hope different from the hope discussed in the Old Testament (Sasse, TDNT, 1:208-9). The Kingdom of Christ will be fully realized in the future, and it will be an eternal kingdom (Luke 1:33). This reference to the future kingdom is the first direct eschatological statement of 2 Peter. It is important for these Christians to understand that God has something planned in the future, and they need to be ready for it (3:14, 17).

1:12—Special note regarding verses 12-14. It is troubling that so many scholars have quickly and easily dismissed 2 Peter as pseudepigraphical. When such is believed, it reduces this powerful section to a forgery and an overt lie. It becomes nothing more than some unknown deceiver attempting to dupe his audience into believing the true apostle Peter penned these words. Yes, I am making a moral judgment on such a person—any person—who would attempt to foster such a lie. Equally, we must consider what such a belief means for the claim of inspiration. Would God inspire a person to lie? Would He include in Sacred Scripture an epistle that is a forgery and overt deception? Of course not. As a result, we readily accept this epistle as it is claimed to be—a letter written by the apostle Peter. And since that is the case, it makes these verses even more emotional and powerful.

In view of the assurances and teachings of the first section, Peter assumes one of his jobs as an apostle of Jesus—that of being a reminder. Peter says **I shall always be ready to remind you of these things**. He is not saying this because they had forgotten these truths. He says **even though you already know them**. The word **know** (οἶδα) is not the same word as used earlier. This word has to do with secured information. They know the facts of the Gospel. Now they need to apply those facts to Christian living. This will transition them into the useful and fruitful knowledge he mentioned in verse 8. By **reminding** them, Peter knows they have **been** established in the truth. The lies of the false teachers loom as a present danger. If one should be duped by their self-serving doctrines, he will share the punishment God has in store for them. Instead, the knowledge Peter gives will **establish** them. This word (στηρίζω) means "to cause to be inwardly firm or committed, confirm, establish, strengthen" (Bauer 945). It is a powerful NT word, found in numerous passages (cf. Luke 22:32; Acts 18:23; Rom. 16:25; 1 Thess. 3:2; 2 Thess. 3:3; 1 Pet. 5:10; Rev. 3:2). Peter would affirm the adage that "knowledge is power." When they know **the truth**, the truth they already have (**which is present with you**), they have the power to defeat the false teachers and destroy their insidious doctrines (cf. 2 Cor. 10:5).

Learning 2 Peter 1

1:13—Peter takes seriously his work. Reminding others of these divine truths is **right** (δίκαιος). "The neuter denotes that which is obligatory in view of certain requirements of justice, right, fair, equitable" (Bauer 247). Telling the truth, when the false doctrines are ever present is not only an obligation but a privilege. As long as Peter is alive **(I am in this earthly dwelling)** he will **stir you up by way of reminder.** The word translated **stir up** (διεγείρω) means "to awaken or arouse." Peter intends for this reminder to be a "shot in the arm," a motivator that encourages them to press on.

1:14—In John 21:18-19 we read about a discussion the Jesus had with Peter regarding his death. That discussion took place over 30 years ago, and Jesus **made clear** what was to happen to Peter. Peter now knows that the fulfillment of that prediction is **imminent**. Death, however, is nothing more than **laying aside of my *earthly* dwelling**. What a beautiful description of death. It is getting rid of this old tent, worn out with service and old age, and replacing it with a perfect "dwelling from Heaven" (did Peter have his Bible open to 2 Cor. 4:16-5:10?)

1:15—Peter's love for these Christians is genuine and the truths he taught are eternal. He therefore is going to be **diligent** to do all that he can that these truths last after he dies **(after my departure)**. If he has succeeded in doing his work, they will be **able to call these things to mind**.

1:16—The first eschatological statement was made in verse 11 (see above). Here is found the second major eschatological statement: "For we did not follow cleverly devised tales when we made known to you the power and coming of our Lord Jesus Christ, but were eyewitnesses of His majesty." As is evident from verses 12-15, this statement reflects a major point that he wants his readers to "understand" and "remember." The reliability of Christ's **power and coming** is found in the fact that "we" were eyewitnesses to His transfiguration. This is why Peter feels qualified to remind his readers. He has first-hand knowledge plus an additional testimony in the "prophetic word" (v. 19). The power and coming of Christ are verified by the transfiguration. This construction is considered a "hendiadys" where two ideas are coordinated but one is dependent on the other. Therefore, the author is here speaking of the **Parousia** (coming) of Christ which will be characterized by **power**.

The **majesty** (megaleiotetos) to which the apostles were eyewitnesses is the verifying point in Peter's argument. Rather than needing **cleverly devised tales** to prove the Second Coming, they based their arguments on something far more trustworthy. These apostles witnessed the transfiguration, and it offered undeniable evidence that God, the **majestic Glory**, was the power behind Christ. Therefore, the transfiguration was an event in which divine glory was evident. It not only looked forward to the Second Coming, it was a pledge of the glorious return of Christ (cf. 1 Pet. 4:13). Talbert says, "The certainty of the Parousia-Judgment is guaranteed by the apostles who saw at the Transfiguration a foreshadowing of the second advent" (138). Liefeld writes, "The Transfiguration, therefore, is a divine confirmation and demonstration of the preceding sayings about the coming of the Son of Man in His Father's glory and the coming of the Kingdom with power (Mark 8:30; 9:1)" (179).

1:17-18—In our country—and in most countries—the testimony of three witnesses is pretty convincing. Peter, along with James and John, were **eyewitnesses** to the Transfiguration (that which occurred **on the holy mountain**). That is not all. They were also earwitnesses (cf. 1 John 1:1-4 where they were hand-witnesses too!). Peter says decisively **we ourselves heard this utterance made from Heaven**. They heard an **utterance** from the **Majestic Glory**, whom Peter earlier claimed was **from God the Father**. God's words provided undeniable proof of the legitimacy of Jesus. He said: "**This**

is My beloved Son with whom I am well pleased" (such was recorded in Matthew's Gospel—17:5, along with Mark (Mark 9:7) and Luke (Luke 9:35).

1:19—The **prophetic word** has been a difficult phrase to identify (Fornberg 82-4; Green 86-9; Roberts 75). Regardless, it is evident that Peter intends to use that **prophetic word** as a second verifying factor in his argument. It too lends support to the future Parousia of Christ and is therefore worthy of the Christian's attention. These Christians are, in fact, urged to pay attention to it **until the day dawns and the morning star arises in your hearts**. The eschatological significance of this phrase is easily seen when contrasted with the preceding phrase. They are not in a "dark place" with the prophetic word as their source of light. Therefore, they are to give heed to the prophetic word until the "day dawns," i.e., the day the prophetic word will come to pass. Fornberg says:

> Since the author must mean that the prophetic word is valid at least as long as this world endures, "the morning star" (φωσφόρος) and "the day" (without the article) must refer to the onset of the new age in the eschatological future…. The dawn of the eschatological day/age will be realized when "the morning star" rises (84-5).

> The "day" that will dawn is most likely the "day of the Lord" (3:10), which is not only a day of salvation to be anticipated (3:12) but also a "day of judgment" (2:9; 3:7). This is the eternal day (3:18). Throughout Scripture the "day" of the Lord is the time of God's coming to judge humanity and execute His wrath (Isa. 13:6, 9; Ezek. 13:5; 30:3; Joel 1:15; 2:1, 11; 3:14; Amos 5:18, 20; Zeph. 1:7, 14; Zech. 14:1; Mal. 4:5; Acts 2:20; 1 Cor. 5:5; 2 Thess. 2:2; 2 Pet. 3:10). But for God's people this will become a day of salvation (Joel 2:21-32; 3:18; Obad. 15-21; Zech. 14:1-21) (Gene Green 228).

Claude Blagden makes a great observation about this phrase: "Until the Second Coming of Christ, who scatters all shadows and illuminates all obscurity. Till then, men must study prophecy: after that, their minds will be lit up to see things as they are" (39).

1:20—Again emphasizing the significance of knowledge, Peter says **but know this first of all**. He will repeat this phrase in 3:3 where the false teachers are mocking the immutable prophecy of Scripture. What they have devised is "their own interpretation," which is decidedly false (3:3-4).

> Peter wants his readers to understand that "no prophecy of Scripture is of the prophet's own interpretation." "Prophecy" (προφητεία, *prophēteia*) here and in verse 21 refers to the inspired utterances of the ancient prophets, which were written down as Scripture (2 Chron. 32:32; Ezra 5:1; 6:14; Tob. 2:6; Matt. 13:14). That the author has in mind the inscripted prophecies, as opposed to other prophetic utterances (1 Cor. 12:10; 1 Thess. 5:20; 1 Tim. 1:18), is made certain by the qualification "of Scripture" (γραφῆς, *graphēs*), which, though in the singular, here means the whole of the OT (Philo, Moses 2.17 §84; Let. Aris. 155; John 20:9; Acts 8:32). "Scripture" is a technical term for the writings that are divinely inspired (Rom. 1:2; 2 Tim. 3:16; G. Schrenk, TDNT 1:750–61) (Gene Green 230).

1:21—This verse closes the argument with the assurance that the OT was written by men who were "borne along" by the Holy Spirit as they spoke from God. This is the claim of other NT Scriptures (2 Tim. 3:16-17; Luke 1:70; 3:18; 4:25). Jesus promised the apostles that the Holy Spirit would "guide them into all truth" (John 16:13). The Bible does not define how this inspiration occurred; but no solution which does not accept the claim at face value can explain the origin of the New

Testament. Thus Peter writes to guarantee the sureness of the truth. It comes from God who gives us all that pertains to life and godliness (1:3).

Fornberg says: "The purpose of verses 20-21 is to show why this prophetic word is valid: It is inspired by the Holy Spirit, and therefore may not be given an arbitrary interpretation. Accordingly, 2 Peter 1:16-21 has a coherent theme: reasons for belief in Christ's power and coming. The author gives two such reasons: the Transfiguration of Christ and 'the prophetic word'" (78-9).

Excel Still More Bible Workshop

Learning
2 Peter 2

DENNY PETRILLO

EXEGETICAL NOTES

***Chapter Two Overview*:** The third major eschatological section is found in 2:1-9 (see 1:11, 16 for the first two). Here Peter initiates the direct attack against the "false teachers" (2:1). In this epistle the false teachers arose from among the people (2:1) and were enticing them away from their faith (2:18-19; 3:17; cf. Jude 4, 12). They denied the Lord who bought them (2:1; cf. Jude 4), discredited the law of God (2:2, 10; cf. Jude 4, 12), and were in search of personal gain (2:3, 12, 14, 15, 18; cf. Jude 16). They were not afraid to discredit others while lifting up themselves (2:1, 2, 10; cf. Jude 8, 19). These false teachers also scoffed at the Parousia, an error which was, in fact, the very basis of all their other sins (3:3-5). The identification of these false teachers has been the subject of much discussion. Some have considered them to be Gnostics (Kasemann 170-72; Talbert 141; Peel 141-65). It is true that certain characteristics of the false teachers are harmonious with known second-century Gnostic tendencies, especially their focus on knowledge (*gnosis*), a discrediting of Scripture and a doctrine that encouraged licentious behavior (cf. Kasemann 170-76). However, this evidence cannot be positively identified with any group since many errorists had similar positions. Guthrie says, "There are in fact many points of contact between the false teachers in 2 Peter, the libertines of Corinth and the Nicolaitans of Asia" (855). Therefore, it seems more likely that 2 Peter is dealing with an unclassified group with various errors, foremost of which was a denial of the second coming and judgment.

2:1—Peter now begins his apology against the **false** teachers/prophets. The word **false prophets** (ψευδοπροφήτης) is a compound word. It captures the idea that these men promote themselves as **prophets**, that is, true prophets of God. By including the word **false**, Peter indicates that their claim is bogus and their teachings are lies. They are like the false prophets mentioned in Jeremiah 14:14. They are not men "moved by the Holy Spirit" that Peter discussed in the previous verse (ignore chapter break! 1:21). Peter refers to these teachers with several phrases that have eschatological significance. First of all, he charges that they will **introduce destructive heresies**. Although some of these heresies (αἵρεσις—teachings outside of that proven and accepted) are connected with the licentious freedom they promise (2:18-19), all are ultimately tied up in their belief that Christ will not return in judgment (3:3). With no judgment to fear, they have no sensual restrictions. Thus, their lusts (epithumia–3:3) can have free reign. In a few verses Peter will say, "Their judgment from long ago is not idle, and their destruction is not asleep (2:3)." Peter says their teachings are **destructive**. This word (ἀπώλεια) is a key word in 2 Peter, found five times (2:1[2], 3; 3:7, 16). The word means "the destruction that one causes, destruction, waste." The false teachers are taking precious souls and ruining them with their false doctrines. They do not realize that they are **bringing swift destruction upon themselves**. This ruin will ultimately bring about eternal punishment in Hell (Matt. 25:41; 2 Thess. 1:7-9).

Second, Peter says that these false teachings they **secretly introduce**.

> *Secretly bring* in translates a Greek verb that appears only here in the New Testament and that means either to bring in without indicating how it is done, or "to bring in under false pretenses." In this context secrecy is perhaps intended; they will introduce these teachings without anyone noticing it. Another word that fits this context is "unobtrusively" (Arichea and Hatton 103-4).

The operating procedure of these false teachers reminds us of a problem at Galatia (2:4) and Corinth (2 Cor. 11:13-15). False teachers are far too clever to openly promote doctrine that is clearly against what the church has been taught. Therefore, as Jesus warned, they have to disguise themselves (and their doctrine) as sheep (Matt. 7:15-20).

Third, Peter says these false teachers **deny the Master who bought them**. To the Jewish mind-set such a denial was ultimately an atheistic attitude which rejected God as judge (Neyrey 415-20). Consider the words of Jeremiah: "They have lied about the Lord and said, 'He is not; misfortune will not come on us, and we will not see sword or famine'" (Jer. 5:12). There are many passages in the Old Testament where men claim God is ignorant and unconcerned for the sins of man (cf. Ps. 10:1-15; 59:7; 64:1-10; 73:10-14; 94:7-11; Job 7:20-21; 22:13; 35:13; Isa. 29:15; Ezek. 8:12; 9:9). Amazingly, they are denying the one true **Master** (Jesus), who **bought them**. The word bought (ἀγοράζω) here is an aorist active participle, and thus requires the meaning "having bought" (it was an action done in the past). The word means "to secure the rights to someone by paying a price, buy, acquire as property" (Bauer 14). The clear, natural meaning is that they were—at one time in the past—saved. Jesus had **bought** them with His shed blood (cf. Acts 20:28; 1 Pet. 1:18-19). Such a view, however, directly contradicts the doctrine of "once saved always saved." This forces some to make statements like this: "In my judgment, verse 2 asserts that Christ 'bought' the false teachers; but this does not necessarily mean that they were saved" (Blum 276). Then what does it mean? Commentators have to get creative to argue that this verse is not saying what it is clearly saying! These false teachers, at one time a part of God's spiritual family purchased with the saving blood of Jesus, are now **bringing swift destruction upon themselves**. Fortunately, there are some scholars who easily see the implications of this statement:

> We should note that many scholars who defend "unlimited atonement" also think that believers cannot lose their salvation. But a problem also arises for their interpretation. The verse seems to say that eschatological judgment will be the destiny of those who were bought by the Lord, who were members of the church, who, apparently, acknowledged Jesus Christ at some point as their Lord and Savior. The verse does not refer to people in general who are the potential beneficiaries of Christ's death. It speaks of false teachers who were part of

Learning 2 Peter 2

Peter's church and had now rejected the Gospel they first embraced. The entire discussion on limited atonement in this verse cannot be segregated from the issue of whether believers can truly apostatize. That is an issue we will face again in this chapter since Peter spoke of those who "have left the straight way" (2:15), of those who have escaped the clutches of the world through knowing Christ but have subsequently been entangled and conquered by the world again (2:20), of those who have known the way of righteousness but have now turned from it (2:21). The issue raised by these verses will be discussed in 2:17-22. We must see, however, that 2:1 raises fundamentally the same question (Schreiner 330-1).

In view of this attitude exhibited by these false teachers, it can be concluded that the denial of the Lord was a denial of judgment (cf. 3:3-4). This explains the purpose of verses 3-9. Peter is going to demonstrate, through a series of examples, that judgment of the wicked "is not idle and their destruction is not asleep" (v. 3).

2:2—Fourth, Peter recognizes the popularity and following secured by these false teachers. He notes that **many will follow their sensuality**. The word **many** (πολύς) underscores the seriousness of the situation. The false teachers are winning the battle for a large number of Christians, who have become disciples. The word **follow** (ἐξακολουθέω) means "to accept as authoritative determiner of thought or action, obey, follow" (Bauer 344). This word shows that these false teachers are winning by advancing a doctrine that encourages *sensuality*. The word **sensuality** (ἀσέλγεια) means "lack of self-constraint which involves one in conduct that violates all bounds of what is socially acceptable, self-abandonment" (Bauer 141).

> These false teachers convinced themselves that sexual activity outside of marriage was acceptable and honoring to God. They borrowed the prevailing opinion of the Greek culture and smuggled it into the church. The impact of this false teaching and immoral living was to lure Christians into similar paths of immorality and thus to bring discredit upon Christ and true Christianity (Walls and Anders 125).

Fifth, their example/teachings cause the **way of the truth to be maligned**. The importance of a godly example is frequently taught in Scripture. Jesus said the truly righteous will be the salt of the earth and the light of the world (Matt. 5:13-16). Paul frequently encouraged conduct that would bring honor to Christ and the Gospel (1 Tim. 6:1; Tit. 2:5, 8, 10; 2 Cor. 8:21; Phil. 2:15) as did Peter in the first epistle (1 Pet. 2:12, 15; 3:16). These false teachers are making a mockery of the doctrine of holiness and purity, causing others to **malign the truth**. The word **malign** (βλασφημέω) is where we get the word blaspheme from, and means "to speak in a disrespectful way that demeans, denigrates, maligns" (Bauer 178). When people like this profess to follow Christ but live immorally, they give Christianity a bad name. The world considers them hypocrites. This is what the Jews had done, causing Paul to say, "The name of God is blasphemed among the Gentiles because of you" (Rom. 2:24). The tragedy of their bad example is increased when it is the **way of the truth** that is damaged. This is the soul-saving message of the Gospel! This is exactly what the world needs to be hearing, but will not hear it, because they consider the messengers of that message to be hypocrites.

> The reputation of Christ and the Christian way of truth is brought to discredit when those who say they identify with Christ involve themselves in obvious immoral behavior. This discrediting occurs in the eyes of other Christians. Most importantly, those who do not know Christ will be influenced negatively. Immoral living by people who are identified

with Christ's church raises a potential barrier, preventing unbelievers from embracing Jesus Christ (Walls and Anders 125).

2:3—Sixth, their motivation and methods are exposed. Peter identifies their **greed**. This word (πλεονεξία) means "the state of desiring to have more than one's due, greediness, insatiableness, avarice, covetousness" (Bauer 824). It is not at all surprising that money is at the root of their evil (cf. 1 Tim. 6:9-10). They are not motivated by the truth. They have no genuine interest in helping people. It is all about themselves and their selfish desires. Peter says they **exploit you with false words**. **Exploit** (ἐμπορεύομαι) means "to engage with someone in a business transaction, buy and sell, trade in" (Bauer 324).

> This greed leads them to exploit Christians, that is, to "make a profit" (TEV) from the members of the Christian community, or possibly, to "take advantage of" the Christians. One way they will do this is with false words. The Greek word translated false primarily means "invented," "fabricated," or "made up" (as in TEV "made-up stories"). False words therefore are stories or accounts or teachings that have no factual basis but are simply the result of the clever imaginations of the false teachers. This of course is related to 1:16, "cleverly devised myths," and the meaning is essentially the same, although Peter uses a different Greek word. What is being asserted here is that it is not the apostles and Christian teachers, but the false teachers, who are depending on concocted fairy tales (Arichea and Hatton 107).

These verses, then, identify the two things that motivate these false teachers: 1) Sexual promiscuity and 2) Greed. There is zero nobility in their actions. Everything they do is carefully calculated to advance their perverted desires and lavish lifestyles. It is troubling, even shocking, that such people could get a foothold in the church, even to the point where "many will follow their sensuality" (v. 2). Yet Peter is doing his job in educating them and warning them. This epistle is not the only one designed to heighten the awareness of the church and enable them to spot **false words** and those who spread them.

> The early church is in a crisis due to the presence of those who claim divine authority for their teaching and prophecies but whose claims are false according to apostolic evaluation. Mechanisms were put in place to aid the young congregations to differentiate the true from the false in the absence of what we know as the Christian canon (Matt. 7:15-23; 1 Thess. 5:20-22; 2 Thess. 2:2; 1 John 4:1-3; Did. 11; Aune 1983: 222). Many NT epistles were sent precisely for this reason as the apostles sought to warn against error and, at the same time, resolve the tension between the mission that moved them onward and the consolidation of the young congregations (Gene Green 238).

The second part of verse 3 would have been a good place to start a new verse. Peter is now done describing the false teachers. He will make two declarations regarding them and then follow with evidences from history that prove those declarations. First, Peter says **their judgment from long ago is not idle**. The word **judgment** (κρίμα) means a "legal decision rendered by a judge, judicial verdict…mostly in an unfavorable sense, of the condemnatory verdict and sometimes the subsequent punishment itself 2 Pet. 2:3; Jude 4" (Bauer 567). God had decreed **long ago** (even in OT times) what would be the fate of those who practice wickedness (Ps. 1:6; Eccl. 12:13-14). While the execution of that decree was delayed, because of God's patience (cf. 3:9), it is **not idle** (ἀργέω—stopped, slacked off). Solomon perfectly described the situation here: "Because the sentence against an evil deed is not executed quickly, therefore the hearts of the sons of men among them are given fully to do evil" (Eccl. 8:11). Yet Solomon knew that it would not end well for such evildoers, as does Peter. Second, Peter says **their destruction is not asleep** (νυστάζω—asleep/drowsy). God has not fallen asleep on the job. He has not been distracted with other things and so has forgotten about His decrees against wicked men. The truth is these men have escaped nothing and the full force of God's wrath will come upon them. Peter calls that wrath God's destruction (ἀπώλεια—v. 1). This is where God will destroy their sensual and greedy lives and replace **it** with eternal torment. A precious soul, given to selfish and sinful desires, is now ruined.

Verses 4-9 compose one single sentence in the Greek (one of the longest, rivaling Eph. 1:3-14). The structure is found with a protasis (the "if" part of a conditional sentence), which serves as the foundation of four examples of his thesis statement (the apodosis—"then") found in verse 9. In the Greek text the word **if** (εἰ) is found only in verse 4. Grammatically the word is designed to be repeated throughout the protasis (which each clause having the conjunction καί—"and"). This is why translations like the NAS, NKJV, KJV, ASV will have the following:

> V. 4—For **if** God did not spare angels…
>
> V. 6—And **if** He condemned the cities of Sodom and Gomorrah…
>
> V. 7—And **if** He rescued righteous Lot…

The ESV, Holman Christian, and NIV include these, but reflect one more "if:"

> V. 5—**if** He did not spare the ancient world

Most commentators will argue that Peter is giving three examples (angels, flood, wicked cities). Two of those examples (the flood and wicked cities) also include persons that God delivered (see Sermon Seed: God Knows). These are all designed to prove the thesis statement found in verse 9.

2:4—Peter's first example is that **God did not spare angels when they sinned**. Much discussion has taken place regarding this example. What event is Peter referring to? The following are suggested:

1) *Peter is referring to some unknown historical event.* Kelcy said: "Peter does not specify when these angels sinned, nor does he say what their sin was. There is no information in the Bible in this subject beyond that which is given by Peter and Jude" (139). Roberts made the following observation: "There is nothing really in the OT itself to indicate that this is the meaning of the story of Gen. 6:1ff, and it is impossible for me to believe that Peter means to give historicity to such tales. The story may well be a perversion of true teaching about the fall of angels who kept not their first or original habitation. They did sin in some way, and their punishment is described" (80-1).

2) *Peter is referring to angelic rebellion before the creation.* Walls and Anders said: "The first example gives an intriguing but partial glimpse into the world beyond our human experience—a world of angelic beings. At one time before the creation of the universe as we know it, they served God the Father. Even in that context, they rebelled against Him. As a result, God judged them" (125).

3) *Peter is referring to the event described in Genesis 6:1ff.* This view sees the "sons of God" as angels (cf. Job 1:6). These angels "saw that the daughters of men were beautiful and took wives for themselves." This act was a clear rebellion against the divine order and brought about divine judgment (both for the angels—described in the following sentences; and for humanity with the flood).

In my view the third position is the most viable. Consider the following reasons that support the view that Peter has Genesis 6:1ff in view. These points come from Michael Hite's class notes on 2 Peter (24-27):

1. The idea that the "sons of God" in Genesis 6 were the descendants of Seth was not popularized until the 4th century A.D.

2. Everywhere the phrase "sons of God" is used in the OT it refers to angels (Gen. 6:2-4; Job 1:6; 2:1; 38:7)

3. The wording of the same example given by Jude confirms the sin of the angels was sexual.

4. This was the mindset of the Jews during the Intertestamental Period. The pseudepigraphic works of the Book of Enoch (6-11) and The Testament of Reuben confirms this mindset.

5. There are a number of early church fathers that hold this view including Tertullian (160-225 A.D.) and Athenagoras (133-190 A.D.).

6. Angels are seen as men with physical form throughout Scripture (cf. Gen. 19:3).

7. 1 Corinthians 11:10—Women are to have a sign of authority on their heads (veil)—"because of the angels."

8. Spiritual beings seem to have an aversion to water.

    a. They must pass through "waterless places seeking rest" (Matt. 12:43; Luke 11:24-26).

    b. When Jesus cast the demon possessed pigs into the sea, Matthew's account says the demons perished in the waters (Matt. 8:32—the nominative noun is "they" the demons not the swine [accusative]).

9. All of Peter's other examples in this section are from Genesis (the Flood, Noah, Sodom and Gomorrah, Lot).

Hite concludes with the following observation:

> POINT: Regardless of your personal view of Genesis 6 the religious culture of the first century believed Genesis 6 was about angels coming to the earth—they were punished for that with the flood. Since Peter uses "angels when they sinned" as the first example to prove the God has always punished evil, it MUST be an event that the first-century church knew about well—that only fits with Genesis 6 (27).

Schreiner (336) also takes the following conclusion:

> Some scholars in the history of interpretation have identified this as the prehistoric fall of angels. It is doubtful, however, that Peter referred to this event in this particular text, even if it is a legitimate deduction theologically. Instead, we can be almost certain that Peter followed Jewish tradition at this point and referred to the sin angels committed with women in Genesis 6:1-4 (1 Enoch 6-19, 21, 86-88; 106:13-17; Jub. 4:15, 22; 5:1; CD 2:17-19; 1QapGen 2:1; T. Reu. 5:6-7; T. Naph. 3:5; 2 Bar. 56:10-14; cf. Josephus, Ant. 1.73)

Learning 2 Peter 2

Peter makes reference to the angels **when they sinned**. He does not mention what sin they committed, which is probably an indication that the readers knew what sin he has in mind. The parallel with Jude provides further evidence that it is the sexual sin of Genesis 6. These angels, like the wicked men of Sodom "went after strange [unauthorized] flesh" (Jude 7). These sinning angels received two decisive acts of judgment from God: 1) **He cast them into hell**. The word for **Hell** (ταρταρόω) is where we get the word Tartarus. "Tartarus was thought of by the Greeks as a subterranean place lower than Hades where divine punishment was meted out, and so regarded in Israelite apocalyptic as well: Job 41:24; 1 Enoch 20:2; Philo, Exs. 152; Josephus, Against Apion 2, 240; Sibylline Oracles 2, 302; 4, 186) hold captive in Tartarus 2 Pet. 2:4" (Bauer 991). 2) He **committed them to pits of darkness**. This terminology reminds us of the numerous times that Jesus described Hell as a place of "outer darkness" (Matt. 8:12; 22:13; 25:30). Combined with the first phrase, these rebellious angels have received the full force of God's wrath and are being kept in a place that is vivid in its awful description. These angels are to remain there until **judgment**.

Special Note: There are still evil angels in the world, including their lord, Satan (cf. 2 Cor. 11:14; Rev. 12:7-9). Therefore, Peter seems to be indicating that those angels who participated in this sin received an immediate judgment where they are being held in Hell. Unlike humanity, whose judgment and punishment awaits the day of judgment (along with Satan—Rev. 20:10), these sinning angels were issued their decree of punishment immediately. Jude says, "He has kept in eternal bonds under darkness for the judgment of the great day" (6). Why then, are these angels being treated differently (then those who initially joined Satan—if our understanding of the initial rebellion is accurate)? Scholars are unsure, but some suggest that Genesis 6 is describing a *second rebellion*, this time from angels who—up to that point—had remained faithful to God. Their direct interaction with mankind was where they "did not keep their own domain" and "abandoned their proper abode" (Jude 6). Angels who do this receive immediate punishment.

2:5—Peter's *second example* is the **ancient world**. The context clearly shows that Peter has in mind the world during the days of Noah. This wicked time is described by Moses: "Then the Lord saw that the wickedness of man was great on the earth, and that every intent of the thoughts of his heart was only evil continually" (Gen. 6:5). Proving Peter's point of verse 9, God did not **spare** (φείδομαι—to save from loss or discomfort; Bauer 1051). This is the same word in verse 4.

Fortunately, with this second example there emerges a good story—one that will also confirm the thesis of verse 9: **Noah**. Peter says that God **preserved** (φυλάσσω—"to protect by taking careful measures, guard, protect"—Bauer 1068) **Noah with seven others**. The readers certainly understand that God took extensive measures to save Noah and his family while he constructed the Ark. That protection lasted through the days of the flood in which mankind perished (**He brought a flood upon the world of the ungodly**). To further confirm verse 9, Peter refers to Noah as a **preacher of righteousness**. The word **righteousness** (δικαιοσύνη) comes from the same root as the word "unrighteous" found in verse 9. "Noah's preaching is not mentioned in Genesis, but was well-known in Jewish tradition. It is especially prominent in the first book of the Sibylline Oracles, a product of Hellenistic Judaism, in which a long sermon of Noah's is given (Sibylline Oracles 1:148–98). Normally Noah was said to have preached repentance to his wicked contemporaries" (Bauckham 250).

2:6—Peter's *third example* comes from Genesis 19. The evil cities of **Sodom and Gomorrah** were **condemned** to **destruction** (καταστροφή). This word means "condition of total destruction, with the implication that nothing is in its customary place or position, ruin, destruction" (Bauer 528). God accomplished this by **burning them to ashes** (τεφρόω). In Jewish literature the fate of these two ancient cities had eschatological significance (Jubilees 16:5; 2 Maccabees 2:5). Oftentimes Sodom and Gomorrah serve as a warning to those who would be disobedient (Deut. 29:22-28; Matt. 10:15; 11:23-24; Luke 10:12; cf. also in some extra-biblical Jewish literature—2 Maccabees 2:5; Wisdom of Solomon 10:6-8). This is Peter's intention as well, who are an example to those who would live ungodly thereafter.

2:7-8—As with the last example, Peter presents the antithesis to the fate of Sodom and Gomorrah (i.e. the ungodly). **Lot**, like Noah, is **rescued** from condemnation. The high moral quality of Lot is found in three descriptive terms: First, he is **righteous** (δίκαιος), a word that Peter will use three times to describe him! Second, Lot was **oppressed by the sensual conduct of unprincipled men**. A reference to **sensual conduct** provides a link to the "sensuality" of the false teachers (v. 2, 10, 13, 14, 18; 3:3). Do they think their unbridled lust will have a different result than that at Sodom? This section is designed to prove that such will not be the case. To say that Lot was **oppressed** (καταπονέω) means that he was worn out by their sinful activities (Bauer 525). Third, Lot **felt his righteous soul tormented**. The word **tormented** (βασανίζω) means "to subject to severe distress, torment, harass" (Bauer 168). Rather than allow the wicked environment to influence him, Lot was distressed about it.

It is important to note these two examples of godliness (i.e. Noah and Lot). They each serve as a demonstration that God has good things planned for those who serve Him. This serves as an important backdrop to what will be said in 3:13. There are the "new heavens and new earth" reserved for those who, like Lot and Noah, are examples of "holy conduct and godliness" (3:11, 14). See Sermon Seed: "Noah and Lot: Righteous in an Unrighteous World"

2:9—Peter now arrives at his main point, the thesis statement of this section (the apodosis). Three convincing examples have been given. The false teachers, who foolishly operate without fear of God's wrath, needed this history lesson. What has been determined is this: **The Lord knows**. The word **knows** (οἶδα) is a Greek word that typically describes factual, intellectual knowledge. In a passage like this, it is designed to illustrate that God has not forgotten what to do in dealing with mankind. He **knows** and has always known what to do. "Peter's declaration that God 'knows' (οἶδεν, oiden) how to deliver the devout is not a simple statement about His cognition but rather a declaration of His ability" (Gene Green 262). Two specific categories are mentioned: First, the **Lord knows how to rescue the godly from temptation**. While Noah and Lot were not called **godly** (εὐσεβής) but "righteous," they certainly were godly men. Both of these men lived among the "ungodly" (vv. 5, 6). Peter notes that God knows how to **rescue** (ῥύομαι), a word that means "to rescue from danger, save, rescue, deliver, preserve" (Bauer 907). It is the same word used in verse 7, where Lot is proof that the Lord knows how to **rescue**. While it is true that God knows how to rescue from various dangers and threats, Peter specifically has **temptation** in mind. This word (πειρασμός) means "an attempt to make one do something wrong, temptation, enticement to sin" (Bauer 793). These men could have allowed the evil to influence them (cf. 1 Cor. 15:33). Instead, they used the power of God and did not give into the temptation (see 1 Cor. 10:13, where God gives us the same promise).

Second, the **Lord knows how…to keep the unrighteous under punishment for the day of judgment**. When men choose to be **unrighteous** (ἄδικος—"acting in a way that is contrary to what is right, unjust, crooked"—Bauer 21), the Lord knows what to do with them. He will **keep** (τηρέω—"to retain in custody, keep watch over, guard"—Bauer 1002) them **under punishment.** They may foolishly think that their sinful choices have gone unnoticed (**is asleep**—v. 3), but such is far from the truth. God has made a reservation for them, which will come due on the **day of judgment**. While the language here is difficult, I do not believe Peter is saying that these are now being punished, but that their punishment is on hold until the day of judgment (which agrees with 3:7). "On the other hand, a majority of commentators take κολαζομένους to refer to punishment at the day of judgment" (Bauckham 254).

Peter's many verbs (found in vv. 4-8) prove undeniably that God knows how to deal with man. See the Sermon Seed: "God Knows—Part Two."

2:10—The world is full of wicked men, who will be charged with a variety of wicked deeds. Peter, however, is focused on the enemies of the church—the false teachers of verse 1—who are causing so much damage to the cause of Christ. Those who are headed toward God's punishment on the day of judgment are **especially** (μάλιστα—here the sense is "specifically") the following:

First, those who **indulge the flesh in its corrupt desires**. Peter had already identified the false teachers as those motivated by sensuality (v. 2). Their unbridled desires are a perfect indication of their **corruption** (μιασμός—that which is polluted or defiled).

> The "corrupt desire" of the flesh followed by these men likely refers to sexual sin. We have already seen a reference to their sexual sin in 2:2. The sin of the angels (2:4) and Sodom and Gomorrah (2:6) included sexual deviation, and 2:7 indicates that Lot was oppressed in part by their sensual perversity. Since the opponents repudiated any future judgment, they lived dissolute lives sexually, without any thought of a reckoning on the last day (Schreiner 345).

Second, they **despise authority.** The word **despise** (καταφρονέω) means "to look down on someone or something with contempt or aversion, with implication that one considers the object of little value, look down on, despise, scorn, treat with contempt" (Bauer 529). **Authority** (κυριότης) has the basic meaning of "the majestic power that the κύριος wields, ruling power, lordship, dominion" (Bauer 579). The challenge here is determining the **authority** these evil men **despise**. Proposed theories include the angels, but such is unlikely since the word is in the singular; church leaders or government rulers, but that also is unlikely because it is in the singular. The most likely meaning is Christ Himself.

> *Despise authority* is related to a similar expression in Jude 1:8. However, there are some differences in meaning and emphasis. Whereas in Jude it is possible to interpret authority as referring to angelic beings or even to human authority in general, here the meaning is more likely to be the authority of God or the authority of Christ" (Arichea and Hatton 118).

If we are correct here, then these false teachers, with uncanny boldness and arrogance, have no problem publicly loathing Jesus Himself. Peter already said that they were "denying the Master who bought them" (2:1). On the day of judgment, they will stand "before the judgment seat of Christ" (2 Cor. 5:10). It will be apparent then what a monumental mistake they made by doing this.

Third, they are **daring** (presumptuous—NKJV; bold—ESV and NIV). The word (τολμητής) is unique, describing one who is audacious, arrogant, and willing to go to extremes (even when those extremes far surpass normal bounds of decorum and decency).

Fourth, they are **self-willed** (αὐθάδης) a word that describes one who is "self-willed, stubborn, arrogant" (Bauer 150). They are, as we would say, "full of themselves." Life is all about them, and their chief concern is pleasing themselves.

Fifth, **they do not tremble when they revile angelic majesties**. The word **revile** (βλασφημέω) is where the English *blaspheme* comes from. These false teachers have no problem (**do not tremble**) at the presumptuous action to **revile angelic majesties**. This phrase, and one similar in Jude 8, is unique and has created much discussion. However, it is likely that Peter has something different in view then does Jude. The word **angelic** is not in the Greek text. Rather, the word is simply "glories" (δόξα). Nevertheless, **angelic majesties** is a viable interpretation of this phrase. The question is, though, what angels does Peter have in mind? Two views have emerged:

a) *Evil angels*—those who rebelled with Satan, or those sinning angels (who were referred to in v. 4).

In that case the passage would mean that these teachers speak disrespectfully of Satan and evil angels (perhaps because they believe that they will neither share their fate nor come under their sway), even though the (holy) angelic beings who are higher in strength and power (both honorable qualities) than they are, and thus their betters, do not bring a slanderous judgment against the "glorious ones" (i.e., fallen or evil angels). (Davids 235)

b) *Good angels*—the false teachers are making fun of, even mocking, God's holy angels. Since they do not believe in a judgment day (3:3-4), any passage that links angels with the coming of Jesus in judgment will be criticized (cf. Matt. 13:41; 2 Thess. 1:7).

We may assume that their rejection of angelic authority is linked to the common understanding of the angelic role in the execution of the final judgment (Neyrey 1993: 213; Perkins 1995: 184). These are not the "fallen angels" (contra Bauckham 1983: 261) but those who accompany the Lord in the great assize (Matt. 13:39, 41, 49; 16:27; 24:31; 25:31; 2 Thess. 1:7; Rev. 7:2; 8:2, 6, 13; 9:15) (Gene Green 271).

Both of these views have some merit. However, I believe the first one—that they are assuming the position of judge and jury over evil angels—makes the most sense. Even good angels, who are far more powerful than these false teachers, would not dare assume the position of judge. That belongs to God, and to Him alone.

2:11—Peter intends to illustrate how foolish is their blasphemy. The **angels** (good ones here, because they are **before the Lord**), who are amazingly powerful beings (**greater in might and power**) would never take on a position of judge. This is even when the judgment **against them** (against these false teachers or against the evil angels) is apparent. The angels know their place; these false teachers do not know theirs.

While the two views of the **glories** are debated, the main point is not. The false teachers are way out of bounds in their arrogant judgments and criticisms. Here are two quotes. One, by Davids (who takes the view that the angels were good angels), and the second, by Bauckham (who takes the view that the angels were evil angels):

Learning 2 Peter 2

If this reading is accepted, then the sense is that teachers arrogantly slander angels, but angels, who would have far more right to accuse them, do not bring against the teachers the charge that the Lord has spoken. For the angels to speak it would be slander, even though it is the Lord's judgment. This would be a warning to Christians not to take over the Lord's place as judge, a theme also found in James 4:11-12 (Davids 235-6).

The phrase ἰσχύϊ καὶ δυνάμει μείζονες ὄντες ("although they are greater in strength and power") compares the angels either (a) with the δόξας ("glorious ones"), or (b) with the false teachers. Either would make good sense: (a) Even the angels, who are more powerful than the devils, do not insult them. How foolhardy of the false teachers, who are less powerful than the devils, to do so! (b) The false teachers venture to insult the devils, whereas even the angels, who are so much more powerful than the false teachers, do not do so. It is probably slightly more natural to read the phrase in sense (a) (in which case both μείζονες ("greater") and αὐτῶν ("them") refer back to δόξας), but the general significance is the same in either case (Bauckham 262)

2:12—Peter now returns to his list where he is describing the false teachers. His *sixth* observation is they are **like unreasoning animals**. Man was God's crowning act of creation. He was the only one who was created in the image of God. He was given intellect, emotion, and a conscience. These false teachers, however, are not displaying the higher knowledge they claimed. Instead, they are like **unreasoning animals** (ἄλογος—devoid of logic and common sense). Animals have no moral compass, no understanding of right and wrong. They have no spirituality. These false teachers are just like them! And, since they have determined to act like animals, they deserve the same fate as the animals who were **born as creatures of instinct to be captured and killed**. "Their actions will not go unpunished. They will perish. This may simply refer to their inevitable death after living animal-like lives, or it may be a reference to their eternal punishment apart from Jesus Christ" (Walls and Anders 128). This is the first time that Peter will show a common pattern: describe the false teachers then identify the consequences of their wickedness. He will do this again in verses 14, 16, 17, 19, 20.

Seventh, they are reviling where they have no knowledge. The word **reviling** (βλασφημέω) is the same as in verse 10. They claim to have a superior knowledge, and that knowledge affords them the right to speak condemning and critical words (against God, against Christ, against angels, against the apostles—you name it!). The truth is, however, they **have no knowledge**. Peter has taken consider time encouraging the Christians to recognize and believe the "true knowledge" (1:3, 8) that was given to them by the apostles (1:12; 3:1-2). Part of their ignorance is seen in that they do not even know their own fate! They will join the wild beasts in **destruction** (φθορά).

The false teachers act like irrational animals without the restraint that angels and righteous men have. They may claim a gnōsis (a special knowledge), but they blaspheme out of their ignorance. Like wild beasts who are slaves to their instincts and are born to be slaughtered, they too are destined for destruction (lit., "in their destruction, they shall be destroyed") (Blum 280).

2:13—The first part actually belongs with the end of verse 12. It completes the thought that the reason these false teachers will be **suffering** is because such **suffering** is the **wages** (μισθός—"remuneration for work done, pay, wages" [Bauer 653]) of **doing wrong**. Since they believed there was no consequence to their sinful lifestyles (because there was no judgment day), they "followed after their own lusts" (3:3).

Eighth, **they count it a pleasure to revel in the daytime**. The word **revel** (τρυφή) means "engagement in a fast, self-indulgent lifestyle, indulgence, reveling" (Bauer 1018). While sinning is never acceptable—day or night—most sinful activity is done under the cloak of darkness (cf. Rom. 13:12-13). These evil teachers are so entrenched in wickedness that the daylight hours, when most people work, is time for them to continue in their debauchery. The word **pleasure** (ἡδονή) is where our word *hedonism* comes from.

Ninth, they are **stains**. This word (σπίλος) is the common one for a spot or stain, but here Peter describes them as an unsightly and defiling. Peter will later encourage the Christians to be found "spotless (same word) and blameless" when Jesus returns (3:14). In the Ephesian letter Paul says the church should be "without spot (same word) or wrinkle or any such thing" (5:27).

Tenth, they are **blemishes**. This word (μῶμος) normally describes a bodily defect, but here is used to refer to a moral defect. In the OT an animal was unfit for sacrifice if it had a blemish (Lev. 1:3), and a man could not serve as a priest if he had a blemish (Lev. 21:21). These false teachers are unfit, defiled, and unclean. Their sinful lifestyles are such that they are examples of the opposite goal stated in 1:4, where Peter encourages the Christians to "escape the corruption that is in the world by lust." They have not escaped this corruption but are contributors to it. As a result they are unfit for Christian service and unusable to God (cf. 2 Tim. 2:20-21).

Eleventh, they are **reveling in their deceptions**. This is admittedly a difficult phrase. Most scholars run to Jude to try to make sense of it. However, it is unlikely that Peter and Jude have the same issue, or people, in mind. **Reveling** (μῶμος) means "to engage in self-indulgent behavior, revel, carouse, cavort" (Bauer 341). **Deceptions** (ἀπάτη) refers to "deception, deceitfulness" (Bauer 99). Taken at face value, these evil men find great delight in their ability to trick and deceive. Peter had earlier noted how they "secretly introduce destructive heresies" (2:1). Their evil tactics have proven successful, as they have duped many (2:2). Now Peter accuses them of taking an extra degree of pleasure in their deceptive powers.

Twelfth, they **carouse with you**. Normally the word **carouse** (συνευωχέομαι) is a good word, simply meaning "to eat together." If we take it in the normal sense, then Peter is noting that these false teachers use common meals as opportunities to deceive (merging this point with the previous). It is possible, even likely, that Peter intends to show how even something that is normally good (common meals) were twisted into sinful activities, characterized by gluttony and immorality. Note: Many scholars believe this is in reference to the early Christian's "love feasts" (as well as Jude 12). There is ample evidence in Scripture that such was done (what we might refer to as "potlucks"—Acts 2:46; 20:11; 1 Cor. 11:17). Such feasts were intended as fellowship occasions where Christians shared not only their food but the love and the joy of being fellow disciples of Christ. How tragic it is, then, that these false teachers took advantage of such occasions to deceive and spread their immoral philosophies.

2:14—*Thirteenth*, they have eyes **full of adultery**. Their minds were so wicked that every girl they looked at they lusted after. They stand in stark contrast to the righteous Job who said that he had made a "covenant with his eyes" and therefore would not look upon a virgin. Jesus condemned such lustful looks and thoughts (Matt. 5:28). The Greek literally reads that his eyes were full of an **adulteress** (μοιχαλίς). They did not look at a woman as a sister in Christ, or a child of God, but as a potential partner for sex.

Fourteenth, they **never cease from sin**. This clause can easily go with the previous point, but for our purpose we'll look at it individually. Peter intends to underscore the moral depravity of these men whom some (in the church!) are seeing as leaders and examples (cf. 2:2, 14, 18). How could they abandon the words of the holy apostles (cf. Eph. 3:5) for such men? Their sinful activities are continual. Most of these activities are of a sexual nature, a point that Peter has frequently made, and will continue to make (2:2, 7, 10, 18; 3:3).

Fifteenth, they are **enticing unstable souls**. Perhaps this is the most amazing part of this section. How could men of such immoral characteristics influence anyone? Shouldn't even the most naïve see through them? Apparently not. So, how do they succeed in **enticing** (δελεάζω—"to arouse someone's interest in something by adroit measures, lure, entice"—Bauer 217)? *First*, they are very good at what they do. They are smooth talkers and charismatic individuals (v. 3; cf. Rom. 16:18; Col. 2:4). *Second*, they have produced a convincing message. This message could have taken several angles. It could have focused on the idea that God made us sexual beings, and therefore intends for us to freely enjoy sexual relationships. Or, it could have suggested that God wants them to be happy, and that happiness could be found in numerous activities (including sexual ones). Most likely, however, is that their promotion of sexual freedom is tied to their belief that there will be no judgment (3:3-4). *Third*, their victims are **unstable souls**. This word (ἀστήρικτος) identifies one who is weak or unsettled. Peter will return to these kinds of people in 3:16. These heretics are seeking out those who are weak in their faith (perhaps new Christians?).

> Since the verse directs our attention to sexual sin and greed, perhaps the teachers enticed people to sin by promising them that they could live for sexual pleasure and the material comforts of this life without any thought of judgment. Such a theology seemed too good to pass up for the unstable, and they swallowed the bait quite eagerly (Schreiner 352).

Sixteenth, they have a heart trained in greed. We had learned earlier that money was a major motivating factor in their evil work (2:3). Peter now reminds us that **greed** is at the core. There is no nobility to be found in their character or work. It is selfish, through and through. The word **trained** (γυμνάζω) is where our word *gymnasium* comes from. They are **trained**, which conveys the idea that they have become proficient and skilled in their seductions.

> "Experts" (*gymnadzo*) is a term borrowed from the athletic world, and it describes the well-trained athlete. These false teachers had trained themselves well. They had worked out for long periods of time. They had exercised to the point of exhaustion in an effort to become well-toned experts in "greed," which simply means "a desire to have more." These false teachers were out for what they could get out of their religion (Walls and Anders 128).

Peter takes a break from his description of these false teachers by expressing a moral judgment. They are **accursed children**. The word **accursed** (κατάρα) is a strong word of condemnation. While these men are enjoying their sinful and materialistic fruits, they are blissfully unaware of the terrible fate that awaits them. Of course, they do not believe that such a fate exists, since they deny there will be a judgment day. What a horrible day it will be when they find themselves face to face with the God they mocked! Their twisting and distorting of Scripture (which enabled them to do what they did) will result "in their own destruction" (3:16).

3:15-16—*Seventeenth*, they are **forsaking the right way**. Peter has been preaching a message of truth (1:12) and "true knowledge" (1:3, 8). He has shown them the right way—a way which will enable them to "escape the corruption that is in the world by lust" (1:4). These heretics, however, have **forsaken** (καταλείπω—"to cause to be left in a place, leave [behind]"—Bauer 520) the **right way** (the way of truth). Notice that the word **forsaken** means "leave behind." This again illustrates that these men were once faithful Christians, but fell away, leaving behind the faith they once embraced (cf. 2:1, 20-22).

Eighteenth, **they have gone astray**. This phrase goes with the previous one, but we'll separate it for the sake of emphasis. As noted in the last paragraph, the evidence is clear that these false teachers once were faithful to the truth. It is not possible to **go astray** from something that you were never a part of to begin with. The fact that they were once true Christians increases the tragedy of this section. They knew the truth and followed it! However, they were overcome with lust and greed and abandoned a faith that would save them.

As with verse 14, Peter is going to deviate from his descriptive list to offer to his readers a history lesson. These men, in many ways, are like **Balaam** (read about him in Numbers 22–24). This Old Testament man, who was given wonderful opportunities by God, **loved the wages of unrighteousness**.

> An Old Testament story illustrates this emphasis (see Num. 22–24). Balaam, who was supposed to be a prophet of God, loved money more than God. He was willing to pursue fame and fortune instead of obeying God. He also taught immorality. As a result, he was rebuked by God through a donkey. For a donkey to rebuke the prophet's madness reflects not only on the foolishness of Balaam but also on that of all false teachers (Walls and Anders 129).

> The way of Balaam is not explained any further; there are three suggested possible points of comparison: greed, leading people to sin, and claiming to be God's prophet or teacher. Perhaps the first of these, namely "greed," is the most probable point of comparison, since it is mentioned in verse 14. This also fits what follows, since Balaam is described as one who loved gain from wrongdoing. We are told in the Old Testament that it was love of money that caused Balaam to lead Israel to sin (see Num 22–24; 31:16, and especially Jude 1:11 for further discussion of Balaam) (Arichea and Hatton 130).

2:17—Nineteenth, they are **springs without water**. The dry climate of Israel is well known. Water was precious, and the lack of it jeopardized their health, crops, flocks—every aspect of their daily lives. These false teachers promised something important and desired, like a **spring** promised refreshing water. However, when one arrives at the **spring**, he is disappointed to find that it is **without water** (cf. Jer. 14:3). So also are these false teachers. One would come to them with the hope of receiving refreshing and valuable instruction. They will leave with nothing of value. A similar situation is with the fig tree that Jesus cursed. It promised figs (since the tree had leaves, and fig trees with leaves typically have figs), yet there were none to be found. As a result Jesus cursed the tree (Matt. 21:18-21; Mark 11:12-14, 20-24)). The meaning of that event is this: The scribes

Learning 2 Peter 2

and Pharisees promised much, but when the people went to them for spiritual guidance, they left empty handed. They, like the fig tree, will be cursed (and such will also be the judgment of Peter's false teachers).

Twentieth, they are **mists driven by a storm**. Like the previous metaphor, **mists** are those which promise to bring moisture to the dry earth. In Israel the morning **mists** are incredibly important to the growth of crops. These false teachers, however, have been blown off course. The idea seems to be that the **storm** of greed and sensuality has blown them off course. The language reminds us of Paul's words in Ephesians 4:14: "As a result, we are no longer to be children, tossed here and there by waves, and carried about by every wind of doctrine, by the trickery of men, by craftiness in deceitful scheming…."

Following his pattern, Peter stops to remind us of the consequences of their sinfulness: for **whom the black darkness has been reserved**. One of the frightening aspects of Hell is the "outer darkness" that describes it. Earlier Peter had said that the sinning angels were "committed to pits of darkness" (2:4). Jesus had described Hell as a place of "outer darkness; in that place there shall be weeping and gnashing of teeth" (Matt. 8:12; cf. 22:13; 25:30). The word **reserved** (τηρέω) has been used by Peter already (2:4, 9) and will be used again (3:7). The word describes a future appointment, one that is inescapable. The heretics do not think they have such an appointment (3:3-4). Yet God has a **reservation** in their name.

2:18—Here a *twenty-first* description is given: These false teachers are **speaking out** arrogant words of vanity. They are not shy in their public declarations (**speaking out**), but their words are 1) **arrogant** and 2) **vanity**. **Arrogant** (ὑπέρογκος) means "haughty, pompous, bombastic" (Bauer 1034). It is made up of words that literally mean "of excessive size, puffed up." These men see themselves as superior to others, and their words demonstrate such. **Vanity** (ματαιότης) means "state of being without use or value, emptiness, futility, purposelessness, transitoriness" (Bauer 621). This further confirms the statement that they are "springs without water" (v. 17). Their teachings are useless.

Twenty-second they **entice by fleshly desires**. The word **entice** (δελεάζω) was used in verse 14. It is a word that describes a fishing lure, or anything used to seduce or attract. Their "bate" is **fleshly desires**. The word **desire** (ἐπιθυμία) is not always negative (cf. 1 Pet. 1:12—"long" to look). However, when coupled with the word **fleshly**, the phrase takes on a sinful desire—a lust. These men are fueled by their insatiable desire for sexual gratification. As Peter noted earlier, they don't have pupils in their eyes, they have adulteries (v. 14). That is all they see. Peter's point here is to describe the insidious work of the heretics. The promise of sexual activity is the bait they use to draw in their unsuspecting victims.

Twenty-third they **entice…by sensuality**. The word **sensuality** (ἀσέλγεια—see 2:2) means "lack of self-constraint which involves one in conduct that violates all bounds of what is socially acceptable, self-abandonment" (Bauer 141). This serves as another "lure" used by the false teachers. The promise of free sex and the fulfillment of any fantasy or desire is a powerful draw to those weak in the faith.

Who is it that these false teachers are influencing? **Those who barely escape**. The word **escape** (ἀποφεύγω—cf. 1:4; again in v. 20) is a rare word that indicates that the person recently escaped from "the corruption that is in the world by lust"—that is, they are new converts. Jesus referred to new converts as "little ones who believe in Me" (Matt. 18:6). He was especially critical of "stumbling blocks" that would make these new converts stumble. Their judgment will be harsh, and a special "woe" is issued to them ("Woe to that man through whom the stumbling-block comes!—Matt. 18:7). Peter's false teachers are targeting new converts, because they will be much easier to "hook" than more mature Christians. Peter had referred to these new Christians as "unstable" in 2:14.

Twenty-fourth, Peter describes them as ones who live in error. The word **error** (πλάνη) is a common word in the Greek NT. It means "wandering from the path of truth, error, delusion, deceit, deception" (Bauer 822). These men are not making an occasional mistake, they **live** (ἀναστρέφω) in error. It is who they are. Peter's point is that these new converts have **escaped** from these men (and others who teach **error**). His concern, however, is that they be drawn back into their pre-Christian lifestyle (vv. 20-22).

2:19—*Twenty-fifth*, they are **promising them freedom**. The **them** are those who "escaped" in the previous verse (new converts). These false teachers are promising them **freedom**, which is something they already have (a freedom from sin when they obeyed the Gospel—v. 20). The Gospel message, which involves self-control and restraint (cf. 1:5-10) could be twisted to be something burdensome (1 John 5:3), unpleasant, and undesirable. They promote a teaching that says: "Who wants to live under the oppressive rules of Christianity?" They would follow that mantra with a reminder that there is no reason to be moral, since there are no consequences for such a choice (sine there is no judgment day—3:3-4). They openly promote the philosophy "eat, drink and be merry for tomorrow we die." Even Paul acknowledged the logic of such "if the dead are not raised" (1 Cor. 15:32; cf. Isa. 22:13).

The logical question is how did these false teachers secure a foothold in the church, even to the point that they wielded such influence? Gene Green offers an interesting observation:

> The suggestion that false teachers in 2 Peter had merged Christian with Epicurean thought is surely attractive…since that philosophy not only denied the possibility of future judgment but also elevated desires (ἐπιθυμίαι, *epithymiai*) to the level of virtue, both features that mark the heretics. Epicurus distinguished between natural desires (both those that were necessary and those that were unnecessary) and empty desires. The blessed life is one that satisfies the natural and necessary desires of the flesh. As Epicurus said, "The cry of the flesh is not to be hungry, not to be thirsty, and not to be cold" (*Sententiae Vaticanae* 33). Sexual desires are, therefore, good, according to Epicurus: "As for myself, I cannot conceive of the Good if I eliminate the pleasures of taste, or the pleasures of sex, or the pleasures of listening, or the pleasures of gazing on the motions and forms pleasing to the eye" (Athenaeus 12.546E). But we are pressed hard to imagine how Epicurean thought could have gained any foothold in the church since Epicureans believed that the gods were not involved in any way in human affairs. One could expect nothing from them, neither favors nor judgment. However, the first century was a period in which disparate religious and philosophical traditions could be patched together and juxtaposed without the kind of consistency that we often erroneously presuppose in our attempts to classify movements, whether ancient or modern. Eclecticism was well established during this period (Dillon and Long 1988), and even Paul was labeled as one whose opinions were randomly bound together (Acts 17:18). The trends that the heretics reflect are not difficult to identify but the exact nature of their belief may well defy

systemization. Certainly the affirmation of bodily gratification was an appealing notion and, coupled with an exaltation of freedom (2:19), would put a very attractive, although lurid, spin on the apostolic faith (296-7).

As Peter had done previously (cf. 2:12, 14, 16, 17), he will issue a moral judgment on these false teachers. It is his hope that such judgments will resonate with the new converts so that they will avoid and reject these false teachers. Here Peter says they are **slaves of corruption**. The irony is found in that they were **promising them freedom**, but they themselves had no freedom. They were, in fact, **slaves**. Their "wild and free" lifestyles were a mirage. In truth they were bound by **corruption** (φθορά—1:4; 2:12). Proof of this claim is found in the logic: **For by what a man is overcome, by this he is enslaved**. Since these men are overcome with sexual thoughts and greed (2:14), they are slaves to these things. A slave is never free from the control of his master. So these men are never free from their true master—Satan.

> Like the beasts in 2:12, they will be destroyed, not because they are mortal, but because of their errors…chief of which is their claim to freedom from judgment and destruction. If freedom for the opponents is placed in a meaningful context, it should be interpreted as implying an acceptance of this world as the only world (no afterlife) and a corresponding rejection of the Parousia which ends this world and brings judgment in the world to come. Intellectual positions such as freedom are not held in a vacuum but belong to a coherent thought structure (Neyrey 420).

2:20—At this point scholars are divided on who "they" refers to in this last section (vv. 20-22). While there is no reason to be dogmatic, I believe the section continues the discussion of the false teachers. Consider this comment by Blum:

> Of whom is Peter speaking in verses 20-22—i.e., who does the pronoun "they" refer to? Does it refer (1) to the false teachers of verse 19, (2) to the unstable people of verse 18, or (3) more generally to both but particularly to the false teachers (cf. Balz and Schrage 140)? In my opinion, it refers basically to false teachers because (1) proximity makes the false teachers (spoken of in v. 19) the normal antecedent of "they," (2) the conjunction *gar* (untranslated in NIV) in verse 20 (*ei gar*, "for if") logically connects verse 20 with verse 19, (3) "mastered" (*hēttētai*) in verse 19 is verbally linked to "overcome" (*hēttōtai*) in verse 20, and (4) the teachers are the main subject of the whole chapter (282).

I would also offer two additional reasons that make me think we're continuing the discussion about the false teachers. First, the new converts are described as those who "escaped" (v. 18). Those described in verses 18-20 are no longer free but virtually recaptured. Second, the vivid pronouncement of judgment and analogies to dogs and swine seems too harsh for young Christians. It is fitting, however, for those more mature in the faith who later abandoned it (cf. Heb. 6:1-8).

Peter offers a clear "then" and "now" description of these false teachers. "Then" refers to the time when **they have escaped the defilements of the world**. It is clear that he has a time in the past in mind. The phrase **if after** confirms it. Regarding the word **if** (εἰ) consider this observation:

> The word *if* is used here not to mark a condition that is contrary to fact, but rather to mark a conditional statement that is true. In other words Peter is not questioning or doubting the initial faith of the false teachers (or, recent converts) but is asserting the fact that they had

at one time left their heathen loyalties and become members of the Christian community (Arichea and Hatton 136).

The word **escape** (ἀποφεύγω) is fitting, for it describes an unpleasant condition from which one desires release (like a person locked in prison or a bird in a net). Notice what they escaped from: **the defilements of the world**. The word **defilements** (μίασμα) is an interesting word, describing not only sinful activity but that which causes shame and disgrace. Paul makes a similar statement in Romans 6:21: "Therefore what benefit were you then deriving from the things of which you are now ashamed (ἐπαισχύνομαι—different word than here)? For the outcome of those things is death." How did they manage to escape? It was **by the knowledge of the Lord and Savior Jesus Christ**. The good information they received in the Gospel showed them the way out. According to 1:4, they did, in fact, escape ("having escaped"). Peter began this epistle by recognizing the value of "true knowledge," which provided all the information needed for "life and godliness" (1:3). Why are we admonished to "preach the Word" (2 Tim. 4:2)? Because the Word is the only means of salvation (James 1:21)!

After describing the "then," Peter moves to the "now." The sad present condition is this: They are **again** (πάλιν—"to return to a position or state, back—Bauer 752) **entangled** (ἐμπλέκω). This word means "to become involved in an activity to the point of interference with other activity or objective, be involved in" (Bauer 324). They are entangled **in them** (the **defilements of the world**) and are **overcome**.

> Although these people had escaped the pollutions of the world, they had returned again to its snares. They had been "overcome" (*hēttōntai*) by its power and "entangled" again by its delights. The Gospel they initially confessed they had now repudiated. The Lord and Savior they had embraced they now rejected. The world they had escaped recaptured them afresh (Schreiner 361).

The **last state** refers to their present condition where they have left the Christian faith; the **first** refers to their pre-Christian days. In other words, they went from the world (lost) to the church (saved) back to the world (lost). However, the tragedy does not end there. God's judgment for those who were never converted is different than those who were converted but then fell away. Peter says clearly that this last state (apostasy) h**as become worse for them than the first**. They will incur a stricter judgment (cf. James 3:1); they will be beaten with "many stripes" (Luke 12:48). The doctrine of degrees of punishment in Hell is confirmed here. "The greater the knowledge and privilege, the greater the responsibility. The more severe judgment will come on the one who knows" (Gene Green 304).

2:21—Peter affirms that it would have been **better** (κρείττων—more advantageous) to go from where they were ignorant (**not to have known the way of righteousness**) to the present condition of leaving the faith (**turn away from the holy commandment**). Those embracing the doctrine of "once saved always saved" argue that these being described were never truly converted. Will such an assessment fit the language here? Note: 1) **Have known**; 2) **Having known it**; 3) **turn away.** Did they know the truth? If they knew it but didn't follow it, what is Peter's point? Did they turn away? Is it possible to turn away from something that you were never near in the first place? The language is clear. These described once embraced Christianity and her teachings. They had once "escaped the defilements of the world" but have chosen to return to a lost condition. See Sermon Seed: The Possibility of Apostasy.

Learning 2 Peter 2

Of course, we might ask what is the point of this section? Does Peter hold out a glimmer of hope that these apostate heretics might repent and return to faithfulness? Such is unlikely. Rather, this section serves as a warning to those who are presently being duped by these deceivers.

> The false teachers are in the state of definite apostasy described in vv 20–22; their followers are doubtless in severe danger of joining them in it, and so these vv serve as a serious warning to the followers, but the author no doubt hopes that the warning will be effective in preventing them from sharing the false teachers' doom. Whether he held out any hope for the reclamation of the false teachers themselves we do not know, but verses 20–22 do not rule it out (Bauckham 277).

2:22—To prove his point, Peter first draws upon a familiar proverb (26:11). The proverb fits, because **it has happened to them according to the true proverb**. **Dogs**, even in Biblical times, were frequently domesticated. People would have been very familiar with the voracious appetites of these creatures, eating virtually anything and everything. Yet such did not always end well, as they would **vomit** what they had eaten. If the dog behavior ended there, one might conclude "lesson learned—the dog won't eat that again!" Yet such is not the case with dogs (or with people, sadly). The dogs, getting hungry again, will return to eat what they had previously vomited.

The second saying is not found in the Old Testament. "It does, however, readily fit into verse, and reappears in the Syrian story of Ahikar, which was certainly in existence by the second century B.C., and so may well have been known to our author" (Michael Green 143). Even though pigs were unclean animals in Mosaic Law, their behavior (like that of dogs) would be well known among the people of the first century. Christian Gentiles would have been very familiar with pigs (cf. Luke 15:15-16). It might be that Peter wants to use both sayings to illustrate not only the extent of the cleansing—both internally (dogs vomit) and externally (sow washes), but also to the tragedy of apostasy, returning to a lifestyle of defilement both in mind and body.

Learning
2 Peter 3

DENNY PETRILLO

EXEGETICAL NOTES

Chapter Three Overview: Peter begins chapter 3 by encouraging them to listen to the words spoken to them by reliable (inspired) sources, like the apostles and prophets (vv. 1-2). Peter will then discuss the claim and influence of the false teachers, especially in regard to the doctrine of the 2nd coming of Christ (vv. 3-4). Peter will expose several flaws in their arguments and present the truth regarding the end of time (vv. 5-13). He will conclude the epistle with a powerful admonition of stay faithful to the Word and continue to grow in their knowledge of it (14-18).

3:1—Peter begins by referring to this as being **the second letter I am writing to you**. As noted in the introduction, this statement has generated much discussion. Since many reject the authenticity of this epistle, this verse is viewed as an "obvious" attempt by this writer to obtain some connection with the genuine Petrine epistle. If he succeeded, it would add authority to this epistle. Yet such an attempt would be an obvious misrepresentation of the truth and an overt attempt to deceive. How could he write about the importance of truth (2:2) and stress the importance of "moral excellence" (1:5) when he is fabricating the truth? How could he boldly pass himself off as the apostle who witnessed the transfiguration (1:16-18)? In addition, how does a book like this make it into the canon of Scripture, in light of 2 Timothy 3:16-17? Because of these reasons, and others, we must accept this letter as claimed—it was written by the apostle Peter. The connection between the two Petrine epistles has been extensively discussed. However, the comment by Gene Green sums it up nicely:

> In the first letter, the author does indeed refer to what was previously received through the Gospel messengers (1 Pet. 1:12), a message rooted in the prophetic testimony (1:10-11). Moreover, 1 Peter serves to remind them of previous teaching (1:18). In the following verse (2 Pet. 3:2) Peter identifies what he wants his readers to remember—the words of the prophets and the command of the apostles. To call both 1 and 2 Peter reminders of such teaching is wholly in line with the purposes of both letters (311).

The love Peter has for his readers is demonstrated by the repetition of the word **beloved** (ἀγαπητός—3:1, 8, 14). He genuinely cares for them and wants his loving reminders to keep them from falling prey to the false teachers. He gives them a high compliment when he says they have a **sincere mind**. The word **sincere** (εἰλικρινής) means "to being sincere, without hidden motives or pretense, pure" (Bauer 282). The love expressed, along with this compliment, will go a long way in encouraging them to faithfulness. The language used in this verse plainly identifies the purpose of this **second letter**. It is a **reminder** (ὑπόμνησις) of the exhortations he gave them in the first letter.

3:2—Specifically what Peter wants them to **remember** (μιμνήσκομαι) are 1) **the words spoken beforehand by the holy prophets**—most likely a reference to the OT prophets, since the word holy is employed in referring to them (Luke 1:70; Acts 3:21; cf. Wisdom of Solomon 11:1). Peter had referenced them in the first epistle (1:10-12). I would not, however, voice a strong objection to those who think that Christian prophets are also in view here. 2) **the commandment of the Lord and Savior spoken by your apostles.** In the Great Commission Jesus commanded the apostles to make disciples by baptizing people and teaching them "to observe all that I commanded you" (Matt. 28:18-20). Following a pattern found by other apostles, Peter places himself among those who had the authority to represent the teachings of Christ (cf. Rom. 1:1, 5; 1 Cor. 14:37; 1 John 1:1–5; 4:6; Rev. 22:18). Both the **prophets** and **apostles** were used to preach the truth (cf. Eph. 2:20; 3:1-5).

3:3-4—The first main section of chapter three is found here. Peter identifies the teaching of the false teachers: They **mock** the idea of a second coming. Their contention is based on two reasons: the long delay since the promise was made and the continuation of the world (**all continues just as it was from the beginning of creation**). The motivating factor behind their mockery is **lust** (ἐπιθυμία). Peter had earlier exposed their self-serving motives (2:2, 13-14, 18). Their philosophy goes something like this: "This life is all there is, so why not enjoy all of its pleasures?" To them that meant enriching themselves by exploiting others (2:3) and to have unbridled sexual encounters (2:13-14).

Is there some validity to their claims? Consider:

1) Where is the promise of His coming? This promise was given by Jesus on several occasions (cf. Matt. 13:41-43; 16:27; 24:37, 39; 25:31; John 14:1-3) and repeated by angels (Acts 1:11) and apostles (2 Thess. 1:7; 2 Tim. 4:8; Tit. 2:13). Yet this promise was initially made over 30 years ago! The early Christians all anticipated these things to take place soon (cf. 2 Thess. 2:2-3). The fact that it had not happened led some to believe that it had already happened (2 Thess. 2:2) or—as here—it was never going to happen. It was a lie, a false claim. After all, the **fathers** (Old Testament patriarchs) have been long dead (**fell asleep**).

2) All continues just as it was from the beginning of creation. There is certainly truth in this statement. Solomon recognized the stability of earth in his day (Eccl. 1:4—"the earth remains forever"). Even David said, "He established the earth upon its foundations, so that it will not totter forever and ever" (Psa. 104:5). Consider how much time had passed since David (c. 1000 B.C.) and Solomon (c. 970 B.C.) uttered those words. And they made these statements after the earth had existed already for thousands of years. Extra note: Now add to that even more years (2,000 years at least), and the earth remains with no change today. If the false teachers had known that the promise remained unfulfilled another 2,000 years after their time, it would have been even more convincing (to them) that it was an empty promise and there will be no 2nd coming.

Learning 2 Peter 3

3:5—The denial of the Lord's coming has some deeper implications which Peter now intends to discuss. For example, a teaching that rejects the Parousia of the Lord discredits the fathers, Jesus, the apostles, the teachers of the early church, and the numerous Biblical passages that originated from God Himself. Neyrey says:

> If there is no resurrection (no other world) then this present world is all the necessarily sufficient; and its continual existence is evident proof against eschatological proclamations of its destruction and renewal. Implicit, then, is a rejection of after life is a responding acceptance of the continual existence of the present world and a rejection of the end of the age (242).

Since the false teachers are doubting the promise (ἐπαγγελία) of the Parousia, Peter defends the prophecy through an argument based on **the Word of God**, an argument that **escapes their notice** (because they want it to). Peter will give three examples to show that cosmic activity is controlled by the **Word of God**.

Argument #1: Creation took place **by the Word of God**. This recalls numerous passages that identify the Word of God as the creative force (cf. 10 times "and God said" is found in Gen. 1; Psa. 33:6, 9). These false teachers are ignoring the tremendous power of God's Word, power that was vividly demonstrated in the creation (of things out of nothing! Heb. 11:1). Peter simply notes that the **heavens existed long ago** without elaborating how God, through His Word, brought them into existence.

> Heavens refers not to the place where God dwells, but to the dome-like structure that is above the earth and shields the earth from the water that is above the dome. In languages where there is a distinction between these two kinds of "heaven," the word for the dome-like structure should be used here. Heavens is plural in form but singular in meaning; its plural form is influenced by Hebrew usage, where the word for *heaven* is always plural. Many translations retain the plural here; however, it may be more natural to speak of *heaven* in the singular, as indeed many other translations have done (Arichea and Hatton 147).

3:6—*Argument #2*: The flood occurred by the Word of God (δι' ὧν—**through which**). God had announced to Noah what He intended to do (Gen. 6:7) and then He commanded that it be done (cf. Gen. 7:1, 10). The Genesis narrative makes it clear that God was controlling the entire event.

> If at creation God introduced stability into the world by separating the waters, during the flood the chaos returned. For the waters were unleashed and the world was destroyed. The false teachers could hardly maintain that the world is marked by regularity, when a flood destroyed human beings (Schreiner 376).

It is important to understand the different words Peter is using, even though most translations translate them as "destroyed." Here Peter says that **the world at that time was destroyed**. The word for **world** (κόσμος) means "humanity in general, the world" (Bauer 562). Peter is not saying that the flood destroyed the planet, but it destroyed humanity. Such is clear by the Genesis account. The word **destroyed** (ἀπόλλυμι) means "perish, be ruined" (Bauer 116), but it does not mean "annihilation." It is clear that humanity perished, but they were not annihilated. They are "now in prison" (1 Pet. 3:19).

3:7—*Argument #3*: By the same Word (τῷ αὐτῷ λόγῳ) the present creation is reserved for a cataclysmic end. It is significant that Peter switches from talking about humanity (κόσμος) to the **heavens and the earth**. The false teachers argued for the stability of the creation (v. 4). The implications of the first two illustrations are clear. God's Word executed two incredible events, and therefore logic would support what future events have been divinely decreed. The element God used initially was water, but now Peter provides information not found elsewhere in Scripture. God will use **fire**. The word **reserved** (τηρέω) means "to cause a state, condition, or activity to continue, keep, hold, reserve, preserve" (Bauer 1002). This is the fourth time Peter has used this word (2:4, 9, 17). It is a fitting word because it answers, in part, the objection by the false teachers. God has control of the situation and is holding the reservation for the ultimate burning up of the creation (v. 10). This will take place on the **day of judgment**—the very day the false teachers say will never occur. Peter has answered what will happen to the present heavens and earth (reserved for fire), but answers what will happen to **ungodly men**. The word **destruction** (ἀπώλεια) is not the same word used in verses 10-11 where Peter is describing the annihilation of the heavens and earth.

Peter's response in 3:5-7, therefore, can be seen to contain the following elements:

1. A formal defense of the prophetic Word of God which specifically predicts the Parousia and speaks of it as a day of destruction and judgment;

2. Cosmological arguments used to defend the Parousia (creation and the flood);

3. An affirmation that the Parousia is a time when judgment will be rendered to the ungodly.

Each of the points has been disputed by the false teachers in various parts of this epistle. Neyrey observes:

> ...the author perceives a strong interconnection between the disputed points: cosmology, judgment, and the interpretation of Scripture. An attack on one aspect is an assault on all of them and the defense of one leads to a defense of all (67).

3:8—Peter begins by appealing to the Christians to **not let this fact escape your notice**. The word **escape** (λανθάνω) is the same word used in verse 5, where Peter charged that the false teachers had, in fact, allowed clear evidence to "escape their notice." The false teacher's statement that "all continues just as it was from the beginning" is the next point of attack. This statement, founded on the obvious delay of the Parousia, could cause serious problems and therefore needs to be dealt with. Peter's first point is to draw from a passage in Psalm 90:4 (following the LXX). In each of his previous dealings with the false teachers, he has made an appeal to Scripture. When the Parousia was challenged as a myth (1:16), Peter cited his eyewitness experience of the transfiguration and the prophetic word as proof for the future coming of Christ (1:16-18). When the opponents denied the possibility of divine punishment (2:3), Peter appealed to the Biblical examples to prove God is not asleep and that judgment was imminent (2:5-9). Furthermore, when the second coming was challenged in 3:3-4, Peter appealed to the Word of God to demonstrate the ignorance of the opponents (3:5-7). Therefore, it is in typical fashion that he again appeals to Scripture to deal with the delay of the Parousia problem.

Psalm 90:4 reads, "For a thousand years in Thy sight are like yesterday when it passes by...." Peter is adapting that to express the idea that God transcends all human time. He is not bound in the confines of time but is timeless. Since this is true, it is illogical to assume that a lapse of time with God indicates that He has forgotten His promise or is unable to fulfill it. 2 Peter plainly demonstrates that the "day of the Lord" will come at the proper time. He is also consistent with the New Testament tradition that nobody, not even the angels in Heaven, know the specific date for the second coming (Matt. 24:36; Mark 3:10; cf. Mark 13:32; 1 Cor. 15:51-52; 1 Thess. 5:1-8).

> The point is rather that God's perspective on time is not limited by a human life span. He surveys the whole of history and sets the times of events in accordance with His agelong purpose. His perspective is so much more comprehensive than that of men and women who, accustomed to short-term expectations, are impatient to see the Parousia in their own lifetime (Bauckham 310).

3:9—The false teacher's charge that God is tardy is the next problem. Peter addresses this charge by showing that God, because of His benevolent nature, has provided man with the gift of time for repentance. The purpose of the delay (i.e., to provide time for man's repentance) has a great deal of support in Jewish non-biblical literature. In the Wisdom of Solomon, God tolerated the sins of the Canaanites in order to "give them a chance to repent" (12:10; cf. 11:23). This same author also says of God: "Thou did punish with great care…granting them time and opportunity to give up their wickedness" (12:20). Like Philo said:

> Not even against those who sin will God proceed at once but gives time for repentance" (L.A. 3:106). God, the Father of reasonable intelligence…takes thought also for those who live a misspent life, thereby giving them time for reformation and also keeping within the bounds of His merciful nature, which has for its attendant virtue and loving kindness well fitted to keep watch as sentry around God's world (Prov. 2:6).

These references are a mere sampling of the many that speak of God's patience in judgment. The Bible itself offers several passages that support this concept (cf. Ex. 34:6-7; Num. 14:18; Psa. 86:15; 103:8; Joel 2:12-13; Jon. 4:2; Nah. 1:3; Rom. 2:4). It is more than evident that Peter is attributing the long-suffering quality of God to this delay. The word **patient** (μακροθυμέω) means "to remain tranquil while waiting, have patience, wait" (Bauer 612). He again mentions God's patience in verse 15 (regard the **patience** of our Lord to be salvation"). It would be unfortunate to interpret a patient delay with an idea that judgment will never happen. The patience of God will eventually wear out.

> But this patience should not be confused with tolerance toward sin, because God's patience will come to an end in the terrible day of judgment (3:10; Psa. 7:12-16; Acts 17:30-31). Somewhat surprisingly, Peter notes that God is patient "toward you." With these words, which will be read publicly during the gatherings of the believers, Peter stretches out the hand to those who are tempted to follow or who have begun to follow the way of the false teachers (2:14, 18) (Gene Green 328).

3:10—Beginning here Peter will enter into a specific statement that covers all of the theological ideas found in this epistle: cosmology, judgment, and prophecy. It might be said that this verse is a more definite response to the heretic's claims of 3:4. They claim stability of the universe, but Peter speaks of instability and destruction. However, in view of the exhortation of 3:11, it seems more likely that he is mainly concentrating on the recipients of this epistle. He is reminding them, in a direct way, that total severance from this world of ungodliness is essential for their salvation. He is able to successfully achieve this goal, while at the same time dealing a decisive blow to the heretic's doctrine. The **day** of judgment, which they claim will never arrive (1:16; 2:3b-9, 19; 3:4) will soon be a horrifying reality.

The concept of the **day of the Lord** has strong futuristic and eschatological implications in the Old Testament and extra-canonical literature. In the New Testament the phrase occurs five times (Acts 2:20; 1 Thess. 5:2; 2 Thess. 2:2; 2 Pet. 3:10, 12). The phrase "the day of the Lord Jesus Christ" occurs six times (1 Cor. 1:8; 5:5; 2 Cor. 1:14; Phil. 1:6, 10; 2:16). All of these occurrences have the future in view. There are other similar usages of **day**, such as "that day," or "in the day of…" that have eschatological meanings (cf. Matt. 7:22; 11:22, 24; 12:36; 24:36; 25:13; Mark 6:11; 13:32; Luke 10:12; 17:30; 21:34; John 6:39, 40, 44, 54; 1 Thess. 1:4; 2 Thess. 1:10; 2 Tim. 1:12, 18; 4:8; 1 Pet. 2:12; 1 John 4:17; Jude 6). It is evident that Peter has this eschatological background in mind when he connects the phrase with a cataclysmic end of the universe.

Consider what Peter says about this **day of the Lord** (See Sermon Seed: The Day of the Lord): First, he says that **it will come like a thief**. This teaching was first used by Jesus (Matt. 24:43-44; Luke 12:39-40) and repeated by Paul (1 Thess. 5:2) and John (Rev. 3:3; 16:15—who was quoting Jesus). In all of these passages the same point is being made: whenever Jesus comes—be it sooner or later—it will be unexpected (like the break-in of a thief). There will be no more time when this happens. God's patience has come to an end. No more opportunities for repentance will be given. The wise will heed the warning and live in a continual condition of readiness (which was the exact point Jesus was making—Matt. 24:44).

Second, the heavens will pass away with a roar. Whereas the phrase "heavens and earth" are equivalent to our word "universe" (cf. Gen. 1:1), Peter here wants to specifically identify what will happen to various aspects of God's creation. He will begin by discussing the fate of **the heavens**. This word (οὐρανός) means:

> Heavens refers not to the place where God dwells, but to the dome-like structure that is above the earth and shields the earth from the water that is above the dome. In languages where there is a distinction between these two kinds of "heavens," the word for the dome-like structure should be used here. Heavens is plural in form but singular in meaning; its plural form is influenced by Hebrew usage, where the word for "heaven" is always plural. Many translations retain the plural here; however, it may be more natural to speak of "heaven" in the singular, as indeed many other translations have done (Arichea and Hatton 147).

By using the word **heavens**, Peter intends to include everything that is above. This would logically include the sky above, but also the distant parts of the sky, including the sun and the planets and every solar system that exists beyond our own. Peter says that the heavens **will pass away**. This word (παρέρχομαι) means "to come to an end and so no longer be there, pass away, disappear" (Bauer 776). This is also what John says in Rev. 21:1. Jesus also taught that the universe would pass away (Matt. 5:18; 24:35; Mark 13:31; Luke 16:17; 21:33). This word does not allow for a remodeling or a renovation of the present heavens. They will be annihilated. Peter says this annihilation will happen **with a roar**. Interesting word here. It is *rhoizēdon* (ῥοιζηδόν), a word found only here. Bauer defines the word as "adv. (in ref. to 'whirring sound made by an obj. going swiftly through the air': pertinent to noise made by something passing with great force and rapidity, with a rushing noise" (Bauer 907).

Learning 2 Peter 3

Third, **the elements will be destroyed with intense heat**. The noun **elements** is an interesting word (στοιχεῖον) that has a variety of possible meanings. Its root refers to things that belong to a series, like a row, rank, line—such as a battle line. Here are the most common views:

1) The connection here with the earth may indicate the celestial bodies (i.e., the sun, moon and stars). Arguments in support of this position are:

   a. The position in the text of this word (between heaven and earth) suggests a third kind of cosmic entity, that is, the celestial bodies. This is also logical because they are situated between heaven and earth and are often a part of futuristic or eschatological language (Isa. 13:10; 24:4; Ezek. 32:7-8; Joel 2:10; Matt. 24:29; Mark 13:24-25; Rev. 6:13).

   b. "The heavens" and "the earth" are comprehensive terms. Any future reference to their constituent elements would be superfluous.

   c. The following explanation of how fire can destroy fire (which is one of the elements of the Stoic stoicheia), is, as Brigg observed, "too scientific for St. Peter" (Bigg 297-8).

2) The elements here refer to water, air, fire, and material things. Arguments in support of this position are:

   a. This is the basic meaning of the word stoicheia (στοιχεῖον), since it favors the idea of elementary principles or components (Delling, "στοιχεῖον," 670-72).

   b. When used in context with the conflagration, στοιχεῖον often refers to the four basic elements of the universe.

   c. The fact that this chapter includes other Stoic concepts, it is logical that Peter means the four basic elements of all the creation (earth, wind, fire, and water). This is in harmony with Stoic beliefs.

The evidence for both positions has some merit, since στοιχεῖον can easily mean either one. This leads us to the same conclusion of Andrew John Bandstra, who said the word "could take on a wide variety of meanings" (31-32). Despite the difficulty of interpreting στοιχεῖον, the meaning of verse 10 remains the same: God intends to completely destroy all of the existing creation. To make sure we understand what is being described, Peter says that these **elements** will be destroyed with **intense heat**. The word used to translate that is kausoo (καυσόω), which means "be consumed by heat, burn up" (Bauer 536). It is found only here and in verse 12.

Fourth, **the earth and its works will be burned up**. In the previous phrase Peter discussed what would happen to the "heavens." Now he turns his attention to the **earth**. Peter had used this word (γῆ) in verses 5, 7, 10, 13. The word simply means the "surface of the earth as the habitation of humanity, earth" (Bauer 196). The **works** (ἔργον) can mean all the results of both human and divine activity on earth, or in a wider sense, everything that is in the earth; hence TEV "with everything in it" (JB), "and all that it contains" (NEB), "with all that is in it" (Arichea and Hatton 155). It logically would include the great building projects of mankind, those that have been marvels of human innovation and creativity (skyscrapers, massive bridges, the Panama Canal, etc.). Peter is making it clear that nothing will survive no matter how strong or beautiful.

The last clause, translated **will be burned up** is clearly the most problematic passage in 2 Peter.

The reason for this assessment is that the text for this phrase is uncertain, and its meaning varies considerably depending on which variant is chosen. While several variants exist, there are two that are the best attested. One is the word that the NAS adopted, which supports the translation **will be burned up**. This is the word κατακαήσεται [*katakaēsetai*]. Peter had earlier said that the elements would be "destroyed with intense heat" and will make this point again in verse 12. In addition, he will say in verse 12 that the heavens "will be destroyed by burning." It is clear that the universe will be consumed by flames. As a result, there is no textual need for *katakaēsetai* here. The second word, which is slightly better attested in manuscript evidence, is the verb εὑρεθήσεται (*heurethasetai*, from εὑρίσκω). This word means "to come upon something either through purposeful search or accidentally find" (Bauer 411). If this is the correct word, it leaves us with an interpretive challenge. What is meant by "the earth and its works will be discovered"? The most logical and feasible solutions are: (1) The inhabitants of the world will have their works manifested, and then they will be judged according to those works. This view is in harmony with passages such as 1 Corinthians 3:13-15. The weakness of this view is that Peter is clearly dealing with the **earth** and not with the deeds of men (cf. Kelly 365); (2) Both the earth and the works done by men on the earth will be manifested. After this "manifestation," both will be found deficient and therefore destroyed (λυομένων, 3:11); (3) Understanding εὑρεθήσεται to be a question. Thus the passage would be translated: "And the earth and the works it contains—will they be found?" This translation implies that, after the destruction, the earth and its works will cease to exist. That is, the question expects a negative response: "Now they will not be found" (Kelly 364-6); (4) Making **works** represent the material things on earth. This allows for a unified flow of thought in this verse progressing from the **heavens** (i.e. the vast expanse of creation) to the **works** (i.e. the small earthly objects). This is the preferred interpretation. This allows εὑρεθήσεται to have a judicial meaning. At God's judgment, all that has done will be manifested before the Judge of all the earth. Nothing escaped His notice, and nothing will escape the destruction He has decreed. This view also allows for a seamless connection with verse 11, for it allows the "all these things" to represent a unified condemnation of all the creation.

3:11—The false teachers foolishly declared that this day would never come. Peter now boldly says **since all these things are to be destroyed**. It is a fact, and these Christians can be assured of it (and stop listening to the false teachers, who clearly do not know what they are talking about). The reference to **all these things** includes both the things in heaven and the things on the earth. It includes 100% of what God created, and it will be **destroyed** (λύω). This word means "to reduce something by violence into its components, destroy... Of the parts of the universe, as it is broken up and destroyed in the final conflagration (2 Pet. 3:10-12)" (Bauer 607). It is important to note that Peter uses this word in reference to the material universe, not in reference to humanity. Even though our translations used the word *destroy* in verses 6 and 7, different words are being used there. God will *annihilate* the physical creation, but he will punish evil humanity. The Bible does not teach the doctrine of annihilation for humanity. Rather, the wicked will go into "eternal punishment" (Matt. 25:46).

In view of the assured and eminent destruction of the universe, Peter makes an appeal to the Christian's moral behavior. He contends that the Christians should live in such a way as to disassociate themselves from the perishing creation. The exhortation is typical of this epistle. In chapter 2 Peter spoke of the destruction of ungodly men but followed it with a note of encouragement to the godly (2:3-9). Here he reminds his readers that **holy conduct and godliness** will provide escape from the coming punishment.

Learning 2 Peter 3

As always in the New Testament, the moral imperative follows the eschatological indicatives. The expectation of the Lord's return always inspires Christians to a holy life (cf. 1 John 2:28). Disbelief in the Lord's return all too often produces indifferentism in behavior, as it had with these errorists (Green 139).

The word **holy** (ἅγιος) is "pertaining to being dedicated or consecrated to the service of God" (Bauer 10). It requires the Christian to be separate from the world and certainly separate from those who are ridiculing the doctrine of the second coming and are following after their own lives. In 3:1 Peter said that this second letter was a "reminder." Certainly this text would remind them of Peter's extensive discussion on holiness in 1 Peter 1:13-22. What also would be a reminder of the first letter is Peter's call for them to have holy **conduct**. This word (ἀναστροφή) is a key word in the first letter, occurring eight times. It means "conduct expressed according to certain principles way of life, conduct, behavior" (Bauer 73).

Godliness (εὐσέβεια) is generally defined as "awesome respect accorded to God, devoutness, piety, godliness" (Bauer 412). It has proven to be a difficult word to explain. However, I believe that 1 Timothy 1:5 captures the essence of a godly person. The threefold attributes listed there ("love from a pure heart, a sincere faith, and a good conscience") genuinely describe a godly person.

3:12—The false teachers arrogantly asserted that there would be no second coming. Peter, however, describes these Christians as **looking for** and even **hastening** its arrival. The word translated looking for (προσδοκάω) means "to give thought to something that is viewed as lying in the future, wait for, look for, expect" (Bauer 877). The word **hastening** (σπεύδω) means "to cause something to happen or come into being by exercising special effort, hasten" (Bauer 938). The word can have two general ideas: (1) Earnestly desiring, looking for, eagerly waiting. If this is the meaning, Christians are looking for Jesus' return and can't wait for it to get here. They are filled with excitement and anticipation; (2) To hasten, speed up, or, as Bauer defined the word, "to cause something to happen." Is this phrase teaching that Christians, by living holy and godly lives, can impact the day Jesus returns? At some level this is true. Peter said in verse 9 that the reason the Lord has not returned was to give men time to repent. On the other hand, Acts 17:30-31 says that God has "fixed a day" for the Second Coming. This is also confirmed by Jesus in Matthew 24:36. Is there a way these two ideas can be reconciled? Of course! Since God is omniscient, He knew the exact moment the last person would repent. It was at that moment that He determined would be when Jesus would return.

Peter is not backing down in directly contradicting the teaching of the false teachers. They claim that the world will not be destroyed, but Peter repeats that **the heavens will be destroyed** (λύω—same word in vv. 10-11) **by burning, and the elements** (στοιχεῖον—same word in v. 10) will melt with intensive heat (same word in v. 10).

> The command to live holy lives in the middle of verse 11 is framed on each side by the assertion that the present world will be destroyed by fire. The false teachers had badly miscalculated. Unfortunately, they had made the kind of mistake in which they would know they were wrong only when it was too late (Schreiner 391).

3:13—Peter again appeals to Scripture to ensure the truthfulness of his argument. The Christian can actively look for the **new heavens and new earth** because its arrival has been assured by **His promise**. The word for **promise** (ἐπάγγελμα) is found in this form only in 2 Peter (1:4; 3:13). The meaning is similar to the more common *epangelia*. The idea of a promise is intimately bound up with God. His power is the essential element behind the promise. When God issues a promise, He is committed to use His power to see it fulfilled. This promise, however, is a future promise. As a result, it remains unfulfilled. Nevertheless, past promises have been fulfilled, assuring the Christian that future promises will equally be fulfilled. This is why Christians can "look for" the accomplishment of God's promise. The giver of this promise could be "the prophetic Word" (1:19), "the words spoken beforehand by the prophets (3:2), or the promises made by God through Christ (3:2-3). All promises found in Scripture ultimately have their origin in God Himself (cf. 1:20-21; 3:15).

There has been much discussion as to what **promise** Peter has in mind. Some have suggested it comes from the words of Jesus in Matthew 5:5 and 19:28. Some believe it comes from the words of Paul in Romans 8:19-22. Some who date the epistle after the Revelation argue that Peter is getting this information from Revelation 21:1. However, the best and most logical view is that it comes from Isaiah 65:17 and 66:22. Whereas Isaiah is describing the future bliss after captivity, his promise can be reapplied by Peter (like a dual-fulfillment prophecy). The creation of the **new heavens and new earth** are exactly the words of God in the Isaiah texts.

The false teachers are not looking for the Second Coming or anticipating a **new heavens and new earth** (3:3-4). Christians, however, based on God's great promise, are looking for this. They are looking for the very thing John saw in his vision in Revelation 21:1. The grouping of **heavens and earth** is not unusual language in the Bible. This phrase is often used to designate the totality of God's creation (Matt. 5:18; Mark 13:31; Luke 16:17; Heb. 1:10; Rev. 21:1; cf. Luke 12:56; Acts 2:19; 1 Cor. 8:5; Col. 1:16, 20; Eph. 1:10; 3:15; Heb. 12:26. In both Hebrew and Greek, the usages of **heaven and earth** represent the sky above and the land beneath. But is this what Peter means here by the word **earth**? There are some interpretations that spiritualize these words, or contend they are figurative. For such to be the case, two things need to be clear:

First, the other parts of this text must also be made figurative. However, I am not seeing those who argue for the figurative use of the word **earth** also relegate other aspects as figurative. Is the Lord's coming a figure or symbolic? Will the creation be consumed by literal flames? Will the heavens be literally destroyed, and will the elements literally melt with intense heat? In my reading everyone takes these things as literal, *but not the new earth*. Such is interpretive dishonesty.

Second, one needs to do a thorough study of the word **earth** in Scripture. This word is found over 2,500 times in the Hebrew Scriptures (אֶרֶץ—this is the word that is the Hebrew counterpart to the Greek word), and 250 times in the Greek New Testament (the word γῆ). What do lexicographers say about the meaning of this word?

> **earth, land:** A word with a variety of meanings, from the whole earth to dirt or soil.
>
> This word is in many ways equivalent to the Hebrew word עֲרָא (*'ereṣ*, "land"). In the Septuagint, it is the usual translation of both 'ereṣ and הָמָדָא (*'ădāmâ*, "land"). It is used in the NT primarily in the books of Matthew, Luke, Acts, and Revelation. This word is used when comparing or contrasting earth (gē) with heaven (e.g., Matt. 16:19, Luke 16:17; John 3:31; 1 Cor. 15:47), or to indicate the whole earth and those who dwell in it (Luke 21:35; Rev. 13:3). It can mean "ground" (e.g., Matt. 10:29; 15:35; John 12:24) or "soil" (Matt. 13:5-23; Mark 4:5-20; Luke 8:8-15). It also is commonly used to refer to a country or territory,

such as the "land (*gē*) of Israel," (e.g., Matt. 2:20), the "land of Judah" (e.g., Matt. 2:6) or another country (e.g., Acts 7:4, 29). This word describes the land (*gē*) that was given to Abraham (Acts 7:3-6; Heb. 11:8-9) as well as the new earth (*gē*), which is the inheritance of the faithful (Matt. 5:5; 2 Pet. 3:13; Rev. 21:1) (Mc-Guire-Moushon).

Notice that among the "variety of meanings," a symbolic or figurative meaning is not among them. As a matter of fact, Hermann Sasse gave the following warning: "It would be wrong to emphasize the word γῆ in exegesis of these passages, or to read into them the metaphysical antithesis of heaven and earth…" (678). The fact is, the word **earth** is not used in the Bible in a figurative or symbolic way. As a result, we should interpret here according to its normal meaning. We are looking for a new earth, and the earth means dirt, rocks, trees, ground, etc.

Another fascinating aspect of this text is the word **new**. This word (καινός) means "what is new in nature, different from the usual, impressive, better than the old, superior in value or attraction" (Behm 447). Another lexicographer defines the word **new** as follows:

> Paul does not use expressions for "born again" or "rebirth," but he uses conceptually similar expressions for "new creation" and "new human being." A Christian is a "new (*kainos*) creation (κτίσις, *ktisis*)" (2 Cor. 5:17; Gal. 5:17); the phrase can also be translated "new creature." Similarly, a Christian is to take off the old human being, to be renewed (ἀνανεόω, *ananeoō*) in mind, and to put on the new (*kainos*) human being (ἄνθρωπος, *anthrōpos*), "who is created in righteousness and holiness from the truth" (Eph. 4:22-24); Col 3:9-10 has similar phrasing but with the word νέος (*neos*, "new") instead of *kainos* and the word ἀνακαινόω (*anakainoō*, "to renew") in place of *ananeoō*. God's renewal of all things through Christ goes beyond the creation of a renewed humanity; He promises a new (*kainos*) heavens and new (*kainos*) earth (2 Pet. 3:13; Rev. 21:1). (Simmons)

So, in what way will the heavens and earth be **new**? When contrasted with the other common Greek word for "new" (*neos*) these difficulties can be lessened.

Kainos (καινός)—what is new and distinctive; new in nature, impressive, better than the old, superior in value or attraction. New in quality.

Neos (νέος)—what was not there before; what has only just arisen or appeared; new in time or origin. Chronological newness (cf. Heb. 12:24).

The use of *kainos* with eschatological terminology is not unusual. In addition to its use with the heavens and earth, there is the new Jerusalem (Rev. 3:12; 21:2); the new wine (Mark 14:25), the new name (Rev. 2:17; 3:12), and the new song (Rev. 5:9; 14:3). Notice that it is still wine, still a name, still a song. What they are is fundamentally the same, only new. These references give some indication of the force of *kainos*. God will create a **heavens and earth** that is like the old, but far superior. It will be more impressive and more attractive.

Peter goes on to say regarding this new heavens and a new earth, "**in which righteousness dwells**." The word **righteousness** (δικαιοσύνη) means "the quality or characteristic of upright behavior, uprightness, righteousness" (Bauer 248). The context of 2 Peter also helps define what is meant by this word. In 2:5, Noah is proclaimed a "preacher of righteousness" and is, by his conduct, the antithesis of ungodliness. In 2:21, the ungodly are those who "turn away from the way of righteousness,"

51

which is paralleled to "the holy commandment." In 3:14, Peter says that Christians are to be found "spotless and blameless." Therefore, the kind of people who will dwell in the new heavens and new earth are godly, spiritual people who were faithful to Christ and His commandments. Certainly, one of the most attractive features of our eternal home is who will **not be there**. John addressed this when he said, "Outside are the dogs and the sorcerers and the immoral persons and the murderers and the idolaters, and everyone who loves and practices lying" (Rev. 2:15).

3:14—The word therefore (διό) has the meaning of "for this reason." The "reason" here is clearly the coming destruction and creation of a new heavens and earth. With that foundation of knowledge, Peter is ready to return his exhortation regarding Christian conduct. He says, as he did in verse 12, **since you look for these things**. These Christians did not merely claim to believe in God's promises; they actively looked for them. He commands them to be **diligent**. This word (σπουδάζω—cf. 1:10) means "to be especially conscientious in discharging an obligation, be zealous/eager, take pains, make every effort, be conscientious" (Bauer 939). Just as they were admonished to apply the virtues of 1:5-7, they must press on to make sure they are prepared for Jesus' return (such would not be necessary if the doctrine of "once saved, always saved" were true). They were to be **found** (εὑρίσκω) in Him. This is the same word in verse 10 and adds support to that being the correct word in that verse. Their **diligence** should be **to be found by Him** (God's day of judgment) with three discernible attributes (see Sermon Seed "What Kind of Person Are You?"). *First*, Peter admonishes them to be found by Him **in peace**. The word **peace** (εἰρήνη) means "a state of well-being, peace" (Bauer 287). The well-being and calm are because their relationship with God is good, based upon their obedience to the Gospel of Christ (1:10-11; Rom. 5:1). *Second*, they should be found **spotless**. This word (ἄσπιλος) "pertains to being of untainted character, pure, without fault" (Bauer 144). Christian behavior is to be holy (3:11). Their lives should be such that they have no moral or spiritual blemish. *Third*, they should be found **blameless**. This word (ἀμώμητος) has the idea of being without flaws. The words "spotless" (*aspiloi*) and "blameless" (*amōmētoi*) contrast with the false teachers, who were "blots" (*spiloi*) and "blemishes" (*mōmoi*) (2:13).

3:15—These Christians can be grateful from God's patience with them. In all likelihood there were many of them who—if God had come earlier in their lives—they would have been lost. Thankfully God wants all men to be saved (1 Tim. 2:4). This **patience** is also available to those mentioned in this letter who have fallen prey to the evil influence of the false teachers. While there is life, there is hope. The salvation these Christians found can also be found by others. **Paul** was one who discussed God's patience, since he himself was a recipient of it (1 Tim. 1:16; cf. Rom. 2:4; 9:22). The **wisdom** given to Paul is a reference to his being inspired of the Holy Spirit when he wrote (cf. 1 Cor. 14:37; Eph. 3:3-5).

> More likely the opponents latched on to Paul's statements about freedom from law to advance libertinism (cf. Rom. 3:20, 28; 4:15; 5:20; 7:5, 7; 1 Cor. 15:56; Gal. 5:1). This fits with the licentiousness of the false teachers, which is amply attested in 2 Peter. It also accords with the context since Peter emphasized that Paul also taught that believers must live in a godly way to experience God's promise and that in the interval before Christ's coming God grants people an opportunity to repent. We may also have an allusion to Romans 2:4 (cf. Rom. 3:25-26; 9:22), where God's patience with sinners is featured (Schreiner 395).

Learning 2 Peter 3

3:16—Peter makes reference to Paul's **letters**. If we accurately date 2 Peter to be around 68 A.D., then most, if not all of Paul's 13 NT epistles would have been written. In view of the false teachers' abuse of Scripture, Peter equally contributes to the importance of handling accurately the Word of God (cf. 2 Tim. 2:15). Here Peter notes that some of the writings of Paul are **difficult to understand**. The word **difficult** (δυσνόητος, dusnoátos) indicates an activity that will provide success but will require effort. It is possible to understand the difficult writings of Paul. Why then, do some handle his inspired words inaccurately? Peter says it is because they are (a) **ignorant**— ἀμαθής (amathás)—a word that means ignorant, incompetent, uneducated. This reminds us of Hosea 4:6, 1 Timothy 2:4, and Ephesians 5:17. There is no excuse for their ignorance but is a result of a lazy approach to Scripture. The truth is that which could be found (cf. Matt. 7:7-8), but they have chosen to remain in ignorance; and (b) **unstable** is ἀστήρικτος (astárikos)—which describes one who has a tendency to change his or her views and attitudes; to be unstable, unsteady, not settled (cf. 2.14) because they are weak (cf. Eph. 4:14).

What is it that these **ignorant** and **unstable** do to the Scriptures? Peter says they distort the **Scriptures**. This word (**στρεβλόω**)—strictly means to *twist or wrench* limbs on an instrument for torturing people called a rack; hence *torture, torment*; figuratively *distort, twist, misinterpret* words to a false meaning (Bauer 948). It is not only Paul's writings that receive this violent abuse and misinterpretation. Peter affirms that these also do it to **the rest of the Scriptures**. Yet such is not without consequence. Peter says they do this **to their own destruction**. The word **destruction** (ἀπώλεια). This word means "to their own ruin" (Bauer 127). This is the word Peter used in 2:1; 3:7, 9. God does not take lightly those who mistreat and misapply His Word, and those who do it are facing eternal condemnation.

Note: There is much in this verse that helps us understand the formation of the NT canon. See the Sermon Seed "The Formation of the NT Canon: 2 Peter 3:16."

3:17—With testimony from Paul, and the other Scriptures, Christians should be on their **guard**. There is no reason, no excuse, for them to be caught unaware of these things. The false teachers and their methods have been identified. Their doctrines have been exposed. Christians should live their lives on alert, ready and prepared for these things. The danger, as noted in chapter 2, is that they be **carried away by the error of unprincipled men**. The word translated **carried away** (συναπάγω) means "to cause someone in conjunction with others to go astray in belief, lead away with" (Bauer 965). Peter had earlier identified the problem when he said that "many will follow their [the false teacher's] sensuality…and in their greed they will exploit you with false words" (2:2-3). The word **error** (πλάνη) means "wandering from the path of truth, error, delusion, deceit, deception" (Bauer 822). The false teaching is called **error** because it involves deviating from the truth of Scripture. God's Word is truth (John 17:17), and Satan is the father of lies (John 8:44). His work, through these false teachers, is to get people to believe lies. What kind of person would personally follow these lies and teach others to do the same? Peter answers the question. They are **unprincipled men**. The word **unprincipled** (ἄθεσμος) means "pertaining to being unprincipled, unseemly, disgraceful, lawless" (Bauer 24). These men have no moral compass. They do not care for God's laws and are willing to openly oppose them.

Peter's main concern is found in the final phrase of verse 17: **you fall from your own steadfastness**. You cannot **fall** from a position you were never on; these Christians are saved, and the danger is that they **fall** from that saved condition. This is the clear meaning here, and again proves that the doctrine of "once saved, always saved" is not biblically correct. The word **steadfastness** (στηριγμός) means "a state of security, safe position" (Bauer 945).

3:18—In a concluding exhortation, Peter sums up his appeal in chapter 1. **Grow** applies to the instructions in 1:2-11; **in knowledge** applies to the educated trust they can have in the Scriptures (1:12-21). Christians are expected to **grow**. Remaining level or stagnant is unacceptable to God. Therefore each Christian must devise a plan for growth. It will not happen by accident. Equally, there needs to be increased **knowledge**. True Christians are devoted to the Word of God. Like the blessed man of Psalm 1, they meditate on it (think deeply about it) continually.

The benediction includes a doxology addressed to Christ: **To Him be the glory** (αὐτῷ ἡ δόξα), which, as Brigg observes, is not unusual considering the high Christology in this epistle (304). The phrase **day of eternity** (ἡμέραν αἰῶνος) is found only here in the New Testament. The customary expression in doxologies is "for all eternity," which may be the meaning here. It seems more likely, however, that Peter was thinking of the approaching day of the Lord (3:10, 12). Thus, **the day** would indicate the day on which the eternal and glorious age, inaugurated by the Parousia, will begin.

BIBLIOGRAPHY

Bandstra, Andrew John. *The Law and the Elements of the World*. Kampen: J.H. Kok, 1964.

Bauckham, Richard J. *2 Peter, Jude*. Vol. 50 of Word Biblical Commentary. Dallas: Word, Incorporated, 1983.

Bauer, Walter. *A Greek-English Lexicon of the New Testament and Other Early Christian Literature*. Edited by Arndt, Gingrich and Danker. Chicago: University of Chicago Press, 1985.

Behm, Johannes. "Καινός, Καινότης, Ἀνακαινίζω, Ἀνακαινόω, Ἀνακαίνωσις, Ἐγκαινίζω," *Theological Dictionary of the New Testament*. Grand Rapids: Eerdmans, 1964.

Blagden, Claude M. *The Epistles of Peter, John and Jude*. Cambridge: The University Press, 1939.

Blum, Edwin A. "2 Peter," in *The Expositor's Bible Commentary: Hebrews through Revelation*, ed. Frank E. Gaebelein. Grand Rapids: Zondervan Publishing House, 1981.

Bromiley, Geoffrey W., ed. *Theological Dictionary of the New Testament*. Grand Rapids: Eerdmans, 1985.

Brown, Colin, ed. *New International Dictionary of New Testament Theology*. Grand Rapids: Zondervan, 1975.

Clark, Gordon H. *2 Peter*. Nutley: Presbyterian and Reformed Publishing Co., 1972.

Davids, Peter H. *The Letters of 2 Peter and Jude*. The Pillar New Testament Commentary. Grand Rapids: William B. Eerdmans Pub. Co., 2006.

Green, Gene L. *Jude and 2 Peter*. Baker Exegetical Commentary on the New Testament. Grand Rapids: Baker Academic, 2008.

Green, Michael. *2 Peter and Jude: An Introduction and Commentary*, Vol. 18 of Tyndale New Testament Commentaries. Downers Grove: InterVarsity Press, 1987.

Grudem, Wayne A. *1 Peter: An Introduction and Commentary*, Vol. 17 of Tyndale New Testament Commentaries. Downers Grove: InterVarsity Press, 1988.

Guthrie, Donald. *New Testament Introduction*. Downers Grove: InterVarsity Press, 1970.

Harrison, Everett Falconer. "*Exegetical Studies in 1 Peter: Part 1.*" Bibliotheca Sacra 97:386 (Apr. 1940): 200-210.

Hastings, James. *The Speaker's Bible*. Aberdeen, Scotland: The "Speakers' Bible" Offices, 1924.

Hiebert, D. Edmond. "Following Christ's Example: An Exposition of 1 Peter 2:21-25." *Bibliotheca Sacra* 139 (Jan. 1982):32-46.

Hite, Michael. *2 Peter Class Notes (unpublished)*. Bear Valley Bible Institute. Denver, Colorado, 2022.

Jobes, Karen H. *1 Peter.* Baker Exegetical Commentary on the New Testament. Grand Rapids: Baker Academic, 2005.

Kelcy, Raymond C. *The Letters of Peter and Jude.* The Living Word Commentaries. Austin: R.B. Sweet, 1972.

Kirk, Gordon E. "Endurance in Suffering in 1 Peter." *Bibliotheca Sacra* 138 (Jan. 1981):46-55.

Kistemaker, Simon J. *Exposition of the Epistles of Peter and of the Epistle of Jude.* Grand Rapids: Baker Book House, 1987.

Louw, Johannes P. and Nida, Eugene Albert. *Greek-English Lexicon of the New Testament: Based on Semantic Domains.* New York: United Bible Societies, 1996.

McGuire-Moushon, J.A. "Promised Land," *Lexham Theological Wordbook.* Bellingham: Lexham Press, 2014.

Neyrey, Jerome H. *2 Peter, Jude: A New Translation with Introduction and Commentary.* Vol. 37C of Anchor Yale Bible. New Haven; London: Yale University Press, 2008.

Nicoll, W. Robertson. *The Expositor's Greek Testament.* New York: Dodd, Mead and Co., 1905.

Owen, Dan R. "Self-Control in 2 Peter 1:6." *Gospel Advocate* (March 1989):11.

Peel, Malcolm L. "Gnostic Eschatology and the New Testament." *Novum Testamentum* 12 (Jan. 1970):141-65.

Roberts, J.W. *1 and 2 Peter and Jude.* Austin: R.B. Sweet, 1964.

Sasse, Hermann. "Γῆ, Ἐπίγειος," *Theological Dictionary of the New Testament.* Grand Rapids: Eerdmans, 1964.

Schreiner, Thomas R. *1, 2 Peter, Jude. In The New American Commentary.* Nashville: Broadman, 2003

Simmons, William A. "Regeneration," *Lexham Theological Wordbook.* Bellingham: Lexham Press, 2014.

Stibbs, Alan M. *The First Epistle General of Peter.* Tyndale New Testament Commentaries. Grand Rapids: Eerdmans, 1959.

Walls, David and Max Anders, *I & II Peter, I, II & III John, Jude,* Vol. 11 of Holman New Testament Commentary. Nashville: Broadman & Holman Publishers, 1999.

Learning Jude

DENNY PETRILLO

EXEGETICAL NOTES

A. Authorship

1. Internal Evidence: The author makes three claims that helps us identify him. First, he says his name is "Jude." Bauer notes that there are eight men so named in the NT that could possibly be this author. However, the most likely, based on other information, is he is the brother of Jesus (Bauer 479). Second, he says he is a *"bond-servant of Jesus Christ."* We know from John 7:5 that the brothers of Jesus did not believe in Him during His earthly ministry. This might explain the humble position he now claims. Fortunately, the brothers of Jesus became believers after His ascension (Acts 1:14). Third, he says he is the *"brother of James."* The Gospels record the names of Jesus' earthly brothers, two of which were named James and Jude (Matt. 13:55; Mark 6:3). Paul also calls James *"the Lord's brother"* (Gal. 1:19). James also became a leader in the Jerusalem church (Acts 12:17; 15:13; 21:18; 1 Cor. 15:7; Gal. 1:19; 2:9, 12). If this "James" is the Lord's brother, it lends further support that the writer of this epistle is also the Lord's brother. This is the most logical and best accepted belief regarding the authorship of this book.

2. External Evidence: Despite the brevity of the book, it has very strong external support. There are references to the book in some of the Apostolic Fathers. It was considered Scripture in the Muratorian Canon (c. 200 A.D.). Tertullian (*On the Apparel of Women 1.3*) and Clement of Alexandria both refer to the book.

3. Objections: This is not to suggest that the book has emerged without its critics. Origen personally accepted it but acknowledges that there are some that question its authority (*Commentary on Matthew* 10:17). Eusebius also noted that some questioned its position in the canon (*Church History* 6.13.6; 14.1). Jerome also noted that some questioned it because it quoted 1 Enoch (*Lives of Illustrations* iv). This point alone is probably why some doubted the book.

4. Conclusion: The fact that some, hundreds of years later, questioned the authenticity of the book is hardly compelling. The evidence is clear: the book has early and consistent support. There is no reason to not accept it, or to believe it was not written by Jude, the Lord's brother.

B. Date and Place of Writing

1. The major discussion about this book is in regard to the false teachers it addresses. Scholars have tried to identify groups of false teachers that held beliefs noted in this letter. That has led some to discard Jude the Lord's brother as the author and assign a second century date (where many of these heresies are found).

2. However, there is considerable evidence of heretical teachings in the first century, and these teachings easily fit into the context of this book. If Jude wrote the book, it would have to be in the first century.

3. The majority of the debate is whether Jude quoted 2 Peter, or whether 2 Peter quoted Jude. If Jude quoted 2 Peter, the letter would have to date around 65-80 A.D. If 2 Peter quoted Jude, the date for the book would be around 40-65 A.D. It is my opinion that 2 Peter was first. Consider: (a) 2 Peter has the false teachers yet to come (2:1), Jude has them already present; (b) Jude's reference to apostolic teachings would logically apply to Peter (vv. 17-18).

4. Without any clear indications in the text, it is virtually impossible to identify where Jude was when he penned this letter. Egypt and Jerusalem are the most common suggestions.

C. Destination

1. The recipients are referred to as *"those who are called"* (v. 1) and *"beloved"* (v. 3).

2. Such general terms lead many scholars to believe that the letter was intended to be a 'circular letter' that would be sent to numerous churches.

3. It is clear that Jude is aware of the struggles and challenges the recipients are facing. That may mitigate against the view that the letter was intended to be a general letter to be distributed abroad.

4. However, the early church, from Rome to Jerusalem, faced similar challenges from false teachers. Therefore, a general letter is certainly possible.

5. It is not possible to settle on a particular location, although Asia Minor, Syrian Antioch, and Israel are common suggestions.

D. Recipients

1. These Christians are facing a great challenge to their faith. This challenge comes from persecution and an influx of false teachers.

2. They are beloved by God (v. 1) and Jude (v. 3). This seems to indicate that they were known to Jude.

3. These Christians are thought to be relatively new Christians, who need to be challenged to stay with the faith (v. 3), because some around them are struggling with doubt (v. 22).

4. Most scholars believe the recipients were Jews, since the letter has references to various Jewish apocalyptic writings (1 Enoch and the Assumption of Moses).

E. Purpose/Occasion of Writing

The letter has three important hints as to its purpose. First is the list of prevalent words that are discussed below. Second, the inspired writer has provided a "purpose statement" in verse 3. Third, the book has a petition verb (v. 3). Petition verbs are used in NT writings to underscore or emphasize especially important statements.

   a. *A reminder that they have all the information they need to live faithfully (1:3)*. Like in 2 Peter, the Christians have "*the faith*" which was given "*once for all*" to the saints (v. 3). Jude says that they "*know all things once for all*" (v. 5). They should not be looking for more revelations from God, and neither should we.

   b. *Reminder that there will always be those who will oppose* God. Jude gives numerous examples of those who rebelled against God (from people to angels), vv. 5-11. In ways similar to 2 Peter, the church is continually having to fight against those who wish to destroy the truth of God (cf. 2 Pet. 2).

   c. *A clear identification of the false teachers*. From verse 4 we can see that these false teachers have joined themselves to the Christian community. However, they are wolves in sheep's clothing. They have denied Jesus as Lord and Master (v. 4). They are motivated by lust and greed (vv. 4, 16, 18) and are ignorant of the truth (v. 10).

   d. *An appeal to stand firm, even in the midst of trials*. God is able and willing to keep them "*from stumbling*" and to make them "*stand in the presence of His glory*" (v. 24). God has not promised Christians an escape from evil men. They will make life hard for the people of God (v. 12).

   e. *An appeal for them to be soul conscious*. Jude encourages them to "*have mercy on some*," and to "*save others, snatching them out of the fire*," and "*on some have mercy with fear*" (vv. 22-23). God expects Christians to counter and oppose false teachers and false doctrine. There is no room for passiveness. Souls are at stake, and the false teachers must not be allowed to win.

F. The Opponents

1. Unlike other epistles, this letter does not present a developed theology (although it does have some important theological truths—see the next point). Instead, the letter is primarily devoted to dealing with the destructive teachings which have infiltrated the church.

2. The false teachers that Jude addresses were outsiders who have "*crept in unnoticed*" into the Christian community. This language suggests that they had infiltrated the church, slipping in with an agenda in mind (to manipulate and exploit—v. 16).

3. Jude spends considerable time comparing them to well-known sinners in Old Testament times.

4. These false teachers were beyond logic and reason (v. 10). They have taken the doctrine of grace to support immoral behavior and have openly denied Jesus as Lord (v. 4).

5. They have divided the church (v. 19).

G. Themes and Theology

There are many great themes to identify, but here are a few:

1. *God has provided "the faith" (the body of doctrine), and it is sufficient for all time* (v. 3). While we live among those who argue that God continues to provide more revelation, this verse proves otherwise. Therefore modern-day prophets, apostles, popes—anyone who claim to receive additional revelations from God—are lying.

2. *The importance of knowledge.* Jude twice tells them that this letter is a *"reminder"* (vv. 5, 17). The truths taught to them need to be used to counter the false doctrines of the opponents. He expands their knowledge by giving them several Old Testament examples.

3. *We must fight for the faith.* Christianity was never designed to be a passive religion. God has always expected His people to stand up for the truth (v. 3; 1 Tim. 6:12).

4. *The power of lust.* These opponents are licentious (v. 4) and follow after their own lusts (vv. 16, 18).

5. *Ungodliness is the core sin.* The word *ungodly* (ἀσεβής) is found six times in this short epistle. It is the primary description of the false teachers, who have departed from God and His Word.

6. *Christ is coming.* The false teachers are living in such a way that they do not expect Jesus to return. These Christians are to await anxiously for the second coming (v. 21).

7. *We must grow in our faith.* Titus explains that they must build themselves up and tells them how to do it (vv. 20-21).

H. Key Words and Phrases

1. *This/these* (οὗτος) — 9 times (vv. 4, 7, 8, 10[2], 12, 14, 16, 19). This is Jude's word to identify the false teachers, typically "these men"

2. *Jesus* (Ἰησοῦς) — 7 times (vv. 1, [2], 4, 5, 17, 21, 25)

3. *Lord* (κύριος) — 7 times (vv. 4, 8, 9, 14, 17, 21, 25). The last three are "our Lord."

4. *Love* (ἀγάπη) — 7 times (vv. 2, 3, 12, 17, 20, 21)

5. *Ungodly* (ἀσεβής) — 6 times (vv. 4, 15[4], 18).

6. *Judge* (δίκαιος) — 6 times (vv. 4, 6, 9[2], 15, 22)

7. *Christ* (Χριστός) — 6 times (vv. 1[2], 4, 17, 21, 25).

8. *Watch/keep* (τηρέω) — 5 times (vv. 1, 6[2], 13, 21.

9. *Age* (αἰών) — 5 times (7, 13, 21, 25[2])

10. *God* (θεός) — 4 times (vv. 1, 4, 21, 25)

11. *Holy* (ἅγιος) — 4 times (vv. 3, 14, 20[2]

12. *Mercy/pity/compassion* (ἔλεος;ἅγιος) — 4 times (vv. 2, 21, 22, 23)

Learning Jude

I. Outlines

1. Various outlines from commentators:

    A. Blum (386).
- I. The Salutation (1–2)
- II. The Reason for the Letter (3–4)
- III. The Warning Against the False Teachers (5–16)
  - A. Examples of God's Judgment in History (5–7)
  - B. The Description and Doom of the False Teachers (8–13)
  - C. Enoch's Prophecy of the Coming Judgment (14–16)
- IV. The Exhortations to the Believers (17–23)
- V. The Doxology (24–25)

    B. Michael Green (177)
- a. The Author and His Readers (1–2)
- b. The Letter Jude Did Not Write, and the Letter He Did (3–4)
- c. Three Warning Reminders (5–7)
- d. The Analogies of Judgment Applied (8–10)
- e. Three More Old Testament Examples (11–13)
- f. The Prophecy of Enoch Applies to Them (14–16)
- g. The Words of the Apostles Apply to Them (17–19)
- h. Jude's Exhortation to the Faithful (20–23)
- i. Doxology (24–25)

C. Schreiner (425) sees the book as a chiasm:

  A. Epistolary Introduction—Participants and Threefold Characterization of Receptors (1)
   B. Salutation—Threefold Benediction (2)
    C. Purpose Introduced—Appeal (3)
     D. Motivation, First Mention—False Teachers (4)
      E. Reminder—Warning from Old Testament Times (5–7)
       F. Description—Heretics: 3 Attributes (8)
        G. Extracanonical example (Ancient)—Michael (9)
         H. Description—Heretics: 3 Attributes (10)
          I. Woe Oracle: 3 Archetypes from Old Testament (11)

        H´. Description—Heretics: 6 Attributes (12–13)
       G´. Extracanonical Prediction (Ancient)—Enoch (14–15)
      F´. Description—Heretics: 3 Attributes (16)
     E´. Reminder—Warning from New Testament Times (17–18)
    D´. Motivation, Final Mention—False Teachers (19)
   C´. Purpose Elaborated—Appeal (20–21)
  B´. Commission—A Threefold Assignment (22–23)
 A´. Epistolary Conclusion (24–25)

D. Neyrey (22)

I. Letter Opening: Address and Greeting (Jude 1-2)
II. Letter Occasion: Insinuation of Deviants (Jude 3-4)
III. Crimes Judged: Three Old Testament Examples (Jude 5-7)
V. Triple Crimes and Their Judgment (Jude 8-9)
V. Triple Example of Deviants Judged (Jude 10-13)
VI. Prediction of Future Judgment (Jude 14-16)
VII. Comparison and Contrast: Faithless Deviants and Faithful Disciples (Jude 17-23)
VII. Letter Closing: Doxology (Jude 24-25)

E. My own outline
    I. Epistolary Salutation (1-2)
   II. **Theme**: (3-4)
       A. Purpose Statement and Petition Verb: contend earnestly (3)
          1) For the faith
          2) For that which was delivered once for all
       B. Introduction of "*certain persons*" (τινες ἄνθρωποι), who are "ungodly" (ἀσεβής)): Three phrases describe them (4):
          1) who were marked for judgment (τὸ κρίμα) long ago
          2) who turn grace into licentiousness
          3) who deny our only Master and Lord, Jesus
  III. Reminder of Old Testament Unfaithfulness: Three Examples and Consequences
       A. Israelites who came out of Egypt (5): Destroyed
       B. Angels (6): Kept in eternal bonds

Learning Jude

      C. Sodom and Gomorrah (7): Punishment of eternal fire

IV. Description of False Teachers (8-17, 19)

      A. οὗτοι ("these men") reject authority (8)

          1) Ill. Michael the archangel (9)

      B. οὗτοι ("these men") revile what they don't understand (10)

          2) Ill. Three parallels: Cain, Balaam, Korah (11)

      C. οὗτοι ("these men") are hidden reefs (12)

      D. οὗτοι ("these men") are like those written about in the book of Enoch (14-15)

      E. οὗτοι ("these men") are fundamentally wicked (16)

      F. οὗτοι ("these men") cause divisions, are worldly (19)

V. "But you"—major shift; direct command #1 (17)

      A. Remember: you were forewarned (17-18)

      B. Remember: Don't forget what kind of people these are (19)

VI. "But you"—major shift continues (20). Direct command #2

      A. Four concluding commands to help them grow and improve:

          1) Keep yourselves in the love of God (21).

          2) Have mercy (22)

          3) Save others (23)

          4) Have mercy with fear (23)

      B. Hate anything that pollutes (23)

VII. Doxology

      A. Praise for what God can do (two aorist infinitives):

          1) Keep you from stumbling

          2) Make you stand

      B. Praise for who God is

          1) The only God

          2) The One who has…now and forever (25)

              a) Glory

              b) Majesty

              c) Dominion

              d) Authority

Book Overview: Jude has made it easy on us by beginning his letter with both a purpose statement (it is about our common salvation) and a petition verb (**appealing** that you contend earnestly for the faith). He then explains why he is making this urgent appeal. There are *"certain persons"* who are undermining their confidence and obedience to that one faith. Jude spends considerable time identifying these opponents and noting the condemnation they face from God (vv. 5-16). He concludes the epistle with four commands that tie back to what *"contend for the faith"* meant in verse 3.

Verse 1—Although there are eight different individuals named **Jude** in the New Testament, the most logical one is that this is the brother of Jesus and James (cf. Matt. 13:55; Mark 6:3). Showing genuine humility, he instead refers to himself as a **bond-servant** of Jesus Christ. The word **bond-servant** (δοῦλος) describes "one who is solely committed to another, slave, subject" (Bauer 260). He says he is the **brother of James**, which is logically Jesus' brother (see the introduction). He describes the recipients in three ways:

a) **They are called.** How were they called? By the preaching of the Gospel (cf. 2 Thess. 2:14). Those who heard the Gospel but did not respond were not considered to be **called**. This terminology has nothing to do with the Calvinistic doctrine of "unconditional election."

> The idea expresses the divine initiative to which man must respond in faith, and in the NT καλεῖν ("to call") becomes a technical term for the process of Christian salvation. It refers to God's call to men and women, through the gospel, to enter his kingdom, to belong to the new people of God. Alongside the OT background, there may be the influence of Jesus' parables in which the call to enter the kingdom is represented by the invitation (καλεῖν) to a marriage feast (Matt. 22:3–9, 14; Luke 14:8, 16–24; Rev. 19:9) (Bauckham 26).

b) They are **beloved in God the Father.** The word *beloved* (ἀγαπάω) is a perfect participle, indicating that they were once the recipient of God's love and continue to be. Despite the hardships they face (which are discussed in this letter), they need to find comfort that their heavenly **God** and **Father** loves them.

c) They are **kept for Jesus Christ.** The word **kept** (τηρέω) means "to cause a state, condition, or activity to continue, keep, hold, reserve, preserve" (Bauer 1002). Those who have obeyed the Gospel of Jesus, have Him as their Lord, protector, and savior.

> This phrase has an eschatological sense: Christians are kept safe by God for the Parousia of Jesus Christ when they will enter into their final salvation in His Kingdom. (Perhaps the metaphor is: Christians are the property of Jesus Christ, kept safe for him until he comes to claim it; cf. 1 Pet 1:4, where the inheritance of Christians is kept safe [τετηρημένην] for them in heaven until, at the Parousia, they can claim it.) For this eschatological sense, cf. 1 Thess. 5:23 (*"may your spirit and soul and body be kept* [τηρηθείη] *sound and blameless at the coming of our Lord Jesus Christ"*); 1 Pet. 1:5 (*"guarded* [φρουρουμένους] *by God's power through faith for a salvation ready to be revealed in the last time"*); and Jude 24 (where φυλάσσειν has the same sense as τηρεῖν, "to keep," here, cf. John 17:12) (Bauckham 26).

Jude refers to the continuous preservation with which Jesus keeps those who trust Him (cf. 2 Tim. 1:12, 1 Pet. 1:5; 1 John 5:18). He keeps what we commit to him. It is interesting to compare this emphasis on Christ's keeping power with its correlative in verse 21, '*keep yourselves in God's love.*' It is God's part to keep man; but it is man's part to keep himself in the love of God. These are the two sides to Christian perseverance (cf. Phil. 2:12-13) (Green 181).

Verse 2—While the wording here could be overlooked because it is relatively common, such would be unfortunate. The words used here are theologically rich, and significant to the life of these first-century Christians. Jude wishes that they have **multiplied** God's **mercy, peace, and love**. **Mercy** (ἔλεος) is found 4 times in this book (2, 21, 22, 23). The word means "kindness or concern expressed for someone in need, mercy, compassion, pity, clemency" (Bauer 316). Jude wants them to extend this to others, while they are "*waiting anxiously for the mercy of our Lord Jesus*" (vv. 21-23). **Peace** (εἰρήνη) generally means "a state of well-being, peace" (Bauer 287). It includes contentment based upon our reconciliation with God—cf. Rom. 5:1-4; Phil. 4:6). The way Jude describes the false teachers and the turmoil they are bringing on the church, it is easy to see how they need **peace**. Even in the midst of such a storm, God can provide calm. **Love** (ἀγάπη) is also a prevalent word in this book, occurring seven times (vv. 2, 3, 12, 17, 20, 21). The word means "the quality of warm regard for and interest in another, esteem, affection, regard, love" (Bauer 6). Like 2 Peter 2:2, Jude wishes for these to be **multiplied to you**. God, who is "rich" in qualities like these (cf. Eph. 2:4, 7), can indeed provide an abundance of them all (see Sermon Seed: "Mercy, Peace and Love").

Verse 3—It isn't often that a writer identifies the original purpose of a letter, only to say that circumstances are such that he needs to change directions. Jude's original plan was to discuss their **common salvation**. The word for **common** (κοινός) "pertains to being of mutual interest or shared collectively, communal, common" (Bauer 551). What they shared was their **salvation**. This language is comparable to Romans 6:17. Christians all followed the same pattern for salvation. They all believed, repented, confessed the Lordship of Jesus, and were immersed in the waters of baptism. That was their shared experience, and it is what all Christians of every generation equally share. Modern "conversions" that do not follow those steps are not following the NT pattern. Jude ends his brief letter with some points that would apply to this **common salvation** (vv. 20-25).

The urgency of the situation has motivated Jude to change course and **write** about the false teachers who have infiltrated the church. The direness of the situation requires Jude to **appeal** to them. This word (παρακαλέω) means "to urge strongly, appeal to, urge, exhort, encourage" (Bauer 765). This petition verb is used in Greek letters to underscore or emphasize an especially important point. Such is the case here. There is significance and urgency in what Jude is about to say. These Christians must not be passive, or even neutral. The damage being done by these false teachers is significant and soul destroying. The **common salvation** that they enjoyed is now in jeopardy. These Christians must protect it!

What is it that Jude wants them to protect? It is **the faith**. Notice how the definite article is with the word **faith**. Usually when this happens the inspired writer has the body of doctrine, the Gospel, in mind. Such is the case here. They are not to contend for "a faith," or some undefined system of belief. They are to contend for the Gospel of Christ—the one and only truth (cf. Gal. 1:6-9, 23; 3:23, 25, 26; Acts 6:6). "'The faith' is the body of truth that very early in the church's history took on a definite form (cf. Acts 2:42; Rom. 6:17; Gal. 1:23). Without doubt, the form of the faith as a body of recognized truth became clearer as time passed" (Blum 388).

Jude urges them to **contend earnestly** for this faith. This word (ἐπαγωνίζομαι) means "to exert intense effort on behalf of something, contend" (Bauer 356). We get our word agonize from this word. These Christians are in a dog fight, a serious struggle for the Gospel. It is under attack. Who will rise up to defend it? The fact that Jude has changed course and is now addressing this shows his level of concern. Does he question the Christian's resolve to engage the enemy? Does he fear that they do not consider the threat credible? Have they grown comfortable in their present situation and don't want to disrupt it (known as apathy)? Do they believe this is someone else's fight, not theirs? This is why Jude says that he is appealing **that you** contend earnestly. It is not someone else's fight. It is not one that can be put off for another day.

Jude's description of the faith that they need to fight for is interesting. He says that it was **once for all delivered to the saints**. The word translated **once for all** (ἅπαξ) "pertains to a single occurrence and decisively unique, once and for all" (Bauer 97. See this word in Heb. 9:26, 28; 10:2; 1 Pet. 3:18, 20). The word does not allow for future revelations. It has no room for doctrinal adjustments based on time or culture. It originates from the omniscient God who knows how to deliver a lasting, eternal message. It is not a message that will be delivered again, nor will it need to be delivered again. The word **delivered** (παραδίδωμι) is a passive participle in this verse. The truth has been delivered, and it will not be delivered again. It did not originate in human councils or conferences. It was not the creation of man but came from the mind of God. God saw that it be **delivered** to mankind. He worked through the Holy Spirit to bring that saving message through the pen of the apostles and prophets (cf. John 14:26; 15:26-27; 16:13; Eph. 3:1-5; 1 Cor. 2:10-13; 2 Tim. 3:16-17; 2 Pet. 1:21. And don't forget passages like Deut. 4:2; 12:32; Prov. 30:6; Gal. 1:6-9; Rev. 22:18, 19). Jude affirms that this truth was delivered to **the saints. Saints** (ἅγιος) means "believers, loyal followers, saints of Christians as consecrated to God" (Bauer 11). This special group of people were made special by the message they are now asked to defend. It saved them, consecrated them, and gave them hope. Is it now special enough to them to fight for it? This makes God's people the custodians of **the faith**. They have been entrusted with the sacred, solemn, and challenging responsibility of delivering the truth—through preaching, teaching, proclaiming, writing. They are expected to model **the faith** through their lives of holiness and dedication.

Verse 4—The use of the word **for** (γάρ) explains the urgency of the appeal in v. 3. Jude is going to prove to them that the situation is serious, and the need to rise up imperative. The problem is found in **certain persons** (τινες ἄνθρωποι), a specific group that is endangering the precious faith that was given to them. The reference to these false teachers will continue with the use of "these" throughout the epistle (vv. 8, 10, 12, 14, 16, 19). Jude notes that they have **crept in unnoticed**. Peter said that such men will come (2 Pet. 2:1), and now Jude affirms that **have** come. Surprisingly, they have managed to become a part of the church without anyone recognizing them for who they are. The word translated **crept in unnoticed** (παρεισδύ(ν)ω) is found only here in the NT. Paul does use a related word *pareisaktos* in reference to the Judaizers who had "infiltrated" Christian congregations to spy on their freedom in Christ Jesus (Gal. 2:4). Like Jesus' wolves in sheep's clothing (Matt. 7:15-20), these men appeared friendly, harmless, and non-threatening. They had tactics of manipulation, designed to dupe the church into believing they were one of them. They acted like Christians, pretended to share the doctrine of the church, raised their voices in worship with others. As we would say, there were no "red flags" with these men—maybe not even orange flags. There were just no warning signs—hence their success in being **unnoticed**. Their agenda, however, is now clear. They intend to destroy the church.

Jude, who loves to group things into threes, makes three observations about these men:

First, he says they were **long beforehand marked out for this condemnation**. In the Old Testament writings God had long ago identified these type of people. They were **marked out** (προγράφω) or written about beforehand.

> Jude's emphasis is not simply that the doom of the heretics was predicted, but also that it was decreed and publicly announced. While the predictive sense is not absent entirely, his principal point concerns the official and public condemnation of the heretics. Their judgment was decreed πάλαι (*palai*, long ago; as Matt. 11:21; Luke 10:13; Heb. 1:1; 2 Clem. 11.2) (Gene Green 58).

These were marked for **condemnation**. This word (κρίμα) means "legal decision rendered by a judge, judicial verdict…mostly in an unfavorable sense, of the condemnatory verdict and sometimes the subsequent punishment itself 2 Pet. 2:3; Jude 4" (Bauer 567). This reminds us of passages like Proverbs 16:4: *"The Lord has made everything for its purpose, even the wicked for the day of trouble"* (ESV). The New Century translates this verse as follows: *"The LORD makes everything go as He pleases. He has even prepared a day of disaster for evil people."*

Second, Jude says they are **ungodly persons who turn the grace of our God into licentiousness**. To identify them as **ungodly persons** (ἀσεβής—key word, found six times) is to claim that they are "violating norms for a proper relation to deity, irreverent, impious, ungodly" (Bauer 141). They put on a front of godliness (cf. 2 Tim. 3:5) yet are wicked and immoral. This is what makes them so dangerous. It is imperative that the church see through their facade. They are hypocrites, pretending to be spiritual. A specific example of their ungodliness is observing what they do with the doctrine of **grace**. In a similar way to Romans 3:1-8; 6:1, they have manipulated the teaching about grace to give license to **licentiousness**. This word (ἀσέλγεια) means "lack of self-constraint which involves one in conduct that violates all bounds of what is socially acceptable, self-abandonment" (Bauer 141). Since God freely gives man His **grace**, why not go ahead and do that which will be forgiven anyway? To such self-serving thinking Paul would say "God forbid!" It is not logical to continue in sin so that grace might abound (Rom. 6:1).

> The second reason for judgment is that the interlopers subverted God's grace and lived licentiously. The word "license" (*aselgeia*) often denotes sexual sin (Wis. 14:26; Rom. 13:13; 2 Cor. 12:21; Gal. 5:19; Eph. 4:19) or some kind of gross debauchery in more general terms (2 Mac. 2:26; Mark 7:22; 1 Pet. 4:3; 2 Pet. 2:2, 7, 18). The context of the letter as a whole suggests that sexual sin is intended. The foundational character of v. 4 manifests itself again since sexual sin is featured as the reason for the judgment of the angels and Sodom and Gomorrah (vv. 6–7). Perhaps Jude also had this in mind when he spoke of defiling the flesh in v. 8 (cf. also vv. 13, 16 possibly) (Schreiner 439).

Third, Jude says they **deny our only Master and Lord, Jesus Christ**. The word **deny** (ἀρνέομαι) means "to disclaim association with a person or event, deny, repudiate, disown" (Bauer 132). What they are denying is the very core of Christianity—the lordship of **Jesus**! Our confession of Him as **Lord** is what was said at baptism and is what is continually lived and practiced (Rom. 10:9-10). It is that confession and practice that has brought us "salvation" Paul says. The word for **master** (δεσπότης) means "one who has legal control and authority over persons, such as subjects or slaves, lord, master" (Bauer 220). These men have no intent of submitting to the lordship of Jesus, for such would prohibit their desired lifestyle of sin.

Verse 5—As Peter did in his second letter (1:12, 13, 15; 3:1), Jude now wishes to **remind** (ὑπομιμνήσκω) them of important truths, all of which establish the point made earlier about how God "long beforehand" had marked out such people for condemnation. Jude does compliment them by affirming that they **know all things once for all**. What he is about to say is not new or novel. They've heard it before and know it to be true. In all likelihood they are being reminded of what Peter wrote. The reference to **once for all** is difficult, and commentators have offered several possible explanations. Probably Jude is simply affirming that they "were at once for all fully informed" (RSV).

> Jude appears to be apologizing to his readers when he acknowledges that they are already *fully informed of,* or "know all about," what he was going to tell them. The records of the past are fully known to them, and they only need to be reminded of these things. It is of course possible that this is a further case of politeness on the part of Jude, and what he is doing here is similar to a modern speaker who says, "I am sure you know," although he is not at all certain that his audience in fact knows what he is going to tell them (Arichea and Hatton 21).

Jude will now provide three (notice again the use of three's) examples of God's judgments against rebellion and disobedience:

First, he reminds them of the rebellious Israelites. In the book of Exodus we read of God's great deliverance of Israel from the oppression of the Egyptians. Through the wonder of the 10 plagues, the parting of the Red Sea, the pillar and cloud, and the mighty demonstration at Mt. Sinai, God had saved them. However, **after saving a people out of the land of Egypt they did not believe.** Their lack of faith—despite numerous illustrations of God's love and care—angered God so that he **subsequently destroyed** them. The word **destroyed** (ἀπόλλυμι) is the same word Peter used in 2 Peter 3:6, 16. It is the word these inspired writers used to describe the fate of people. It is not the word that means annihilated (which is a word Peter used to describe the present heavens and earth—they will be annihilated—2 Pet. 3:10-14). Rather, the word means "ruined" and captures the sad fate of those who were the precious creation of God but used their free will for selfish ends, ruining themselves and the relationship with their heavenly Father. This reminds us of a passage from Hebrews 3:16-19:

> *For who provoked Him when they had heard? Indeed, did not all those who came out of Egypt led by Moses? And with whom was He angry for forty years? Was it not with those who sinned, whose bodies fell in the wilderness? And to whom did He swear that they would not enter His rest, but to those who were disobedient? So we see that they were not able to enter because of unbelief.*

Verse 6—*Second, he reminds them of the sinning angels.* Jude talks about **angels** committing two sins. First, they **did not keep their own domain**. God, as Master over all of His creation, has assigned roles and positions of authority. The word **domain** (ἀρχή) is a common word but appears to be used here in a unique way. Bauer says here it means "the sphere of one's official activity, rule, office" (138). The angels had assigned roles and duties. They, however, did not **keep** (τηρέω—watch over, maintain) those duties. Second, they **abandoned their proper abode**. God had not only assigned duties, but He assigned a set place. The word **abode** (οἰκητήριον) means "a place for living, dwelling, habitation" and is found only here and 2 Corinthians 5:2 (Bauer 695). The word for **proper** is a phrase that means "their own" (τὸ ἴδιον). Therefore, God has not only assigned duties, but areas in which angels could travel. Angels, like men, are free moral agents. They determined to defy God in both of their assignments. As a result, has **kept** (τηρέω—"to retain in custody, keep watch over, guard"—Bauer 1002) them in **eternal bonds under darkness**. They can no longer do what they were assigned to do, nor live where they were assigned to live. God now has a new location for them, a place described with **eternal bonds**. The word **bonds** (δεσμός) is "that which serves as a means of restraint by tying or fastening, bond, fetter" (Bauer 219). These once mighty creatures are now locked up, restrained by heavenly chains. The sentence for their rebellion is **eternal** (ἀΐδιος—cf. Rom. 1:20 that describes God's "eternal power"). The **great day** means Judgment Day, when all of God's creation, both in the earthly and spiritual realms, will face God's **judgment**. Paul even says that Christians will judge angels (1 Cor. 6:3).

Of course, the primary question is what event Jude is referring to. He says he is reminding them of this, and that these are things they already know (v. 5). He also noted that these examples come from teachings that were made "long beforehand." The other examples are from the Old Testament, and there is no reason to not conclude the same here. Yet where in the Old Testament do we read about angels not keeping their proper abode and rebelling against God? There is no such passage outside of Genesis 6. For evidence that this is the correct interpretation, see my notes on 2 Peter 2. Schreiner says: "We can be almost certain that Jude referred here to the sin of the angels in Gen. 6:1-4" (447-8).

The second example is of the fallen angels. The most likely reference here is to the angels ("sons of God," cf. Gen. 6:4; Job 1:6; 2:1) who came to earth and mingled with women. This interpretation is expounded in the pseudepigraphical Book of Enoch (7, 9.8, 10.11; 12.4), from which Jude quotes in verse 14, and is common in the intertestamental literature and the early church fathers (e.g., Justin Apology 2.5) (Blum 390).

Verse 7—*Jude's third example: Sodom and Gomorrah.* These famous cities refer to what was recorded in Genesis 19. The **cities around them** are Admah and Zeboiim (Deut. 29:23). The level of debauchery and evil found in these cities became a common example throughout the Old and New Testament (cf. Deut. 29; 23; 32:32; Isa. 1:9; 3:9; 13:19; Jer. 23:14; 49:18; 50:40; Eze. 16:46ff.; Amos 4:11; Matt. 10:15; 11:24; 25:41; Luke 10:12; 17:29; 2 Pet. 2:6; Rev. 11:8; 20:10, etc.).

Jude identifies two sins of **Sodom and Gomorrah**. First, they **indulged in gross immorality**. In the Garden of Eden God established the high standard of human relationships. With Adam and Eve God laid the foundation for morality and sexual interactions. Homosexual relations were frequently condemned by God in the Mosaic Law (cf. Lev. 18:22; 20:13; Deut. 23:18). The word that is translated **gross immorality** (ἐκπορνεύω) means "to indulge in illicit sexual relations / debauchery" (Bauer 309). The people of these cities were evil, and their homosexual practices were an abomination to God. Second, they **went after strange flesh**. The word translated strange (ἕτερος) "pertaining to being dissimilar in kind or class from all other entities, another, different." Its Hebrew equivalent refers to that which is unauthorized (cf. Lev. 10:1). It is possible that Jude has in mind their desire to have sex with the angelic visitors (Gen. 19:5), which Lot said would be to "*act wickedly*" (v. 7). The men of Sodom did not know they were angels. They referred to them as "*men*" (v. 5). It is possible that Jude is merely using these two phrases to identify and emphasize the evil actions of these cities. These cities are **exhibited** (πρόκειμαι—made public) **as an example** (δεῖγμα—evidence, proof), and will be **undergoing the punishment of eternal fire**. What example did they give? They failed to submit to God's established order and to honor His divine laws. Just

69

as the two previous examples, there is an expectation from God that His creation submit to Him. The obvious point, then, is that these false teachers are *"denying our only Master and Lord"* (v. 4) and living in defiance to God's laws.

Additional Study: The question of who are the sinning angels is made more clear by a little, often overlooked phrase found in verse 7. It is the phrase **since they in the same way as these**. It is clear that **they** is referring to Sodom and Gomorrah. Grammar demands it, and the context supports it. The question, then, is to whom does the **these** refer to? Some scholars have said it is a reference to the surrounding cities: since they [Sodom and Gomorrah] in the same way [sexual immorality] as these [the cities around them]. The problem: cities is feminine plural, **these** (τούτοις) is masculine plural. Therefore, Jude cannot be referring to the cities. We are left to look for another masculine plural. There is one—found in verse 6: the angels (ἀγγέλους—masculine plural). This makes the phrase mean: since they [Sodom and Gomorrah] **in the same way as these** [angels] **indulged in gross immorality and went after strange flesh**. When, in all of recorded Scripture did angels go after **strange** (unauthorized) **flesh**? The only answer is Genesis 6, providing further evidence that the *"sons of God"* in that passage refers to angels. It also explains what the angels did in v. 6. By leaving their heavenly position and home (v. 6), and co-habiting with earthly women (v. 7), they are faced with an **eternal** (word used both places) judgment of bonds and **fire**.

Verse 8—Jude now moves to an application from his three examples. He argues that **in the same manner** (judgment/punishment from God) **these men** (οὗτοι—see introduction for a breakdown of how Jude uses this word) are rebelling against God. Jude says it is **by dreaming** (ἐνυπνιάζομαι) that they engage in their sinful activities. This rare word should be understood in the sense of an inspired vision or dream. That is, they are claiming that their viewpoint is from God Himself.

> The word for "dream" occurs only one other time in the New Testament, in Acts 2:17, where it is used of prophetic dreams. It is very likely that these people have claimed that through dreams or "visions" (TEV) they receive special revelations from God and thereby gain spiritual insight. Therefore the verse is not suggesting that they perform all these evil acts while experiencing visions, or that they sin in their dreams (which a literal translation may suggest), but that they justify their sinful acts by special revelations they claim to receive from God (Arichea and Hatton 29).

Jude, following his pattern of three points, makes the following observations about **these men**:

*First, they **defile the flesh**.* The word **defile** (μιαίνω) means "to cause the purity of something to be violated by immoral behavior, defile" (Bauer 650). The body (**flesh**) was designed by God to be pure and the temple of the Holy Spirit (cf. 1 Cor. 6:19-20). These men have taken that which is good and holy and corrupted it. The language used here frequently refers to sexual corruption.

> The word "defile" (*mianiō*) often designates sexual sin in the Old Testament (e.g., Gen. 34:4, 13, 27; Lev. 18:24, 27–28; Job 31:11; Jer. 3:2; Hos. 5:3; 6:10; cf. Pss. Sol. 2:13; 1 Enoch 9:8; 10:11; 12:4; 15:3–4). It also fits with what Jude said about the angels and Sodom and Gomorrah in vv. 6–7. The phrase "defile the flesh" to describe sexual sin is also found (Sib. Or. 2:279; Herm. Mand. 29:9; Sim. 60:2). Naturally the opponents did not think they were defiling the flesh. Presumably, they appealed to their dreams to say that their sexual freedom was from God himself, that they transcended moral norms (Schreiner 456).

*Second, they **reject authority***. The word **reject** (ἀθετέω) means "to reject by not recognizing something or someone, reject, not recognize, disallow" (Bauer 24). **Authority** (κυριότης) is in reference to "the majestic power that the κύριος wields, ruling power, lordship, dominion" (Bauer 579). While it is possible that Jude means they reject human authorities (either church leaders or government officials), the word used here never has that meaning. Some believe the reference is to angelic authorities, but that would most likely be in the plural (cf. Eph. 1:21; Col. 1:16). The singular noun logically points to the Lordship of Christ (or God). This fits with what Jude said in verse 4.

*Third, they **revile angelic majesties***. The word **revile** (βλασφημέω) means "slander, revile, defame, speak irreverently/impiously/disrespectfully of or about" (Bauer). Our word *blaspheme* is a transliteration of this word. These men have no problem using the ugliest words against **angelic majesties**. The word for **majesties** (δόξα) is a common NT word, but here means "a transcendent being deserving of honor, majestic being" (Bauer 258). The high position afforded angels is found in Scripture (cf. Ex. 15:11; 1 Tim. 5:21; Heb. 2:2). But does Jude have reference to good angels or the evil, fallen ones? Some commentators argue that it must be in reference to good angels, since Jude would not have a problem with their blaspheming evil angels. When merged with verse 9, however, it seems that evil angels are in view. This makes Jude's argument one of recognized authority and position. These men are 'out of line' to think they have any right or authority to mock angels—good or bad. For example, even Michael the archangel refused to pronounce judgment on the devil. Instead, Michael knew that was not his to do, but belonged to the ultimate authority of God.

> Why were the angels receiving scorn from the opponents? We must admit our lack of knowledge here. Those who see the angels as good have proposed various answers. Some have suggested that the opponents were Gnostics who criticized the angels for their part in the creation of the material world. But this interpretation stands only if Jude is an anti-Gnostic polemic, and the evidence for such a theory is lacking. Others think the angels were criticized as mediators of the law of Moses (Gal. 3:19; Acts 7:38, 53; Heb. 2:2; cf. *Jub.* 1:27–29; Josephus, Ant. 15.136). This would fit with the antinomian character of the opponents, but it fails if the angels here are demons since there is no warrant (not even in Gal. 3:19) to think that God's law was transmitted by demons. Alternatively, others argue that the opponents held to a form of overrealized eschatology, and they disparaged angels because they knew believers would judge them (1 Cor. 6:3). Another possibility is that angels were reviled because they would play a major role on the day of judgment. But if the "glories" were demons, another answer might be correct. It is difficult, of course, to discern from verse 8 alone whether the "glories" were good or evil angels, but verse 9 tips the scales in favor of demons. Michael did not take upon himself to pass judgment on the devil but entreated the Lord to judge him. Yet the intruders in Jude's community felt no compunction about reviling demons. The adversaries may have reviled these glories because they claimed that demons could not hurt those belonging to God. If this is the case, they underestimated the power of evil; for these angels, though evil, still retained glory, even though that glory had now been deformed by evil (Schreiner 457–458).

Verse 9—In contrast to the arrogant, sinful actions of the false teachers, Jude offers **Michael the archangel** as an example. As an **archangel** no one would question **Michael's** great power and position. Among the angelic hosts, he has been put in charge (cf. Rev. 12:7). Yet he **did not dare pronounce** against Satan a **railing judgment**. He knew his place and knew that it was not his role to make judgment against **the devil**. Instead, he simply said to Satan: **The Lord rebuke you**. The **Lord** who has already demonstrated His power over angels (v. 6) can easily **rebuke** (ἐπιτιμάω—reprove, censure) and judge Satan.

Part of the curiosity of this verse is the subject of debate between Michael and the devil. Jude says they **argued about the body of Moses**. Bauckham does a superb job of discussing this text. I will provide some selected quotes.

> Evidently the words of Michael, quoted in Jude's source, derive from Zechariah 3:2. The vision in Zech. 3:1-5 is a courtroom scene in which the accusing angel, "the adversary" (וְהַשָּׂטָן), and the angel of the Lord confront each other in a legal dispute in which the defendant is the high priest Joshua. Evidently Joshua's guilt, as representative of Israel, has placed him in the power of Satan his accuser. When the angel of the Lord (Jude's source must have read מלאך יהוה "the angel of the Lord" for MT יהוה "Lord" in Zech. 3:2), as the Lord's representative, silences Satan with the words, "May the Lord rebuke you, Satan," he dismisses Satan's case against Joshua (Bauckham 65).

> At Moses' death, Satan makes a last attempt to assert his power over him. As we shall see, he does so by accusing Moses of murdering the Egyptian. By this accusation he intends to claim Moses' body and deprive him of the honor of burial by the archangel. Michael, however, silences Satan by his appeal to God to assert his authority over Satan ("May the Lord rebuke you!"), and thereby not only rescues Moses' body from Satan's power, but also vindicates Moses as the servant of God against Satan's attempt to claim him as a sinner (Bauckham 66).

While several sources have been given as the possible background to this (since the Old Testament says nothing of a debate over the body of Moses), the most likely is a now extant work named *The Assumption of Moses* or a second writing known as *The Testament of Moses*. Numerous early church writers claimed that this text was from those documents. Our problem is that what little remains of these works (fragmented Latin translations) leaves out the most important part—what they were debating about. I believe that Bauckham's explanation is the strongest.

Verse 10—Jude returns to his discussion of **these men** (οὗτοι). He says they **revile** (βλασφημέω––v. 8) **the things which they do not understand**. The lessons learned from Michael are lost on these men. They do not know their proper place, and do not respect the authority of God or His law. He is Judge and the only Judge (cf. James 4:11). What they **do not understand** (based on v. 8) is the role of angels in God's scheme. A failure to **understand** is such a common problem in Scripture that we are not surprised to see it here. Nearly every epistle, both those of Paul, Peter and John, deal with ignorance—ignorance of God, His law, and His Son. We can add the angels to that list.

Jude does acknowledge that there are some things they **know by instinct**. The overall context supports the notion that their sexual indulgence has taught them the joy of sinful pleasure. "Though they claim to be guided by special spiritual insight gained in heavenly revelations, they are in fact following the sexual instincts which they share with the animals" (Bauckham 63). There is no nobility in such knowledge. Rather they are like u**nreasoning animals**. Animals are not governed by a moral code. They feel no remorse when they kill. Their lives are governed by what they want. These false teachers share these same traits. However, it is **by these things they are destroyed**.

Learning Jude

Their rebellion against God and their licentious behavior will be their spiritual undoing. They will be **destroyed** (φθείρω). This is not the word found in verse 5. Rather, this word means "to cause deterioration of the inner life, ruin, corrupt" (Bauer 1054). That corruption, however, will assuredly lead to judgment and punishment (v. 15).

Verse 11—Jude provides a strong interjection: **Woe to them!** (οὐαὶ αὐτοῖς). This word is common in the Gospels, where Jesus used it often (cf. Matt. 23). Outside of the Gospels it is found in 1 Corinthians 9:16, here and Revelation 8:13; 9:12; 11:14; 12:12; 18:10, 16, 19. This **woe** is a warning, for these false teachers are heading toward God's wrath. This is because they have followed the terrible example of three OT characters:

First, they have gone the way of Cain. The word **way** (πορεύω) indicates a moral or religious path. Cain, as discussed in Hebrews 11:4, developed his own faithless approach to God. His works were therefore rejected. That rejection by God led to other sins, like hatred and murder (cf. 1 John 3:12-13). The men are following the same course as **Cain**. They are not living by the faith that was once for all delivered (v. 3) but have developed their own self-serving theology (v. 4). They know what they want to do. They want to live sexually promiscuous lives and then ask God's grace to sanction such (v. 4).

Second, for pay they have rushed headlong into the error of Balaam. **Balaam** is seen in Scripture as a person who sees religion as an opportunity to enrich oneself (2 Pet. 2:15-16) and to justify his own immoral behavior. His philosophy is such that it influences others into error and immorality (what happened at Baal-Peor is evidence—Num. 31:16-19). When Jude says they do this **for pay**, he is noting that these false teachers have found a way to make money off of the Christians and the church (cf. 1 Tim. 6:5; Tit. 1:11).

*Third, they have **perished in the rebellion of Korah***. **Korah**, along with Dathan, Abiram, and 250 others, led a rebellion against Moses (Num. 16:1-35). In an unusual twist, he portrays these false teachers as also having **perished** in that rebellion. The use of the aorist is designed to say it is assured. They might as well have been in the crowd of 250, because they are going to receive the same fate, guaranteed.

Verse 12—Notice how Jude continues the pattern with **these men** (οὗτοί). It is imperative that the Christians understand the nature and character of these men who have gained a position in the church. They "**crept in unnoticed**," but hopefully Jude's identification of them will mean they are unnoticed no longer. In this verse Jude is going to continue to apply his "woe" oracles and names several more dangers of having these false teachers in their midst.

First, Jude days they are **hidden reefs in your love-feasts**. The word translated **hidden-reefs** (σπιλάς) means "a rocky hazard hidden by waves, a rock washed by the sea, a (hidden) reef" (Bauer 938). The NIV goes with "*blemishes*," accepting an alternative definition of the word that can mean a "stain" or "spot." This interpretation also agrees with 2 Peter 2:13. However, this is a slightly different word, and the common meaning is "rocks." If we go with this definition, Jude is giving a powerful illustration. For centuries ships have feared the rocky shores as they are trying to safely make it to the harbor. These men are those which can bring about considerable damage to the Christian unity. Jude especially notes their **love-feasts**. This is one word in Greek (ἀγάπαις) "a common meal eaten by early Christians in connection with their worship, for the purpose of fostering and expressing mutual affection and concern, fellowship meal, a love-feast" (Bauer 7). In many ways this was similar to modern "potlucks" where Christians enjoy each other's company around a shared meal. These types of social gatherings were intended to strengthen the bond of unity for fellow Christians. The false teachers, however, saw these love-feasts as an opportunity to spread their teaching and immoral beliefs (v. 4). Jude goes on to say that they **feast with you without fear**. They have succeeded in gaining a position in the church. They are not seen as wolves in sheep's clothing. When Jude says they do this **without fear**, it seems that they have no concern of being discovered. This could also mean that they do this without any guilt of conscience. Like those of 1 Timothy 4, their consciences are desensitized.

Second, the statement **caring for themselves** confirms their motives without conscience. They have an evil agenda and are not troubled that they might destroy other's faith, other's relationships, even other's marriages. Some translations render this "*shepherds who feed only themselves.*" If such is the correct rendering, it would show a parallel to the false shepherd of Ezekiel 34:8, who had no genuine care for the flock.

Third, they are **clouds without water**. The dry climate of Israel made rain especially valuable and needed. Without the rains the crops could not grow, the animals could not drink and life as a whole becomes a major struggle. Clouds provide a glimmer of hope that there is rain. When those clouds produce no moisture, there is great disappointment, even despair. These false teachers are like these clouds. They promise something that the people want and need but are incapable of delivering. They leave nothing but disappointment. Like clouds that hover overhead with the prospect of dropping rain, but then are blown away by the winds, these false teachers are present for a while but leave having provided nothing. While some see the **winds** as a veiled reference to Satan (he is the one controlling them), there is no reason to see that kind of interpretation behind these words.

Fourth, they are **autumn trees without fruit**. The reference to **autumn** shows that these trees are well past the time that they should have produced fruit. However, those are waiting in vain. The false teachers, like a tree without fruit, are unable to produce anything needed or valuable. While some believe the next two clauses of this metaphor are unrelated to trees, it is best to see Jude as continuing to describe these trees. He says they are **doubly dead**. A tree that is unproductive is, as far as its owner is concerned, a **dead** tree. He will, as the Gospels noted, cut down the unproductive tree (Matt. 3:10). Now it is truly dead—dead a second time. The false teachers should be considered "dead" to the Christian community. The **doubly dead** might then refer to their judgment of eternal death and condemnation on Judgment Day (Rev. 20:6, 14).

> In light of the fact that the "trees" have no fruit and are uprooted, Jude declares them "twice dead." ...The metaphor of being fruitless and uprooted trees points rather to Jude's desire to demonstrate their absolutely corrupt and useless nature. He holds out no hope for them (Gene Green 97).

Verse 13—Jude continues his metaphors, emphasizing the dangerous and destructive nature of the false teachers.

Fifth, they are **wild waves of the sea**. Ancient man had a great fear of the sea. Many ships had sailed and failed to return. Those that did return reported the massive waves and high winds. The perils at sea were legendary. These false teachers offer similar dangers. They are powerful, relentless and

wild (untamed). They are **casting up their own shame like foam**. The white **foam** that covers the beach is sticky and grimy. It can ruin a beautiful beach. So also with these false teachers. As Isaiah said in a similar passage, *"But the wicked are like the tossing sea, for it cannot be quiet, and its waters toss up refuse and mud"* (Isa. 57:20).

Sixth, they are like **wandering stars**. Moving from the metaphor of things on the earth, Jude now addresses astronomy. The ancients called the planets "wandering stars" because of their movement. Sailors learned about the unreliability of these **wandering stars**. So also could the ancient church learn about the unreliability of the false teachers. They were worthless when it came to navigating spiritual waters.

> The reference here could be to meteors, shooting stars, comets, or planets; but planets is the most likely meaning. An unpredictable star would provide no guidance for navigation so false teachers are useless and untrustworthy. Their doom is the eternal darkness that is reserved for them (cf. 2 Pet. 2:4) (Blum 393).

Jude offers several conclusions regarding these false teachers. *First, they have a **reservation**.* This word (τηρέω) means "to cause a state, condition, or activity to continue, keep, hold, reserve, preserve someone or something" (Bauer 1002). This is a reservation that they cannot reject, and appointment that they cannot cancel. They are going to stand before the Almighty God who is going to judge them according to their deeds (Rev. 20:11-15). *Second, their reservation is in a place with **black darkness**.* Jesus talked about "outer darkness" as a place where the wicked would go (Matt. 8:12; 22:13; 25:30). Since God is light and has no darkness in Him (cf. 1 John 1:5), and since the wicked will be cast away from the presence of the Lord (cf. 2 Thess. 1:7-9), their fate is to go to a place without God and any light. Most people find such a thought to be terrifying! *Third, the reservation is **forever**.* The phrase used here (εἰς αἰῶνα) describes the everlasting nature of their reservation. They will go into the place of black darkness and will remain there "into eternity."

Verse 14—Once again Jude uses the common word **these** or **these men** (τούτοις). The false teachers remain the focus of attention. Jude here makes reference to **Enoch**. This writing was a well-known book among the Jews and was frequently referenced. It is part of a collection that is known as Jewish pseudepigraphical writings. Books in this category claim names of famous persons in order to give their writings more credibility among the Jews. This writing, known as the Book of Enoch (and also "The Ethiopic Book of Enoch") is an attempt to connect itself with the famous Old Testament man who *"walked with God"* (Gen. 5:18-24). That Enoch was also the **seventh generation from Adam**, and so this writing accurately links with the Old Testament character. The exact date of this writing, however, is far after that famous man lived. While we do not know the precise date, the writing is generally believed to have been composed during the intertestamental period (400 B.C.–4 B.C.). The statement that he **prophesied** is not claiming that he was a genuine prophet of God, but that he made a prediction about the coming judgment. It is important to note that Jude is careful to not refer to this book as "Scripture" (*graphe*). As Paul said, all "*Scripture*" is inspired (2 Tim. 3:16). There is no claim that this writing is inspired. It is merely another writing, outside of Scripture, that is referred to by inspired writers (Paul did this frequently—cf. Acts 17:28; 1 Cor. 15:33 and Tit. 1:12). Why then would Jude quote it (or why would God inspire Jude to quote it)? The most likely answer is that this writing in an accurate way describes the powerful judgment of God.

Enoch was not the author of this pseudepigraphic work, and it is not likely that the book preserves material from that historic personage. At best, we can only hope to identify the milieu in which the various fragments of 1 Enoch were composed and compiled (Gene Green 102).

Perhaps he referred to Enoch because the adversaries treasured the work, and thereby he used their own ammunition against them. Vögtle suggests that the opponents rejected Christian tradition about Christ's coming and hence Jude cited the prophecy from Enoch. Indeed, the content of the prophecy is not remarkable, assuring the readers that the Lord will truly judge the ungodly. Citing a quotation from another source does not indicate that the entire work is inspired, even if the saying drawn upon is true (Schreiner 469-70).

The quotation from Enoch is from 1 Enoch 1:9. He presents a powerful judgment scene, where the **Lord came with many thousands of His holy ones**. The **holy ones** are in reference to the angels (Deut. 33:2; Zech. 14:5). The New Testament teaches that Jesus will come in judgment with His angels (Matt. 16:27; 25:31; Mark 8:38; Luke 9:26; 1 Thess. 3:13; 2 Thess. 1:7). The appearance of the Lord with thousands of angels is a description that defies imagination but elicits wonder and awe.

Verse 15—Notice the emphasis on the word **all** and the word **ungodly**. Both of these words are found here four times. It underscores that the judgment will especially be for the **ungodly** (ἀσέβεια) "is understood vertically as a lack of reverence for deity and hallowed institutions as displayed in sacrilegious words and deeds: impiety" (Bauer 141). It equally underscores that this judgment will capture all—that is 100%—of those who are godly. Any hope of escaping is gone. **The Lord** will also **convict all the ungodly of all their ungodly deeds**. The word **convict** (ἐλέγχω) means "to bring a person to the point of recognizing wrongdoing, convict, convince" (Bauer 315). This will include their **deeds** (works), which were fueled by their ungodly workers and executed in an **ungodly way**. God will also convict them of **all the harsh things** that were spoken against Him. The word **harsh** (σκληρός) "pertains to causing an adverse reaction because of being hard or harsh, hard, harsh, unpleasant" (Bauer 930).

Verse 16—For the fifth time (of six), Jude repeats the transition word **these [men]** (Οὗτοί). He now wants to identify more characteristics that establish that these men are fundamentally wicked. The Christians there must not see some sense of spirituality or nobility in these false teachers. They are wicked through and through. The following points prove it:

First, they are **grumblers**. This word (γογγυστής) is a rare word, occurring in the noun form only here in the NT. It has the basic meaning of a "whisperer" but entails the idea of complaining in a low voice as if to make it seem like it is a secret message being conveyed. However, this word reminds us of those who murmured against the Lord in the Old Testament (cf. Ex. 16:7-9, 12; 17:3; Num. 11:1; 14:23; 16:41; 17:5, 11; Ps. 105:25). They were faultfinders, critics, and scoffers. Such persons do not contribute to the betterment of the church but tear it down. Their hypercritical negativity permeates through the Christian community, robbing the church of its joy and peace. The question is what were they grumbling about? Some argue that it was their typical definition of grace, which they argued was much more permissive (cf. v. 4). Perhaps it was the lofty position given Jesus, whom they denied His Lordship (cf. v. 4). Others leave this text and propose varied arguments, such as a discontent with the restrictions of the Mosaic Law, or that—as Gnostics—grumbled that they were imprisoned in a physical body. Ultimately, however, they are grumbling against the faith that was to be defended (v. 3). Continuing the thought about their being complainers, Jude adds that they were **finding fault**. This is one word in Greek (μεμψίμοιρος) and means "complaining about one's lot, discontented" (Bauer 629).

Second, they are **following after their own lusts**. Based upon what said about them in verse 4 and their licentious lives, the comparison to Balaam (v. 11), and what is repeated in verse 18, we are not surprised that their **lusts** are a key element in their character. While **lusts** can be understood in various ways, here Jude has in mind mainly sexual desires. They are driven by their unbridled passion and see people as objects to fulfill their sexual desires. There is no interest in helping, strengthening, or guiding others in the right way. They intend to manipulate for to satisfy their sensual cravings.

Third, they speak **arrogantly**. This word (ὑπέρογκος) means "haughty, pompous, bombastic" (Bauer 1034). Their arrogance is seen in their pompous statement about the Lordship of Jesus (v. 4), coupled with their own inflated view of themselves. They clearly have a pride problem, such that they see themselves as the correct interpreter of Christian doctrine and have discovered a higher consciousness (that allows them to manipulate the doctrine of grace—v. 4).

Fourth, they are **flattering people for the sake of gaining an advantage**. This statement reveals the full scope of their hypocrisy. Their words of praise are devoid of sincerity or genuineness. They are contrived and issued with one goal in mind: **gaining an advantage**. The **advantage** gained might find itself in financial support, praise returned and stacking up "voters" who will back them for leadership positions. Ultimately the flattery is designed to enable them to accomplish their selfish goals within the Christian community.

Verse 17—Jude shifts directions, now bringing together a list of admonitions to the church. He has not finished describing the false teachers, but now does so to compare how they should conduct themselves differently than the evil opponents. His words **but you, beloved** show this shift in attention. His term of endearment (**beloved**—cf. v. 3) and the emphatic **but you** identifies a charge to take a completely different direction than that of the false teachers. Jude encourages them **to remember the words that were spoken beforehand by the apostles of our Lord Jesus Christ**. The **apostles**, as Jesus' authorized agents and spokesmen, were crucial pieces in the dissemination of Christian doctrine and practice. Their reception of the Holy Spirit enabled them to remember fully the teachings of Christ (John 15:26; 16:13) and empowered them to speak with authority (cf. 1 Cor. 14:37). The church was built upon the foundation of the apostles and prophets (Eph. 2:20).

Verse 18—The apostles had issued warnings about false teachers. Paul did this with the elders at Ephesus (Acts 20:29-30) and did so repeatedly to Timothy (1 Tim. 1:3-9, 18-20; 4:1-5; 2 Tim. 3:1-5). Peter equally issued severe warnings in 2 Peter 2:1ff. Notice how what the apostles said was considered admonitions to these Christians as well, not just those to whom the letters were written. Jude says that these apostles **were saying** (language that indicates repeated warnings) that **in the last time there will be mockers, following after their own ungodly lusts**. This reference is nearly identical to 2 Peter 3:3, and, in my opinion, is a quotation of that text. If this is accurate, it clearly places Jude *after* 2 Peter (see Introduction). Jude intends to use this quote to show how it fits perfectly with the men he's been describing. They are **ungodly** (as was emphasized in v. 15) and are motivated by their **lusts** (v. 16). The reference to the **last time** is a phrase in reference to the last Christian dispensation. The New Testament Christians believed the next event to occur was the coming of Christ and would usher in judgment and eternity. Therefore, they were in the "*last days*" (Heb. 1:2; Acts 2:17; 1 Pet. 1:20; 1 Tim. 4:1; 2 Tim. 3:1). It is noteworthy that both Peter and Paul warned about the influx of false teachers in these last days.

Verse 19—The "*ungodly lusts*" mentioned in the last verse serves as the basis of the list of activities discussed here. Jude continues to press hard in describing **these men** (Οὗτοί), hoping that they will see them for what they truly are. Obviously, there was a time when such was not the case, because they came in unnoticed (v. 4). Jude describes them as follows:

First, they are the ones **who divide you**. Their overall goal was to "divide and conquer." Their arguments managed to persuade some, while others were able to see through them. This naturally created an unhealthy environment within these churches. This idea is found in several of the preceding verses. Their influence prompted Jude to write the letter, they had infiltrated their love feasts (v. 12) and mimicked the dividing nature of Balaam who turned Korah and his followers against Moses (v. 11). Many letters of Paul address the seriousness of division in the church, and Paul speaks boldly about this (1 Cor. 1:10; Phil. 1:27-2:4). Of course, they are following the words of Jesus who prayed that the disciples would be one (John 17:21).

Second, they are **worldly minded**. This is one word in Greek (ψυχικός). It "pertains to the life of the natural world and whatever belongs to it, in contrast to the realm of experience whose central characteristic is πνεῦμα, *natural, unspiritual, worldly*" (Bauer 1100). The word is found in the writings of Paul (1 Cor. 2:14; 15:44, 46) and James (3:15). The call of Christianity is to "separate" oneself from the world and its evils (2 Cor. 6:14-17; 1 John 2:15-17). These men have no genuine spirituality but are "playing church" to enrich and/or empower themselves.

> In light of this understanding, Jude's accusation is that the heretics are nothing more than earthly people who are not governed by the Spirit. They are entirely "natural" and belong solely to this world, as "worldly people." In other words, they are not disciples of Christ but simply unregenerate people (Gene Green 117).

Third, they are **devoid of the Spirit**. The word **devoid** (μὴ ἔχοντες) literally means "not having." It is possible to see **spirit** to be in reference to their being unspiritual. Jude just said they were "*worldly*," and so this concept would logically fit. However, the idea of "not having spirit[uality]," does not seem to fit what Jude is saying. Rather they men do not have the Holy Spirit. The Bible teaches that the Holy Spirit is evidence of their belonging to God (Eph. 1:13) and that Christ is in them (Rom. 8:9). Jude will note that Christians "*pray in the Holy Spirit*" (v. 20). Those that obey Christ have the Spirit (Acts 5:32).

> The readers should not have been surprised by the intrusion of the opponents. The apostles foresaw that it would happen. Foreseeing their arrival should strengthen the faith of the church since it confirms the truth of the faith that was once and for all given to them (v. 3). No false teaching, no threat from the outside can be considered a genuine threat to the truth since it has all been foreseen and predicted. God never promised that the church would progress in the world without enemies from within. People are apt to think that blessing from God would mean that the people of God exist in a blissful state with no conflict. On the contrary, the apostles foretold that opponents would come, and now they had arrived. They were evident by their words and their works. It should be clear to all,

therefore, that they were not part of the people of God. The church should recognize them, reject their teaching, and reach out to those wavering under their influence (Schreiner 480).

Verse 20—Jude repeats the term of endearment, with **beloved** (ἀγαπητός—cf. vv. 3, 17). Here Jude includes the emphatic phrase **but you** (ὑμεῖς δέ,). This phrase was typically used by Paul to present a vital contrast to how God's child would act as opposed to the evil workers (cf. 2 Tim. 2:1; 3:10, 14; 4:5). The majority of the letter has focused on the character of the false teachers and the need for Christians to be aware of them. However, there is more to Christianity than dealing with false teachers, and Jude wants to remind them of that. When we look at this text exegetically, we see that Jude has one command/imperative: **keep** (τηρήσατε), followed by three present participles: building, praying, and waiting (see Sermon Seed). The word **keep** means "to cause a state, condition, or activity to continue, *keep, hold, reserve, preserve someone or something*" (Bauer 1002). The word naturally includes the concept of value. Something needs to be preserved or protected, because it is valuable. In this case it is the Christian himself. He must be proactive in preserving his own relationship with God (cf. v. 1). The admonition is to **keep yourself in the love of God**. Jesus explained clearly how this is done: "*If you obey My commands, you will remain in My love*" (John 15:10). God's love will not continue for those who defy Him and abandon faith in Him. One will not remain in His love if he practices sin (1 John 3:8, 9). It will force God to hide His face from them (Isa. 59:1, 2).

So how are Christians to **keep yourselves in the love of God**?

*First, by **building yourselves up in the most holy faith***. The word translated **building yourselves up** (ἐποικοδομέω) means "to engage in a building process of personal and corporate development, edify, build up/on" (Bauer 387). The importance of Christians working to grow, build, and improve is a continual and constant teaching in Scripture (cf. Matt. 16:18; Acts 9:31; 15:16; 20:32; Rom. 14:19; 15:2, 20; 1 Cor. 3:9–15; 8:1; 10:23; 14:3-5, 12, 17, 26; 2 Cor. 10:8; 12:19; 13:10; Gal. 2:18; Eph. 2:18; 2:20-22; 4:12, 16; Col. 2:7; 1 Thess. 5:11; 1 Pet. 2:5). The idea of one assuming individual responsibility is common in Scripture, and there is an aspect of that individual element here. However, the word **yourselves** is plural here, indicating that Jude is commanding them to build each other up. As seen in the next phrase, this is done by a use of the Word of God (a theme that fits with the overall admonition of v. 3). The fact is Christians need encouragement (cf. Heb. 3:13; 10:23-25). Satan is hard at work to discourage each and every one so that he/she will depart from the faith. God knows that there is great power in the Christian community, where His people rally behind each other, support each other, and offer words that build up and encourage. Jude says that this **building up** should be **in the most holy faith**. It is holy because it comes from the holy God (cf. 1 Pet. 1:13-17). Thus, with God at its origin, it is capable of enabling one to grow (2 Tim. 3:16-17). As in verse 3, Jude has the Gospel of Christ in mind—the faith/belief/conviction of the church of Christ, rooted in Christ Himself (v. 3). The holy Word can produce a **holy faith** because it originated from a holy God.

Second, believers keep themselves in God's love by *praying in the Holy Spirit*. The wording here reminds us of Paul's admonition in Ephesians 6:18: "With all prayer and petition pray at all times in the Spirit, and with this in view, be on the alert with all perseverance and petition for all the saints." **Praying in the Holy Spirit** means to pray in a way that is consistent with the will of the Spirit (cf. 1 John 5:14-15). It would be a **holy** prayer that is based on a **holy faith**. Self-centered prayers that are filled with selfish requests are not examples of these kinds of prayer. Prayers for one's faith, and for the faith of others, is in harmony with the will of the Spirit. Faithful Christians pray, and pray continually (cf. 1 Thess. 5:17).

Verse 21—*Third*, believers keep themselves in God's love by ***waiting anxiously for the mercy of our Lord Jesus Christ to eternal life***. Their waiting anxiously if for the eventual return of Jesus. The language is similar to Peter: "T*herefore, beloved, since you look for these things, be diligent to be found by Him in peace, spotless and blameless*" (2 Pet. 3:14), and Paul: "*In the future there is laid up for me the crown of righteousness, which the Lord, the righteous Judge, will award to me on that day; and not only to me, but also to all who have loved His appearing.*" Christians do not fear or dread Jesus' return. They are anxious for Him to return!

> Throughout early Christian literature "waiting" describes the eschatological expectation (προσδέχεσθαι: Mark 15:43; Luke 2:25, 38; 12:36; 23:51; Acts 24:15; Tit. 2:13; 2 Clem. 11:2; προσδοκᾶσθαι: Matt 11:3; Luke 7:19-20; 2 Pet. 3:12-14; 1 Clem. 23:5; Ign. Pol. 3:2; ἐκδέχεσθαι: Heb. 11:10; Barn. 10:11; 2 Clem. 12:1; ἀπεκδέχεσθαι: Rom. 8:23; 1 Cor. 1:7; Gal. 5:5; Phil. 3:20; Heb. 9:28; ἀναμένειν: 1 Thess. 1:10; 2 Clem. 11:5), though not often in exhortations (2 Pet. 3:12; 2 Clem. 12:1; cf. Hab. 2:3; 2 Apoc. Bar. 83:4) (Bauckham 114).

When Jesus returns, He will bring His **mercy** with Him (Tit. 2:13). This word (ἐλεάω) involves showing leniency and compassion toward someone. Since all have sinned (Rom. 3:23), all have need of the **mercy** of Jesus (cf. Tit. 3:4-7). Some today, unfortunately, are willing to accept His mercy and grace but "*continue in sin*" (Rom. 6:1). However, as Paul continued to explain in Romans 6, those who are a recipient of God's mercy and grace will die to sin and will present their bodies to God as instruments of righteousness. Jude says this is to **eternal life**. The ultimate promise of God for those who are in Christ is this gift of life which will endure forever (John 3:16). This command, and its three prepositions, are of utmost importance because one's **eternal** destiny is in the balance.

> Apparently Christians cannot remain in God's love if they immerse themselves in this world and cease to long for their future perfection before God (vv. 24–25). One of the means by which we continue in our love for God is if we continue to long for the day when Jesus Christ will show us His mercy, when He will grant us the gift of eternal life, and we will be perfected forever. Those who take their eyes off their future hope will find that their love for God is slowly evaporating, and it will be evident that their real love is for the present evil age (Schreiner 484).

Verse 22—This verse has some textual challenges, which is why several translations render it differently. Some have two clauses, but it seems the best supported rendering has three. This is because Jude has three imperatives: show mercy, save, show mercy (repeated). Further confirmation that this is a list of three points is that each one, in addition to the imperative, has the relative pronoun οὓς. See Sermon Seed. *First*, Jude says **have mercy on some who are doubting**. The verb **have mercy** (ἐλεάω) comes from the same word used in v. 21. While we are waiting for the **mercy** of Christ, we need to extend **mercy** to others. The word is not just talking about forgiveness, although it would include that. It involves acts of charity (usually that is the same word); charity that might involve financial help, providing food or clothing, maybe a listening ear. Simply put, it would include anything someone needs. In this case it involves those who are **doubting**. This is another of our textual difficulties in this verse. The word **doubting** (διακρίνω) which means "to be uncertain, be at odds with oneself, doubt, waver" (Bauer 231). The Majority Text has a nominative plural (*diakrinomenoi*), which would then describe the person who is showing mercy; that is, they should do this without any question on the value of the mercy being shown, or could mean not to pick and choose who should receive the mercy. However, the more likely meaning is that reflected in the NAS. There are always those in the church who struggle with the faith—what to believe and how to apply what they have been taught. Part of "*contending for the faith*" is to help solidify the faith in the minds of the doubters. The false teachers were certainly doing their part to cast doubt on established Christian doctrine (as seen in v. 4).

Verse 23—*Second*, Jude commands them to **save others**. When Christians think souls, they are aligning themselves with Jesus, who came to seek and save that which was lost (Luke 19:10; 1 Tim. 1:15). The souls being saved here certainly would include those who are in the world, separated from Christ. They need to hear the good news of Jesus (Rom. 1:16). However, this phrase would also involve saving those who are in the clutches of the false teachers. They are like sheep, in danger of wandering away from the flock. Like the good shepherd, they need those who will leave the ninety and nine and go after the one who is straying (Matt. 18:12). The next phrase is especially noteworthy: **snatching them out of the fire**. The word translated **snatching** (ἁρπάζω) means "to grab or seize suddenly so as to remove or gain control, snatch/take away" (Bauer 134). The word **fire** is certainly in reference to the fires of Hell (cf. v. 7; cf. Matt. 3:10, 12; 5:22; 2 Thess. 1:18; Heb. 10:27; Rev. 20:14-15). This terminology shows several important truths: (1) People need help. It is the children of God who are to help them find their way to salvation; (2) Hell is no joke. It is not some made up doctrine intended to scare people. It is a real place and real people are going there. To "snatch" them out of the fire demonstrates rescuing them from a terrible fate; (3) It shows the value of souls. Jesus taught that we have nothing more valuable than our souls (Matt. 16:26). Caring Christians are going to do their best to save others. Not all will respond favorably to ministry attempts, but some will (cf. 1 Cor. 3:12-15).

> Those who are to be snatched from the fire are evidently church members who, under the influence of the false teachers, are indulging in sinful behavior, but will repent when their error is pointed out to them. It is not necessary for Jude to explain how his readers are to snatch them from the fire, because it was understood everywhere in the early church that an erring brother must be rebuked and warned in a spirit of brotherly love (Matt. 18:15–17; Luke 17:3; Gal. 6:1; 2 Thess. 3:15; 1 Tim. 5:20; Tit. 3:10; James 5:19–20; Did. 2:7; 15:3) (Bauckham 115).

Third, Jude says **have mercy on some**. The same word is repeated from the last verse. The repetition of the phrase **have mercy** has sent Bible critics pointing to a contradiction or proof that this could not be inspired (since God makes no mistakes). It has sent Bible scholars searching for explanations, with many arguing that it was a scribal error. Fortunately there are those who argue that it was intentional, and that Jude has a different group in mind. It is possible, even likely, that this **mercy** is extended to those ensnared in sin. This is a much more serious problem than the one earlier who is doubting. These people would include the false teachers and those who have been duped by them. They are in the worst possible place spiritually. What should be the Christian's response to such? They should **have mercy**. This would include some patience and gentleness. It would never include accepting the sin or minimizing the consequences of sin. The use of the word **some** (οὓς) is not meant to imply that there are exemptions to showing mercy; that some should not receive any. Rather, there are some who need it, and some who don't. Jude has two points that go along with this third category of showing mercy: (1) **with fear**. There is always the danger that the one intending to influence others ends up himself being influenced (1 Cor. 15:33). There also is the possibility that one can be polluted by these people. In addition, the fear here could be of God. As Paul noted in Galatians 6:2, those who are trying to help others must also do it with meekness. We also know that it is a terrifying thing to fall into the hands of the living God (Heb. 10:31). Jesus taught us to "*fear Him who can destroy both the body and soul in Hell*" (Matt. 12:28); (2) **hating even the garment polluted by sin**. A beautiful Old Testament illustration of this is the filthy garments worn by Joshua the high priest. His clothes are an indication of his sinful life. Satan is there accusing him (and Satan has the evidence on his side). However, the forgiving God commands that the dirty be removed and replaced by the clean. Joshua is being forgiven (Zech. 3:3-5). Christians should **hate** (μισέω) sin. There should never be acceptance of sin or minimizing it. They hate it in themselves and hate it in others. They are well aware that sin **pollutes**, and—if unforgiven—will sentence one to eternal damnation.

> The text constructs a nice balance between showing love and mercy and maintaining standards of purity and righteousness. Showing love for the sinner does not exclude an intense hatred for the corruption brought about by sin. Furthermore, believers need to beware of getting too entangled with some who sin, lest the sinner influence them rather than vice versa (Schreiner 489).

Verse 24—it would be easy to see these last two verses as nothing more than a traditional doxology—without any direct connection with the body of the letter. I believe this would be unfortunate and would cause one to miss the link between these verses and the admonition given in verse 3. The dire warnings in these verses could be depressing and discouraging. They could leave the impression that the fight for truth is vain, and that the fight against evil is a battle they won't win. Yet eternity is within their grasp, and all of God's great promises can be realized. But how? The answer is so beautifully given here: It is according to the **power of God**. Jude uses the familiar word δύναμαι (from dunamis) that is here translated that God **is able**, that is, God has the power and the desire to see Christians through the challenges. Notice what the power of God can do, based on two aorist active infinitives (see also Sermon Seed).

First, God is able to **keep you from stumbling**. It would be a grave abuse of this text to see God manipulating things outside of a person's own choosing (the doctrine of Calvinism). Rather, when one is equipped with the full armor of God, he is "*standing firm in the Lord and in the strength of His might*" (Eph. 6:10) and will be able to "*stand firm against the schemes of the devil*" (Eph. 6:11). Peter, after calling on Christians to grow in their faith, lists seven areas in which they need to add to their faith (2 Pet. 1:5-9). Notice what Peter says after discussing those areas: "*As long as you practice these things you will never stumble*" (2 Pet. 1:10). The word **stumbling** (ἄπταιστος) is from the same root that Peter uses. The word translated **keep** (φυλάσσω) means "to protect by taking careful measures, guard, protect" (Bauer 1068). In other words, God has provided us with the equipment and knowledge for success. He is not going to do it for us, but He is going to make certain that if we use His tools, we will succeed. Satan will fail in his desire to see us **stumble**. In the context of this book, that **stumbling** would be seen when one follows the false teachers and becomes unfaithful. God has provided "the faith," which is the divine guide to strength and stability in Christ. They need to contend earnestly for that faith.

Second, He is able to **make you stand**. As noted earlier, the only way Joshua was able to stand before the Lord was because of His forgiveness (Zech. 3:3-5). Equally, the only way that we can stand before the Lord is because of His forgiveness. The word **stand** (ἵστημι) means "to cause to be in a place or position, set, place, bring, allow to come" (Bauer 482). Paul says that the servant of the Lord will stand "*because the Lord is able to make him stand*" (Rom. 14:4). If one has fallen because of sin, God can set him back on his feet if he will confess and repent (cf. 1 John 1:9). Jude says that when we **stand**, it will be before the Lord's **glory**. This is in reference to God's glorious (awesome, magnificent) presence (cf. Rom. 16:17; Eph. 3:21; 2 Pet. 3:18). When we **stand** before God and His glorious throne, we will be (a) **blameless**—a word that does not mean sinless, but that one has had his/her sins removed—and is therefore without blame. Bauer says that this word (ἄμωμος) "pertains to being without fault and therefore morally blameless, blameless" (56). Jude also says that when we **stand** before the Lord, without fault, we will have **great joy**. How can we better describe our feelings? We made it! We are going to be forever with the Lord! The **great joy** will be unbridled happiness. All of the struggles, tears, and disappointments will be over (cf. Rev. 20:4). Eternal bliss will be ours.

Verse 25—The God who had the power to do those two great things for us is now described. This list is impressive. It captures many features of God which makes Him worthy of our praise and devotion. This verse would be a terrific basis to give a lesson on "knowing God" (see Sermon Seed). *First*, Jude says He is **the only God**. In a world full of polytheism, Christianity championed the truth. There is only one God. Hinduism and Buddhism have many gods. *Second*, He is **our Savior**. The Old Testament frequently described God as Savior (Deut. 32:15; Ps. 24:5; 25:5; 27:9; 65:5), as well as the New Testament (Luke 1:47; 1 Tim. 1:1; 2:3; 4:10; Tit. 1:3; 2:10; 3:4). Despite what the false teachers are saying about God, He is able to save them. *Third*, He is approached **through Jesus Christ our Lord**. If one rejects God's Son, He has lost God as His savior (Rom. 7:25; 16:27; 2 Cor. 1:20; Col. 3:17; 1 Pet. 4:11). *Fourth*, to Him belongs **glory**. The idea here is that He is deserving and worthy of our praise and adoration. There are not enough words we could say that could adequately capture the praise He warrants. *Fifth*, to Him belongs **majesty**. This word (μεγαλωσύνη) means "a state of greatness or preeminence, majesty, used only of God" (Bauer 623). The amazing splendor of God, with His power, dominion, and sovereignty is all wrapped up in this word. *Sixth*, He has **dominion**. This word (κράτος) means the "exercise of ruling ability, power, rule, sovereignty" (Bauer 565). God has absolute power. He is truly omnipotent. Any power of dominion exercised by others is only because God allows it. *Seventh*, He has **authority**. This word (ἐξουσία) means "potential or resource to command, control, or govern, capability, might, power" (Bauer 352). As with the previous, there may be human authorities, but the ultimate authority belongs to God. All men must answer to Him.

Jude ends by affirming that these qualities permanently belong to God and are His for all eternity. In a unique (but powerful) description, He says that they were His **before all time**—that is, before there even was time. Before creation, before Genesis 1:1, God possessed these attributes. They are **now**—God has not lost some of these or is reduced in effectiveness. In the present age, even today, God is what He has always been. Finally he says **and forever**. The future does not possess a time that God will have reduced attributes. As this age ends and eternity begins, we will be able to observe firsthand God's amazing attributes.

The solemn time notation "before all ages, now and forevermore" indicates that these attributes of God suffer no change and that therefore His divine plan will surely be carried out. Salvation is completely secure because God's own purpose stands and because He is able to do all that He wills (Isa. 46:9-10) (Blum 396).

Glory, majesty, power, and authority have always belonged to God, before the world began and will be His forever and ever. This is not a prayer, which would be rendered by the term "may be," but a fact, and so the fitting verb is "are." Because of who God is and what He has done, the praise and power are His forever. Readers rest secure in this truth, and Jude did as well, signifying it by saying "Amen" (Schreiner 492).

BIBLIOGRAPHY

Arichea, Daniel C. and Hatton, Howard. *A Handbook on the Letter from Jude and the Second Letter from Peter, UBS Handbook Series*. New York: United Bible Societies, 1993.

Bandstra, Andrew John. *The Law and the Elements of the World*. Kampen: J.H. Kok, 1964.

Bauckham, Richard J. *2 Peter, Jude*. Vol. 50 of Word Biblical Commentary. Dallas: Word, Incorporated, 1983.

Bauer, Walter. *A Greek-English Lexicon of the New Testament and Other Early Christian Literature*. Edited by Arndt, Gingrich and Danker. Chicago: University of Chicago Press, 1985.

Behm, Johannes. "Καινός, Καινότης, Ἀνακαινίζω, Ἀνακαινόω, Ἀνακαίνωσις, Ἐγκαινίζω," *Theological Dictionary of the New Testament*. Grand Rapids: Eerdmans, 1964.

Blagden, Claude M. *The Epistles of Peter, John and Jude*. Cambridge: The University Press, 1939.

Blum, Edwin A. "2 Peter," in *The Expositor's Bible Commentary: Hebrews through Revelation*, ed. Frank E. Gaebelein. Grand Rapids: Zondervan Publishing House, 1981.

Bromiley, Geoffrey W., ed. *Theological Dictionary of the New Testament*. Grand Rapids: Wm. B. Eerdmans, 1985.

Brown, Colin, ed. *New International Dictionary of New Testament Theology*. Grand Rapids: Zondervan, 1975.

Clark, Gordon H. *2 Peter*. Presbyterian and Reformed Publishing Co., 1972.

Davids, Peter H. *The Letters of 2 Peter and Jude*. The Pillar New Testament Commentary. Grand Rapids: William B. Eerdmans Pub. Co., 2006.

Green, Gene L. *Jude and 2 Peter*. Baker Exegetical Commentary on the New Testament. Grand Rapids: Baker Academic, 2008.

Green, Michael. *2 Peter and Jude: An Introduction and Commentary*, vol. 18 of Tyndale New Testament Commentaries. Downers Grove: InterVarsity Press, 1987.

Grudem, Wayne A. *1 Peter: An Introduction and Commentary*, vol. 17 of Tyndale New Testament Commentaries. Downers Grove: InterVarsity Press, 1988.

Guthrie, Donald. *New Testament Introduction*. Downers Grove: InterVarsity Press, 1970.

Harrison, Everett Falconer. "Exegetical Studies in 1 Peter: Part 1." *Bibliotheca Sacra* 97:386 (Apr 1940): 200-210.

Hastings, James. *The Speaker's Bible*. Aberdeen, Scotland: The 'Speaker's Bible Offices, 1924.

Hiebert, D. Edmond. "Following Christ's Example: An Exposition of 1 Peter 2:21-25." *Bibliotheca Sacra* 139 (Jan 1982):32-46.

Hite, Michael. *2 Peter Class Notes (unpublished)*. Bear Valley Bible Institute. Denver, Colorado, 2022.

Jobes, Karen H. *1 Peter*, Baker Exegetical Commentary on the New Testament. Grand Rapids: Baker Academic, 2005.

Kelcy, Raymond C. *The Letters of Peter and Jude*. The Living Word Commentaries. Austin: R.B. Sweet, 1972.

Kirk, Gordon E. "Endurance in Suffering in 1 Peter." *Bibliotheca Sacra* 138 (Jan 1981):46-55.

Kistemaker, Simon J. *Exposition of the Epistles of Peter and of the Epistle of Jude*. Grand Rapids: Baker Book House, 1987.

Louw Johannes P. and Nida, Eugene Albert. *Greek-English Lexicon of the New Testament: Based on Semantic Domains*. New York: United Bible Societies, 1996.

McGuire-Moushon, J.A. "Promised Land," Lexham Theological Wordbook. Bellingham: Lexham Press, 2014.

Neyrey, Jerome H. *2 Peter, Jude: A New Translation with Introduction and Commentary.* Vol. 37C of Anchor Yale Bible. New Haven; London: Yale University Press, 2008.

Nicoll, W. Robertson. *The Expositor's Greek Testament*. New York: Dodd, Mead and Co., 1905.

Owen, Dan R. "Self-Control in 2 Peter 1:6." *Gospel Advocate* (March 1989):11.

Peel, Malcolm L. "Gnostic Eschatology and the New Testament." *Novum Testamentum* 12 (January 1970):141-65.

Roberts, J.W. *1 and 2 Peter and Jude*. Austin: R.B. Sweet, 1964.

Sasse, Hermann "Γῆ, Ἐπίγειος," *Theological Dictionary of the New Testament*. Grand Rapids: Eerdmans, 1964.

Schreiner, Thomas R. *1, 2 Peter, Jude*. In The New American Commentary. Broadman, Nashville, 2003.

Simmons, William A. "Regeneration," *Lexham Theological Wordbook*. Bellingham: Lexham Press, 2014.

Stibbs, Alan M. *The First Epistle General of Peter*. Tyndale New Testament Commentaries. Grand Rapids: Wm. B. Eerdmans, 1959.

Walls, David and Max Anders, *I & II Peter, I, II & III John, Jude,* vol. 11 of Holman New Testament Commentary. Nashville: Broadman & Holman Publishers, 1999.

Applying
DETERMINED TO INCREASE

2 PETER 1:1-11

JOE WELLS

"We all have dreams. But in order to make dreams come into reality, it takes an awful lot of determination, dedication, self-discipline, and effort."[1]

- Jesse Owens -

INTRODUCTION

Special Section: Synonyms of *determined*:

Resolute—fully committed to achieving a goal

Being resolute is a powerful trait that can help us achieve our goals and overcome obstacles. Resolute people have a clear sense of purpose and are determined to achieve their objectives, no matter what. They have a clear vision of their goals and are committed to reaching them. They have a strong will. Setbacks or failures do not easily deter resolute people. They have a strong sense of self-discipline and are willing to put in the effort needed to achieve their goals. They are also willing to sacrifice and endure discomfort if it means getting closer to their objective.

The quality of being resolute means having a positive mindset. Resolute people are optimistic and believe success is possible and probable. They do not let negative thoughts or self-doubt hold them back. Instead, they focus on their strengths and capabilities and use their failures as opportunities to learn and grow. They are adaptable and willing to adjust when necessary.

Being resolute is not just about being determined to achieve your goals. It's also about being committed to your values and beliefs and staying true to them even in adversity. Resolute people have a strong sense of integrity and are guided by their principles, which gives them a sense of

---
[1] "Jesse Owens Quotes." BrainyQuote.com. BrainyMedia Inc, 2024. 10 January 2024. https://www.brainyquote.com/quotes/jesse_owens_166163.

integrity and are guided by their principles, which gives them a sense of purpose and direction. They are honestly aware of their strengths and weaknesses and use this knowledge to make informed decisions regarding areas they need to improve, being determined to reach their goals.

Perseverance and patience are crucial. Resolute people understand that success does not come overnight and that achieving their goals may require hard work and sacrifice. They are willing to put in the effort and stay committed to their objectives, even when slow progress or setbacks occur.

HISTORICAL EXAMPLE

Thomas Edison, one of the most prominent inventors of the 19th century, was well known for his relentless determination to succeed. Born in 1847 in Milan, Ohio, Edison was one of seven children. Samuel and Nancy Edison were his parents, and his father worked as a shingle maker and carpenter. Edison had very little formal education and was mainly homeschooled by his mother. Despite his lack of formal education, Edison was a bright child and showed an early interest in science and technology.

Edison's first job was as a train newsboy, selling passengers candy and newspapers. However, he soon became interested in telegraphy and began working as a telegraph operator at 15. During this time, Edison first began experimenting with electrical devices, and he soon became known for his ingenuity and creativity in electronics.

In 1869, Edison moved to New York City, establishing his first laboratory and working on his many inventions. Over the next few years, Edison would develop several groundbreaking technologies, including the phonograph and the incandescent light bulb. However, despite his many successes, Edison faced numerous setbacks and failures along the way.[2]

One of Edison's most famous failures was his attempt to develop a storage battery for electric cars. Despite working on the project for over a decade, Edison was ultimately unsuccessful and the battery was never brought to market. However, instead of giving up, Edison continued to work on other projects and eventually invented the alkaline storage battery, which became widely used in the 20th century.

Another of Edison's failures was his attempt to create a machine that could transcribe spoken words onto paper. Despite working on the project for years, Edison could never get the machine to work correctly and eventually abandoned the project. However, his work on the machine ultimately led to the development of the phonograph, which became one of his most successful inventions.

Perhaps one of Edison's most famous quotes is, "I have not failed. I've just found 10,000 ways that won't work."[3] This quote perfectly sums up Edison's attitude towards failure. Instead of viewing failure as a negative thing, Edison saw it as an opportunity to learn and grow. He believed every failure was simply a step towards success, and that the key to success was never giving up.

---

2 Matthew Josephson and Robert E Conot, "Thomas Edison." Encyclopedia Britannica, 25 Dec. 2023, https://www.britannica.com/biography/Thomas-Edison.

3 https://www.goodreads.com/author/quotes/3091287.Thomas_A_Edison.

Determined to Increase

Edison's determination and perseverance are what ultimately led to his success. Despite facing numerous failures and setbacks throughout his lifetime, he refused to give up on his dreams. He constantly pushed the boundaries of what was possible and always looked for new and innovative ways to solve problems.

Edison's legacy continues to inspire people today. His inventions revolutionized the world, and his determination and perseverance serve as a reminder that anything is possible if you are willing to work hard and never give up. Edison's life is a testament to the power of determination and the importance of perseverance in achieving success.

In 2 Peter, we read of a determination far more significant than Edison's—that of the apostle Peter. With the writing of this letter being dated between 64–68 A.D., we are left with the conclusion that Peter's time on this earth is short (2 Pet. 1:14). In instances such as these, we often see people leaving their last impressions, their last "words of wisdom" some might say. In Peter's situation, it's no different. He cares deeply for the recipients of this letter, referring to them as "*beloved*" no less than five times in chapter 3 (vv. 1, 8, 14, 15, 17). He is determined for them to remain established in the truth. It compels him, with one of the final strokes of his pen, to stir or "*awaken*" them to decide, be firmly determined, to increase in their spiritual walk as God demands of those whom He calls through the Gospel (2 Thess. 2:14; 2 Pet. 1:3, 10, 13).

DISCUSSION

As our attention turns to the text of 2 Peter 1:1-11, we learn five crucial components that must be present if we are determined to grow spiritually. In 2 Peter, we see this determination to increase is pivotal in combating atrocities of the false teachers, their "*destructive heresies*" (2 Pet. 2:1) and their immoral lifestyles engulfed in "*sensuality*" (2 Pet. 2:2). In reflecting on our own culture today which is inundated with greed, saturated with rampant teachings that go against Scripture, and the sexualization of even the most innocent aspects of society, absolute determination to grow is unapologetically necessary. In other words, if the Holy Spirit inspired the apostle Peter to instruct these Christians to set their purpose and determination to grow spiritually firmly, you and I must do the same today if we are going to hold fast to our walk with God and lead our families to do the same in our cultural context.

What five crucial components must be present to be a determined person who desires to grow spiritually?

1) We must sincerely appreciate what God has already done for us.

Fundamental to every aspect of growth in your life is a complete appreciation for where you are in life and where you are going. When a person sets out to better himself occupationally, he must understand not just how far he's come from the early days in his job but why and how he arrived at the place he

---

4 William Arndt et al., *A Greek-English Lexicon of the New Testament and Other Early Christian Literature* (Chicago: University of Chicago Press, 2000), 243.

is. This period of reflection allows him to learn from his past and appreciate where he currently is. It also will serve as a significant motivating factor to continue to press on to that next level.

The same holds true when applied to several other areas of our lives. Weight loss, healthy lifestyles, creating new habits, developing a deeper level of Bible study, improving our personal relationships, and a host of other aspects of each of our lives are all impacted by reflecting in the mirror and appreciating how we arrived we are and what we've learned along the way. Only after taking inventory do we find the motivation to change or improve in areas in which we are underperforming.

In 2 Peter, this need to remember and appreciate reverberates throughout the first chapter. Peter draws these Christians back to the work that God has already accomplished through the righteousness of Jesus Christ (v. 1). This precious faith they possess, like that of the apostle Peter himself, is not cheap, nor is it to be weak.

Through the tremendous demonstration of sinlessness while walking this earth (2 Cor. 5:21), Jesus continually entrusted Himself to the Father as He endured extensive persecution and hatred (1 Pet. 2:23). With an unswerving determination to live according to the divine standard of the Father, Jesus accomplished precisely what He was sent to this earth to do: *"seek and save that which was lost"* (Luke 19:10). It's because of the love of God, demonstrated in and through the crucifixion of His only begotten Son Jesus, that you and I, just like the Christians to whom Peter is writing in our text, bask in the grace and peace that God abundantly supplies (John 3:16; 2 Pet. 1:2). God has richly provided everything we need that pertains to life and godliness, both here on this earth and in eternity (2 Pet. 1:3).

Therefore, as we reflect on our escape from the corruption of our previous life and the fact God has allowed humanity to know Him through the written Word, Peter says we have the *"precious and magnificent promises of God"* in which we place our complete trust (v. 4). We have the firm assurance from God who is not like man and who cannot lie (Heb. 6:18). Because of who He is and what He has done, we don't have to die in our sins (Rom. 6:23).

It's fascinating that Peter begins with this message, emphasizing the nature of God, which expresses God's nurturing of humanity through Jesus Christ. He shows that God has done far more for you than you will ever be able to do for Him, and He wants the recipients of this letter to appreciate this fact unequivocally and deeply. By beginning with this point, Peter draws a very important message to the pinnacle: If you are going to be the person who is determined to increase spiritually, you must first appreciate what God has done for you in Jesus Christ. Another way to express this would be that if spiritual growth is not occurring in our lives, it's not because it's too complicated and unrealistic. We do not fully and sincerely appreciate what God has done for us.

Is that challenging? It's meant to be. That's what Scripture does in the heart of the person seriously seeking God and allowing His Word to convict him. Do you want to know if you are genuinely determined to increase? The answer begins with whether the fire of your appreciation for God's work in your life through Jesus has died down or worse—gone out.

2) We must be ready to apply and supply diligently.

The thought of accomplishing something personally positive is attractive to many. For example, consider the resolutions people make immediately after the New Year begins. On January 2, the workout facilities are packed, whereas just days before, the "regulars" could use any machine anytime. Now, because of all the "newbies" who have made resolutions to grow and increase their physical health, they must wait in line. Some may promise to eat healthier, run/walk every day, and some will even resolve to study their Bibles or go to worship/Bible class more regularly. While these are all excellent goals and aspirations, the question is, "Why do so many people fail at keeping their resolutions?"

In an article posted on psychologytoday.com entitled, "Why Do Resolutions So Often Fail?" author Gurnek Bains, Ph.D. noted what he believes is the number one answer to this question.

> The answer is simple. The one constant we carry is the same old self. Too often, we confuse a change in context with a change in self.
>
> It's very common. Think about a time when you've looked forward to a new job, a new relationship, a big move, or even just a new wardrobe. We assume that once we get this shift in our environment or situation, this will somehow automatically trigger a transformation of our character. We can leave our insecurities behind and emerge, the myth goes, into happier, more confident, successful people.
>
> If only meaningful change were so easy. The truth is that as long as we take the same self into any new situation, the problems we encounter are likely to re-emerge. This is why people often encounter the same conflicts in different relationships, the same insecurities being replicated in new jobs or the same junk food items being scoffed from the fridge two days after your pledge to eat more healthily.[5]

Did you catch that? Here's the quote, "The truth is that as long as we take the same self into any new situation, the problems we encounter are likely to re-emerge." In other words, if a resolution will stick and there is lasting change, we can't simply show up at the gym or the church building and expect that to do the trick. There must be a change inside us if there will ever be lasting change outside us.

Peter begins by drawing the Christians back to what God has done in their lives. When a person obeys the Gospel, God causes him to be born again to a living hope (1 Pet. 1:3). Paul writes to the Christians in Rome regarding this new birth that a new walk will be present because a newness of life is now a reality (Rom. 6:4). However, in Romans 12:2, the apostle Paul emphasizes where the root of any external change occurs in our lives when he writes,

> *And do not be conformed to this world, but be transformed by the* **renewing of your mind**, *so that you may prove what the will of God is, that which is good and acceptable and perfect.* (emp. added)

Peter also homes in on the importance of the internal readiness of the mind when he pens,

> *Therefore,* **prepare your minds** *for action, keep sober in spirit, fix your hope completely on the grace to be brought to you at the revelation of Jesus Christ. (*1 Pet. 1:13; emp. added)

---

[5] Gurnek Bains, "Why Do Resolutions So Often Fail? | Psychology Today" *Psychology Today*, 31 Dec. 2021, www.psychologytoday.com/us/blog/global-lens/202112/why-do-resolutions-so-often-fail.

Again, in 2 Peter 1:15, he writes of the importance of what the mind is thinking about righteous living,

> *All I will also be diligent that at any time after my departure you will be able to call these things to **mind**.* (emp. added)

It could be said that where the mind goes, the body will follow. Therefore, if you want purity of body, purify your mind. If you want to improve your relationships, improve how you view others. If you're going to increase spiritually in your physical walk before God, you must grow in your internal determination and commitment to such an end. That's the significance of 2 Peter 1:5.

> *Now for this very reason also, **applying** all **diligence**, in your faith **supply** moral excellence, and in your moral excellence, knowledge.* (emp. added)

For now, notice the following impactful words in this verse:

- "**Applying**"—[*pareisphérō*] make every effort, do your best [6]
- "**Diligence**"—[*spoudé*] earnest commitment in discharge of an obligation [7]
- "**Supply**"—[*epichorēgéō*] to provide (at one's own expense) [8]

What do these all have in common?

They each require an internal conviction that causes an external action. If we are going give our very best effort, show up with an earnest commitment, and be willing to sacrifice whatever is necessary to provide at our own expense what is required to reach the goal, we must be unapologetically convinced in mind, heart, and our very being that the end for which we strive is right and good. If we have doubts or lack of conviction mixed into our thought process, we will fail in one of these areas, if not all. Initially, we may be like the sprinter who bursts out of the blocks when the starting gun sounds. However, like the runner who fades when the muscles get tired and the lungs begin to burn, if we are not determined to diligently apply and supply what God tells us is necessary for spiritual growth, the enemy will overtake us (2 Pet. 3:8).

God will not force you to grow. He has done His part through Jesus Christ and has made it possible for us to know Him. However, we must decide, here and now, and every day from this point forward, that we will give our total and determined commitment to God. We will pay the price, whatever that may be. Like Paul, we will "*press on toward the goal for the prize of the upward call of God in Christ Jesus*" (Phil. 3:14).

3) We must possess, not merely dabble.

In Acts 3, we read of Peter and John in Jerusalem going up to the temple at the hour of prayer. Just as they were about to enter the temple, a man described as "lame from his mother's womb"

---

[6] Arndt et al. 774.
[7] Arndt et al. 939.
[8] Arndt et al. 387.

Determined to Increase

(Acts 3:2) began begging them to give him alms, that which is benevolently given to meet a need, primarily of a material nature.[9] Demanding the lame man's attention, Peter said, "I do not possess silver and gold, but what I do have I give to you: In the name of Jesus Christ the Nazarene – walk!" (v. 6).

Focus for a moment on the word *possess*. In the Greek, it means "to really be there, exist, be present, be at one's disposal."[10] Understandably, then, what Peter is telling the lame man is he has no silver and no gold. If he did have any, he could not say, "I do not possess" because that would be a lie. In other words, there is a clear and definitive distinction between possessing and not possessing something.

While this may sound like a lesson parents would teach their child trying to make the case that they didn't take their sibling's toy when they did, sometimes using the most straightforward logic and explanation helps make the most profound point. There is a big difference between possessing something and not.

Now, focus your attention on 2 Peter 1:8,

> *For if these qualities* **are yours** *and are increasing, they render you neither useless nor unfruitful in the true knowledge of our Lord Jesus Christ. (emp. added)*

Here, we see the same word translated as "*possess*" in Acts 3:6 included in the translated phrase "*are yours.*" The meaning is the same, only the emphasis is more clearly stated. Peter tells the Christians receiving this letter that the referenced qualities must be genuinely present in their lives. They must own them, having made a clear and firm decision that these qualities aren't merely something they dabble in throughout their lives but ones they own.

Unfortunately, many Christians will spend the entirety of their lives believing, or at least practicing, that if they attend worship and are pretty good people at home, they will be pleasing in the eyes of God. Their spiritual growth is seen as a passive exercise if they even see it as exercise. They obeyed the Gospel, show up for worship, and go about their lives.

That couldn't be further from what this text is teaching. At some point, a line of determined commitment must be drawn in the sand of our lives. There must be a "point-of-no-return" where we decide we are all in and that a plan B doesn't exist. There is no going back for the determined Christian who dares make this commitment. The ships have been burned, and the only way to move is toward the increase.

Faith is your starting point, not the end. Like a house that cannot be built except upon a solid foundation, your life must have the firm foundation of a stable and sure faith. A high level of trust in God and obedience to His Word is fundamental; however, the apostle Peter makes it very clear that if, like the Christians to whom he is writing in 2 Peter, we are going to be able to withstand the continual onslaught of those who seek to derail our faith and encourage the participation in the unrestrained corruption offered by the world by lust (1:4), then we must be determined to continually grow as a follower of Jesus Christ.

---

9 Arndt et al. 316.
10 Arndt et al. 1029.

Where should we be focusing our efforts when it comes to being determined to increase? Consider what Peter writes by inspiration of the Holy Spirit in 2 Peter 1:5-7.

> *Now for this very reason also, applying all diligence, in your faith supply moral excellence, and in your moral excellence, knowledge, and in your knowledge, self-control, and in your self-control, perseverance, and in your perseverance, godliness, and in your godliness, brotherly kindness, and in your brotherly kindness, love.*

Moral Excellence	uncommon character worthy of praise, excellence of character, exceptional civic virtue
Knowledge	comprehension or intellectual grasp of something spoken of practical knowledge, discretion, prudence
Self-control	restraint of one's emotions, impulses, or desires, self-control
Perseverance	the capacity to hold out or bear up in the face of difficulty, patience, endurance, fortitude, steadfastness, perseverance
Godliness	awesome respect accorded to God, devoutness, piety, godliness
Brotherly Kindness	sense of affection for a fellow-Christian used of the love of Christians one to another, brotherly love out of a common spiritual life
Love	the quality of warm regard for and interest in another, esteem, affection, regard, love

Don't get wrapped up in the order of these virtues. Like the instruments in an orchestra, they are individually significant and can stand on their own. Like a violin soloist captivates and deeply draws the audience in, each of these qualities or Christian virtues does the same. However, imagine a cellist joining the violin soloist on the stage. As they combine their beautiful sounds and melodies, the song intensifies as it intertwines in the listener's mind. As the soft sound of the flute is added, the thundering percussionists join, and the rest of the artists play their distinct instruments in the orchestra; the collective sound of the orchestra is complete, each instrument complementing the next.

That's the concept we should have when considering this list. It's not considered a stair-step system where we master the first and then move on to the second. Instead, you and I are to possess, not dabble in, each of these qualities simultaneously as part of our being. If that's going to happen, a determined decision must be made. Just as was mentioned at the beginning of this section, there is a difference between possessing something and not possessing it. You can't sort of possess something. Either you possess it, or you do not.

So, do you possess faith, moral excellence, knowledge, self-control, perseverance, godliness, brother kindness, and love?

4) We must be increasing in each of these qualities.

In 2 Peter 1:8, the Greek word for "increasing" is πλεονάζω, "*pleonázō*," from the root πλέον, "*pleon*."[11] It's defined as "to become more and more, so as to be in abundance, be/become more or be/become great, be present in abundance, grow, increase."[12] At first, using this word may not seem like a significant key to unlocking the deeper meaning behind what Peter is writing; however, a fuller picture begins to appear when we understand this word.

Imagine sitting in an old-fashioned diner, drinking a cup of coffee, and enjoying breakfast. Your waiter comes by the table and notices that your coffee cup is about half-full, so he kindly asks if you would like more coffee. As he begins to pour the fresh, hot coffee into your cup, you notice the coffee getting very close to the top edge. You assume he will stop before it's too late; however, without hesitation, your waiter continues to overflow the coffee into the saucer below. He's not apologetic. He simply wanted to make sure you have an abundant amount of coffee.

If you were sitting at the table in the diner and something like this happened, you may not be too happy. After all, who wants to participate in the daring endeavor of lifting a full cup of hot coffee from the table to his lips? However, this is offered to illustrate the meaning behind the word "increasing" in this text. The intricate details of this word encompass the idea of overflowing or abundance. There's more than is needed, and the coffee is not limited to the edge of the cup. Instead, it overflows. The word *pleonázō* is that word. Here, Peter is saying these virtues not only must be present in your life but there is also no limit to how much they must be increasing and overflowing in your life.

In Romans 5:20, by inspiration of the Holy Spirit, the apostle Paul used this same word to emphasize how great the grace of God is when he wrote, "*The Law came in so that the transgression would* **increase**; *but where sin* **increased**, *grace abounded all the more*" (emp. added). Here, the word is used in correlation with the Law of Moses and man's inability to keep it perfectly. Thus, when the Law was made known, sin increased as man missed the mark of such. Paul answers that "*grace abounded all the more.*" The word *abounded* is impressive because it means the abounding is supercharged. No matter how much sin increase—and no limit is set by this word—grace is supercharged and can more than cover the enormous amount of sin.

Consider these other verses where we find this word.

- Mark 4:8—"*Other seeds fell into the good soil, and as they grew up and* **increased**, *they yielded a crop and produced thirty, sixty, and a hundredfold.*"
- Luke 2:52—"*And Jesus kept* **increasing** *in wisdom and stature, and in favor with God and men.*"
- John 3:30—"*He must* **increase**, *but I must decrease.*"
- Acts 6:7—"*The word of God kept on spreading; and the number of the disciples continued to* **increase** *greatly in Jerusalem, and a great many of the priests were becoming obedient to the faith.*"
- 2 Corinthians 9:10—"*Now He who supplies seed to the sower and bread for food will supply and multiply your seed for sowing and* **increase** *the harvest of your righteousness.*"

---

9 Arndt et al. 824.
10 Arndt et al. 824.

In each of the above, the idea being relayed using the word *pleonázō* is growth without reference to a cap or a limit. What is significant is that in all the above verses and the many more throughout the New Testament that could have been referenced here, the word *increasing* is not a neutral term. It never implies staying at the same level or reaching maximum growth without needing to grow continually.

If we are people determined to increase, there must be a mindset present where we understand we are not working toward a minimum level of increase where God will be pleased. Instead, our mindset must be set on continually growing in moral excellence, knowledge, self-control, perseverance, godliness, brotherly kindness, and love.

5) We must practice, not merely memorize.

Perhaps one of the greatest struggles for many who study God's Word is not found in memorization but in implementation. Since we were little children, many of us have been taught songs that encouraged committing to memory the books of the Bible, the 12 apostles, and the days of Creation. From the earliest years of our lives, we were taught to memorize and recite Scripture. We studied for Bible Bowls and took tests to see how much we retained. Perhaps we even gave speeches at competitions designed to help us grow our knowledge of God's Word and the presentation of Bible lessons/sermons. These are all great and should be encouraged among every child in a Christian home. However, memorizing songs, Scripture, facts, and speeches alone will never please God if the facts, Scripture, and lessons don't change that person's walk before Him.

In business, there are "Thinkers," "Doers," "Talkers," and "Watchers." While most leadership and business websites address the necessity for each in the business environment, they also talk about the dangers that exist if there is a lack of balance and cohesion between these groups. While some in the company need to come up with a plan, effectively communicate it, and measure its success or failure, at the most basic level of the company, someone must implement the plan putting it into action. Meetings can take place all day long, and charts can be created; however, if no one is willing to work hard on the plan, the plan remains a hypothetical theory that may or may not be worthwhile.

According to one author, the difference between "Talkers" and "Doers" can be summarized in three areas: risk, focus, and execution. The "Doer" understands and accepts the risks. He isn't blind to them. He simply decides to manage them instead of allowing them to paralyze him from doing anything. "Talkers" discuss all the beautiful things they want to accomplish; however, they fear what could go wrong. Thus, they stay in meetings, dreaming of what could be. "Doers" are focused and accomplish something every day. They do not explain why they couldn't "get around" to a task like the "Talkers." Instead, "Doers" make a plan and are determined to accomplish something, even if just a tiny portion of the task every day. The "Doer" knows that all the small steps cover a significant distance when added together. Execution is about regular and steady progress daily, and the "Doer" is determined toward execution.[13]

---

[13] Mike Figliuolo, "The Difference Between Talkers and Doers" thoughtLEADERS, LLC: Leadership Training for the Real World. https://www.thoughtleadersllc.com/wp-content/uploads/2022/04/logo.png, 8 July 2020, www.thoughtleadersllc.com/2012/11/the-difference-between-talkers-and-doers/.

Determined to Increase

In your spiritual walk, you must become a "Doer." It's not enough to merely study the Word of God and be able to quote a lot of verses. This statement is not meant to belittle the importance of studying the Word of God (2 Tim. 3:15). However, the Word of God was never handed down to us so that we could memorize sections and impress one another with how much we know. It was meant to be a lamp to our feet and a light to our path (Ps. 119:105). The Word of God is to be written on our hearts and souls, meaning the core of who we are (Deut. 11:18). Scripture was handed down to us to inform us and move us because of the Good News found therein.

That's why Peter, in 2 Peter 1:10, tells the Christians and us that we must be practicing—doing—these virtues he outlines. Christianity is an active lifestyle, not a passive study. With faith as my starting point, I must practice moral excellence, knowledge, self-control, perseverance, godliness, brotherly kindness, and love. Being a "Talker," "Thinker," or "Watcher" is not enough. Here, Peter says we must be "Doers."

CONCLUSION

To the average person, it could be said that Thomas Edison failed more than he succeeded. However, one thing that separated Edison from most people was his resoluteness. He was determined to continue moving forward and learning along the way. He believed the outcome was obtainable and all the sacrifices along the way were completely worth the cost. To Edison, the seeming failures only brought him closer to his desired end. He was determined to grow, learn, advance, and accomplish.

Are you determined to increase your spiritual walk? Do you have an unwavering resolve to stay committed through whatever difficulties come your way? Do you have a sincere appreciation for what God has done for you? Are you ready to diligently apply and supply everything He instructs? Do you possess these Christian virtues outlined in 2 Peter 1? Do you own them, or have you been dabbling in them occasionally? Are you increasing in each of these areas today? Are you practicing these, or are you merely talking about them?

I call these "crossroad questions" that are meant to place you at a pivotal point in determining which way you will go. That's important because if you are going to be a determined person in your walk with the Lord, you must get off the fence and make a definitive decision. John 15 clarifies that no unproductive branches will be left to hang out on the vine. You are either growing and producing or merely taking up space on the vine. Spiritually speaking, a determined man doesn't stand at the crossroads and take solitude simply in knowing how God wants them to go, all while he remains stagnant and cemented in the ground. Instead, the determined man will commitment to increasing in the direction God has outlined in Scripture.

Applying
DETERMINED TO PAY ATTENTION

2 PETER 1:12-21

JOE WELLS

"An invincible determination can accomplish almost anything and in this lies the great distinction between great men and little men." [1]

- Thomas Fuller -

INTRODUCTION

Special Section: Synonyms of *determined*:

Purposeful—having a purpose; meaningful; intentional; full of determination [2]

Being purposeful in life is one of the most important things you can do to live a meaningful and fulfilling existence. It means having a clear sense of direction and working towards goals that align with your values and beliefs. Purposeful living can help you stay motivated, focused, and happy.

Here are some tips on how to be purposeful in life.

First, take the time to reflect on your values and beliefs. What matters most to you? What do you believe in? What are your passions and interests? Once you understand what you value, you can start setting goals and making decisions aligning with those values.

Next, set realistic and achievable goals. Your goals should be specific, measurable, and time bound. For example, if your goal is to write a novel, you could set a goal to write for an hour every day and have a completed manuscript within a year. Having clear goals will help you stay on track and measure your progress along the way.

---

1 https://www.azquotes.com/quotes/topics/determination.html.
2 "Purposeful." *Merriam-Webster.com Dictionary*, https://www.merriam webster.com/dictionary/purposeful.

Third, take action towards your goals. Break your goals into smaller, manageable steps and take action towards them every day. Staying committed to your goals is essential, even when things get tough. Remember that setbacks and failures are a natural part of the process and can help you learn and grow.

Fourth, surround yourself with supportive people. A network of people who support and encourage you can help you stay motivated and focused on your goals. Seek like-minded individuals who share your values and interests and can offer guidance and support.

Living a purposeful life is not only beneficial to your personal growth, but it can also positively impact those around you. You inspire others when you have a clear sense of direction and work towards goals aligning with your values and beliefs. Your dedication and commitment can motivate others to pursue their goals and live purposeful lives.

HISTORICAL EXAMPLE

Colonel Harland Sanders is a man who is widely known for his famous fried chicken chain, Kentucky Fried Chicken. However, most people don't know that he was determined and faced numerous obstacles and setbacks before succeeding.

Sanders was born in 1890 in Indiana. His father died when he was only six years old, forcing him to take up various odd jobs to support his family. Despite this, he managed to finish sixth grade and went on to attend high school. However, he dropped out before graduating to work as a farmhand.

In 1917, Sanders enlisted in the U.S. Army and served during World War I. He was honorably discharged in 1919 and returned to his hometown in Indiana. He then took various jobs, including selling insurance and running a ferryboat company. However, none of these ventures were successful, and he struggled to make ends meet.

In 1930, Sanders opened a small restaurant in a gas station in Corbin, Kentucky. He started selling his famous fried chicken, which he had perfected over the years. The restaurant became popular, and he expanded his business by opening franchises. However, in 1952, disaster struck when a new interstate highway was built, bypassing Corbin and causing a significant drop in business.

Undeterred, Sanders embarked on a journey to promote his chicken recipe to other restaurants across the United States. He drove around the country in his car, sleeping in it and cooking for restaurant owners willing to try his recipe. He faced numerous rejections but was determined to succeed.

Finally, in 1955, Sanders signed a deal with a restaurant owner in Utah, who agreed to pay him a royalty for every piece of chicken sold using his recipe. This began the KFC franchise, one of the world's most successful fast-food chains. Sanders continued to work tirelessly, traveling around the world to promote his brand and ensure that the quality of his chicken was consistent across all locations. He also became known for his eccentric personality, dressing in a white suit and black string tie and sporting a goatee.

Determined to Pay Attention

Despite his success, Sanders remained humble and committed to his values. He believed in providing high-quality food at a reasonable price and treating his employees and customers respectfully. He also donated generously to various charities and organizations.

In 1980, Sanders passed away at 90, leaving a legacy of hard work, determination, and innovation. Today, KFC has over 23,000 locations in more than 140 countries, serving millions of customers every day.

Colonel Harland Sanders is an inspiring figure who embodies the values of determination, perseverance, and hard work. Despite facing numerous setbacks and rejections, he never gave up on his dream of bringing his famous fried chicken to the world. His legacy inspires countless individuals worldwide to pursue their dreams and never give up, no matter how difficult the journey may be.

Driving in the snow and ice is not for the faint of heart. I spent my middle and high school years in western Pennsylvania learning to drive. To stay off the roads during the winter months is not an option there, so I quickly learned the value of having good tires that firmly and securely grip the road. We were taught that it wasn't a matter of if we would slide while driving but when. We approached the journey expecting it to be complicated. Therefore, we learned to read the road, anticipating the most dangerous parts. Time and time again, it was drilled into our minds what to do if you begin to slide and what the most effective maneuver would be to get your vehicle back into alignment where the tires could firmly grab the road.

This concept of having good and solid contact between the tires and the road can be applied to many different areas of life. In 2 Peter 1: 12-15, the apostle writes concerning this same principle,

> *Therefore, I will always be ready to remind you of these things, even though you already know them, and* ***have been established*** *in the truth which is present with you. I consider it right, as long as I am in this earthly dwelling, to stir you up by way of reminder, knowing that the laying aside of my earthly dwelling is imminent, as also our Lord Jesus Christ has made clear to me. And I will also be diligent that at any time after my departure you will be able to call these things to mind.* (emp. added)

The phrase "*have been established*" expresses this same "tire-gripping" concept. The Greek word for "established" means "to cause to be inwardly firm or committed, confirm, establish, strengthen" and is used multiple times throughout the New Testament.[3]

- Luke 22: 31-32—"*Simon, Simon, behold, Satan has demanded permission to sift you like wheat; but I have prayed for you, that your faith may not fail; and you, when once you have turned again,* ***strengthen*** *your brothers*" (emp. added).

- Acts 18: 23—"*And having spent some time there, he left and passed successively through the Galatian region and Phrygia,* ***strengthening*** *all the disciples*" (emp. added).

- 2 Thessalonians 3:3—"*But the Lord is faithful, and He will* ***strengthen*** *and protect you from the evil one*" (emp. added).

---

3 William Arndt et al., *A Greek-English Lexicon of the New Testament and Other Early Christian Literature* (Chicago: University of Chicago Press, 2000), 945.

In each of these instances, there is a determination expressed intent on firmly fixing and setting fast those who are disciples of Jesus Christ. Just as the winter storms rage in western Pennsylvania as they did when I was growing up, some storms crash into the lives of those who seek to be set apart for the purpose of God. Those who desire to be faithful will find "slick spots" along the way, and there must be a purposeful determination to read the road. More importantly, like the tire to the road, a determined connection must be made and maintained with the Word of God.

DISCUSSION

A simple principle in following a map while driving says that whatever route you take, you will end up where it leads. It may not be the most profound statement you've ever heard; however, it is true. If you want to go to Los Angeles, you better take a road that leads west towards California. If you began going east toward New York believing you were going to Los Angeles, you would be sorely mistaken upon seeing the Statue of Liberty. However, if you pick the path that leads to Los Angeles and stick to it, you will see the beautiful Hollywood hills which you were seeking. If you desire a destination, you had better pick the path that leads you there.

In driving, this is a simple concept. However, what about the areas of philosophy and religion? Is it possible for the path to appear to take you in the right direction only to find out after following it for too long that it leads the opposite way? If you're not careful and paying attention, then "yes." In philosophy and religion, there may be just enough truth sprinkled in with complete fabrications of man that all paths may seem right to the one who is leisurely strolling along the way.

It's so sad to think about, but that's precisely what is happening today. Postmodernism, evolution, humanism, materialism, and countless other philosophies are promising answers with no power to deliver on them. Happiness and fulfillment remain elusive to those rummaging through the garbage pile of beliefs abundant in our culture today. There's just enough substance for these and the numerous religious beliefs floating about to captivate those strolling through life. To those who are not determined, all paths appear correct. However, the differences are very apparent to those determined to pay attention.

In 2 Peter 1:19, Peter writes, "*So we have the prophetic word made more sure, to which you do well to **pay attention** as to a lamp shining in a dark place, until the day dawns and the morning star arises in your hearts*" (emp. added). Interestingly, Peter stresses the responsibility these Christians possess regarding where they give their attention. He emphasizes the importance of such by using this word that, in Greek, means "*to pay close attention to something, pay attention to, give heed to, follow.*"[4] A constant state of being alert and continual care is stressed. However, why would he tell them such, and why would they determine to pay attention as he has strongly encouraged? The answers in 2 Peter 1: 12-21 are just as applicable and meaningful for us today. When we more fully understand what they were facing and how they would avoid the derailments, we will be more firmly grounded and determined to pay attention to the prophetic Word ourselves.

---

4 Arndt et al., 880.

Determined to Pay Attention

What does it take to be determined to pay attention to anything, especially to the prophetic Word, as Peter instructed?

1) Being convinced it is worthy of my attention.

In 1997, I was a freshman at Texas Christian University in Ft. Worth, Texas. I was considered "undeclared" in my major, which meant I was in the process of taking as many introductory liberal arts courses as possible that the school required. One of those classes was basic science in a lecture hall with over one hundred other students. It was your typical first-year level class taken by the masses because we didn't know what we wanted to do with our lives yet, but we had to mark a science class off our list.

About mid-semester, we were introduced to four guest lecturers who were all considered professionals in their specific area when it came to the subject of evolution. I had just turned 18 and was grossly unprepared for the onslaught of evolutionary teaching I received. At first glance, their material sounded pretty good. After all, they were the ones with the initials behind their names, and I was a kid trying to figure out life away from home. It became easy to be drawn into their explanations and theories, although I didn't even really understand what a theory was at the time. They taught as if their conclusions were settled and there were no rebuttals or arguments to be made against them. So, like the hundreds of other first-year students in the class, I took notes and tests, regurgitating the information I had ingested.

My confusion became bothersome because all my life, I had been taught that God created everything in the six days of Creation as outlined in Genesis chapters 1 and 2. I never questioned it, so in my first year of living on my own, I was bombarded with this new belief system that is touted as scientific fact. Fortunately, my grandparents lived in Waco, Texas, and I went to see them on the weekends. During one of those visits, my grandmother and I sat in their driveway while I told her about my class and the confusion that boiled up. I remember even asking her if it were possible that the Bible and my teachers were correct simultaneously. With great patience and confidence, my grandmother took the time to explain the Word of God to me. She reminded me that the Bible claims God made each creature after its kind and that the days of creation were literally 24-hour days. I later found out this is known grammatically by the use of the Hebrew word *"yom"* combined with a clarifier, *"there was evening and there was morning"* (Gen. 1:5, 8, 13, 19, 23, 31).[5]

I invite you into a pivotal time in my early years to illustrate the power of philosophies rooted in manufactured myths and fables. Evolution, macro-evolution, as taught in many schools throughout the world, is universally known as a theory, meaning it has never been proven and given accreditation to make it a law. In the field of science, once something has been repeatedly tested time and time again and demonstrated the same results, it is moved into the category of a law, such as the law of gravity. However, if a belief gets stuck in the theory stage, some hurdles and obstacles can't be overcome. Thus, for many, a belief that remains stagnant in that stage for an extended period should be dismissed. Instead, for this myth, this fable simply known as the theory of evolution, our society allows it to be used to sway the innocent and impressionable minds of our youngest toward a belief that God is not nonexistent, the Bible is not credible, and that humans are simply a higher form of animals and thus act as such.

---

3 Dr. Terry Mortenson, "Six Literal Days." *Answers in Genesis* (Answers In Genesis, 8 Feb. 2017), https:answersingenesis.org/days-of-creation/six-literal-days/.

"Cleverly devised tales" is Peter's phrase in 2 Peter 1:16 to describe these empty and man-made philosophies and ideologies in which some ground their trust and confidence. Like the guest lecturers in my freshman science class who crafted their conclusions based upon unfounded myths and legends passed down in writings of misguided individuals, those who devised the tales present at the time of Peter's writing did so for various reasons. As we will see in the following chapters, dishonest men introduced destructive heresies for their own gain (2:1). That's nothing new. These "false words" (2:3) are broadly cast because of the greed in the sower's heart. We've got to be more discerning than merely allowing every proposed truth to seep into our hearts and be the road our "tires" grip.

When I accept and agree with the premise that whatever road I take, I will end up at a specific destination, I will understand the road is worthy of my attention. If I am going to be a determined, purposeful person, then the route I take matters. It matters in my relationships, occupation, parenting, hobbies, and, most importantly, my relationship with God. So, should the road we take, the philosophies and religious teachings we adhere to, be worth our attention? Absolutely! However, we must be genuinely convinced of this fact.

2) Being convinced the one telling me is trustworthy.

Each of us, in both large and small ways, encounters discerning moments daily. We hear or read news reports that are processed through filters that have been set in our minds and hearts. We read books where philosophies are applied, and perhaps religious conclusions are propagated. Through these filters, we weigh what is said to determine if it is logical and routed in authenticity. We will discern whether to allow those teachings to influence and change us. That's why it's essential to be convinced of the trustworthiness of the person declaring such.

Peter was not a man without flaws. While there are books upon books written about the historical data surrounding his fishing business, his marriage, and his teachings, to test the trustworthiness of the man calling others to listen to his words and count them as truth, we must evaluate his character. It's been said before, "The only thing that walks back from the tomb with the mourners and refuses to be buried is the character of a man. What a man is survives him. It can never be buried."[6] Peter's character lives beyond his grave, whether in Rome or wherever. The man's character demands that we pay attention to his writings.

Peter had numerous wonderful qualities. He was **bold**, as demonstrated in Matthew 16:21-23 when Jesus told the disciples He was going to go to Jerusalem and *"suffer many things from the elders and chief priests and scribes, and be killed, and be raised up on the third day."* Peter, refusing to allow any such thing to happen to his friend and teacher, pulled Jesus aside and seriously began to rebuke Him. What a ridiculous reaction from Peter! However, it reveals a fundamental quality of his character. Peter was very bold.

Peter was also **decisive**. In Matthew 14, in the face of fear (v. 26), Peter cried out to Jesus and said, *"Lord, if it is You, command me to come to You on the water."* The Scriptures leave us no reason to conclude there was hesitation on Peter's part after Jesus said, *"Come"* (v. 28). Peter decisively stepped out of the boat on the stormy sea and briefly walked on the water.

---

6 John C. Maxwell, *The 21 Irrefutable Laws of Leadership* (Nashville: Thomas Nelson, 1998), 71.

Determined to Pay Attention

He was **courageous**. On the night Jesus was betrayed, Peter was with Him in the garden. John 18:3 records the scene this way, *"Judas then, having received the Roman cohort and officers from the chief priests and the Pharisees, came there with lanterns and torches and weapons."* Having a Roman cohort present means there could have been as many as 600 soldiers with weapons of war strapped to their bodies. These would have been battle-trained and tested men, and Peter's response was to be the first to pull his sword and strike. Jesus healed Malchus (v. 11) and told Peter to put his sword away; however, think about Peter's courage on that momentous occasion.

Peter was **insightful**. While many thoughts about Jesus circulated during his day, Peter keenly observed and listened to what Jesus did and taught. It doesn't mean he fully understood everything the Master did; however, he also knew Jesus was more than John the Baptist, Elijah, Jeremiah, or other prophets. When Jesus asks, *"But who do you say I am?"* Peter answers, *"You are the Christ, the Son of the living God"* (Matt. 16:15-16). Jesus affirms that this insight had not come from the wisdom of men. Instead, Jesus responded, *"Blessed are you, Simon Barjona, because flesh and blood did not reveal this to you, but My Father who is in heaven"* (v. 17).

While these and numerous other positive traits give a glimpse into Peter's character, they also only paint a partial picture. Peter was a man who could be **distracted with fear and doubt,** as he displayed in Matthew 14 when he took his eyes off Jesus and began to look at the stormy sea. He was filled with an **over-abundance of self-confidence** as revealed in the upper room of Matthew 26 when, upon hearing Jesus tell the disciples they will all fall away because of Him (v. 31), Peter brazenly replied, *"Even though all may fall away because of You, I will never fall away"* (v. 33). Seeing this overconfidence, Jesus replied, *"Truly I say to you that this very night, before a rooster crows, you will deny Me three times"* (v. 34). Peter vowed that he would die before ever doing such; however, we know how that ended next to a fire in the courtyard.

Along with these, Peter **struggled with hypocrisy**, especially when it came to the interactions of Jews and Gentiles. The most notable was in Antioch when Paul had to confront him to his face. Paul records details about this interaction in Galatians 2: 11-21 and states,

> *But when Cephas came to Antioch, I opposed him to his face, because he stood condemned. For prior to the coming of certain men from James, he used to eat with the Gentiles; but when they came, he began to withdraw and hold himself aloof, fearing the party of the circumcision. The rest of the Jews joined him in hypocrisy, with the result that even Barnabas was carried away by their hypocrisy.* (v. 11-13)

Perhaps the most considerable dent in the armor of his character is when he **fearfully denied Jesus** three times on the night He was betrayed (Matt. 26: 69-75). Some have pointed out that Peter displayed great courage in showing up to the courtyard in the first place. Perhaps that is true. After all, when he cut off the ear of Malchus, he would have become known among the group who took Jesus, the same group that would logically have been at the gathering that night. Even if this is a moment of courage, Peter's denial of Jesus, amplified by cursing in the third denial, was about saving his own skin. Fear overcame, doubt clouded, and self-preservation kicked in.

The true character of any man is understood, not by diving deep into each aspect and allowing that one to define him completely. Instead, a man's character is like a soldier's armor. Some portions reveal battle scars, clashes, and piercings. Perhaps there are stains of blood, sweat, and the filth of the battlefield ingrained in the seams. However, there are sections where the sword has not pierced, and the club has not dented. Some portions have withstood the filth of battle and reflect what appears to be perfection. Overall, the soldier's armor tells a complete story that can only be understood when taken as a whole.

In the same manner, the character of Peter, just like ours, is best understood in totality, and the whole picture is that Peter repented and would go on to bravely advance the cause of Christ throughout the known world of his day. He would stand with the others on the Day of Pentecost, declaring the saving message of the Gospel of Jesus Christ (Acts 2). After having been imprisoned and threatened to never speak in the name of Jesus Christ again, he, along with John, stood their ground and declared, *"Whether it is right in the sight of God to give heed to you rather than to God, you be the judge; for we cannot stop speaking about what we have seen and heard"* (Acts 4:19-20). He's the same Peter who history will record that shortly after writing the book of 2 Peter, would watch his wife crucified and would himself be crucified, possibly upside down, because he would rather die for the cause of Christ than deny him, saving his own life (see John 21:18-19).

An individual who devotes his life to advancing a message and is willing to die for such is either a lunatic or has a firm conviction rooted in what he knows. In 2 Peter 1:16, Peter makes it very clear that he is not a madman. Instead, he claims to be an "eyewitness" of the majesty of Jesus Christ. He was there on the Mount of Transfiguration and saw firsthand what occurred. The Scriptures record that Jesus was *"transfigured before them; and His face shone like the sun, and His garments became as white as light"* (Matt. 17: 2). He was an "earwitness" in that he heard with his ears when the Father said, *"This is My Beloved Son, with whom I am well-pleased; listen to Him"* (v. 5).

Apart from having a flawless character, Peter is a trustworthy witness when taken as a whole. Through a testing and tumultuous journey, his character was shaped and molded into the older man we read in 1 and 2 Peter. Even with the "warts" Peter possessed, Jesus saw an honest man who, when convicted, would decisively move to advance what was right and good, even if it meant dying for that cause. That tells me everything I need to know about the man admonishing the recipients of this letter, as well as you and me today, to pay attention.

3) Being convinced it is God's Word.

If I devote my life to a teaching that advances a belief rooted in a resurrected Messiah, I better be convinced, without any doubt, that teaching is truly from God. In 2 Peter 1:20-21, Peter writes, *"But know this first of all, that no prophecy of Scripture is a matter of one's own interpretation for no prophecy was ever made by an act of human will, but men moved by the Holy Spirit spoke from God."* Drawing a stark contrast between the *"cleverly devised tales"* (v. 16) of the false teachers of his day, Peter makes it crystal clear that the Scripture (v. 19) is very different than anything these Christians would ever hear and read. Whereas many philosophies and religious beliefs are rooted in man's interpretations and their desired conclusions, Scripture is not. Instead, Peter claims Scripture is given to us by men *"moved by the Holy Spirit"* who *"spoke from God."* Since that is the case, we should be able to see clear and credible evidence that these men weren't simply coming up with prophecy as they went along.

What would such evidence look like, and where can we turn to observe it? Consider the following reasons why you should be convinced that Scripture is unlike any *"cleverly devised tales"* made by the *"interpretations"* of man according to their *"human will."*

Determined to Pay Attention

Fossil Record: The Bible tells us that God created all living things and that each species was created according to its kind (Gen. 1). This idea is supported by fossil records, which show that living things appear suddenly and fully formed rather than gradually evolving. Along with this, for a fossil to form, an organism that was once living had to be quickly and wholly covered with sediment so that the oxygen could not cause decomposition like we see when an animal is hit by a vehicle and lies on the side of the road, or a tree falls to the ground and rots due to being exposed to the elements. The number of fossils found in dry, arid locations indicates that, at one time, those areas had to be completely submerged in water. Thus, the fossilization and the location where fossils are found support a global catastrophe, such as the flood in the days of Noah recorded in Genesis 7.

Medicine: When a male child is born today, he usually leaves the hospital in a few days if no health issues are preventing such. During those few days after birth, the parents will be allowed to decide whether they want their baby boy to be circumcised. If they decide they do, their child will be given a shot of Vitamin K before the surgery commences. That is because for blood clotting to occur, we know the human body must have high enough levels of prothrombin and vitamin K. Both are very low when a male child is first born; however, on the eighth day, both should occur at high enough levels naturally that the male child will be able to not continually bleed after surgery. We know this now because of scientific advancements; however, Moses wrote about this long ago in Genesis 17:12.

Fulfilled Prophecy: The Bible contains hundreds of prophecies that have been fulfilled with remarkable accuracy, including the birth (Mic. 5:2; Matt. 2:1), life (Zech. 9:9; Matt. 21:7-9), death (Isa. 53:7; Matt. 27: 12-14), and resurrection (Ps. 16:10; Acts 2:22) of Jesus Christ. Prophecies concerning nations and the scattering of people have also been fulfilled in detail (Deut. 28: 47-68; 2 Kings 17:24; 18:13; Isa. 13; Dan. 5:28). These prophecies demonstrate the divine inspiration of the Bible and provide a powerful witness to the truth of its message.

Archaeology: Excavations in the Middle East have uncovered numerous artifacts (Moabite Sone, Cyrus Cylinder) and structures (Sargon's Palace) that support the historical accuracy of the Bible. These include the discovery of the city of Jericho (which began in 1868 and continues today), which was destroyed just as the Bible describes, and the discovery of the Dead Sea Scrolls (1947-1956)[8], which contain copies of many of the books of the Old Testament. These and many other discoveries demonstrate the historical reliability of the Bible and provide robust evidence of its accuracy.

Cohesiveness of the Bible's Message: Despite being written over a period of 1400 years by 40 different authors, the Bible presents a consistent and unified message. The Bible teaches that God is love (1 John 4:8), that He desires a relationship with His people (2 Pet. 3:9), and that He has provided a way for us to be reconciled to Him through faith in Jesus Christ, including obedience to the Gospel (John 3:16-17; Rom. 1:16). This message of love and redemption is woven throughout the entire Bible, providing a powerful testimony to its truth and accuracy.

---

7 World History Edu. "The Ancient City of Jericho: History and Major Facts." *World History Edu*, 10 Oct. 2023, worldhistoryedu.com/the-ancient-city-of-jericho-history-and-major-facts/.

8 Nathan Steinmeyer, "What Are the Dead Sea Scrolls?" *Biblical Archaeology Society*, 17 Apr. 2023, www.biblicalarchaeology.org/daily/biblical-artifacts/dead-sea-scrolls/what_are_the_dead_sea_scrolls/.

Geography/Topography: The Bible contains detailed descriptions of the geography and topography of the Middle East, including the locations of cities, rivers, and mountains. One example is in Luke 10:30-35, when Jesus described the man as "*going down from Jerusalem to Jericho.*" Bible critics love to point out that Jerusalem is north of Jericho on a map; however, upon looking at a topographical map, one finds that Jerusalem is higher in elevation than Jericho. Thus, what Jesus said is true. These descriptions, along with others, have been confirmed by modern maps and archaeological discoveries, providing further evidence of the accuracy of the Bible.

Historical Writings: The Bible is not the only ancient text that describes events and people of the time. Other historical writings include those of Josephus, a Jewish historian born in 37-38 A.D. and died early in the second century. In his writing known as *Antiquities*, he references John the Baptist (Ant. 18.116ff.), James the Lord's brother (Ant. 20.200), and Jesus Christ (Ant. 18.63f)[9]. Roman historian Tacitus (56-118 A.D. is another such writer who corroborates the historical accuracy of the Bible. In Annals, he referred to the crucifixion of Jesus by order of Pontus Pilate: "Christus, the founder of the name [i.e., Christian], had undergone the death penalty in the reign of Tiberius, by sentence of the procurator Pontius Pilatus."[10] These writings provide further evidence of the accuracy of the Bible and its message.

CONCLUSION:

Those early years when I was learning to drive in western Pennsylvania were foundational, especially when driving on ice and snow. I remember driving home one night in a blizzard so thick the headlights reflected off the falling snow, making it difficult to see. I've slid and skirted this way and that, and I've learned the tremendous value of making sure to pay attention and drive in such a way so your tires have the best opportunity to grip the road with good contact. To do so took a high level of determination and focus.

If you and I are determined to pay attention as the apostle Peter admonishes in 2 Peter 1:19, we must focus on the tires of our lives, making good contact with the road. Along with this, we must make sure we are on the right road. This is only accomplished when we are convinced paying attention is worth our time, the person telling us the direction to go is trustworthy, and the word we follow is the very Word of God, not some human interpretation.

---

[9] F. F. Bruce, "Josephus, Flavius," ed. D. R. W. Wood et al., *New Bible Dictionary* (Leicester, England; Downers Grove: InterVarsity Press, 1996), 611.
[10] Derek Brown, "Tacitus," ed. John D. Barry et al., *The Lexham Bible Dictionary* (Bellingham: Lexham Press, 2016).

Applying

DETERMINED TO DO RIGHT

---

2 PETER 2:1-22

JOE WELLS

"Failure will never overtake me if my determination to succeed is strong enough." [1]

- Og Mandino -

INTRODUCTION

Special Section: Synonyms of *determined*:

Intent—directed with strained or eager attention; having the mind, attention, or will concentrated on something or some end or purpose [2]

One of the critical traits of an intent person is his ability to stay focused. An intent person can block out distractions and stay on task, even when things get tough. This is an essential skill in today's fast-paced world, where distractions are everywhere. Being an intent person allows you to stay on track and accomplish your goals, even when the odds are against you.

Another important trait of intent people is their commitment to their goals. They are willing to put in the time and effort required to achieve their objectives, no matter how challenging. This type of commitment is essential for success, allowing you to push through obstacles and overcome adversity.

Another key trait of intent people is their ability to work hard and persevere. They understand that success is not always easy or immediate and that there will be setbacks and challenges. However, they are willing to work and keep pushing forward, even when things get tough.

---

[1] https://www.overallmotivation.com/quotes/determination-quotes/.
[2] "Intent," Merriam-Webster, https://www.merriam-webster.com/dictionary/intent.

Being an intent person means you are willing to step outside your comfort zone. You can't be rigid or inflexible, especially regarding your growth and approach to overcoming obstacles. This mindset is essential for growth and development, allowing you to learn new skills and discover new opportunities.

Being an intent person means being focused, committed, and willing to adapt to achieve your goals. It requires discipline and unrelenting perseverance. If you want to be successful, it is essential to cultivate this mindset. Your dedication and commitment can motivate others to pursue their goals and live purposeful lives.

HISTORICAL EXAMPLE

Henry Ford, the founder of the Ford Motor Company, is a name that is synonymous with success and innovation. However, many people do not know that Ford faced numerous failures and setbacks on his way to success. Despite these challenges, he remained determined and focused, eventually becoming one of the most successful entrepreneurs of his time.

He was born in 1863 to a family of farmers in a rural area of Michigan. Ford left his family's farm and moved to Detroit to work as an apprentice machinist at 16. He quickly became interested in the burgeoning automobile industry and began working for the Detroit Edison Company, which was developing electric cars. However, Ford was not content to work on other people's projects. He was determined to create his own automobile.

In 1899, Henry Ford founded his first automobile company, the Detroit Automobile Company. Unfortunately, it failed two years later due to financial difficulties and investor disagreements. Despite this setback, Ford did not abandon his dream of building a successful automobile company.

In 1903, Ford founded the Ford Motor Company with a group of investors. However, the company did not become an overnight success. It faced numerous challenges in its early years, including a shortage of capital and a lack of demand for automobiles. Ford was forced to borrow money to keep the company afloat, and he even went so far as to mortgage his own home to secure a loan.

His first car, the Model A, was not a success. However, Ford was undeterred and remained focused on his goal of creating an affordable, mass-produced automobile. In 1908, he introduced the Model T, the first affordable automobile for the average American. The Model T was an instant success, quickly becoming the best-selling car in the United States.

However, Ford's determination did not end with the success of the Model T. He was determined to make his car affordable for the average American. To do this, he had to streamline his manufacturing processes and reduce the cost of production. By 1913, he introduced the assembly line, allowing his workers to complete their tasks more quickly and efficiently. This not only reduced the cost of production but also allowed Ford to increase his workers' wages. This was a revolutionary idea at the time, and it helped to create a new middle class in America.

Determined to Do Right

Ford's success was not without its challenges, however. In 1914, he faced a major setback when his workers went on strike. The strike lasted for six months, and it had a significant impact on the company's production and reputation. Ford responded by increasing wages for his workers and implementing other reforms, such as reducing the workday from nine hours to eight hours.

Despite these challenges, Ford's determination and vision led to his ultimate success, and it did not stop at his business ventures. He was also determined to make a difference in the world. He was a strong advocate of peace and a believer in the power of technology to improve people's lives. He created the Ford Foundation in 1936, which has since become one of the largest philanthropic organizations in the world.

Henry Ford's determination and drive to succeed in the automobile industry revolutionized manufacturing and changed the course of American history. His innovative ideas and approach to mass production have had a lasting impact on the economy and society. Ford's perseverance through failures and setbacks is a testament to his unwavering determination. His legacy as a business leader, philanthropist, and advocate for technology and education is a reminder of the power of determination and the impact one person can have on the world.[3,4]

I've always been interested in why people do what they do. I guess it's because I used to work at a group home for teenagers who had behavioral struggles in society. It's easiest to merely focus on the problem behaviors of children and seek to get them to stop the bad and do good. However, I've learned that there is always an underlying reason why someone does and thinks as he does. You can help them with their behavior struggles if you can discern that.

I'll never forget hearing the stories of mothers choosing random men over their children and the lasting negative impact that had on some of the boys. It's enough to break even a strong man's heart to see a teenager who has struggled in life work the recovery program in place for them to earn a visit on Sunday with their family only to hear that the boy's mother or father never showed up because they had something better to do or someone else with whom they preferred to spend the day. That boy comes back to the home broken. Why should he try? If he's not shown love and attention by those who are supposed to love him the most, he will act out and try to get any attention possible.

I've heard and seen the impact of stories that would make most cringe. There are stories of parents allowing their sons to be sexually abused in the back room while they were getting high or drunk in the front of the house. I've seen scars on the arms of a boy whose father used to put cigarettes out on them, leaving a permanent reminder of the pain caused by those who were supposed to nurture and protect him. I've even seen mothers try to buy their way into the lives of their sons with expensive shoes and clothes, all the while emphasizing to those boys that "love" (which really was not love but a mother feeling guilty for her behavior) can be bought and sold just as a pair of shoes. What impact will that have on their future relationships?

---

3 Carol W Gelderman, "Henry Ford," *Encyclopedia Britannica*, https://www.britannica.com/biography/Henry-Ford.
4 Nathan Steinmeyer, History.com Editors, "Henry Ford," *History.com*, A&E Television Networks, 26 Mar. 2020, www.history.com/topics/inventions/henry-ford.

In all these and countless other scenarios, the truth that a person always has a reason for doing what they do reverberates. The older I get, the more that lesson has been etched in my mind. In ministry, I've seen men wrapped up in pornographic addictions melt when they acknowledge what's really going on behind the scenes. A son whose father always told him he wasn't good enough runs to find someone who will. A husband who is broken because his marriage is filled with unhealthy criticism at every turn seeks acceptance in "the arms of a woman" on a video. An employee finds the stress of his job too much to bear, so he seeks what he thinks is relief in the comfort of a woman on the screen of his phone. I've seen it. Men who are broken or hurt are addicted to pornography as a coping mechanism; only the behavior doesn't help them. They find themselves more hurt, and the wake of pain they leave behind destroys those around them.

In all, the reality is that we are still accountable for our actions, regardless of the reason we did them. We emphasized that to those boys in the group home. We told them that they can't control the behaviors of others, but they are in control of their response. They didn't have to choose a harmful and destructive path in life just because other people struggled and failed in their journey. The same can be said for the man addicted to pornography because he is coping with something in his life. It can also be said to the man who looks at me in the mirror. We don't have to choose negative behaviors just because we are hurt or desire something. We are in control of our actions, and we are accountable for our actions.

The Old Testament prophet Ezekiel said it this way when he wrote concerning the judgment of God,

> *Yet you say, "Why should the son not bear the punishment for the father's iniquity?" When the son has practiced justice and righteousness and has observed all My statutes and done them, he shall surely live. The person who sins will die. The son will not bear the punishment for the father's iniquity, nor will the father bear the punishment for the son's iniquity; the righteousness of the righteous will be upon himself, and the wickedness of the wicked will be upon himself. "But if the wicked man turns from all his sins which he has committed and observes all My statutes and practices justice and righteousness, he shall surely live; he shall not die. All his transgressions which he has committed will not be remembered against him; because of his righteousness which he has practiced, he will live. Do I have any pleasure in the death of the wicked," declares the Lord God, "rather than that he should turn from his ways and live?"* (Ezek. 18: 19-23)

Since the person who does the actions will be judged for the action, it stands to reason that each of us has a choice regarding our actions. After all, a loving God doesn't judge us for something we can't control. On the other hand, a righteous Judge cannot sit back and not hold individuals who do wrong accountable. So, we must all swallow the fact that we are in control of our actions; therefore, we get to choose them. If we are determined to do right, vital values and critical elements must be present.

In 2 Peter 2, we are introduced to the actions and motivations of the *"false prophets"* who bask in greed and sensuality. Their lifestyle is rooted in the very denial of the Master who bought them (v. 1) and a belief that an eternal judgment will not happen (3:3-4). These, who once had escaped the defilements of the world, have now become trapped in them once again (2:20). Both their message and their actions indicate this horrific state (2:21). Their belief and motivations dictate their actions, and they will be held accountable for their sins (2:3, 9).

We want to avoid their way of life and the inevitable ending. But how will we do so? We must not walk in their footprints, but we can learn from them by observing where they ventured off the trail. We can set our minds to do right instead of giving in to every passion or potential motivating factor that has come our way in the past or will in the future. It will take severe intent and determination to do right; however, the reward waiting at the end of the journey is more than worth it. It's beyond anything these or any other "false prophets" promise.

DISCUSSION

To be a person determined to do right…

1) I Must Value the Way of Truth

In life, some things are just bigger than you and me. A soldier who is sent into battle knows an objective must be accomplished. He will prepare himself physically and mentally to the best of his ability. The military will equip him with the best technology and defenses to ensure the mission is accomplished and his life is spared. With all the scenarios they can think of mapped out ahead of time, it's inevitable that something will occur on the mission that was outside of the plan. It's also very likely the soldier may lay down his life, knowing the importance of accomplishing the mission. The mission is bigger than any one of the soldiers.

Another instance where something is larger than any one individual is when it comes to sports. Everybody loves positive press, and to get their name in the headlines for a wonderful accomplishment, at times, can drive actions. A quarterback seeking the record for most passing yards in a season may call an audible and throw more than the coach initially intended. If he catches so many passes or has a certain number of total yards in a single season, a receiver with a significant financial bonus on the line might let his frustration known to the coach, quarterback, team, and the media. The whole squad fails when a person becomes so wrapped up in his success that he quits functioning as a single part of the bigger picture. The team and winning as such is more significant than any one person, even if it means benching your starting quarterback or receiver because he isn't performing at a high level during that specific game.

More important than both of the previous illustrations is the bigger picture of the will of God. In his first letter to the scattered Christians, Peter stressed the importance of their new birth (1:3, 23). This new birth meant they were living for a different cause and purpose, much bigger than any of them. In chapter 2, Peter stressed that they were living stones being built up as "*a spiritual house for a holy priesthood, to offer up spiritual sacrifices acceptable to God through Jesus Christ*" (v. 5). He later told them they were the holy priesthood (v. 9); thus, instructing them as a holy people to live differently than the rest of those around them (vv. 11-13). This was so that they would not "*wage war against their own soul*" (v. 11), and so those who were seeking their harm might "*glorify God in the day of visitation*" (v. 12).

The bigger picture is that God wants all souls in Heaven with Him, even if it means you and I must encounter challenging and life-threatening situations during our stay on this earth (1 Pet. 3:17). In his second letter, Peter emphasizes this point even more clearly when he writes, *"The Lord is not slow about His promise, as some count slowness, but is patient toward you not wishing for any to perish but for all to come to repentance"* (2 Pet. 3:9). That's the good news of the Gospel. God does love the world so much so that He gave His only begotten Son, Jesus Christ, to die on the cross for our sins (John 3:16-17). He raised Him from the grave after three days in the tomb (1 Cor. 15:1-4), so you and I have a living hope (1 Pet. 1:3). This hope is available to the entire world. God has set it up so you and I, as disciples of Jesus Christ, would go with this saving message to our friends, family members, co-workers, neighbors, and beyond to bring others to Him (Matt. 28:19-20).

The *"way of truth,"* as Peter calls it in 2 Peter 2:2, is so important. Consider a lengthy list of Scriptures explaining what the Bible says regarding truth and the impact this has on one's eternal salvation.

- Psalm 25:10—*"All the paths of the Lord are lovingkindness and **truth** to those who keep His covenant and His testimonies."*

- Psalm 31:5—*"Into Your hand I commit my spirit; You have ransomed me, O Lord, God of **truth**."*

- Psalm 86:11—*"Teach me Your way, O Lord; I will walk in Your **truth**; Unite my heart to fear Your name."*

- John 1:14—*"And the Word became flesh, and dwelt among us, and we saw His glory, glory as of the only begotten from the Father, full of grace and **truth**."*

- John 1:17—*"For the Law was given through Moses; grace and **truth** were realized through Jesus Christ."*

- John 8:31-32—*"So Jesus was saying to those Jews who had believed Him, 'If you continue in My word, then you are truly disciples of Mine; and you will know the **truth**, and the **truth** will make you free.'"*

- John 14:6—*"Jesus said to him, 'I am the way, and the **truth**, and the life; no one comes to the Father but through Me.'"*

- John 17:17—*"Sanctify them in the **truth**; Your word is **truth**."*

- Romans 1:18—*"For the wrath of God is revealed from heaven against all ungodliness and unrighteousness of men who suppress the **truth** in unrighteousness."*

- Romans 2:5-8—*"But because of your stubbornness and unrepentant heart you are storing up wrath for yourself in the day of wrath and revelation of the righteous judgment of God, who will render to each person according to his deeds: to those who by perseverance in doing good seek for glory and honor and immortality, eternal life; but to those who are selfishly ambitious and do not obey the **truth**, but obey unrighteousness, wrath and indignation."*

- Ephesians 1:13—*"In Him, you also, after listening to the message of **truth**, the gospel of your salvation—having also believed, you were sealed in Him with the Holy Spirit of promise."*

- Ephesians 4:17-24—*"So this I say, and affirm together with the Lord, that you walk no longer just as the Gentiles also walk, in the futility of their mind, being darkened in their understanding, excluded from the life of God because of the ignorance that is in them, because of the hardness of their heart; and they, having become callous, have given themselves over to sensuality for the practice of every kind of impurity with greediness. But you did not learn Christ in this way, if indeed you have heard Him and have been taught in Him, just as* **truth** *is in Jesus, that, in reference to your former manner of life, you lay aside the old self, which is being corrupted in accordance with the lusts of deceit, and that you be renewed in the spirit of your mind, and put on the new self, which in the likeness of God has been created in righteousness and holiness of the* **truth**.*"*

- *1 Timothy 2:3*—*"This is good and acceptable in the sight of God our Savior, who desires all men to be saved and to come to the knowledge of the* **truth**.*"*

- *2 Timothy 4:3-4*—*"For the time will come when they will not endure sound doctrine; but wanting to have their ears tickled, they will accumulate for themselves teachers in accordance to their own desires, and will turn away their ears from the* **truth** *and will turn aside to myths."*

While not an exhaustive listing of all the verses in the Bible that address the concept of truth, from this, we can clearly see the immense value of the way of truth. Truth is rooted in the very nature of God and is made known to man in Jesus Christ. It can set us free from the wages of sin and death and should change how we live in this world. The way of truth is revealed to us through the preaching of the Gospel and leads to eternal hope. While God wants all men to know the truth, not everyone will love it and want to follow its lit path. Some will abandon the truth, preferring myths or cleverly devised tales, as Peter addresses in 2 Peter 1:16. Sadly, because of their influence, they will lead others down the same condemned path as they malign, bring blasphemy or demean, the way of truth (2 Pet. 2:2). The result for these and those who follow them will be condemnation. Not because God is not love, but because in rejecting and bringing blaspheme on the way of truth, they have attacked the very nature of God and His saving work in Christ Jesus.

That's why if we are going to be people who are determined to do right, we must first value the way of truth. When we do, everything we do in life will be weighed against what impact it will have on the way of truth, our journey along the way, and the influence we have on others to either walk on the path or veer away. I want to do right, not because I want my name in the headlines. Instead, I want God's name "in the headlines" as my life is lived as a sacrifice before Him. The way of truth is more significant than you and me, and if we are going to do right, we must not simply acknowledge that fact. We must value that truth.

2) I Must Hold Fast to the Right Way

Logic tells us that if there is a right way, by default there must be a wrong way. This is true because you can't have right without the opposite existing. It's like knowing what hot water is without knowing that cold water exists—or understanding light without a grasp of darkness. Some concepts can only exist in pairs; thus, a wrong way must exist when there is a right way. This is true because the idea of comparison is inherently built into these words. Right, as compared to what? Hot water as weighed against what? Light by comparison to what measurement? In all these, a standard must exist and stand as the measurement by which all these are compared.

In 2 Peter 2:15, when talking about the false prophets (2:1), we read, *"forsaking **the right way**, they have gone astray, having followed the way of Balaam, the son of Beor, who loved the wages of unrighteousness"* (emp. added). Since a *"right way"* exists, there must be a wrong way. That's the point Peter is making. These false prophets are accused of *"forsaking,"* meaning "to cause to be left in a place, leave (behind)," and have *"gone astray,"* meaning "to proceed without a sense of proper direction, go astray, be misled, wander about aimlessly."[6] Ironically, this means they once were on the right way, and like sheep who wander and chase what they believe to be greener pastures, they have left the fold, leaving the protection of the shepherd, and are now choosing to be exposed to the wolves and countless other dangers that are present in the wild. The problem is they have conditioned themselves to this end. Peter says they are like *"unreasoning animals, born as creatures of instinct to be captured and killed"* (2:12).

What a sad and terrifying state to be in! However, they don't care. Peter reveals that these purveyors of perversion "revel" in the daytime meaning (2:13), a word meaning *"engagement in a fast, self-indulgent lifestyle, indulgence, reveling."*[7] They choose wrong and blatantly engage in actions consistent with that choice in front of everyone. That's what Peter refers to as *"the way of Balaam, the son of Beor"* (2:15). While the original audience would have undoubtedly understood this very well, it will do us good to revisit this account in Numbers 22–24. However, we will benefit even more by investigating the opposite of *"the way of Balaam"* as well. After all, since Peter is drawing a comparison between *"the right way"* and *"the way of Balaam,"* you and I can gain a fuller understanding and appreciation if we study both. Consider the following.

A. The Way of Balaam (Numbers 22–24):

> *Forsaking the right way, they have gone astray, having followed **the way of Balaam**, the son of Beor, who loved the wages of unrighteousness; but he received a rebuke for his own transgression, for a mute donkey, speaking with a voice of a man, restrained the madness of the prophet.* (2 Pet. 2:15-16, emp. added)

Balaam is most notably the prime example from the Old Testament used by New Testament authors Peter and Jude to explain a core motivating problem with the false teachers of their day. Being known to Balak king of Moab as a prophet/divinator, Balaam was sought to curse Israel as they camped in the plains of Moab. Much wealth and honor were promised to him; however, the Bible records that God came to Balaam and asked, *"Who are these men with you?"* (Num. 22:9). Balaam explained the situation; however, God made it very clear that he was not to go with these men nor was he to curse the Israelites (v. 12).

As we read of Balaam reporting this to the entourage Balak sent (v. 13), we are almost left with a sense that Balaam's submission and obedience to God, his resolve in the face of an offer of significant financial gain, was destined to serve as a very positive and good example throughout time. However, when the men returned a second time, many more people who were in greater positions of influence and power with them. They sought Balaam's services again, only this time, there was a promise of even greater wealth and gain (v. 17).

---

5 William Arndt et al., *A Greek-English Lexicon of the New Testament and Other Early Christian Literature* (Chicago: University of ChicagoPress, 2000), 520.
6 Arndt et al., 821.
7 Arndt et al., 1018.

Determined to Do Right

Balaam should have said something like, "I already told you 'No.' Now leave!" However, as the New Testament reveals (2 Pet. 2:15; Jude 11), Balaam's internal greed drove him to entertain the idea and even beseech God (Num. 22:19-20). God had already told him "No" once; however, He will not stop Balaam from making his own decisions. So, God commands Balaam to go but to obey only the word and speak the word God gives him.

God would not allow Balaam to curse the Israelites; however, for Balaam, the damage was already done. Everything Balaam said sounded good: *"Though Balak were to give me his house full of silver and gold, I could not do anything, either small or great, contrary to the command of the Lord my God"* (v. 18). It seemed he was going to do the right thing, but God is not only interested in doing the right thing. He's interested in His disciples doing the right thing for the right reasons, and Balaam's reasons were greed-filled and abhorrent before God.

Thus, God sends an angel with a sword to stand in the way of Balaam's donkey. The donkey can see him, but Balaam is spiritually blinded. Out of anger and because his vision is clouded with greed, Balaam strikes the donkey three times until finally, the donkey is given a voice (v. 28). In verse 31, we see a crucial moment in this narrative when the Bible says, *"Then the Lord opened the eyes of Balaam, and he saw the angel of the Lord standing in the way with his drawn sword in his hand; and he bowed all the way to the ground"* (v. 31). A man who, like a wild animal, was driven by greed is now bowing to the ground because his eyes have been opened.

Like Balaam, the false prophets Peter writes of in his second letter have hearts filled with greed and eyes continually lusting after what is forbidden (2 Pet. 2:14). There's never enough to satisfy their sinful appetite, so they continue to deceive, exploit, and entice weaker individuals, perhaps young in their faith, to follow them. They are blind and desire others to join them in their unrepentant and pitiful existence, promising the world but ensuring damnation.

B. The Right Way (Noah and Lot)

> *Forsaking the **right way**, they have gone astray, having followed the way of Balaam, the son of Beor, who loved the wages of unrighteousness.* (2 Pet. 2:15; emp. added)

To draw a stark contrast between the righteous, those who walk according to the way of truth (v. 2), and the unrighteousness of those who walk in like manner as that of the false prophets in chapter 2, Peter highlights two key individuals from the Old Testament: Noah and Lot (vv. 5, 7). Both individuals lived in challenging cultural contexts. However, both made a determined decision not to be absorbed by the sensual saturation and self-seeking normative behavior of their day.

Noah, a preacher of righteousness (v. 5), is described as one who found favor in the eyes of the Lord (Gen. 6:8), being a righteous man, blameless in his time, and one who walked with God (Gen. 6:9). He is also described as being seen by God to be the only one in his time to be righteous (Gen. 7:1). While not being a perfect man who had lacked need for the grace of God (Rom. 3:23), Noah is remembered as one who boldly proclaimed what was right and just according to God. However, he didn't simply preach the sermon. He lived the sermon in a time when *"the earth was corrupt in the sight of God, and the earth was filled with violence"* (Gen. 6:11).

It was God's observation that all those who inhabited the earth had chased after corruption and gained the outcome of such (Gen. 6:12). At first glance, all these descriptions may not stand out to the casual reader; however, upon closer examination, one can't help but see that as bad as the corruption had gotten—demonstrated by the just response of God in causing a global flood—the righteousness found in Noah was just as significant.

Like Noah, Lot lived during a time of tremendous and disgusting circumstances. By choice, Lot moved his family and herds to the valley of the Jordan, which would have included Sodom (Gen. 13:10-11). He made his selection based on the beauty of the land and the abundant resources; however, he should have investigated the moral standards by which those in this valley operated.

While Noah is described explicitly in the Scriptures in specific ways depicting the reasons he is included in 2 Peter, Lot is not. His being included by Peter seems to be based upon his actions (inviting the messengers to stay at his house and refusing to hand the men over to the men of the city) that reveal his character. When we read the account of the destruction of the cities of Sodom and Gomorrah, these actions communicate a distinction between him and the land's inhabitants. Above this, upon observing the dialogue between the Lord and Abraham in Genesis 18 regarding any righteous who dwell in Sodom, one can conclude a connection exists between them and Lot's being included by Peter as "*righteous Lot*" (2 Pet. 2:7).

It's fascinating to see the distinguishable "ways" Peter is describing. If we are determined to do right, we can't stand silently at the crossroads of Balaam and the right way. The false prophets and those who followed their way of greed and sensuality made their choice. Thus, they will end up where that road leads. However, the depth of sorrow in this passage is realized when one stops to consider these who Peter describes as "*stains and blemishes*" (2 Pet. 2:13), were once washed as white as snow, having been "*bought*" by the Master (2 Pet. 2:1) before they forsook the right way (2 Pet. 2:15). In other words, they didn't have to end up the way Peter describes them. They did so because they did not hold fast to the right way.

3) I Must Cherish the Freedom

Of all the descriptions of people that should cause the greatest sorrow, a person once having escaped the defilements of the flesh only to turn back and become entangled in the very way of life that separates them from God is at the top of the list. Poor money management skills are not good; however, it's not damnable. Not having the knowledge to work on your vehicle may be an expensive position, but it will not cost you on the day of judgment. Not being the best student, the best athlete, or even the best-looking person may be impactful to some on this earth; however, none of these matter in eternity. What does matter is whether one holds fast to the hand of Jesus in continued submission to the will of God. That's why the one who knows the joy of escape and turns back to the destitute of enslavement is the saddest of them all.

When we consider what the Bible says regarding the transition in the eternal standing of a person who obeys the way of truth, the terrible magnitude of the decision to turn back to sin weighs heavy. Think about the beautiful state of the person who has been set free from the bondage of sin.

Determined to Do Right

- Romans 5:9—"*Much more then, having now been **justified** by His blood, we shall be saved from the wrath of God through Him.*"

- Romans 5:11—"*And not only this, but we also exult in God through our Lord Jesus Christ, through whom we have now **received the reconciliation**.*"

- Ephesians 2:4-5—"*But God, being rich in mercy, because of His great love with which He loved us, even when we were dead in our transgressions, **made us alive** together with Christ.*"

- Colossians 2:13—"*When you were dead in your transgressions and the uncircumcision of your flesh, He **made you alive** together with Him, having **forgiven** us all our transgressions.*"

- 1 Corinthians 6:11—"*Such were some of you; but you were **washed**, but you were sanctified, but you were **justified** in the name of the Lord Jesus Christ and in the Spirit of our God.*"

Peter claims the ones who have, in "obedience to the truth, purified their souls" (1 Pet. 1:22), have a hopeful expectation of an "inheritance which is imperishable and undefiled and will not fade away, reserved in heaven" (1 Pet. 1:4). So, when contemplating the response of the false prophets in 2 Peter, we are left dumbfounded by their decision to chase after temporary pleasures and forfeit the favor of God. However, that's precisely what they did.

But why? Why did they turn back, like a dog returning to its vomit (2 Pet. 2:22)? Why would anyone, after having tasted the kindness of the Lord (1 Pet. 2:3), want to taste the filth of sin? The answer we find in 2 Peter 2 is what we must guard against if we are determined to do right.

In returning to verse 15, where Peter used Balaam as an example in discussing the contrary way, he said Balaam "*loved the wages of unrighteousness.*" The word *loved* is the Greek word *agapao* and is defined here as "to have high esteem for or satisfaction with something, take pleasure in."[8] It's the same word used in John 3:19 when we read, "*This is the judgment, that the Light has come into the world, and men **loved** the darkness rather than the Light, for their deeds were evil*" (emp. added). In both verses, the key is that value was assigned and actions followed.

What a person values will genuinely impact the way they live. If we value our desires above being in a right relationship with God, our lives will reflect this sad reality. Ultimately, that's what the lives of the false prophets of 2 Peter display. Their wrong thinking about the second coming of Jesus (2 Pet. 3:3-4) and their love for the wages of unrighteousness unleashed a beast of passion and self-pursuit. Their every thought was for their fulfillment and satisfaction.

CONCLUSION

There are always reasons behind behaviors. If we are determined to do right, our reasons must be worth the sacrifices we are called to make. People who desire to compete in the Summer Olympics must work hard to train their bodies and hone their skills. Often, it takes a lifetime of commitment to compete in a race that will take a few minutes or less. That's a lot of work for a short competition.

---

8 Arndt et al., 5.

However, to the determined athlete, this dedicated lifestyle is entirely worth the sacrifices because they know a great reward is at the finish line.

To those sowing to the flesh, our choice to deny the temporary benefits of sin doesn't make sense. When desire is rooted in only what this life can bring, to forgo unrestrained passions is pointless. However, for those sowing to the spirit and who genuinely know the kindness of God, nothing on this earth is worth the exchange of our souls. That's why we must determine now to do right. We must value the way of truth, hold fast to the right way, and cherish the freedom we have in Christ Jesus.

If we are determined to do right, we must value the freedom we have in Christ Jesus more than we love ungodly, temporary feelings of pleasure here on this earth. In obeying the Gospel, we have died to ourselves (Matt. 16: 24-25; Gal. 2:20). This fact means we are now living for the will of God, daily choosing to leave the old man of sin in the grave.

Applying
DETERMINED TO BE RIGHT

2 PETER 3:1-18

JOE WELLS

"Determination is the wake-up call to the human will."[1]

- Tony Robbins -

INTRODUCTION

Special Section: Synonyms of *determined*:

Adamant—sticking to an opinion, purpose, or course of action in spite of reason, arguments, or persuasion.[2]

While some may view this trait as stubbornness or inflexibility, being adamant can have many benefits. When you are determined and persistent, you are more likely to stick to your plans and see them through to completion. You are less likely to give up when faced with obstacles or setbacks and more likely to find creative solutions to problems. This determination can be beneficial in achieving long-term goals in life and when thinking about your eternal goal of heaven.

Being an adamant person can also boost self-confidence. You are less likely to be held back by fear or self-doubt and more likely to seize opportunities when they arise. This confidence can benefit personal and professional relationships, as it can help you assert yourself and communicate effectively.

Being an adamant person can also lead to more tremendous success and achievement. When you are determined and persistent, you are more likely to put in the time and effort required to excel in your pursuits. Whether it's a new hobby, a new skill in your career, or, most importantly, your spiritual growth, being an adamant person can help you achieve greater success than less persistent ones.

---

[1] "Determination Quotes: A-Z Quotes," *A*, www.azquotes.com/quotes/topics/determination.html?p=7.
[2] "Adamant," Merriam-Webster, https://www.merriam-webster.com/thesaurus/adamant.

Ultimately, being adamant is about being authentic and diligently seeking to achieve your goals while growing along the way. It is a balance between persistence and flexibility, requiring self-awareness and a willingness to learn from successes and failures. When this quality is one you possess, it's challenging to be deterred, and that is crucial for all who desire to excel in their pursuits, both in this life and in the one to come.

HISTORICAL EXAMPLE

Walt Disney is a name that is synonymous with creativity and imagination. He is the man behind one of the most successful entertainment companies in the world, and his legacy continues to inspire generations of people. But many people don't know the story behind Walt Disney's success and the determination and resolve he displayed throughout his life.

In Chicago, Illinois, Walter "Walt" Elias Disney was born on December 5, 1901. From a young age, he had a passion for drawing and spent much of his childhood creating cartoons and sketches. However, his childhood was not an easy one. His family struggled financially, and he had to work odd jobs to support himself.

Despite these challenges, Walt never gave up his dream of becoming an artist. He attended the Academy of Fine Arts in Chicago but dropped out after one year to pursue his passion for animation. He moved to California and started his animation studio, which he called Laugh-O-Gram.

The studio was initially successful, but it soon faced financial difficulties. Walt was forced to file for bankruptcy in 1923 and lost everything he had worked so hard for. However, he didn't let this setback stop him. He packed his bags and moved to Hollywood, where he started working on his next project.

Walt's next project was a cartoon character called Oswald the Lucky Rabbit. He created the character and sold it to a distributor, but he soon realized he had made a mistake. The distributor had taken ownership of the character and had hired Walt's animators to work on it without his permission.

Walt was devastated by this loss, but he didn't give up. He knew he needed to create a new character he could call his own. That character was Mickey Mouse. Walt began crafting the character of Mickey Mouse in 1927, and in 1928, "Steamboat Willie," an early cartoon equipped with voices and music, was released. Mickey Mouse and Walt Disney both quickly became sensations. The character's success allowed Walt to build his animation studio, which he called Disney Studios.

Disney Studios was a massive success, and Walt continued to create new characters and movies that captured the hearts of audiences worldwide. However, his success was not without its challenges. He faced numerous setbacks and obstacles throughout his life but never let them stop him.

Walt faced one of the most significant challenges during World War II. The war substantially impacted the entertainment industry, and Disney Studios was no exception. Walt was forced to halt production on many of his projects, and he even had to loan money to his employees to help them through tough times.

Determined to Be Right

Despite these challenges, Walt never gave up. He continued to work tirelessly on his projects and even created a series of propaganda films to support the war effort. His dedication and hard work paid off, and Disney Studios emerged from the war more robust than ever.

Ultimately, Walt Disney is remembered in history as one who displayed incredible determination and resolve throughout his life. He faced numerous challenges, but he never let them stop him. His passion for animation and storytelling inspired generations, and his legacy continues today. Walt Disney is a true inspiration to anyone who has ever faced a setback or obstacle in their life, and his story is a reminder that anything is possible with hard work and determination.[3]

There is a big difference between "looking right" and "being right." Unfortunately, in a time inundated with social media likes and portrayals of our ideal selves, this distinction gets lost easily. One is selfishly concerned with what everybody else thinks about them, and the other is concerned only with what God sees in them. One is only interested in going through the motions; the other is dedicated to making sure his character and motivation are in alignment so that his deeds are an overflow of his steadfast devotion to God. Perhaps the most significant difference between these two is one has a firm conviction that who he is before God is more important than how others perceive him. It's not that the person who desires to "be right" is not concerned with his influence on others. However, where he excels is understanding and accepting that God is the only Judge, and one day, all of humanity will be held accountable for the deeds done in the flesh (2 Cor. 5:10).

I think the character in Hollywood history that best summarizes the difference between the two is Eddy Haskell from the show *Leave It to Beaver*. With a smooth compliment, Eddy always appeared to be a nice boy in front of the adults. However, when the parents weren't within hearing distance, he schemed and talked down about people, especially the Beaver. His desire to "look right" only served his overall purpose of manipulating the perception others held regarding him and ultimately served to advance his selfishness.

In 2 Peter, the false prophets represent the Eddy Haskells of Peter's time. They are self-seeking and driven by the lusts of the flesh. They have smooth tongues that make grand promises; however, they are "*springs without water and mists driven by a storm*" (2 Pet. 2:17). With greed as their driver, they present a message both in word and example of sensuality and debauchery. Unfortunately, their "looking right" captivates the spiritually immature (2 Pet. 2:18) as they constantly dig their own grave of enslavement and corruption. However, as the letter advances to chapter 3, we clearly see that's not the way God desires His true disciples to be. Instead, God demands "being right."

Why is this the case? The answer is simple: because Jesus is coming back, and when He does, it will not be favorable for those who spent their life sowing to the lusts of the flesh as these false prophets have done. On that day, the secrets of men will be judged by God through Christ Jesus (Rom. 2:16). The stubborn and unrepentant hearts have nothing but the expectation of wrath and revelation on that dreadful day (Rom. 2:5). However, for those who have loved the way of righteousness, a crown of righteousness awaits and will be awarded on that day by the righteous Judge (2 Tim. 4:8).

---

[3] Bosley Crowther, "Walt Disney," *Encyclopedia Britannica*, 19 Jan. 2024, https://www.britannica.com/biography/Walt-Disney.

The false prophets did not accept this simple truth. Instead, they argued that because Jesus had not returned according to their expected timetable, He must not be coming, and the whole concept of a Judgment Day was a farce (2 Peter 3:3-4). By their logic, since there was no Judgment Day, there was no accountability for the way they lived, so fulfilling their lustful desires was their objective, and "looking right" served to trap the weak. Their wrong thinking about the second coming of Jesus led to evil and sinful behavior.

In chapter 3, Peter explains that he is writing, "*stirring up your sincere mind by way of reminder*" (2 Pet. 3:1), regarding what they have been taught about the coming of the Lord and what kind of people they are to be while they eagerly await His coming. He also stated this desire earlier in chapter 1:13. His desire to awaken these Christians and ensure they are not asleep serves as the springboard to the instruction we find in this chapter regarding our lives. While, as disciples of Jesus Christ, we want to be "light" and "salt" in this world (Matt. 5:13-16), we do not let the way others talk about us drive us. Instead, in allowing the way of truth to be our path and the light of the Word of God to serve as our light (Ps. 119:105), we seek to "be right" before God.

But what does that mean specifically in 2 Peter 3? Consider these five key characteristics Peter by inspiration of the Holy Spirit highlights and urges these Christians to adopt as they await the return of our Lord and Savior.

DISCUSSION

1) Be Holy in Conduct and Godliness

In Leviticus 19:2, we read of God commanding Moses to speak to the sons of Israel and say to them, "*You shall be holy, for I the Lord your God am holy.*" Having set their eyes on the promised land of Canaan, the children of God were unaware of all that awaited them. I don't mean they didn't have knowledge of the false gods of the people who were currently inhabiting the land or that they hadn't heard stories and myths of lifestyles that involved not just unrestrained sexual lust but also child sacrifice. I'm referring to the difficulty of being drawn into a similar lifestyle. The strong magnetic pull of a culture that normalized sinful behavior and the tendency of humanity to rationalize and justify why going along with the cultural context in which we find ourselves planted is captivating. It's easier, and God, knowing this to be accurate, wanted to make a bold statement regarding His expectations.

The above-quoted verse tends to focus on the first part, "*You shall be holy,*" and we will allow the text to explain what that meant for them in their time and what it meant for us in ours as well. However, if we are going to grasp the first part of that statement entirely, we must completely appreciate the second part. In Leviticus 18–20, we read no less than 25 times where God says, "*I am the Lord*" or "*I am the Lord your God.*" While having a scholarly knowledge of Hebrew and Greek is undoubtedly a blessing, it's unnecessary in this case. When a statement or a point is made this many times in a relatively short section of Scripture, it's evident that the author intends for a point to be implanted in the readers' minds and serve as the backbone for instruction.

Determined to Be Right

The concept of God being their Lord and the call for that to mean a significant amount in their lives predates the events in the book of Leviticus. We can venture back to the book of Exodus 20:1-6 when Moses was on Mt. Sinai, receiving the covenant commandments from God, and see this same point of emphasis serving as the anchor or the "Why?" behind the behavior and character God expects.

> *Then God spoke all these words, saying,* ***"I am the Lord your God****, who brought you out of the land of Egypt, out of the house of slavery. You shall have no other gods before Me. You shall not make for yourself an idol, or any likeness of what is in heaven above or on the earth beneath or in the water under the earth. You shall not worship them or serve them; for I,* ***the Lord your God****, am a jealous God, visiting the iniquity of the fathers on the children, on the third and the fourth generations of those who hate Me, but showing lovingkindness to thousands, to those who love Me and keep My commandments."* (emp. added)

In this covenant language, we see the goodness of God displayed in His rescuing the people from bondage, the kindness of God allowing a covenant relationship with Him, and the expectation of God that being in covenant with Him means their behaviors and—more importantly—their lives were to reflect their devotion to Him. However, even this event on Mt. Sinai is not the first time we see this reasoning established.

In Genesis 17: 1-8, we read,

> *Now when Abram was ninety-nine years old, the Lord appeared to Abram and said to him, "I am God Almighty; Walk before Me, and be blameless. I will establish My covenant between Me and you, And I will multiply you exceedingly." Abram fell on his face, and God talked with him, saying, "As for Me, behold, My covenant is with you, And you will be the father of a multitude of nations. No longer shall your name be called Abram, But your name shall be Abraham; For I have made you the father of a multitude of nations. I will make you exceedingly fruitful, and I will make nations of you, and kings will come forth from you. I will establish My covenant between Me and you and your descendants after you throughout their generations for an everlasting covenant,* ***to be God to you and to your descendants after you****. I will give to you and to your descendants after you, the land of your sojournings, all the land of Canaan, for an everlasting possession; and I will be their God."* (emp. added)

Even during the early period of the call of Abraham and the promises God made regarding multiplying his descendants and an extraordinary land that would be given to them, there was an anchor that held fast. That anchor served, and still does today, to cement and root the reasons God expects His people to be and act differently than the world. If we claim to be children of God, being in covenant with Him through the blood of His Son, then our lives and the motivation at our very core should reflect such.

That's the backbone of why God told Moses what He did in Exodus 20 and the children of Israel in Leviticus 18–20. In each case, the behavior God expects from His people flows from a covenant relationship with Him. That changes everything about the person. When God is your God, that means something beyond merely "going through the motions" or doing good to get good in return. That's where the hypocrites in Matthew 6 displayed a disconnect. They were doing good to get the good that man would give them. They looked the part while being displeasing to God throughout the entire exercise. That is because the true child of God practices holiness in his conduct and has godly reverence and awe because he undoubtedly understands who God is and the tremendous, overwhelming blessing that comes with being in covenant with Him.

That's why what Peter writes in 2 Peter 3:11 when he says, "*What sort of people ought you to be in holy conduct and godliness?*" is so important. Peter's not asking a question. Instead, he's making a definitive statement based upon the incredible realities of God that the false teachers are denying but remain sound and trustworthy.

- (v. 5) The Power of God Has Been Displayed in His Speaking Creation into Existence.
- (v. 6) The Judgment of God Has Been Realized with the Onset of the Flood.
- (v. 9) The Patience of God Remains Strong in That He Desires All to Come to Repentance.
- (v. 10) The Promise of God Regarding the Day of the Lord is Going to Place Both His Power and Judgment on Display Once Again.

Since this is certain and the evidence is plain, the one who truly loves and reveres Him will intentionally and deliberately respond to reflect this conviction.

"*Holy conduct*" means a lifestyle that is "pure, perfect, worthy of God."[4] "*Godliness*" encompasses an "awesome respect accorded to God, devoutness, piety, godliness."[5] Both entail purpose, intent, determination, and sacrifice. At their core, these are not merely going through the motions of doing right. Even hypocrites can "do right." However, if these qualities and the display of such are to be, one must be right.

2) Be Looking and Hastening for the Day

Expectations influence preparations. Think about it. If you know you're going on a car trip tomorrow with the family, you will spend time preparing for that trip. If you expect it to be cold, you will prepare accordingly. If you're going to stay in the mountains, it wouldn't make much sense to pack for the beach. What you expect influences the preparations you make.

Now consider what your life is like when you live every day "*looking for*," "to give thought to something that is viewed as lying in the future, wait for, look for, expect"[6], and "*hastening for*" "to cause something to happen or come into being by exercising special effort,"[7] the day of the Lord's return. For starters, don't think "*looking*" and "*hastening*" for the day of the Lord's return means that you stand outside looking up at the sky all the time just trying to catch the first glimpse of the smoke from the fire (2 Thess. 1:7). That would be rather pointless because the description of this day coming as a "*thief in the night*" emphasizes the surprise and unawareness each will have. God doesn't want your eyes physically peering off into the distance, paralyzed by your longing. Instead, He demands your hands be placed on the plow with eyes on the row ahead of you and planting the seed of the Word of God in those you meet daily. He wants you and I to be busy watering and caring for the growth of those developing a faith in the Lord.

---

4 Arndt et al., 11.
5 Arndt et al., 412.
6 Arndt et al., 877.
7 Arndt et al., 938.

Determined to Be Right

Instead of a paralyzed gaze, Peter calls these Christians to live in a way that demonstrates a strong conviction and a bold proclamation that Jesus will return. This will impact everything from our attendance and participation in worship to our relationships within our marriages and with our children. The people with whom we work, see at the gym, or even go hunting should be able to see our expectations regarding the day of the Lord. In short, when we live with a *"looking"* and *"hastening"* for the coming of the day of God, there will be a significant, noticeable difference in our lives.

3) Be Diligent to be Found in Peace, Spotless, and Blameless

In 2 Peter, diligent or diligence is used multiple times.

- 1:5—*"Now for this very reason also, applying all **diligence**, in your faith supply moral excellence, and in your moral excellence, knowledge."*

- 1:10—*"Therefore, brethren, be all the more **diligent** to make certain about His calling and choosing you; for as long as you practice these things, you will never stumble."*

- 1:15—*"And I will also be **diligent** that at any time after my departure you will be able to call these things to mind."*

- 3:14—*"Therefore, beloved, since you look for these things, be **diligent** to be found by Him in peace, spotless and blameless."*

In each occasion, the emphasis behind the word involves being "especially conscientious in discharging an obligation, be zealous/eager, take pains, make every effort, be conscientious."[8] With conscientious effort being such a pivotal component, it should hit home that the determination required to be right before God will not happen by chance. That doesn't mean I'm advocating for any theory or teaching that claims to be able to earn our way into the category of "right" before God. However, I want to impress upon each of you that your relationship with God can't coast or exist passively and be pleasing to Him. You must pursue Him and pursue a life that aligns with what He expects, which aligns with His character. That's why in 2 Peter 1:5-7, Peter emphasizes that we must be determined to devote ourselves to continual growth in the spiritual virtues God sets forth.

In chapter 3, Peter specifically mentions three essential character traits that must be our pursuit. He does so while emphasizing the earnest effort and intention necessary. He admonishes the Christians to be determined to be found on the day of visitation…

1) In Peace (εἰρήνη, *eirḗnē*)

When the day of the Lord is upon us, Jesus appears with His mighty angels in flaming fire, *"dealing out retribution to those who do not know God and to those who do not obey the gospel of our Lord Jesus"* (2 Thess. 1:8), the only thing that will matter is whether you are at war with God or not. It might sound strange to look at one's relationship with God in these terms; however, that's precisely what the Scriptures say regarding our condition when unforgiven sin stains our souls (Rom. 5:8-10).

---

8 Arndt et al., 939.

As enemies of God, we desperately need forgiveness and justification that only God extends through the Gospel (Eph. 6:15). If we neglect such salvation, the abundance of tears poured forth on Judgment Day won't have the power to change our eternal state. However, if we embrace salvation in this life, as the Christians whom Peter is writing have (2 Pet. 1:1), peace ("a state of concord, harmony"[9]) will be ours. This is not a peace that results from an inner acceptance of ourselves or our circumstances. It's not peace that results from all the personal relationships in our lives being in harmony. Instead, the peace described here explicitly refers to the relationship between God and the individual sinner. This peace is only possible because God offers it and delivers it to the One who is the Prince of Peace, Jesus Christ (Isa. 9:6).

2) Spotless (ἄσπιλος, *áspilos*)

As a stark contrast to the false prophets described by Peter as "stains and blemishes" (2 Pet. 2:13), he further elaborates on the condition in which they are to be found upon the day of the Lord's appearance. Like a dirty garment needing to be cleansed by water and soap, we—because of our sins—have the same problem the children of God had in the day of the prophet Jeremiah when we wrote, "'*Although you wash yourself with lye and use much soap, the* **stain** *of your iniquity is before Me,' declares the Lord God*" (Jer. 2:22, emp. added). This condition puts us at odds with God and in alignment with those who live in rebellion.

As a comparison, in 1 Peter 1 Peter uses the word "*spotless*" to describe the nature of Jesus regarding His perfection and sacrifice when he wrote,

> *If you address as Father the One who impartially judges according to each one's work, conduct yourselves in fear during the time of your stay on earth; knowing that you were not redeemed with perishable things like silver or gold from your futile way of life inherited from your forefathers, but with precious blood, as of a lamb unblemished and* **spotless**, *the blood of Christ.* (1 Pet. 1:17-19, emp. added)

In this usage, we see the emphatic point being made that those who chose to live according to sensuality and greed, as the false prophets of 2 Peter, will find themselves outside of purification on the day recompense is heaped upon them. Regardless of how pleasing their words may be and how enticing their promises may seem, their conduct demonstrates that they live outside of the character and nature of Jesus Christ. Thus, they are as opposite as they can be to what God has shown He desires from His followers through the life of Jesus Christ.

3) Blameless (ἀμώμητος, *amṓmētos*)

If you've ever built anything, you know blemishes exist. You know where the measurements were a 1/16th of an inch off or where the glue was pressed out between the joints and dried. If a board was twisted a little or had a bow in it and you had to make last-minute adjustments, that might not have been the best, but they worked. Any of us who have made anything knows this reality. Blemishes just seem to be a part of crafting something.

---

9 Arndt et al., 287.

Determined to Be Right

The blemishes sometimes add character or make one handcrafted piece unique and special. You realize this immediately when you walk through an antique store. Taking a quick trip through history, when many tools and pieces of furniture were handmade, reveals that imperfections will naturally be a part of the product when human hands are involved.

While that may be true when crafting items, it's also true when it comes to matters of a spiritual nature. Romans 3:23 makes it very clear that *"all have sinned and fall short of the glory of God,"* which indicates that spiritual blemishes will happen when it's left up to us as people. If that weren't true, we would not need Jesus. If we could live without spiritual blemishes, repentance, forgiveness, and redemption would be topics we wouldn't need to study and take personally. However, that's not the case. We need to hear and learn about these crucial topics because we can't save ourselves from our sins.

When Peter instructs the Christians to be found *"blameless,"* he's telling them to be people who are "without fault and therefore morally blameless."[10] In light of this charge, a tremendous and seemingly impassable mountain seems to be before us. Many of those who read this will think to themselves, "I can never be blameless!" Of your own accord, you absolutely can't. That's why we need the blood of Jesus to cleanse us. However, that doesn't mean we can't set our aim to live morally pure lives. That's the charge we see in Leviticus 18–20. The Israelites are called to live differently than those in the land of Canaan. We see the same thing in Peter's first letter to these Christians in 1 Peter 1:14-15. Even with you set your aim to live a morally pure life, you will fail. The great news is that it was never about your getting it all right anyway. It's always been about God making you blameless, without blemish, through the Gospel of Jesus Christ.

4) Be on Guard

Imagine your family being in an extremely crowded environment, much like you've seen in New York City on New Year's Eve. Everywhere you turn, with each move, you bump into someone. You can barely move, and when you can, you want your family to move as a unit because you know of the dangers that persist if you're separated or worse, there's a "bad guy" who is looking for ways to grab children in such an environment and disappear with them.

If you're like me, you are on heightened alert. You're constantly looking around and seeing if dangers exist or trying to find ways to maneuver your family through the crowd in the best way possible. You're also insistent on your family holding hands or grabbing onto one another's shirt/jacket and holding on. You need each family member to keep eyes on one another because the task is too great for one person to see everything and make the decisions necessary to navigate such a task.

If you've ever been in such an environment or can vividly imagine a situation as you read this, your blood pressure is probably increasing just a bit. You may even feel slightly uncomfortable as your nerves strike you more. Your breathing rate may have even increased as you began imagining some of the "what ifs" that a vivid illustration stirs. In this case, that's a good thing because I want you

---

10 Arndt et al., 56.

to relate to what it means to be on guard as Peter instructed the Christians in 2 Peter 3:17, "*You therefore, beloved, knowing this beforehand, **be on your guard** so that you are not carried away by the error of unprincipled men and fall from your own steadfastness*" (emp. added).

A heightened sense, keen awareness, a greater attention to detail, a determination to keep something or someone from being taken from you or from you losing it yourself, all these descriptions and human responses are wrapped into being on guard. While many of us are completely capable of associating these to our response to a crowded environment and our family, do we also understand the relation of this to our faith? Do we know the potential dangers that linger around the corners regarding our faith?

After identifying the false prophets—their teaching, techniques, and motivations—Peter calls to arms the determination and alertness of these Christians. He doesn't want them to fall away into the same mire; however, Peter understands, and he wants them to accept that if they are going to remain faithful in the face of such falsity, they must, just like we must, be alert, be aware, and be adamant about avoiding such threatening teaching and be grounded in the truth of God's Word as delivered by men inspired by the Holy Spirit (2 Pet. 1:20-21).

5) Grow in Grace and Knowledge

The best way to combat false teaching that seeks to ensnare us is to continually grow in the grace and knowledge of our Lord and Savior, Jesus Christ. Stagnation opens the door to considering all sorts of theories and beliefs, not having the drive nor the working knowledge that is sharp and keen to combat such. That's why Biblical illiteracy is such a dangerous condition. It's not only that one's faith grows stale. It's that the immaturity and lack of pursuit of a closer relationship with Jesus leaves us vulnerable to the attacks of Satan.

Think about your physical health. Lousy health will eventually take hold if you're not actively pursuing good health. A person who continues exercising, getting the right amount of sleep, drinking the right amount of water, and avoiding abundant sugar and fatty foods will move toward better health. His heart will get stronger, blood sugar will be regulated, and cholesterol will be kept in check. However, the opposite is true of the person who sits around, doesn't exercise, and has a "eat whatever I want" diet. While not necessarily actively pursuing early health problems, that person has not actively pursued better health.

The same applies when it comes to our spiritual well-being. It's like riding a bicycle. If you're moving forward, you stay up on the bike. The second you stop, it's much more challenging to balance and you fall off. If we aren't actively pursuing better spiritual health, by default we will find spiritual decline. Peter is admonishing them, as he did in 2 Peter 1:5-8, to determine to be right by growing, continually pushing forward, in the grace, the divine favor extended to people by God through Jesus Christ (2 Pet. 1:2), and knowledge, the unfiltered true knowledge, of our Lord and Savior Jesus Christ.

CONCLUSION

There is a fixed chasm between the person who merely wants to "look right" and the one who wants to "be right." One is self-seeking, and the other is rooted in integrity. "Looking right" is interested in pleasing man, while "being right" is focused on consistency regardless of whether men are pleased.

The imagery of those spoken of in Matthew 6 rises to the top when I think of the vast difference between these two. The hypocrites do good; however, it's all a show. They give so others will honor them (Matt. 6:2). They pray and want to make sure others see them (Matt. 6:5). The hypocrites fast. Still, they do so to be noticed by men (Matt. 6:16). In all these examples, the emphasis is placed on the reward man gives versus the much better reward God wants to give them. The problem is there's no room for God's reward in their lives.

When you and I think about being determined to be right, we're talking about your inner man, who you are at the core. Your motivations are being targeted. Your reasons for doing what you do are being questioned. While this may be uncomfortable, the answers you give when dealing with both reveal whether you are about "looking right" or "being right." God is the only One you need to be concerned with pleasing. He alone sets the standard in the lives of those who want to be His people. There is no room for a divided spirit in the ranks of Jesus Christ, so we must have a convicted determination to be the people He desires.

Applying

DETERMINED TO STAND

JUDE 1:1-25

JOE WELLS

"The difference between men is in energy, in the strong will, in the settled purpose and in the invincible determination."[1]

- Vince Lombardi -

INTRODUCTION

Special Section: Synonyms of *determined*:

Tenacious—persistent in maintaining, adhering to, or seeking something valued or desired.[2]

Tenacity, often associated with perseverance, determination, and resilience, plays a crucial role in shaping an individual's success and ability to overcome challenges. A tenacious person exhibits unwavering persistence in the face of adversity, possesses a strong sense of purpose, and refuses to be deterred by obstacles.

At the core of being tenacious lies an unyielding determination to achieve one's goals, regardless of the difficulties encountered. This persistence is fueled by a deep passion and commitment toward a particular objective, driving the individual to push through setbacks. Self-discipline is also a critical characteristic of tenacious people, often setting clear and actionable plans to achieve their aspirations. They are willing to work hard, understanding that success rarely comes easy.

Furthermore, tenacity is closely intertwined with resilience, the ability to bounce back from failures

---

1 Vince Lombardi Quotes," BrainyQuote.com. BrainyMedia Inc, 2024, 10 February 2024, https://www.brainyquote.com/quotes/vince_lombardi_786504.

2 "Tenacious," *Merriam-Webster*, https://www.merriam-webster.com/dictionary/tenacious.

and setbacks more robust than before. A tenacious person views challenges as stepping stones towards growth, using each setback as a valuable lesson to improve and refine their approach. This resilience enables them to stay focused on their goals, even when faced with adversity, criticism, or rejection.

A tenacious person also possesses a strong sense of grit, a combination of passion and perseverance over the long haul. Grit drives individuals to stay committed to their goals, even when the initial excitement fades, or progress seems slow. It is the ability to maintain momentum, day in and day out, working steadily towards the desired outcome. Success is not achieved overnight; tenacious people know it results from consistent effort and dedication.

With all these qualities of a tenacious person in mind, consider their value when it comes to our walk with God. When faced with challenges or obstacles, having tenacity allows individuals to persevere and remain steadfast in their faith. This resilience enables believers to weather difficult times, trusting in God's plan and continuing to seek His guidance and support. Furthermore, tenacity fosters a deep commitment and dedication to living out one's faith daily, even when circumstances may be discouraging.

HISTORICAL EXAMPLE:

Born on June 20, 1925, in Kingston, Texas, Audie Murphy's upbringing was marked by poverty and hardship. Raised in a large family, he found himself thrust into the responsibilities of adulthood at a young age following his father's abandonment and his mother's death. Despite these challenges, Murphy's indomitable spirit and unyielding determination remained undeterred. When war engulfed the world in the 1940s, he saw an opportunity to escape the confines of his circumstances and make a difference.

Enlisting in the United States Army at the age of 17, Audie Murphy embarked on a journey defining his legacy. His unwavering determination became evident from the moment he set foot on the battlefield. Assigned to the 3rd Infantry Division, Murphy found himself in the thick of combat in North Africa, Sicily, Italy, and eventually, France.

Murphy's courage and determination were put to the ultimate test during the Allied invasion of Italy. He led his men with unwavering resolve in the face of withering enemy fire, earning a battlefield commission and a reputation for fearlessness. Despite being wounded multiple times, Murphy refused to yield, pressing forward with an iron will that inspired those around him.

However, his actions in France would etch his name in military history. On January 26, 1945, near the village of Holtzwihr, Audie Murphy's valor reached its zenith. Faced with overwhelming German opposition, his company commander ordered a retreat. But Murphy, refusing to abandon his comrades, single-handedly held off an entire company of German soldiers for over an hour, directing artillery fire with a field telephone and mounting a desperate defense.

Determined to Stand

With bullets flying and shells exploding around him, Audie Murphy's determination never wavered. Armed with little more than a rifle and a handful of grenades, he repelled wave after wave of enemy attacks, inflicting heavy casualties and buying precious time for his fellow soldiers to regroup. Despite sustaining severe injuries, including wounds to his leg, Murphy refused to surrender, fighting on until reinforcements arrived.

For his extraordinary bravery and unwavering determination in the face of overwhelming odds, Audie Murphy was awarded the Medal of Honor, the highest military decoration awarded by the United States government. He demonstrated unparalleled determination and bravery throughout his military career, earning numerous awards and decorations, including the Distinguished Service Cross, two Silver Stars, and three Purple Hearts. His exploits made him a symbol of American resilience and grit, inspiring countless soldiers to rise above adversity and face their challenges with courage and determination.[3,4]

Catherine Susan "Kitty" Genovese was born in Brooklyn, New York, on July 7, 1935, to Vincent and Rachel Genovese. Kitty was a standout student at Prospect Heights High School. She was the eldest of five siblings and was known for her wit and humor. After witnessing a murder, her family relocated to New Canaan, Connecticut, but Kitty remained in New York City.

In the early morning hours of March 13, 1964, around 2:30 a.m., Kitty Genovese was making her way home from work when she encountered Winston Moseley, armed with a knife. Fleeing toward her apartment building, she was caught by the assailant who stabbed her while she cried for help. Despite her severe injuries, Genovese managed to crawl to the rear of her apartment building, out of sight of potential witnesses. However, ten minutes later, Moseley returned and subjected her to further violence. Genovese would succumb to her injuries en route to the hospital.

The New York Times initially reported that 37 people watched and did not intervene, sparking public outrage. While there is evidence that The Times got the details wrong, there were two neighbors who were there and did not act. One of those was named Karl Ross.

Intoxicated that night, Ross heard noises and, after deliberating, cracked open his door to investigate. He saw Genovese lying on the ground, still alive and attempting to speak, and Moseley stabbing her. He shut the door and called a friend to ask what to do. The friend said not to get involved.

Ross eventually climbed out his window and went to a neighbor's apartment. He called the police after hearing Sophie Farrar, the neighbor who found Kitty, call for someone to do so. Ross' explanation, "I didn't want to get involved," became the pivotal claim of what would later become known as the Bystander Effect—where individuals are less likely to help in a group setting.[5]

Psychologists Latané and Darley's research shed light on this phenomenon, attributing it to diffusion of responsibility. Their studies found that the more people present when distress occurs,

---

3 Evan Andrews, "WWII Hero Audie Murphy: 'How Come I'm Not Dead?'" *History.Com*, 23 Jan. 2015, www.history.com/news/audie-murphys-world-war-ii-heroics-70-years-ago.
4 Richard L Rodgers, "Biography," *Audie Murphy Research Foundation*, 1996, www.audiemurphy.com/biography.htm.
5 Editors, History.com, "Kitty Genovese—Case, Murder, and Bystander," History.Com, 5 Jan. 2018, www.history.com/topics/crime/kitty-genovese.

the less likely anyone is to act to intervene. Of course, this study was initiated by the thought that so many of Genovese's neighbors heard the attack and did not get involved, much like Ross claimed. While the initial facts regarding the number of witnesses are disputed, the studies that have surfaced since have shown there may be something to the Bystander Effect.

Psychologists who have studied this effect claim three psychological factors are thought to facilitate bystander apathy. They are the feeling of having less responsibility when more bystanders are present (*diffusion of responsibility*), the fear of unfavorable public judgment when helping (*evaluation apprehension*), and the belief that because no one else is helping, the situation is not an emergency (*pluralistic ignorance*).[6] Unfortunately, because of fear and a lack of personal responsibility, many dangers go unchecked by onlookers, and many needs go unmet by those who can help. Groupthink influences actions, and the consequences of such can haunt those who stood by while people got hurt, remained hungry, or froze in a homeless condition.

When we take the lessons learned from the Kitty Genovese murder and couple them with the studies done to try and identify why people could act but do not, a picture is painted of human hesitation. When we apply this to the instruction given in the book of Jude 3, admonishing the Christians to "*contend earnestly for the faith*," the amplification of the urgent charge to appropriately defend and confront those who threaten the goodness and simplicity of the Gospel of Jesus Christ can introspectively be felt by all. If these Christians were aware, alert, and attentive to the "*certain persons*" of verse 4, people who have already infiltrated their ranks as they pretend to be part of the family of God, Jude's instruction would not be necessary.

The problem is, just like Karl Ross in the Genovese case, too many Christians see the problem and close their doors, not wanting to get involved. The dreadful thinking that someone else will deal with the false teachers who are described as "*ungodly persons who turn the grace of our God into licentiousness and deny our only Master and Lord, Jesus Christ*" (v. 4) paralyzes many otherwise dedicated followers of Jesus. Thoughts about what other people might say about them if they do stand for the truth cause tremendous angst and fear take over, convincing the Christian that at least in doing and saying nothing, they don't run the risk of doing or saying the wrong thing. While doubting the severity of the situation, many believe that if it were really that urgent to put a stop to the influence of those who are "*grumblers, finding fault, following after their own lusts*" who "*speak arrogantly, flattering people for the sake of gaining an advantage*" (v. 16), someone in a leadership position would do it. However, that's not what Jude calls these Christians to think or do.

Being determined to take a stand can be terrifying to many. Reading the above paragraph might make you very uncomfortable, realizing you have always thought those same things as you stayed silent. Let me put your mind at ease, "*contending earnestly for the faith*" does not mean you have to be "big and bad" in your Christianity. It's not about looking for a fight or living life confrontationally, always being suspicious of everyone who teaches or preaches God's Word. It requires you to study the Word of God so you can tell when something is advocated or taught that does not follow what God says (2 Tim. 2:14-19). When someone teaches error, with great humility and the intent to help a brother, you pull him aside and point him to a fuller, more complete understanding of God's Word just as Priscilla and Aquila did for Apollos (Acts 18:23-

---

[6] Ruud Hortensius and Beatrice de Gelder, "From Empathy to Apathy: The Bystander Effect Revisited," *Current Directions in Psychological Science* Vol. 27,4 (2018): 249-256.

28). However, that's not all *"contending earnestly"* entails. It also means living a merciful lifestyle as one who has received mercy from God (Jude 21-23). Don't be quick to "write them off" as a lost cause. Be patient with them, as you want others to be with you.

Some are not interested in adhering to the Word of God. Like those in the book of Jude, they are *"ones who cause divisions, worldly-minded, devoid of the Spirit"* (v. 19). Unfortunately, those who will not cease spitting on God and His Word require a firm rebuke, one that will prayerfully cause them to repent as they reconsider their stance before God. However, even if they do not repent, there will be times when the doctrine of the Gospel of Jesus Christ must be defended from evil attacks, even at the expense of friendships, acquaintances, and possibly your reputation. Perhaps that's why Jude wrote to the Christians, appealing to them to *"contend earnestly for the faith."* They would already be doing it if it were easy, but it's not. It's costly but necessary.

The Gospel is still the greatest answer to man's most dire need: forgiveness from sin. It's here we read and learn of the mercy of God, revealed through His Son Jesus. Herein, a desperate man, sin-sick in his very soul, finds hope and direction out of the mire of lost condition. It's not a neutral act when people twist and distort the Word of God to their own ends. Instead, it's an attempt to defame God and His glorious name. You would stand up for your loved ones if someone tried to do that. How much more should you stand up for the God of the faith that has been *"once for all handed down to the saints"* (v. 3)?

DISCUSSION

1) Taking a Stand Involves Risks

Satan operates very well in the shadows of fear. Fear of the unknown, of the "what-ifs," and of the stories heard regarding what happened to other people is the disguise Satan uses to manipulate and stagnate disciples of Jesus Christ. He doesn't have to tempt you to commit a "big" overt sin. Although, that seems to be what feeds him. He only must convince you that the risks are not worth action. Satan wants you to allow the possibilities of difficulties to dissuade you from advancing the cause of Christ. He doesn't care if you and I claim to be disciples as long as we are stuck in fear and do nothing.

In the Old Testament, we read of dedicated men and women who refused to allow the risks to silence them. Daniel refused to stop praying to God even when the decree from Darius went forth, knowing that being cast into the den of lions was the risk for doing so (Dan. 6:4-10). Esther, knowing that to come into the inner court of the king without being summoned could result in death, bravely stood for the people of God as she requested the king's and Haman's presence at a banquet she would host (Est. 5:11; 6:4). Shadrach, Meshach, and Abednego risked being thrown into the furnace of blazing fire as they refused to bow when the music played (Dan. 3:8-18). Moses risked his own life when returning to Pharaoh, demanding the release of the large slave force of the Egyptians. As a result, the labor and toil of the Israelites increased, and Moses received criticism and isolation from those hurting even more (Ex. 5). David faced the giant, knowing the risk of losing life and freedom for his people (1 Sam. 17). Noah risked ridicule from those around him as he showed tremendous trust in God and His word regarding the pending flood (Heb. 11:7).

The New Testament is also filled with examples of the disciples of Jesus boldly standing in the face of immense risks. In Acts 7, we read of the death of a man named Stephen, a disciple of Jesus Christ and one known as having *"good reputation, full of the Spirit and of wisdom"* (Acts 6:3). He was a man described as being *"full of faith and of the Holy Spirit"* (Acts 6:5), "grace and power" (Acts 6:8), and one who was not hiding, "performing great wonders and signs among the people" (Acts 6:8). Even in the face of the angry mob who would eventually murder him, he continued proclaiming the goodness of God through Jesus. Peter and John refused to stop spreading the good news of Jesus Christ, risking imprisonment and further punishment (Acts 4:18-21). Paul embraced the excruciating risks to stand up for Jesus and advance His cause (2 Cor. 6:3-10). John realized the danger of standing for Jesus as he was exiled to the island of Patmos (Rev. 1:9). Then there are the martyrs of Revelation 6:9-11, those who *"had been slain because of the Word of God, and because of the testimony which they had maintained."*

How can one read these and not be moved in motivation?

The cold truth is there are always risks involved when you are determined to stand for something, regardless of what it is. Standing requires conviction, commitment, and an unwavering dedication to a cause or a side. Anytime you are that determined, others who do not see it the way you do and disagree with your conclusions will be unsettled at least and vengeful at worst. Those so determined to take a stand will face embarrassment as they are isolated, slandered, gossiped about, and publicly or privately ridiculed. Those who have come before us have faced years of imprisonment and even death for standing for Jesus Christ and the Word of God. Their examples serve as focusing reminders that to suffer for the sake of advancing the Kingdom of God is honorable and desirable and places you in a more intimate relationship with Jesus, as He is the most outstanding example of facing deadly risks for the sake of the worthy cause of salvation (1 Pet. 2:21-24).

2) Taking a Stand Involves Rewards

What thought comes to mind when reading Hebrews 11 and the names listed therein? Perhaps, for you, it's the bravery each displayed as their belief in God was coupled with faithful action, thus defining what true Biblical faith is. Others may think of the difficulty each faced and ponder whether they would have been able to do the same. I stop in my tracks and am humbled when I read, *"They were stoned, they were sawn in two, they were tempted, they were put to death with the sword; they went about in sheepskins, in goatskins, being destitute, afflicted, ill-treated (men of whom the world was not worthy), wandering in deserts and mountains and caves and holes in the ground"* (Heb. 11:37-38). I am challenged because I internally ask myself if I would do the same and what my breaking point would be. I am drawn into introspection as I consider the risks involved and the cost paid. Then I'm brought back to the grounding principle on which they all acted, as pointed out in Hebrews 11:16, *"But as it is, they desire a better country, that is, a heavenly one."*

The rewards of standing for the Lord and the faith *"which was once for all handed down to the saints"* (Jude 3) far surpass any consequences that may present themselves due to the risks involved. This truth is amplified when we reflect on the brevity of our lives on this present earth. When put into the proper perspective as James 4:14 does, and we accept the temporariness of our situation, we are also, just like David, drawn to begging God to make us know our end, the extent of our days, and just how transient we are on this present earth. As David reflected, so do we, "*Behold, You have made my days as handbreadths, and my lifetime as nothing in Your sight. Surely every man at his best is a mere breath*" (Ps. 39:5). As we personalize the brief nature of our time in this flesh, and we consider sacrificing whatever is required in the short term for eternity of reward, the "trade-off" is incomparable (Rom. 8:18).

What are these rewards?

For starters, in looking at Jude, we see that those who are determined to stand and "*contend earnestly for the faith*" (Jude 3) are in the category of people who have "*mercy*," "*peace*," and "*love*" multiplied to them. "*Mercy*" spoken of here is from God and is the "kindness or concern expressed for someone in need."[7] "*Peace*" is also rooted in God and means "a state of well-being."[8] "*Love*" is the word *agápē* and means "the quality of warm regard for and interest in another."[9] All of these are multiplied or increased for those who are "*called*," "*beloved*," and "*kept for Jesus Christ*" (Jude 1).

Other rewards addressed explicitly in the book of Jude are found at the end of the letter. In verse 21, we read, "*the mercy of our Lord Jesus Christ to eternal life.*" This sweet, promised reward resulted from God forgiving our sins through His Son Jesus. The hope we have in His return is to anchor and compel us to continue "*building*" ourselves up in the faith, "*praying*" in the Holy Spirit, and "*waiting anxiously*" with great expectations (Jude 20-21). Expanding further on the rewards, Jude tells these Christians that in so standing for the Lord and "*contending for the faith*," God is able to "*keep you from stumbling, and to make you stand in the presence of His glory blameless with great joy*" (v. 24). Because of the forgiveness He extends to those who endure the risks involved with following Him, having fully and continually submitted to the very Gospel they preach to others, God promises to the determined to endure, tremendous and sure rewards.

3) Taking a Stand Involves Resolve

It has been said, "If you want to make everybody happy, don't be a leader. Sell ice cream." While there is debate as to credit former Apple founder Steve Jobs or former University of Alabama head coach Nick Saban with this quote, the truth of the statement is not impacted. When you stick your neck out for a person, a purpose, or a pursuit, there will be those who stand ready to chop it off. Criticism is in no short supply for those who stand up and be leaders.

There will always be challengers who are contentious and contrary. Knocking someone down who dares to be different and go against the cultural norm seems to be a reality we live with daily. That's why so many Christians either stay seated or, worse, bow down to the idols presented by those who distort and blaspheme the excellent name and nature of God. They would rather be liked by making people happy, than standing and leading. However, that's not you. That's not the drive and motivation of those determined to be pleasing to God.

---

7 William Arndt et al., *A Greek-English Lexicon of the New Testament and Other Early Christian Literature* (Chicago: University of Chicago Press, 2000), 316.
8 Arndt et al., 287.
9 Arndt et al., 6.

Standing requires a deep-rooted resolve that is unwavering and unbending. It begins with an unapologetic conviction that what you are standing for is truth; it matters and is desperately needed by the world around you. In our case, for the consideration of this book, Jude makes it very clear that *"the faith"* is valuable and worth *"contending earnestly"* for, meaning it's worth the intense effort required to do so. It is not forfeited to anyone, especially the *"certain persons"* of Jude 4.

Therefore, this task takes great resolve, a "fixity of purpose.[10]" But a resolve to do what? Where are we to focus our resolve? Consider the following three areas.

A. Resolve to Teach the Faith

Biblical illiteracy is a significant problem in many homes and individual lives. Far too many people who profess to be followers of Jesus have dusty Bibles, lacking the natural oils from their fingers marking the well-worn pages. Even in our day, where Bibles are readily available through technology, some even being read to you, we still find a way to remain lacking. This doesn't mean that everyone who is a disciple of Jesus Christ is this way; however, in my time in ministry with adults and teens alike, I have found that knowledge of the Word of God is very surface as we are well positioned to know what the preacher says in his sermon, but not necessarily what God says in His Word. We can point fingers as to why this is the case; however, at the end of the day, the result of a lack of knowledge will be the same for us as it was for the children of God during the days of Hosea when the prophet wrote regarding God's reflection on His people,

> *My people are destroyed for lack of knowledge.*
> *Because you have rejected knowledge,*
> *I also will reject you from being My priest.*
> *Since you have forgotten the law of your God,*
> *I also will forget your children.* (Hos. 4:6)

Let it never be repeated that *"there arose a generation after them who did not know the Lord"* (Judg. 2:10). If there ever is, each preceding generation—no matter what level of faithfulness they claimed—failed to pass along the faith.

There are no bystanders in this task. It is not someone else's responsibility. It's yours, and it's mine. Every disciple of Jesus Christ must learn from the church in Thessalonica. We must be like those from whom *"the word of the Lord has sounded forth"* (1 Thess. 1:8). Like Timothy's grandmother Lois and his mother Eunice, we must teach the faith to our families (2 Tim. 1:5). With the aim of glorifying God and leading others to a close walk with Him, we must strive to be the faithful men of 2 Timothy 2:2 who teach others. We must begin with the elementary principles of the Scriptures; however, we must move to the more mature teachings of the Word (Heb. 6:1).

With a resolve to teach the faith, not only will we be forced to study more deeply the Word ourselves, but we will also help ensure our loved ones, our neighbors, and our fellow Christians

---

10 "Resolve," *Merriam-Webster*, https://www.merriam-webster.com/dictionary/resolve.

aren't swept away by false teachers who twist and distort the Scriptures to their end. If they dreadfully do turn their backs, it won't be because they didn't know the truth. Sadly, it will be because they selfishly pursued their desires or even the comforts of personal relationships.

We must go out of our way, whatever the cost may be to us or our resources, to teach the faith because, as we read in 2 Timothy 3:16, *"All Scripture is inspired by God and profitable for teaching, for reproof, for correction, for training in righteousness: so that the man of God may be adequate, equipped for every good work."* As Jesus did in John 8, we must understand and teach others that freedom is not found in man's conclusions but rather in continuing in the Word (vv. 31-32).

B. Resolve to Live the Faith

Perhaps one of the biggest draws of Christianity for those who are immature or not Christians at all is the unmerited kindness disciples of Jesus show every day. From stocking food pantries, serving the homeless, clothing the needy, caring for widows in nursing homes, visiting the orphans in children's homes, collecting furniture for people who've lost everything in house fires, knitting blankets for cancer patients, sewing teddy bears for those in the children's hospital, working on a neighbor's car, building a handicap ramp at the home of someone in a wheelchair, going grocery shopping for an elderly neighbor, babysitting for a young married couple who never gets to go out on a date, and countless other service-oriented exercises, Christians have a remarkable impact on those who do not know Jesus by showing Him to them in the way they live and serve. Jesus did say it best when He said,

> *You are the salt of the earth; but if the salt has become tasteless, how can it be made salty again? It is no longer good for anything, except to be thrown out and trampled under foot by men. You are the light of the world. A city set on a hill cannot be hidden; nor does anyone light a lamp and put it under a basket, but on the lampstand, and it gives light to all who are in the house. Let your light shine before men in such a way that they may see your good works, and glorify your Father who is in heaven.* (Matt. 5:13-16)

This kindness, or *"mercy,"* as Jude puts it in verses 22-23, is not only to be shown to those who look favorably on Jesus and the Word of God. Regardless of their current view of Christianity, the disciple of Jesus is resolved to live the faith before all because he knows a day of judgment is coming. He wants even those who twist and distort the Word of God for their dishonest gain to glorify God on the day of visitation. As Peter wrote concerning those who would wish to cause Christians harm, we must keep our *"behavior excellent among the Gentiles, so that in the thing in which they slander you as evildoers, they may because of your good deed, as they observe them, glorify God in the day of visitation"* (1 Pet. 2:12).

That's because, as a Christian, your life is all about bringing honor and glory to God, both in your short stay on this earth and in eternity. You've died to yourself and are determined to stay behind the cross of Christ (Gal. 2:20). You want others to do the same, not residing on the receiving end of the wrath of God when Jesus returns (2 Thess. 1:7-8). Therefore, you must be resolved to show them the faith is not lip service meant to make you appear suitable but is a life-changing message that infiltrates your entire being. It's transforming your mind, energizing your actions, and softening your heart to those who desperately need us who have received mercy from God through Jesus to pour forth mercy on others around them.

C. Resolve to Defend the Faith

What does it mean to defend anything? What comes to mind when you consider a football game and the term "goal line" defense? My mind thinks of the severity of the situation. Defenses are only needed when something is worth defending, and the goal line qualifies because points are awarded if the offense crosses the line. The game could be won or lost on the ability of the defense to hold the line, not giving any ground to the opposing side.

In the special historical study at the beginning of this chapter, you read of Audie Murphy, a decorated World War II hero who exemplified the significance of defending with unwavering resolve. On January 26, 1945, near the village of Holtzwihr, Murphy's valor shone brightly amidst the chaos of battle. Surrounded by advancing German forces, Murphy's small unit faced overwhelming odds. Despite the dangerous situation, Murphy refused to yield an inch of ground, embodying the indomitable spirit of defense. Just as Murphy stood firm against the tide of tyranny, we too must stand resolute in the face of those who would seek the destruction of the faith.

Please do not misunderstand. Quarrels and debates are not the goal. When they become the goal, the focus turns to winning an argument and not necessarily on winning the person or the people who listen for the cause of Christ. That doesn't mean I think conversations, call them "debates" if you'd like, that we see some having today are valueless. I do believe they have their place; however, at any time we turn an opportunity to discuss or debate the faith with others, and it turns into something that is about us, we are wrong.

We must resolve to defend the faith because of where it's seated and what is accomplished in the life of the person who obediently conforms to its teaching. God is the author of the faith, and Jesus is the good news of the faith. The grace and mercy of God have been extended to mankind in the simple fact that we have the faith that was delivered once for all handed down to the saints. God desires a relationship with each of us, that includes those who may not care right now. That perfect love is worth defending because it is rooted in the One who is perfect.

Through the faith, those who will submit and obey will find hope, peace, mercy, grace, and forgiveness. They will find the answer for better well-being, marriages, parenting, and societies. In the faith, we find a community of believers called the Church, a community that is family, bears the burdens of one another, and supports each other. We find purpose, meaning, and ultimately, what love truly is as we discover what God has done for us in sending His Son to die on the cross for our sins (John 3:16).

It's not about simply winning an argument. It's about being so grateful for what God has done for you that you want to honor Him. Like David was furious and taken back (1 Sam. 17) when he found the armies of Saul sitting back, allowing pagan Goliath to insult the

Determined to Stand

very God whose banner they marched under, you and I must resolve to respond. David didn't understand how anyone who truly has faith in God could allow an attack on God, and neither should we. Fear and uncomfortableness are often realities of standing up and defending the faith. We must put those behind us because the cause is too valuable. Hold the line. Hold the post—not for your benefit, but so that the faith is not defamed—and others will want the blessings found therein.

CONCLUSION

The Bystander Effect is real. I'll never forget watching a video report of an older man who was robbed by an individual in a convenience store parking lot. The assailant was a much younger and stronger man who was bound and determined to take whatever he could from this older man. At one point in the video, the older man was standing in the gap between the car and the open driver's side door when the young man began slamming the door on the older man's legs. If he couldn't get the man's money or car, the criminal was going to make sure the older man paid with pain and possibly his life.

The news report wasn't about how horrible crime has become in some parts of America, although that definitely could have been its focus. Instead, during the report, the camera panned out, showing a crowd of witnesses who were stood by and did nothing while the older man was fighting for his life. The segment was a wake-up call that highlighted the condition of many in our culture who are too complacent in the face of danger.

We've become that way religiously as well. In our time, to be labeled intolerant, judgmental, or any number of negative terms terrifies far too many. The fear of what could happen if we got involved causes many to keep walking by as if they saw and heard nothing. What a shame!

Instead, we need to be people determined to stand for the faith. Yes, society is growing ever more secular, and the watered-down interpretations of the Word of God are popular. That's exactly what Paul told Timothy would happen (2 Tim. 4:1-4). The good news is that people are watching and wanting to see authenticity in many different facets of society. They want to see how the faith makes a difference in your life. They need to see if what you say, you believe—really believe. Will you live it out? Will those who've received mercy show mercy? Will those who preach the love of God display that when it comes to interactions, even with those who disagree with them? In short, they may not be as closed to God as they've been painted to be. Instead, they may be closed to those who profess to be His disciples who don't believe the faith is worth standing for.

Be determined to stand. The rewards outweigh the risks, and with great resolve, we can show our families, communities, country, and world that Jesus makes all the difference. Be determined!

Excel Still More Bible Workshop

Building

PAY ATTENTION TO WHAT TRUE FAITH MAKES YOU!

2 Peter 1

GARRETT BERNETHY

"For by these He has granted to us His precious and magnificent promises, so that by them you may become partakers of the divine nature, having escaped the corruption that is in the world by lust."
- 2 Peter 1:4 -

INTRODUCTION

While doing my study of the books of 2 Peter and Jude, there is as usual so much to take in as these two books are full of tremendous insights to the things that we ought to *"remember"* (2 Pet. 1:12, 13; 3:1, 2; Jude 5, 17). In fact, Peter writes to these Christians (1 Pet. 1:1-4; 2 Pet. 1:1; cf. 1:10 *"brethren"*; 3:1) telling them that they are in need of *"paying attention"* (NASB 1:19) to the *"prophetic word"* which has been spoken to them and *"granted them everything"* (1:3) that they were in need of in order that they might know who they are, what they should be, and where they need to go.

Why would a person need to be told to *"pay attention"*? Here are a few examples to think about.

Let's think back to our school days. Your teacher is in the middle of a lesson, teaching you something new regarding a certain subject, but some of the students are messing around talking to each other. When your teacher sees and hears them talking, he or she says, "Pay attention; this is going to be on the test!"

You are in a CPR class where you are being trained to do a maneuver to remove an object from the throat of a toddler that has been caught. While showing you the proper way or ways to remove the obstruction, the instructor may say something like, "You need to pay attention so that you may do this properly and clear the airway."

Or let's say that it is Thanksgiving and you have decided to deep fry a turkey this year. You set everything up and purchase all the necessary items to cook, but when it comes time to finally fry the turkey, you watch a YouTube video on actually "how" to do it. You watch several videos that give you a step-by-step tutorial, and each says, "Pay attention to the time; if you cook too long, you will burn the turkey!"

Why would they say something like that? It is simple. The teacher calls on the students and tells them to "pay attention" because they are *distracted*! The CPR instructor tells the class to "pay attention" so that they will not allow themselves to be *distracted*. The Thanksgiving turkey guy is told by the YouTubers to "pay attention" so they don't get *distracted* and forget the time. When a person is distracted, it means that they are not "paying attention" to the very things that they are in need of paying attention to.

A distraction is anything you do to temporarily take your attention away from something else or something you do that has lifelong effects turning your mind to something completely different regardless of whether either of them is right or wrong. From a spiritual perspective, this means that one may turn his focus from being on Heaven or right living to the lust of the world.

Distractions are everywhere, aren't they? Keeping us from doing what we need to be doing throughout our days, weeks, months, and years. Some are worse than others, of course, but a distraction is a distraction, nonetheless.

In an article written by Kendall Peterson entitled "Everyday Distractions that Hold Us Back,"[1] she gave this list of distractions people deal with to which I have given further definition.

Social Media—While not inherently bad, how often have you done a quick check of social media only to find yourself still scrolling an hour later? How many times have you found yourself feeling as if you aren't doing as well as others while looking at their "perfect" photos? On one hand, you have wasted your time looking at things that are taking you away from the things you need to be doing. On the other hand, you find your mind being pulled from reality, wishing your life was as good as theirs. Either way, this can hinder your productivity and positivity in life.

Regrets—Looking back on something you should or shouldn't have done in your life, wishing you would have done it differently, can make you have regrets. It could be the thing you said in the last argument you had with your spouse or the regret of something you wished you would have done at some point in your life. Either way this is wasting time thinking about the past which will not allow you to live in the present or look towards the future.

Grudges—No matter the reason for holding a grudge, it is always a waste of time and energy when you hold on to things like this. By holding on, we first are not practicing the teachings of Matthew 18 nor any of the concepts of *"brotherly love."* "This mindset is extremely negative, making it difficult to focus when you're consumed with worry or anxiety over someone's past actions. While some events are unforgettable, nothing is unforgivable. Let it go!"

Toxic Relationships—Nothing is more distracting than being around toxic people. People like this can make you feel horrible and monopolize your time. These types of relationships are not

---

[1] Kendall Peterson, "Everyday Distractions that Hold Us Back." *LinkedIn*, 10 Jan. 2023, www.linkedin.com/pulse/everyday-distractions-hold-us-back-kendall-peterson-1c.

Pay Attention to What True Faith Makes You!

only dangerous physically but can have effects on your spiritual life in an eternal way, distracting you from what truly matters with emotions of all kinds leading to more heartache, pain, and stress.

Pursuits of Perfection—A dangerous distraction that is based mainly on perception, pursuing perfection is working towards something that may not even exist or be obtainable. This is a pointless pursuit which can distract you from moving on and focusing on more important goals that can bring you closer to where you want to be. While there is nothing wrong with wanting things to be done correctly, or being the best at what you do, perfection is in many cases different in everyone's mind. Do your best, so that you have given your best.

The Thoughts of Others—Being bothered by what other people think makes a person change their behavior because of their concern about others' perception of him. By constantly worrying about the thoughts of others, we are extremely distracted from what we need to do or how we need to live because we are too worried about what others think about us. When this occurs, our actions of any kind are no longer for the right reasons, but rather to play into the narrative that may or may not be in the minds of others regarding you as an individual or family.

Poor Boundaries—Poor boundaries are the result of not allowing people to know what you can and cannot do because of your schedule, things that are important (family time or worship), or prominent projects you may be working on. This can and should even be applied to improper relationships that should not exist because of non-existent or weak boundaries or scruples. When poor boundaries are set up, others will have no problem infringing on your time and energy, which is a result of not knowing how or when to say "no." These will assuredly bring distractions to your life.

The Promise of Tomorrow—Vision, plans, and future steps are all very positive and are needed to be successful in the future. However, when a person gets so caught up in what is happening tomorrow, they can often lose sight of today and be distracted from what is happening right now. Plan for the future, but be in the present (cf. Matt. 6:33-34).

Negative Thinking—This way of thinking is likely the most toxic distraction of them all. When we begin to think negatively, we do nothing but waste time and energy as we are distracted from all that is positive in life. If you are a negative thinker, change the way you think! Negativity is like a cancer that spreads not only through your mind but also can have terrible effects on those around you, ultimately destroying many good things, meaningful relationships, and the unity that exists among the Church, families, and friendships. Negativity is a distraction that destroys; don't let it have its effect on you!

While this is a short list, I think that we can all agree that not every type of distraction is inherently bad. While we would probably all say that the drama a person or a family brings to the table is a bad distraction, we would also most likely agree that hunting, watching our kids play basketball, fishing, shopping, caring for our elderly family, or getting away to do something different can be good ones.

While searching for and through many different lists of things that distract people, I have found that there are many different facets to this idea. In looking at lists for the workplace, schools, families, and our own personal lives, I have found that experts look at distractions in two ways.

First, they look at the negative side of a distraction. You know, the things that take you away from what you should or need to be doing. This can, of course, affect your secular life as well as your spiritual life. In your secular life, you can be distracted from your family by all the extra activities you are involved in as a result of your hobbies and the work that you do, which can consume who you are and all your time, or even an addiction that you have given yourself to that results in mental and/or even a physical separation from those that you love. These distractions take your positive movement to the negative and can make you stagnant in your life, physically and spiritually.

Second, they look at the positive side of a distraction.[2] These can be used as a coping mechanism that can be useful for anxiety, panic attacks, overwhelming emotions, negative thoughts, pain, or even emotional triggers. From a physical and spiritual standpoint, the blessings of doing something to distract yourself from all the things you are dealing with is not only good, but it can be a great blessing. In fact, one of the things that many older ministers have said and continue to say, regarding preachers, is about the importance of "getting away." Taking a vacation, going on a small trip, doing something different simply take your mind off the things you devote yourself to. Why? To clear your head, make sense of things, and give yourself a break. This is the positive impact of a distraction.

Biblical Examples of Distractions

Biblical examples of this can be found in the life of Jesus. It seems that for Jesus, the town of Bethany was a place where He could get away, be with friends, and relax and simply be Himself along with His friends Mary, Martha, and Lazarus. This seems to be a place for Jesus that He could go to forget about the world and all the work He is had to do, even if for only a minute. This is an example of a "good distraction" in His life.

On the other hand, there were, of course, bad distractions in the life of Jesus. For instance, the temptation of the devil as he strives to distract Him with lust, pride, and power (Matt. 4:1-11). Or the Pharisee's introduction of the adulterous woman as they tried to distract Jesus by her deeds with their lies and law-bending schemes, trying to get him to make a rash decision or speak out of emotion (John 8:1-11).

However, in looking at the life of Jesus, one cannot help but think of the story of Mary and Martha for a topic like this. In Luke 10:38-42 we read,

> *Now as they were traveling along, He entered a village; and a woman named Martha welcomed Him into her home. She had a sister called Mary, who was seated at the Lord's feet, listening to His word. But Martha was **distracted** with all her preparations; and she came up to Him and said, "Lord, do You not care that my sister has left me to do all the serving alone? Then tell her to help me." But the Lord answered and said to her, "Martha, Martha, you are **worried and bothered about so many things**; but only one thing is necessary, for Mary has chosen the good part, which shall not be taken away from her."* (emp. added)

The application of this story is somewhat simple. While Martha was distracted with everything she was preparing, she lost sight of all that truly mattered. She lost sight of her guest; she lost sight of her Lord.

---

[2] Estee Panda, "200+ Ways to Distract Yourself: The Ultimate List." Hopeful Panda, 16 May 2023, hopefulpanda.com/distraction/#:~:text=So%20here's%20a%20list%20of%20possible%20productive%20things,Tend%20the%20yard%20Mow%20the%20lawn%20Do%20laundry.

Pay Attention to What True Faith Makes You!

The two of these women represent (at least for our purposes) the great contrast that the apostle Peter is making within chapter 1. Martha represents the person who has given in to the "*cleverly devised tales*" (1:16) that had been presented by the false teachers of the day, distracting them from the truth that had previously and, of course, are now being presented. While Mary represents for us the person who "*pays attention*" (1:19) to the "*lamp shining in a dark place.*"

The world, according to Peter, is filled with "*corruption*" (φθορά, *phthora*; decay, ruin, deterioration) in the "*lust*" that has taken its place within it (cf. 1 John 2:16; Gen. 3:6). It is by these things that the distraction comes to our lives—making us believe false things. Bringing us to the point of doing nothing when something needs to be done. It brings us to hate instead of leading us to love. It takes us down the wrong road of sin instead of the right road to salvation.

According to the *Merriam-Webster Dictionary*, the word distracted simply means "having one's thoughts or attention drawn away: unable to concentrate or give attention to something."[3] So, in thinking about the concept within itself, being distracted is nothing more than our inability to direct our minds to what our minds need to be directed towards as our attention is drawn elsewhere.

Martha's mind was drawn somewhere else. It was drawn to presentation instead of preparation. It was drawn to doing instead of listening. It was focused on her and not Him. It was focused on pride instead of humility. Her mind was drawn from the one thing she needed to the several things she wanted. This is *distraction*!

Has there been anything throughout the history of the world that has caused us to waste more time, hurt the progress of projects, look away from those things that matter in life, and lose both our physical and spiritual family than those things that distract us?

Think about it: when Jesus was wandering in the wilderness fasting (Matt. 4:1-11), what was it exactly that Satan was trying to do to Him? The NASB says that the "*tempter*" (Matt. 4:3) came to Him, suggesting the idea of temptation that was to come, but what exactly was Satan trying to do? First, he tempted him with food—bread in particular (Matt. 4:3-4). Second, he tempted Him to test God (Matt. 4:6-7); and third, he tempted him with power (Matt. 4:7-10).

So, what exactly, as we look at this event from our current perspective, was Satan trying to do? If we look at this contextually from each of the vantage points mentioned in 2 Peter 1:19 and Matthew 4:1-10, we can find that each place is essentially discussing the same thing.

Matthew 4:1-2 states,

> *Then Jesus was led up by the Spirit into the wilderness to be tempted by the devil. And after He had fasted forty days and forty nights, He then became hungry.*

---

3 "Distracted," *Merriam-Webster*, www.merriam-webster.com/dictionary/distracted.

3 Denny Petrillo, "Matthew 6:16," *World Video Bible School Course Notes: Matthew* (Maxwell, TX: World Video Bible School, 2011) 79.
 The Law of Moses required fasting once a year—on the Day of Atonement (Lev 16; Num. 29:7). The purpose of fasting was the denying the body food for a specific reason, such as mourning or for study and meditation. Fasting is that which has a spiritual emphasis. And since it has this, our fasting is a matter between us and God, it is not to be announced to others. It is done by choice, by Christians who want to spend time denying the physical to focus on the spiritual. It was a part of the early church life (Acts 14:23).

One of the purposes of what Jesus was doing had to do with Him beginning His work and fulfilling His purpose. The spiritual connection and preparation of His ministry, which would begin with the choosing of His disciples (Matt. 4:18-22), can be seen in His fast, which took place for forty days.[4] Peter was one of the first to be chosen. Second, He was there for the purpose, it seems, of temptation, as He was "*led up by the Spirit.*" The mindset of Jesus in His reaction to those temptations of the devil shows us that His focus was truly on spiritual things as well as all scriptural fulfillments and His purpose here on earth.

So naturally, the first thing that the tempter tries to do is distract Him with what He wants! So, the *distraction of lust* (Matt. 4:3-4) is thrown at Him with the very thing His body craves: food. Much like the first, the second was a *distraction of pride* (Matt. 4:6-7) to test God. The third in the same pattern is the *distraction of the eye* (Matt. 4:7-10) with the ability to rule over all the earth (cf. 1 John 2:16), which connects to the promise and pursuit of His spiritual reign as King of Kings and Lord of Lords.

To distract Jesus from His purpose would have been the greatest triumph that Satan could have ever accomplished. However, due to our Lord's knowledge, dedication, love, and focus, Satan had no chance of distracting Him from His purpose here.

Magic Tricks

Everybody loves a good magic trick! Magicians have been a treasured source of enjoyment and amazement for hundreds of years, leaving us all wondering the very same thing! How did they do that?!

What makes a good magic trick? Is it the waving of hands? Is it the wand or that hat? I guess in some instances, they may play a key role in the trick itself, but the main goal for a great magic trick, as we all know, is "misdirection." Getting you to look in a certain place at a certain time draws both your mind and eyes away from what is going on right in front of your eyes.

In 2 Peter, a word that we can connect to the idea of "misdirection" would be "deception." *Deception* (ἀπάτη; *apatē*) is defined by BDAG as being *deceitful* or even *deceptive trickery* as it references 2 Thessalonians 2:10, which is identified in the NASB as "*wickedness.*"

The *Wycliffe Bible Encyclopedia* looks at the word *deceit or deceiver*, showing that there are many Hebrew and Greek words that appear in our English Bibles for the word *deceit*. Basically, it is defined as a deliberate misrepresentation of the truth, especially in moral and spiritual matters, to mislead another person. So what we are seeing is the "magic tricks" of the "*false prophets*" (2:1) who have been deceiving (2:13) Christians into thinking something is right when in fact it is

---

2 **BDAG, ἀπάτη, ης ἡ** (s. ἀπατάω; Hom.+). **deception, deceitfulness** (Jdth 9:10, 13; 4 Macc. 18:8; Jos., Ant. 2, 300; SibOr 5, 405 ἀ. ψυχῶν) ἡ ἀ. τοῦ πλούτου the seduction which comes from wealth **Matt.** 13:22; **Mark** 4:19; ἀ. τῆς ἁμαρτίας deceitfulness of sin **Heb.** 3:13 (note that sense 2 is also probable for the synoptic passages and **Heb.** 3:13; cp. PRein inv. 2069 V, 73 LRobert, Hellenica XI/XII, '60, 5ff). ἀ. τοῦ κόσμου Dg 10:7 (cp. Herm. Wr. 13, 1 ἡ τοῦ κόσμου ἀπάτη). [τ]ὰς ἐπὶ τὴν ἀπάτην ἀγούσας (paths?) that lead to deceit AcPl Ha 9, 13 (the text is fragmentary, s. ed.'s note and also s. ἄγω 3 end); w. φιλοσοφία (cp. Heraclid. Crit., Descriptio Graeciae 1, 1 [p. 72, 15 Pfister]) empty deceit **Col. 2:8**. ἐν πάσῃ ἀ. ἀδικίας w. every kind of wicked deception **2 Thess**. 2:10 (of deceptive trickery, like Jos., Ant. 2, 284). ἐπιθυμία τ. ἀπάτης deceptive desire **Eph. 4:22**. W. φιλαργυρία 2 Cl. 6:4; w. εἰκαιότης Dg. 4:6; listed w. other sins Hm. 8:5. Personified (Hes., Theog. 224; Lucian, De Merc. Cond. 42) Hs. 9, 15, 3.

2 John Rea, "Deceit, Deceiver," ed. Charles F. Pfeiffer and Howard F. Vos, *The Wycliffe Bible Encyclopedia* (Moody Press, 1975).

Pay Attention to What True Faith Makes You!

very wrong. But these weren't outright lies; they were "*secretly introducing destructive heresies*" (2:1) into the minds of the brethren, directing their minds from the things that they already knew (1:12).

This is the problem with the "deceptive tricks" of false teachers. While telling you all that you want to hear, "*tickling your ears*" (2 Tim. 4:3), they, in many ways, secretly introduce things while making you see something else. Making things sound so good or offering false proofs to try and change your mind on things that may not be fully explainable or that might be outside of something you have studied and may not have the answers to. However, these people knew of "*these things*" (1:10, 12, 15; 3:11, 14, 16), which were told to them, preached to them, and taught to them, giving them all the knowledge they needed, which pertained to "*life and godliness.*"

Deceivers distract and distractions are what can take our minds away from all that we know to be true. They can take us away from all that we need to do. They can take us away from all that we have worked for. In this case it seems that the distractions were meant to take their minds off the fact that God is *truly in control* of all things, and our knowledge of that leads us to understand true righteousness which will bless us and save us on the day of judgment. However, the evil that is in the world continues to try and drive us back or push us over to the side getting us off the narrow road (Matt. 7:13-14) which leads to salvation because of the life of Jesus (Rom. 5:10).

False teachers or the deceivers have impacted people throughout time on an extreme eternal level, preying on their weakness with the power that lies within the lust of the eye and flesh (1 John 2:16), shifting their focus on to all things that are physical and not eternal. However, when people can rely on the knowledge they have in Christ which has been preached in its fullness "*granting us everything pertaining to life and godliness, through the true knowledge of Him who called us by His own glory and excellence*" (1:3), only then can they look to the coming of our Lord as they follow Him to the fullest.

Magic tricks, distractions, deceptions only work on those who allow themselves to take their eyes off the prize. They only work on those who aren't focused on the goal. On those who aren't relying on their own personal knowledge. Why? Because they aren't *paying attention*!

Pay Attention and Remember

The apostle Peter presents many truths within this little epistle that would be unfortunate for us to look past. One of those great truths that we would all do well to "pay attention" to is found in chapter 2:20-21. Here Peter explains this simple truth: While one can come to the true knowledge of our Lord and give him/herself to Him and His work, one can just as easily fall away and out of the good graces of our Lord (cf. Gal. 5:4).

Peter seems to write about these false teachers in two ways. First, he writes about them as coming, but second, he writes of them as if they were already there.[7] In Johnny Ramsey's book *Cover to Cover*, he discusses 2 Peter and the false teachers, whom Revelation identifies as the Nicolaitans

---

3 Johnny Ramsey, *Cover to Cover: Bible Questions Answered.* (Abilene: Quality Publications, 1981), 297.

who had come upon the spiritual scene in a powerful way to persuade the brethren in deeper spirituality. False teachers, as we know, are *"enemies of the cross"* (Phil. 3:18-19) who teach and practice things which the Lord hates (cf. Rev. 2:6,15).

As a result of the false teachers who came in tormenting the brethren, many false doctrines have come into play, duping the brethren into believing something that was not true. For instance:

- In Galatians, you have the Judaizers who were teaching that one should cling to the law of Moses, especially regarding circumcision, claiming they follow Christ but, in fact, follow a different gospel (Gal. 1:6-10).

- In 1 Thessalonians, you have groups coming in, teaching that those who have passed away will miss out on the salvation to come with Jesus. Then, in Paul's second letter to the Thessalonian brethren, false teachers had persuaded them to believe that Jesus had already come, and they had missed out on His coming (1 Thess. 4:13-18; 2 Thess. 2:1-9).

- In 1 John, we begin dealing with the Docetic and Cerinthian Gnostics who were teaching that Jesus was not a man and/or that Jesus was not deity (1 John 2:15-24).

While these are just a few to name in particular, false teachers were, are, and have been molding the truth to fit their lies, dragging many people to build their spirituality on emotion or feelings rather than faith. One of the false teachings of the day had to do with the unscriptural doctrine of "once saved, always saved." Since the birth of such an idea, it has pulled so many people out of the faith because of the false sense of comfort that it brings. I mean, think about the idea that when people come to Jesus and obey the Gospel or possibly think they have obeyed the Gospel, they can live a life as they desire for themselves. This is a doctrine that certainly will bring attention to itself because it states that no matter what you do, you can live life the way you want. This certainly plays into the concept of one's "*lust*" (1:4).

However, this is not something that stopped with the teachings of the Nicolaitans or anyone else who believed a version of this idea. One can even think about the teachings of John Calvin, who taught that salvation is given or bestowed unconditionally. In fact, one of the planks of Calvinism is unconditional election regarding salvation.[8]

When people "pay attention" to what they have been taught and takes in many things that are known to be true, they can put into practice what they have learned. Much like Jesus, as He was tempted by the devil, He did not allow Himself to be overcome by emotion. He didn't give in to something He may have desired. He didn't fall into a word-smithed trap. Why? Because He remembered what He had known from the Scriptures what they said *and* what they meant. He also paid attention to His purpose and His goal—why He was there in the first place—not allowing His mind to be persuaded by the things that "looked good." Instead, He focused on the things that were good.

---

[8] Wayne Jackson, "Conditional Election" *Notes From the Margin of My Bible* (Jackson: Fortify Your Faith, 2021), 366.

Pay Attention to What True Faith Makes You!

FAITH BUILDING

What Does True Faith Make You?

First, let's think about the words of 2 Peter 1:16-21,

> *For we did not follow cleverly devised tales when we made known to you the power and coming of our Lord Jesus Christ, but we were eyewitnesses of His majesty. For when He received honor and glory from God the Father, such an utterance as this was made to Him by the Majestic Glory, "This is My beloved Son with whom I am well-pleased"— and we ourselves heard this utterance made from heaven when we were with Him on the holy mountain. So we have the prophetic word made more sure, to which you do well to pay attention as to a lamp shining in a dark place, until the day dawns and the morning star arises in your hearts. But know this first of all, that no prophecy of Scripture is a matter of one's own interpretation, for no prophecy was ever made by an act of human will, but men moved by the Holy Spirit spoke from God.*

We must know that true faith is built on knowledge, which means that the things we believe in are sure and true because they really happened and/or were indeed spoken. Therefore, Peter reminds his readers that he was an *"eyewitness of His majesty"* and therefore heard the words of Jesus, saw the actions of Jesus, witnessed the divine nature of Jesus, and is now sharing the truth of the things taught by Jesus Himself, by all the Holy Spirit has given to him to say (2 Pet. 1:21; cf. 2 Tim. 3:16-17; John 16).

The importance of these words is simple as you and I look at them today. Because the words that Peter both spoke and wrote were not of His interpretation but rather of the Holy Spirit through him. We understand that this truth is not facilitated by the thoughts of man, which can be persuaded by events, people, propaganda, and pure feelings, but by the unwavering stability of God Himself. Therefore, every word that proceeds out of the mouth of God is foundational, stable, unwavering, and fruitful in every aspect of life.

As a result of this, Peter says to his recipients and ultimately you and me that we must pay attention and remember what our faith makes us so that we are not deceived by the secret and crafty words of men who are against the teachings of Christ. Remember, faith is built on knowledge, and it is this knowledge that allows us to be fruitful and stable in our faith, thus not allowing us to *"stumble"* (1:10) nor to be *"unstable souls"* as we are focused on *"everything pertaining to life and godliness"* (1:3) which leads to salvation in Christ.

1. Faith Makes You and I the Same as the Apostle Peter

We must understand that the faith we have, the salvation that we have, and the hope that is laid before us are no *different* than that of Peter, James, John, or Paul. It is exactly the same! The word ἰσότιμος (*isotimos*) as Denny, also described for us in 1:1, means equal honor or equal value. So, this means that our *faith* is of equal honor or value as Peter's. Isn't that awesome?

While Peter may be an apostle who did great things for the Kingdom and witnessed many wonderful things that we can only imagine as we read the text in our mind's eye, Peter also counts you and I *"blessed"* (1 Pet. 1:8), because we have not physically seen Him with our eyes and yet still believe.

It would do us well to think of Peter not as an apostle but as a brother. Should Peter be recognized as an apostle? Absolutely! Without a doubt, because he was (1 Pet. 1:1; 2 Pet. 1:1). However, much like the brothers of Jesus (i.e., James and Jude) who wrote letters themselves, none of them fixed their minds on the title of apostle, nor did they stake their claims as *"brothers,"* using it as a badge of honor demanding themselves to be known as more than they should be.

While Peter identifies himself as an apostle in both letters, he also identifies himself as a *"bondservant"* in his second letter first. Therefore, he saw himself as a servant first and apostle second. This is not out of the ordinary for a follower of Christ; James, Jude, and Paul each do the same thing. His mind was not on or about who he was individually. His mind was completely consumed with who Jesus was both to him and the rest of the world. Therefore, when Peter wrote, he wrote to those he knew to be his brethren!

Notice his wording throughout his writings.

- *Who has caused us to be born again to a living hope through the resurrection of Jesus Christ...* (1 Pet. 1:3).

- *He Himself bore our sins in His body on the cross so that we might die to sin and live to righteousness...* (1 Pet. 2:24).

- *Seeing that His divine power has granted to us everything pertaining to life and godliness...* (2 Pet. 1:3).

- *Therefore, brethren, be all the more diligent to make certain about His calling and choosing you...* (2 Pet. 1:10).

While in some cases he was writing to *"you,"* in many cases he was writing about *"us"* all together, including himself, as he too was a recipient of the grace given by God through our Lord. Peter understood that without Jesus, he, too, would be lost and consumed by the plague of sin without hope in the world. But with Jesus and because of Jesus, we like him and him like us are together *"children of God"* (cf. 1 Pet. 1:14-18; 2:9; 2 Pet. 1:10).

We need to pay attention to the fact that Peter was a great man of faith and an apostle of Jesus Christ who recognized our similarities and likeness in Christ Jesus our Lord. So, for all that he endured until the end (2 Pet. 1:13-15), we, like him, can and must have the same type of faith that is built in what we know, loving our Lord for all that He is, even to the point of death. When Peter looks at you on the glorious day that we are called to our Lord, together we will walk in and together we will worship, because together we are His children.

2. Faith Allows You to See Everything that Pertains to Life and Godliness

Can you think of a world in which God has not allowed Himself to be known by the world in any way, shape, or form? If this were the case, we would genuinely have no knowledge at all of His greater existence or involvement in our lives. We may believe in something greater but would not know Him.

Pay Attention to What True Faith Makes You!

It is my opinion that one of the great faith builders that we find in the text from its beginning to end is found in the fact that God has not only made Himself known, but in the case of Jesus has made Himself seen and, of course, heard. God truly wants to be involved in your life, desires to speak to you daily, and listens to you at any moment throughout the day. I am unaware of any other "deity" that has ever desired that from its believers.

2 Peter 1 is very much focused on who you are and what you need to be so that you may not stumble but find your way to the *"entrance into the eternal kingdom of our Lord and Savior Jesus Christ"* (1:11). So what are the things that pertain to *"life and godliness"*? In reference to *"these things,"* it seems that there is a list of things to focus on.

1. Faith
2. Moral Excellence
3. Knowledge
4. Self-Control
5. Perseverance
6. Godliness
7. Brotherly Kindness
8. Love

Some have made this a list of greatest importance to least importance or even presented them as a stairstep type of growth. I do not take this list as one thing leads to another. Instead, these are the "qualities" or "virtues" that one in Christ must possess to find the *"entrance into the eternal Kingdom"* as it will be *"abundantly supplied"* to those who are seeking to live a godly life.

God, through both Jesus and the Holy Spirit, has made known to us everything needed to attain eternal life. It is through Jesus that all things have come to be, and through the Holy Spirit the words were given to man as they wrote about our Lord. God set all of this into play; thus, the Godhead has worked to bring us home to be with Him as His Son (Rev. 21:7).

Every word that God has sent us leads to eternal life and, therefore, is fruitful to produce in us all godliness and righteousness to live as He desires for us to live. However, while a person can look forward to eternal life and make that his eternal goal, there are things that we must do daily to be obedient to Him and His will; this is what He has abundantly supplied to us—the knowledge of how to live and walk through life for Him.

- We have the knowledge to know what He expects of our lives.
- We have the knowledge to know how He will save us in the end.
- We have the knowledge of how we are to treat our brethren during our lives.
- We have the knowledge of how we can look past the trials of life.
- We have the knowledge of how we can be like God.

With His direction, I can know how to live life daily for Him so that I can say I have lived my life for Him, and with His words, He helps me to do that. We must also pay attention to the intention of His words and the instruction they give us so that we can live up to the standards of His rule in our hearts to be His people! Our God cares who we are and how we live. This is His desire—to have your heart so that you will be His.

3. Faith Makes You a Partaker of the Divine Nature

The word *partaker* comes from the word κοινωνός (*koinonos*)[9] literally meaning to be a "partner" or "sharer" in something. How humbling it is to know that the God of the universe has created something that you can partake of to be with Him.

In Denny's notes on chapter 1:4, he wrote, "Our connection to God is established when we make His promises an active part in our lives."

Our connection…

- First is through the written Word which allows us to know.
- Second is by His active call which is to obey.
- Third is a result of our choice to accept His call.
- Fourth is the Savior of the world who brings the connection together and establishes the fellowship of both parties.
- Fifth is the Church of our Lord.

To be a partaker or partner, both sides must be aligned in the primary goals of the relationship. Two participating groups or individuals. Each having a desire to be with the other. In this case, God desires to be with us, and because of that desire, He has acted on our behalf to produce the possibility of a true relationship to exist between you and Him.

For the opposite party, that pattern remains the same. Our desire to be with Him requires our actions of faith to produce a relationship with Him. It was because of His love that He acted on behalf of you, and it is also because of our love that we act upon our understanding of Him.

This brings us to the main point of all of the writing of the Bible—our obedience. When we partake of the divine nature, we focus on the things that connect us to the divine. Again, these concern love, perseverance, faith, and godliness. When God saw man's need regarding salvation, He didn't just talk about what He needed to do; He made plans for what must be done and then acted out those plans without hesitation.

To be an actual partaker, our actions must be the same. Less talking about what we need to do and more actions directed towards what needs to be done. This is the way of God. Our lives must be consumed by faithful conviction in every word that has proceeded out of the mouth of God. A complete belief that doesn't turn away, doesn't fade away, and doesn't walk away, but remains stable in all its ways as it is established on God's truth.

To be a partaker is to be a partner, and to be a partner means that you have a way to escape the corruption that has filled the unstable world with its lust, working against itself in every way.

---

9 William Arndt et al., *A Greek-English Lexicon of the New Testament and Other Early Christian Literature* (Chicago: University of Chicago Press, 2000) 553.

Pay Attention to What True Faith Makes You!

However, our connection to God is both stable and powerful, especially when both you and God are connected faithfully through the blood of Jesus Christ our Lord.

We must pay attention to our connection. Realizing that the connective tissue that holds us together has an eternal purpose of protection and life. I don't know that there is a more powerful faith builder than the understanding that God has desired you to be a part of His family since before the world began.

4. Faith Makes You Chosen

Every person who hears the message of Jesus (i.e., the Gospel) is called to decide. Those who obey the message themselves become the "chosen" or "elect," thus making them the chosen of God. God is calling you home like a parent calls their children home. One child may come home sprinting to get in the door, while the other may stay away and not listen. But both children were called; only one child responded properly, in obedience.

When faith is put into action (James 2:14-26), the response to the call makes the outcome certain. Spiritual stability, foundational strength, and true Biblical knowledge. While there is always the opportunity to fall away from the truth, the person who chooses to be chosen and faithfully obeys His every command will have the ability to be certain about his call. Just as the apostle John writes that we can know that we have eternal life (1 John 5:13), we too can have this knowledge and confidence.

However, one must *"pay close attention"* to the Word spoken so that they might recall all that God has required. It isn't good enough to keep some of His commands or only live a life "half faithful" to God, but rather to live a life for God in its fullest, giving all that you must for Him. When one practices these eight virtues and places the right amount of focus on who they should be for Him, that is the time that stability can genuinely exist spiritually in a person's life. You are the chosen, you are the called, never forget, He wants you!

CLOSING THOUGHTS

From a faith-building perspective, we must pay close attention to what our faith makes us in the eyes of God. When we realize just how much we mean to Him, we may begin to think about what He means to us. Every word that we have been given. The "eye-witnessing" accounts of each writer were given to us for the purpose of godliness. To allow us access to the divine, giving us the opportunity to respond to the call of God.

As a result of our faith, we have become *"brothers in Christ"* (1:10), and therefore, we should not be shortsighted or blind to the goodness of God (1:9), who has cleansed our sins in Christ. We must be those who *"pay attention"* to what and who we have become in Christ. All knowledge has been given to us in the story of our Bible so that our faith might be as stable as those who saw our Lord on the *"holy mountain"* (1:18).

So, pay attention to what true faith will make you, remember who and what you are, and be founded in His truth because we can have a relationship with God through Him!

Building

PAY ATTENTION TO THOSE WHO TRY TO FAKE YOU!

---

2 Peter 2

GARRETT BERNETHY

"But false prophets also arose among the people, just as there will also be false teachers among you, who will secretly introduce destructive heresies, even denying the Master who bought them, bringing swift destruction upon themselves."
- 2 Peter 2:1 -

INTRODUCTION

As Peter closed his first letter to the Christians *"scattered abroad"* (1 Pet. 1:1), he wrote of an animal. One that is known for its fierceness, power, and strength. One that is prone to stalk its prey but also attack with a force that is both disturbing and amazing simultaneously due to the violence of its pounce. It is the lion!

As we look towards the end of his first letter, Peter describes the devil with these words,

> *...Be on the alert. Your adversary, the devil, prowls around like a roaring lion, seeking someone to devour* (1 Pet. 5:8).

As God designed it, the lion can think outside the box when it comes to entrapping its prey, blending into its surroundings, and using multiple friends to accomplish its task. They typically do not go after the "large and in charge" of the group but rather the weak and weary. The reason for this is simple. They put up the least amount of fight. They are the slowest, the least experienced, the smallest in many cases, or possibly the lame of the group. They are carefully watched and picked out so that the lion will be sure to eat a good meal.

In his second letter, Peter doesn't talk about the "lion" but instead references the animal species altogether by calling those who are in accord with the devil (cf. 2 Thess. 2:9) *"unreasoning animals born as creatures of instinct to be captured and killed"* (2 Pet. 2:12). They too have seemingly "blended in" with the brethren as they "*secretly introduced*" the "*destructive heresies*" that amazingly enough were denying Jesus! Undoubtedly, these false teachers were good at what they did. They blended in, chose the weak in faith, looked for those who were lame and wounded spiritually and chose the right time to pounce and take down their prey.

How were they able to do this? I mean, how can a person become or be so unreasonable? Here is the answer. These people had no boundaries and were willing to do whatever it took to accomplish their goal, which was to live life as they wanted to live it and convert as many as possible to their corrupt ways of thinking.

When people have no boundaries in life, they have no moral compass. They are willing to do whatever it takes to please themselves because, in all reality, they have become their own God. Nothing means more to them than themselves and their lustful desires.

The term *moral compass* is defined as a set of beliefs or values that help guide ethical decisions, judgments, and behavior: an internal sense of right and wrong.[1]

When you begin to look at the list of how Peter describes these people you can and will quickly see that these people are anything but moral and certainly have no compass. Peter describes these false teachers with these twenty-five descriptions in the text as pointed out by Denny in our Learning section.

Peter says…

1. They indulge the flesh in its corrupt desires…2:10
2. They despise authority…2:10
3. They are daring…2:10
4. They are self-willed…2:10
5. They do not tremble when they revile angelic majesties…2:10
6. They are like unreasoning animals…2:12
7. They revile where they have no knowledge…2:12
8. They count it pleasure to revel in the daytime…2:13
9. They are stains…2:13
10. They are blemishes…2:13
11. They are reveling in their deceptions…2:13
12. They are carousing with the brethren…2:13
13. They have eyes full of adultery…2:14
14. They never cease from sin…2:14
15. They entice unstable souls…2:14
16. They have hearts trained in greed…2:14

---

[1] "Moral Compass," *Merriam-Webster*, www.merriam-webster.com/dictionary/moral%20compass.

Pay Attention to Those Who Try to Fake You!

17. They forsake the right way...2:15
18. They have gone astray...2:15
19. They are springs without water...2:17
20. They are mists driven by a storm...2:17
21. They speak out arrogant words...2:18
22. They entice by fleshly desires...2:18
23. They entice by sensuality...2:18
24. They live in error...2:18
25. They promise freedom while they themselves are slaves of corruption...2:19

This is all because they "*deny the Master who bought them,*" and therefore, they follow their *sensuality* (ἀσέλγεια; *aselgeia*—lack of self-constraint which involves one in conduct that violates all bounds of what is socially acceptable, self-abandonment[2]), leaving them morally boundless which has allowed them to lie and deceive with no moral regard whatsoever.

When one has no moral compass or regard for right and wrong, it begins to present a significant problem for all the souls involved, mainly the false teacher, and those weak in faith who allow themselves to be overtaken by the false teachings and ways of the teachers themselves. However, if people are not careful, they can get caught up in the so-called "free lifestyle" where they can begin to believe that *what they desire is what really matters*.

The major issue is that these individuals have come from among them in the past, during the present, and in the future. This is one thing that we cannot overlook within the text itself. The major question at this point is where the leadership is. Is Peter looking toward these people, knowing they don't have any? Is he preparing those who are stronger to be watchful of those who are unstable? Is this preparation, warning, and/or both?

For us today...

- How many of our churches have fallen to false teachers from among us?

- How many of our brothers and sisters have been duped into believing the false teachings of denominationalism, Dispensational Premillennialism, Calvinism, or other forms of false doctrine?

- How many of our new converts have fallen away only after a short time of becoming a Christian as a result of a lack of people leading them in their new spiritual walk?

- How many Churches of Christ have become more closely connected to or resemble the community churches of the world rather than the Church of the New Testament?

- How many of our leaders have folded to the pressures of people in their congregations to change the way worship is or what we accept through our doctrine because of the threat of leaving and/or of money?

---

2 Johnny Ramsey, *Cover to Cover: Bible Questions Answered*. (Abilene: Quality Publications, 1981), 297.

- How much doctrine has been changed because of our world's political views to ensure we aren't going to be sued, put on the news for our beliefs, or even lose members of our congregations?

- How many families have turned from truth as a result of a minister beginning to teach and persuade the brethren towards another walk that leads to destruction rather than life to gain a following or maybe prove a point?

While some of these might not have a definitive answer, the questions remain the same, and their significance is important. How many?

When the moral corruptness of specific individuals begins to be adopted by those around you, significant problems will soon follow. Why? Because of the lack of boundaries, those who have no morals are enticing and intriguing in and of themselves. This is dangerous. When a person does not have a **foundational faith** and belief system, the opportunity for them to leave the faith increases as the thought of living how you desire seems incredible. Mainly if that belief teaches that no matter what I do, I can get to Heaven, at least this is what "*unstable souls*" will believe as they are young in the faith.

Georgia Anne Geyer wrote an article in 1992 in which she said,

> "I have concluded that it is impossible to have a moral community or nation without faith in God because without it, everything rapidly comes down to "me," and "me" alone is meaningless. Today, Americans have stopped acting in terms of their own moral, ethical and religious beliefs and principles. They've stopped acting on what they knew was right—and the "me" has become the measure of everything.
>
> However, moral societies are the only ones that work. If anyone thinks there is not a direct and invaluable relationship between personal integrity in a society and that society's prosperity, that person has simply not studied history. And this should not surprise us. Great moral societies, built upon faith in God, honor, trust, and the law blossoms because they are harmonious; because people love or at least respect their fellowman; because, finally, they have a common belief in something beyond themselves. It simplifies life immensely; you do not waste and spend your days fighting for turf, for privilege, for money and power over your fellowman."[3]

A Major Problem

We all know that we have a significant problem today in our world and even in the Church. While it may not be the case for everyone, it is unfortunately the case for many, and that is a lack of Bible knowledge. It is unfortunate, sad, and frustrating to see brethren going the way of another doctrine. You believe, being one who is watching this happen, that they should know better! In many cases, that is the truth. However, there are many cases in which it may not be.

We say, "But we are preaching the truth from our pulpits and teaching the truth in our classrooms and have lots of extra things that we are doing to teach the Bible; everyone should know better!"

---

[3] Georgia Anne Geyer, "Morality," *Bits & Pieces*, September 17, 1992, 23-24; http://www.sermonillustrations.com/a-z/m/morality.htm.

Pay Attention to Those Who Try to Fake You!

While I agree with this statement 100%, I have also learned something else to be true. The Church itself, which officially meets on the first day of the week (cf. Matt. 28:1-8; Mark 16:1-8; Luke 24:1-10; John 20:1-8; Acts 20:7; 1 Cor. 16:2) and in most cases on Wednesday evenings plus the occasional Gospel meeting or seminar, is only together just less than four hours per week, depending on your times and the size of your congregation (larger congregations may have two services to which the sermons are shorter).

Can people learn all they need to know in this time? If they were truly engaged, they would learn a lot after years of being in those settings. However, the preacher and the eldership are often plagued by people who complain about so many things regarding our services. The length of the lessons and/or classes, the person talking is too boring, loud, soft, slow, fast, big, or small, or you fill in the blank. In many cases, those who are complaining are those who do not have their Bibles out and are on their phone doing who knows what or sleeping because they stayed up too late or don't care what is being said and just want to get through the sermon to get to lunch.

Now, I realize that this is only the case for some. Some are on their phones or tablets with their Bibles on, doing and going through the study, taking great notes, and others may work long hours, and it is everything they can do to get to worship. However, for some or many, it is a fact, as we have all heard so many times before, that the only time their Bibles open is on Sunday morning. Brethren, this cannot be your practice!

For years in the Old Testament, generation after generation fell away from God, which turned into a vicious cycle of death, war, destruction, and captivity. Over and over again, God sent judges and prophets to save the people and bring them out of captivity, only for them to return to their ways of corruption. Therefore they had come to a point that they could not escape the truth of Hosea 4:6, as God states,

> *My people are destroyed **for lack of knowledge**. Because you have rejected knowledge, I also will reject you from being My priest. Since you have **forgotten the law of your God**, I also will forget your children.*

When a person studies the book of Judges, we find the cycle of unstable people regarding their faith and obedience to the Lord.

SALVATION: GOD SENDS A JUDGE TO SAVE THEM.

SIN: ISRAEL GOES INTO IDOLATRY.

SORROW & SUPPLICATION: ISRAEL CRIES OUT TO THE LORD FOR HELP.

SERVITUDE: GOD LETS OTHER NATIONS ENSLAVE THEM.

After the time of the Judges, the people did not want God to be their God anymore, nor their King, or army for that matter. As a result, the nation of Israel would go through king after king, only for things to worsen. The kingdom would split under King Rehoboam, the son of Solomon (1 Kings 11:43; cf. 1 Kings 12); Jeroboam would take reign of the northern Kingdom of Israel while Rehoboam would reign over the southern Kingdom of Judah. With each king, the people would wander further away from the Lord until their ultimate demise, once again being overtaken by another kingdom. Assyria would destroy Israel, and Babylon would take Judah into captivity for 70 years (Jer. 25:11-12; 29:10; Ezra 1:1; Dan. 9:2).

After generations of kings had existed, the law of God through Moses had been lost! This shows us so much about the people's lack of emphasis on the law of God. Just before the capture of the southern Kingdom, which is discussed in 2 Kings 24:1-5 and 2 Chronicles 36:1-10, the Bible tells us that Hilkiah, the priest *"found the book of the Law of the Lord given by Moses"* (2 Chron. 34:14-15) after generations of it being lost.

However, even though they had found the book, it didn't matter; the kingdom and its kings continued to do *"evil in the sight of the Lord"* (cf. 2 Chron. 36:5) and, as a result, were overtaken by the Babylonian king Nebuchadnezzar. For 70 years (Jer. 25:12; 29:10; Dan. 9:2; Ezra 1:1), the southern Kingdom would remain in captivity as recorded from 2 Kings 24:1-5, 2 Chronicles 36:1-10 through the book of Daniel, until we reach the prophet Ezra, a leader of the second wave of release back to Jerusalem, a priest (Ezra 7:1-5) and a scribe (Ezra 7:6) who was allowed access to the royal archives of the Persian Empire (Ezra 1:2-4; 4:9-22; 5:7-17; 6:3-12). A man who had *"set his heart to study the Law of the Lord and to practice it, and to teach His statutes and ordinances in Israel"* (Ezra 7:10) and who placed a significant amount of emphasis back on teaching the people the ways of God.

Jerusalem would grow to be inhabited once again by the people who made up the tribes of Judah and Benjamin, who would rebuild the temple, the religion, and the wall, as stated in both the books of Ezra and Nehemiah. However, as history continues to replay itself, the people would leave the ways of God once again for the traditions of man, the philosophies of the world, the pride of their leaders, and the desires that existed in the hearts of man.

As a result, this would lead to the rejection of Jesus, the murder of many Christians, the persecution of apostles, the burning and destroying of many Bibles and scrolls, and, of course, the rejection of all truth that His Word offers because something was presented in a way that sounds more pleasing to "me" as I find some personal benefit within it.

In Peter's second letter, he describes the fact that *"many will follow their sensuality"* (2:2) and as a result, *"their greed will exploit you with false words,"* which is, of course, a great tool of *deception* that is and has been offered by all false teachers both then and now. But these false words are what they are: *false!* Meaning there is no truth within them. You see, the only way something false can seem true is if it is presented in a way that can draw you in and make you think that something is better than what you already have. In some ways, this is a "grass is always greener" concept.

So, this means that Peter's message is about the fact that we as Christians must pay attention to what we know God has done, can do, is currently doing, and will do for us as a result of our faithfulness to prevent us from thinking that there is for some reason something better out there

Pay Attention to Those Who Try to Fake You!

for us. In other words, *don't let their false words fake you* out and make you believe something is right when it is wrong (cf. 2:13, 15a)!

Again, a major theme of this letter must stand out! Remember what you know! Why? If you remember the things that you have been taught and dwell on them, you will never go astray nor give in to the false teachings of these immoral teachers to be led away from God. We ought to keep ourselves from fitting the picture of Hosea 4:6! And be a person who, as the King James states, will,

> *Study to shew thyself approved unto God, a workman that needeth not to be ashamed, rightly dividing the word of truth.* (2 Tim. 2:15)

If a person sets his mind to do this in both his heart and mind, it will allow him to defend the faith that he has produced, which is a result of his knowledge, and protect those who are not where he is.

Pay Attention

From the pages of the Bible, God has presented Himself to us so that we can have a chance to grow in His grace. When we learn the truth (John 17:17), then we can truly practice self-control and/or temperance, which means that we will then have the ability to abstain from all evil things, such as teachings, ideals, concepts, people, etc. However, Peter is pointing the brethren in the way of remembrance of the fundamental principles that may stir their minds up so that they may hold on to the Lord and His teachings as they have learned them.

Therefore, Peter is essentially saying within his words this…

- Pay attention to the Lord's teaching.
- Pay attention to the history you have been taught so you will not repeat it.
- Pay attention to the eyewitnesses who have presented themselves to you and taught you about Him.
- Pay attention to what doesn't work regarding the past, present, and future.
- Pay attention to what makes sense and what does not.
- Pay attention to people who seem to be teaching something different than what you have come to believe.
- Pay attention to my words now and hold them in your mind to know what you should look for!

Johnny Ramsey wrote, "To gain a following, some people will do almost anything!"[4] This truly is the case here and is backed by the idea that these individuals are said to be like *"unreasoning animals…who count it a pleasure to revel in the daytime"* (2:12,13). So, Peter's focus is simple. First, to show that God will not spare the ungodly, as we can relate to the book of Nahum about the capital city of Assyria (Nineveh) to whom *He will not clear the guilty*. Second, nothing can rival the matchless love of God, who looks to the faithful and saves them on account of their faith, as in the cases of both Noah (cf. Gen. 6–8) and Lot (Gen. 19).

---

[4] Johnny Ramsey, *Cover to Cover: Bible Questions Answered.* (Abilene: Quality Publications, 1981), 299.

Thus, the thesis statement:

> *Then the Lord knows how to rescue the godly from temptation, and to keep the unrighteous under punishment for the day of judgment.*

First, let's break down how God plans to separate the "godly" and the "ungodly." The godly are those who have submitted to His will, comprised of those who:

1. Accept God's Word as truth, and therefore both live by it and work to understand it (1 Tim. 3:16-17; 2 Tim. 2:15; 2 Pet. 1:19-21; cf.1 John 5:1-5).

2. Have an active faith which leads them to be connected to God through Christ (Rom. 3:26; cf. John 17:19-26; Rom. 8:16-17; Col. 1:22-23; 1 John 1:3; 2:24).

3. Believe that God did not spare Jesus as He died for sins once and for all so that He might bring us to God (Rom. 5:10; Heb. 10:10; 1 Pet. 3:18; 1 John 1:5, 7, 9).

4. Believe Christ will present you (the Church) without spot or wrinkle, holy and blameless (2 Cor. 4:14; 11:2; Eph. 5:27; Col. 1:22; cf. Eph. 1:4).

5. Recognize the death of Jesus so that we can have a life with God (Rom. 5:9-10; 6:3-11).

6. Have been born again through the watery grave of baptism and been cleansed by His blood (John 3:3,7; 1 Pet. 1:3,23; Mark 16:16; Acts 2:38; Rom. 6:3-5; 1 Pet. 3:21; Gal. 3:26-27; 1 John 1:7).

7. Live a life of faithful obedience to God (2 Pet. 1:1; Rev. 2:10).

The ungodly are those who have not submitted to God's plan and thus are not subject to the "*spiritual blessings in the heavenly places*" (Eph. 1:3) but rather the condemnation (cf. Rom. 8:1) and wrath of God (cf. Rom. 5:9).

The apostle Paul wrote to the Romans,

> *For the wrath of God is revealed from heaven against all ungodliness and unrighteousness of men who suppress the truth in unrighteousness....and although they know the ordinance of God that those who practice such things are worthy of death....* (Rom. 1:18-32)

He would also write to the Galatians,

> *Now the deeds of the flesh are evident, which are: immorality, impurity, sensuality, idolatry, sorcery, enmities, strife, jealousy, outbursts of anger, disputes, dissensions, factions, envying, drunkenness, carousing, and things like these, of which I forewarn you, just as I have forewarned you, that those who practice such things will not inherit the kingdom of God.* (Gal. 5:19-21)

However, it seems that Jesus distinguished best those who would be saved and those who would not by saying these words...

> *He who has believed and has been baptized shall be saved; but he who has disbelieved shall be condemned.* (Mark 16:16)

Pay Attention to Those Who Try to Fake You!

The word believe (πιστεύω, *pisteuo* (believe (in) something, be convinced of something, w. that which one believes (in) indicated)[5] is an aorist tense participle which describes an active form of faith which is a continuous action within a person's life. It is a snapshot of how a person truly is in each moment of his/her life. What Jesus is saying here is simple. Faith or belief is essential to the salvation process as faith is the only thing that moves a person to act out of obedience, which is an essential command of God.

Peter writes in 2 Peter 2:9,

> *Then the Lord knows how to rescue the godly from temptation, and to keep the unrighteous under punishment for the day of judgment.*

So, from a spiritual standpoint, God clearly states what will happen and who it will happen to from these two scriptures. For us not to know these infallible truths is a travesty because they are right at our fingertips! James writes that we must have a faith that works, meaning it must be active. An active faith requires active study, reading, contemplation, praying, and self-evaluation. For us to not indulge ourselves in spiritual thinking is nothing more than a condemnation of ourselves.

Remember, Peter wrote in his first letter,

> *But you are* A CHOSEN RACE, *a royal* PRIESTHOOD, *a* HOLY NATION, A PEOPLE FOR GOD'S OWN POSSESSION, *so that you may proclaim the excellencies of Him who has called you out of darkness into His marvelous light; for you once were not a people, but now you are* THE PEOPLE OF GOD; *you had* NOT RECEIVED MERCY, *but now you have* RECEIVED MERCY.

In looking at this from a faith-building perspective, here is what we can bring out of a passage like this.

- For those who are struggling with the idea of *belonging, pay attention* to the fact that the Bible says you are *chosen* and a part of a people who are of *God's own possession*! You, in Christ, belong to God!

- For those who are struggling with the *connection* in life, *pay attention* to the fact that the Bible says you are a part of a *holy nation*. Holy (ἅγιος *hagios*) meaning that you are set apart or reserved[6], nation (ἔθνος *ethnos*) meaning "people." You in Christ are a "set apart or reserved people" for God! You are connected to God through Jesus! You are not alone!

- For those who are struggling with *direction* in life, *pay attention* to the fact that the Bible says you are one individually who has been *"called out of darkness into His marvelous light."* This call was not given or directed to the mega-rich, the extremely powerful, or those who you count as more blessed in this life than you are. This call is for the meek and lowly, for the rich and powerful, for the humble and the prideful, healthy and the sick. This call is for all people, and you have been given a direction in life that leads to God and away from all unrighteousness. You have a direction!

---

5 William Arndt et al., *A Greek-English Lexicon of the New Testament and Other Early Christian Literature* (Chicago: University of Chicago Press, 2000), 816.

6 Arndt et al., 10.

- For those who are struggling with a negative *perception* of life, *pay attention* to the fact that the Bible says you are or can be God's people! You can receive His mercy! Too many people think this life gives them nothing and place everything through that lens or way of thinking. However, the Bible says you can be given everything regarding the eternal! We must see through our perceptions to obtain God's truth of reality.

- For those who are struggling with believing you are *nobody* and are an *outcast*, *pay attention* to the fact that the Bible says you are part of a *race* that is *chosen*, a *priesthood* that is *royal*, a *nation* that is *holy*, and a *people* who are *God's own possession*. You in Christ aren't a nobody; you are somebody to God, and we know this because Jesus had you in mind when He was nailed to that cross! His words were very specific, "*So that the world may know that You sent Me, and loved them, even as You have loved Me*" (John 17:23).

FAITH BUILDING

For us to begin "building," first, I want us to look at the flow of words in this chapter that all begin with the letter R, as taken from the New American Standard Bible. These words are:

1. **Reserved** (τηρέω, *tereo*)—to retain in custody, *keep watch over, guard*[7]...v. 4

2. **Reducing** (τεφρόω, *tephroo*)—*to cover with* or *reduce to ashes*[8]...v. 6

3. **Rescued** (ῥύομαι, *rhyomai*)—*to rescue, save, deliver, or preserve someone from someone or something*[9]...vv. 7, 9

4. **Righteous** (δίκαιος, *diakaios*)—to being in accordance with high standards of rectitude[10]...vv. 5, 7, 8, 21

5. **Revile** (βλασφημέω, *blasphemeo*)—in relation to human *slander, revile, defame*[11]...vv. 10, 12

6. **Revel** (τρυφή, *tryphe*)—engagement in a fast, self-indulgent lifestyle, *indulgence, reveling*[12]...v. 13

7. **Rebuke** (ἔλεγξις, *elenxis*)—expression of strong disapproval, reproach, *rebuke, reproof*[13]...v. 16

8. **Returns** (ἐπιστρέφω, *epistrepho*)—to return to a point where one has been, *turn around, go back*[14]...v. 22

What story are these words telling us, or what picture are they painting? In the text, you will notice that only two words, *righteous* and *rescued*, are connected to those who have an active, obedient faith, such as Lot and Noah. However, six of these words tell us exactly who the ungodly are and what will happen to them as a result of their unrighteousness.

---

7 Arndt et al., 1002.
8 Arndt et al., 1001.
9 Arndt et al., 907.
7 Arndt et al., 246.
8 Arndt et al., 178.
9 Arndt et al., 1018.
9 Arndt et al., 315.
9 Arndt et al., 382.

Pay Attention to Those Who Try to Fake You!

Therefore, the unrighteous are said to have the *pits of darkness reserved for them*, where they will be *reduced* to nothing as a person is truly nothing without God. This results from their *reviling* and *reveling*, in which they will be strongly rebuked for on the day of judgment. This is not because they didn't have the chance or opportunity to follow God; they did, yet they returned to their old lifestyle of lust, pride, and arrogance, and walked away from their faith in God.

So, as Peter paints this picture, we can develop a pure thought on the subject of unfaithfulness which is this. *God has reserved a place away from Him for those who are unfaithful to Him.* It is a result of their own actions, that will create an outcome where they will be reduced to nothing.

Their following, money, popularity, material items, and reputation will all be reduced to nothing without God. This is a result of their slanderous speech and self-indulgent lifestyles, for which they will be strongly rebuked due to God's disapproval. Those who have come to know the Lord and leave His way of righteousness are nothing more than a dog or pig who returns to their ways of uncleanness away from God.

The picture is simply this. When one sins and lives a lifestyle of sin, they are reduced to nothing and will ultimately be cast away from the presence of God to the pit reserved for them. However, for those who would walk according to His way, no matter how hard the walk might be, God is strong, righteous, and faithful enough to rescue you from the temptation and corruption that the world offers you.

Many people will tell you today, "God loves everyone, and there is no way that He will send anyone to Hell. He accepts all people no matter what they do."

However, when people *pay attention* to their Bibles, they will realize quickly, as we do right here in 2 Peter, that God has clearly distinguished who will be the saved and who will not be the saved as we look to the words of the chapter. All we have to do is note the contrasts made: righteous and unrighteous, the godly and ungodly, those rescued and those destined for destruction. A right way and a wrong way, those who are knowledgeable and unknowledgeable, and, of course, the saved and the unsaved.

Each represents two clear distinctions of what God sees as right and wrong. The beauty of this is that they are all laid out very clearly in the text for us to see and study. So, as we lay a foundation from chapter two to build our faith, let us first remember that God clearly understands those who belong to Him and those who do not, no matter how confused mankind may be on the issues itself.

This matters because He has shared His view with you and me. Remember, "*God is not a God of confusion but of peace*" (1 Cor. 14:33), and He has made known who is who and what is what so that you and I can see the two paths before us (cf. Matthew 7:13-14). In other words, His clarity brings us clarity, allowing us to find peace as we know what He knows.

Some might say this way of thinking is dogmatic, harsh, and unchristian-like, but is it? I hardly believe that if God stands on one side of the road, I have the power or persuasion to tell Him, "That's not the right side!" Is it that hard to believe that God has described two different ways? Is it that harsh to know that God has deemed one way right and one way wrong? Is it a cruel and harsh mind that has drawn a line and said, "Don't cross it?" I hardly think so. Why? Because in the mind of God, you have what is right and wrong, good and evil, light and dark, and these are two separate things. So, understanding how God has distinguished all created life is both a blessing and a benefit and not something that should be seen as negative.

Maybe this is the reason the apostle John wrote,

> *This is the message we have heard from Him and announce to you, that God is Light, and in Him there is no darkness at all.* (1 John 1:5)

So, for the false teachings and understandings that have been taught for years like…

- "God will save everyone and would never send anyone to Hell."
- "Once you are saved, you are always saved."
- "All you need is faith, and He will save you."
- "You will have a second chance when the Lord reigns here on earth, and at that point can be saved."

For those who seek to know God's way, will find that this cannot be the truth. Why? God has clearly stated that there is His way—the right way, and then there is every other way, which are the wrong ways.

From this idea, we can lay our "faith building" foundation, which will help us to counteract the false teachers of our day, as Peter is refuting the false teachers of his. For instance, because we know that the blood of Jesus is what cleanses us and washes us clean (Acts 22:16; 1 John 1:7), allowing us to have our sins forgiven is to have a relationship with God, we also know that the only way to connect with the blood of Jesus is through the watery grave of baptism (Acts 2:38; Gal. 3:27; cf. Rom. 6:3-5) which now saves us (1 Pet. 3:21). Because I know this, it automatically rules out that I can be saved by faith alone or any other teaching that has risen through the cracks over the past two thousand years.

So, to *build a foundational faith, one must read the foundational material* to begin building what God requires you to build: your own faith, which is built with knowledge (Phil. 1:9; Col. 1:9; 3:10). Therefore, we must pay attention to God's Word so that we might identify those who are teaching something contrary to it.

The only way to identify what is wrong is to know what is right. The only way to spot a lie is to know the truth. The only way to avoid the *pits of darkness* is to know the paths of light. Pay attention to what the words of God tell you because they alone have the power to free you from all that is trying to harm you.

Now, let's look at some building blocks from this chapter that will help us see some things from which we can build a stronger faith.

Look to Your Great Examples in the Faith and Follow Their Lead

Positive Examples: To express two great examples of faith, Peter discusses both Noah and Lot as two examples of faithfulness that God saw fit to write through the hand of Peter. Why? First, because the recipients would have remembered them and what they did. Second, their extraordinary faith was followed by extraordinary measures.

Pay Attention to Those Who Try to Fake You!

Have we thought about all that God did for Noah and his family? We have all studied the ark and the animals and discussed the world at that time. But how about the extraordinary measures that God took to save Noah and his family? Peter writes that Noah was a *"preacher of righteousness,"* meaning he proclaimed God and His way. It means that he stood where God stood and said what God said. Therefore, because Noah was with God, God stood with him. As a result, when the day of the flood came (Gen. 7:10), Noah and his family found favor in the eyes of God because his faith produced God's mercy upon himself. God would send enough water to cover the entire world with enough wind and storm to demolish all things upon the earth, yet it never touched nor harmed the eight people in the ark nor the animals it hosted.

What about Lot? Again, Peter uses an identifier with this man by using the word *righteous* (δίκαιος). Because of his righteousness, he too stood with God and walked in His ways. Thus, he was saved from the destruction of the two cities engulfed in sin. Because of his obedience to God in a place where sin reigned as king, God looked upon him with grace and mercy, allowing him to be removed from all of the wickedness that existed in those two cities. He and his family were blessed with salvation as their faith would not allow them to give into the evil ways of the world, even though he was tormented by their temptations and lust day after day. Peter shows us by this example that God has great things in store for those who obey Him, even if they live in a great time of peril.

Could these men have been grouped into how God saw the world and been thrust into punishment? While some might say, "Yes, that is possible." In my understanding of the straightforward ways of salvation, my answer is a resounding *no*! Is it possible that God could have been frustrated with either of these men at some point in their lives because of how they may have acted? I would say that is a possibility. However, they were the only "clear lights" that could be seen, in Noah's case, in the world. And in the case of Lot, in the city. There is an amazing faith-building perspective that can be seen here. While God had planned to destroy both the world and the cities, He equally planned to save His righteous servants. While He knew how He would destroy the world and these cities, He also knew how He would save both men and their families. So the positive element here is simple: If we are faithful in His ways, we will be saved from the world's ways.

Negative examples: Peter includes angels, Sodom and Gomorrah, and Balaam—all examples of the unfaithfulness of the ages. The angels gave up God, Sodom and Gomorrah turned away from God, and Balaam went his way without God. Is this not the characteristic of those who will or have been condemned to judgment? Truly, when we look to the comparisons of chapter two and the list given describing those who live sinful lifestyles, is this not their way? Of course, it is. Even if we state some of the keywords of the chapter itself, we can find this truth, such as the words *sin, judgment, destruction, ungodly, condemned,* or *unreasoning*. These are descriptive words, identifiers, and characteristics of those living in the pre-flood world, the destroyed cities, and Balaam himself. Equally, when people live lives formed after these examples of ignorance and sinfulness, the result of their ways only ends with their destruction.

To follow their example is essentially stamping your ticket to your sentence of death. It is putting the needle in your arm, flipping the switch to the electric chair, and pulling the trigger to a gun pointed in your direction. It is a direct flight to a dark place that has been purposefully separated from God and made for those who are unruly and unprecedented in their ways of life.

While this may be on the down and dark side of the text, a fantastic faith-building perspective can also be seen here.

The apostle Paul wrote,

> *When the Lord Jesus will be revealed from heaven with His mighty angels in flaming fire, dealing out retribution to those who do not know God and to those who do not obey the gospel of our Lord Jesus. These will pay the penalty of eternal destruction, away from the presence of the Lord and from the glory of His power.* (2 Thess. 1:7-9)

God is for the good guys, and He is against the bad guys! Lot was tormented and Noah was rejected; however, in the end, God wins. Those who are worthy of salvation due to their faith will be saved. Those worthy of destruction due to their lack of faith will be punished. Either way, God's righteous judgment will take place, and at that time, the Justifier (Rom. 3:26) will assume His duty, and all will be made right! Our faith can be built upon the clarity of the expectations and understandings of God.

God Is Actively Working to Save the Lost and Punish the Unrighteous

One of life's great myths surrounds the idea that God is not here and is doing nothing. In the 2003 hit movie with Jim Carrey entitled *Bruce Almighty*, Bruce makes a statement that surrounds many people's idea of God. Bruce says, "God is a mean kid sitting on an anthill with a magnifying glass, and I'm the ant. He could fix my life in five minutes if He wanted to, but He'd rather burn off my feelers and watch me squirm." [15]

While this is a terrible and disrespectful way to depict or characterize God, it seems to fit the bill in the minds of some people, and they really feel this way. They think that God is playing or toying with their lives and essentially does nothing for them, that He is inactive and not present with His creation.

If there is one thing that I am sure of, it is that God did not make the world and walk away. He made the world, created man, man rejected His way, and He has been working to save man from their ways ever since. This is the complete truth of the entire Bible, from the first page to the last page.

Just think about it for a moment. God desired to have His people live in a promised land so He led them there (Gen. 13:14-15) where they could live, worship, and survive the world as His own possession. When it came time to fulfill that promised God used Moses and Aaron to bring the people out of Egyptian captivity after a span of 430 years (Ex. 12:40-41) to the land of promise. God would lead the faithful with the leadership of Joshua establishing the land as their own where they could live as God's people. But time after time they turned away from God only for God to bring them out and back to the land again and again. From the judges to the prophets, to the apostles and Christ Himself, God has continually worked to provide of way of passage into His wondrous glory. That does not sound like a God who does nothing!

---

15 *Bruce Almighty,* IMDb.com, 1990, www.imdb.com/title/tt0315327/quotes/.

Pay Attention to Those Who Try to Fake You!

It would do us well to understand an important truth. Glory is ours to lose, and Heaven is gain for those who seek it (cf. Matt. 6:33; Phil. 1:21).

The reality here is simple. God is truly *active* in the lives of all people. Actively seeking (Luke 19:10), searching (Luke 15:8), forgiving (1 John 1:9), adding (Acts 2:47), and cleaning (1 John 1:7) all those who will come to Him. Equally He is *active* in judgment. Just as He did not allow the nation of Israel to enter into the promised due to their lack of faithfulness, He will not allow any into Heaven in the same result. This isn't mean; it is reality.

Paul wrote that God is examining our hearts (1 Thess. 2:4), which is an active thing. This means that God is working in our lives, even though we may not know exactly how. Some use the word *providence*—a word that describes the workings of God in the lives of man. Can I see it right now? Maybe not, but when I look back at my life I can see many things that are a result of both God's blessings and work through the lives of others and opportunities that I have had.

Is it that hard to believe that God is working? The Bible shows us over and over again that He has worked diligently in the lives of many and even came down to be with us Himself (Jesus is "God with us," thus the meaning of the name *Emmanuel* [cf. Matt. 1:23]). If God took these measures to lead people into His ways of righteousness, why is it so hard to believe that He is active in our lives today? Is He talking to us? Yes! Through His Word. Can we talk to Him? Yes! Through prayer. Is He keeping the faithful in the right state or condition? Yes! He is keeping us clean (1 John 1:7). This shows us His activity. The faith builder is this: God continuously works, looks, and watches our lives to bless the faithful and curse those who are not. Either way, I can build my faith knowing God is actively working with me!

Rescue, Escape, Freedom

God has offered a way! God has provided a way! Will you take it? Will you accept it? That is the question. Noah had a choice—to build the ark or not build it. Lot had a choice to leave the city or not leave the city. While not in this chapter, Jesus also had the option to go to the cross or not go to the cross.

Each of these words has a powerful meaning.

- Rescue: *lit. to save* (2:7, 9)
- Escape: *lit. to avoid* (2:18, 20)
- Freedom: *lit. a state of being free* (2:19)

While Peter uses some of these words to describe the promises of false teachers or the opportunity you have with the Lord, each tells us what we have with God. God's name is used 35 times in this book alone, and that tells us something powerful: God will rescue us, allowing us to escape the deceptions of those in the world and have freedom from our sins! God alone has the power to rescue and to give you true freedom! He is your way of escape.

True faith (2 Pet. 1:1) gives us true power. How? In our relationship with God through Christ (cf. Matt. 6:13; Rom. 1:16; 1 Cor. 1:18; 2 Cor. 13:4; Eph. 3:7; Col. 1:29; Heb. 1:3; 1 Pet. 1:5). Not that the power is ours, but that through Christ we are in fellowship with God who is the great power and has great power over all things.

While the devil is the great power of the world (1 John 5:19), God has great power over him (cf. Job 1; Matt. 4:1-11; Luke 9:1). Therefore, He has the power to provide us a way of escape (1 Cor. 10:13), by rescuing us through Christ (Col. 1:13), giving us freedom with Him (Rom. 8:21; Gal. 5:1).

Peter shows us through these words that with God, the faithful who build their trust in His Word over the words of any person or preacher can and will be blessed with a heavenly future where we will exist for all eternity with Him!

CLOSING

As we go through life and all of the struggles it offers. We hear the false narratives surrounding the idea of God and His plan. As we struggle to see through the blurred lines of so many false teachings, let us remember one thing. Where God stands is where I need to stand. This doesn't mean we must be dogmatic about everything, rude, or condemning. It means that we must be "truth seekers" so that our hearts may actively seek God's truth and not our own.

As we close this lesson, chapter two's message regarding a building perspective is clear. With God is where I need to be, and away from God is where troubles will be. Don't let the world fake you; let God's Word make you!

Building

PAY ATTENTION TO WHERE A STRONG FAITH TAKES YOU!

2 Peter 3

GARRETT BERNETHY

"But according to His promise we are looking for new heavens and a new earth, in which righteousness dwells."
- 2 Peter 3:13 -

INTRODUCTION

Is it not a wonderful thing to think about? You know, eternal life?! It is something that I frequently think about. Especially regarding those I will get to see again. I think about what it will be like, how everything works, and what we will look like regarding the words and experience of John (1 John 3:2) and Peter (Matt. 17:1-13; Mark 9:1-13; Luke 9:28-37; cf. 2 Pet. 1:17). It is truly something that will be amazing!

When any of my boys ask me where we are going, my answer is generally always the same (partly to bug them, but partly to remind them), "We are going to Heaven." Now, while that is not something that originated with me but was picked up from a friend, it was in my mind something good to adopt—the reason why could not be any simpler. I want to get my family Home! That is where we belong, it is where you belong, it is where we all belong, *and* where God wants us to be.

It is so disheartening to know that the devil has created so much contention over this place. He is working from all directions, trying to pry us away from our Lord! Even when it comes to a place that is so good and majestic (More will be covered in detail in my special study entitled "What Do We Know About Heaven?"). I believe the point must be made in the most direct way possible! *Do not* let Satan pull you away from what Jesus is building (John 14:3), whether it be by lust, pride, or any other kind of sin, especially regarding the ideas and/or traditional thoughts of what this place looks like and where it will be. From a faith-building standpoint, I want to follow up with this statement regarding this idea. *Nothing will hinder a person's faith more than other Christians fighting over the place we are all striving to get to*! Don't let our limited understanding of Heaven drive us apart. Let it bring us closer together!

In Johnny Ramsey's discussion of 2 Peter 3, he wrote, "One can find the proper motivation for going forward in spiritual nobility; Christ is coming."[1] In understanding this undeniable fact, a person can and should be able to find the proper motivation to live each day in a fervent manner. We are expecting our Lord to come at any given moment, aren't we? I hope you are! It is so easy to fall into the mindset of those who mock the idea of His coming and possibly even come into agreement with their ideas, as Peter stated.

> *Where is the promise of His coming? For ever since the fathers fell asleep, all continues just as it was from the beginning of creation.*

Is their statement true? Yes, it is the truth; however, that doesn't mean that while something might be true, it nullifies something else that might be true simultaneously. Yes, the world has been in a constant state of motion as it was created to do. As God spoke *"in the beginning"* and made all things come into being that once were not (Gen. 1), He created a universe of self-sufficiency in which all things were held together by the word of His power, and at the same time continue to work, as He designed them to. The reality is all things will be this way until God Himself is ready for it not to be this way. So until the day dawns that Jesus appears from the clouds after the loud voice and trumpet sound (1 Thess. 4:16), plants will continue to lay seed and regrow. The seasons will continue to change in rotation, the sun will continue to rule the day and the moon the night. And mankind will continue to be born as well as grow old and pass away because that is how God designed all things.

The motivating factor that can and should be found here is simple: We ought to pay attention to what lies ahead to be prepared for what is coming, Jesus Christ our Lord. With everything we deal with constantly and continuously, isn't it nice to know that there is something ahead of us that we can look forward to? In my experience, I tend to operate better and have a better attitude when something great is ahead of me. For instance, just a few years ago, my family and I planned a vacation together to Disney World. For a year, we planned for the trip so that we could be ready when it came. Everything had to be purchased and paid for, from travel to the hotel to the tickets before our departure. If we had not prepared ourselves to be at Disney when we got to Disney, the doors would have been closed to us. The Bible speaks of a similar concept in Matthew 25:1-13, in the parable of the ten virgins. On that day, our ability to walk through the door will depend on just how prepared we have made ourselves. Motivation will drive preparedness to the fullest, but without it, being prepared might not be anything more than a dream.

A Foundation of Motivation

What is the motivating factor for us to attain our heavenly goal? Is it the *"streets of gold"* (Rev. 21:21)? Is it the people or family we once knew here on earth? Is it found in the songs we sing or the encouraging thoughts from a preacher standing behind a pulpit? I think that I can speak for Peter and myself when I say that it really is not any of these things, even though they are all great reasons. The real motivation however is because that is where our Lord is; that is where our God resides.

---

[1] Johnny Ramsey, *Cover to Cover: Bible Questions Answered* (Abilene: Quality Publications, 1981) 300.

Pay Attention to Where a Strong Faith Takes You!

Remember, Jesus said, *"I will come again and receive you to Myself, that where I am, there you may be also"* (John 14:3). Isn't this great? Our Lord has promised to come back! To get us! *And* bring us with Him! *But how does all of this work? What does He expect from me?* In our first building session, we discussed the idea that our faith is built on what we know. Therefore, knowledge is power when it comes to our eternal state. So, the more we know, the more comfort we can have, and the more we can look forward to the life to come.

First, let's think about what I believe is the main point of this section. It is what Peter states in verses 11b-12a as he writes,

> *What sort of people ought you to be in holy conduct and godliness, looking for and hastening the coming of the day of God?*

So, let's think about our first question:

How does all of this work?

In other words, what is going to happen? After all, everyone is looking for all of the signs of His coming; what are they, and when will we know? After all, that is the first part of their question. Peter says the mockers will say, *"Where is the promise of His coming?"*

To first answer this question, many minds have been damaged or, to use a word from chapter two, *"enticed"* (2:14) to believe that we will be able to tell when He will come, which has, I believe, brought a false sense of comfort to many people in the world. Some of this is built on a lack of understanding of Matthew 24, 1 Thessalonians 4, Revelation, and several other passages that could be mentioned. However, we must remember the words of Jesus Himself regarding His second coming.

> *Heaven and earth will pass away, but My words will not pass away. But of that day and hour, **no one knows, not even** the angels of heaven, **nor** the Son, but the Father alone.* (Matt. 24:35-36, emp. added)

We must *pay attention* to the words of Jesus so that we, too, do not fall into the deceptive schemes and words of those who preach and teach false doctrines surrounding the end of time. One of the most harmful of these teachings is Dispensational Premillennialism. This doctrine claims one may have a second chance at salvation, that Jesus will reign here on earth for a thousand years, and that many will be secretly raptured or taken to Heaven without anyone knowing it. While these are only three areas of this false teaching, these are prefaced with signs of His coming.

This is such a dangerous, ignorant, and disrespectful doctrine, and it is hard for me to understand how so many so-called "preachers" or "pastors" who claim to study their Bibles can come to a belief like this. It is filled with error and is completely against the pattern of the Gospel and the teachings of the entire Bible. Not to mention, it makes the bold claim that Jesus was and is a failure when it came to the establishment of His Kingdom! How ridiculous and irresponsible can we be to come up with an accusation such as this, which has no basis or Biblical foundation? However, many people have come to believe in it. Why? Because they aren't *paying attention* to His Word.

When we dive into the question, "How does all of this work?" We are discussing the day of judgment. We are essentially asking the questions: What will happen, and is there an order to the events that will take place?

But first, I think it is good for us to think on a couple of things regarding the days leading up to the great Day of the Lord. As the apostle Paul wrote to the Thessalonian brethren, he wasn't necessarily dealing with the false doctrine of Dispensational Premillennialism but rather another form of doctrine that was very persuasive and led the people to believe things that were not true.

In 1 Thessalonians, the people were led to believe regarding the eschatological event that those who had died or *"fallen asleep"* before His coming would miss out on their opportunity to find Heaven itself as Jesus would essentially forget them. However, Paul refocuses the minds of people back to the basic principles of the Gospel regarding His resurrection (1 Thess. 4:14). He states that *"by the Word of the Lord we who are alive will not precede those who have fallen asleep"* (1 Thess. 4:15). These words are preceded by Paul saying, *"We do not want you to be uninformed brethren,"* meaning we want to make sure you understand how this works, just as Jesus was raised from the dead, so will you be.

In 2 Thessalonians, another false teaching arises amongst the brethren, leading them to believe that Jesus had already come! Thus, putting the people into a state of depression, it seems as if many were going through life in a daze, being lost and filled with no purpose. However, Paul once again shows them the way of truth, saying, *"With regard to the coming of our Lord Jesus Christ and our gathering together with Him"* (2 Thess. 2:1), clarifying the main point of his argument towards the false teaching, the coming of Jesus. In chapter 1, he says, *"When the Lord Jesus **will be** revealed"* (1:7) and *"**When He comes** to be glorified in His saints on that day"* (1:10), showing them that Jesus has not come yet but will come in the future. By these words, Paul is showing them that the words spoken before they came to believe this (2 Thess. 2:5), which were from God, gave them the right knowledge about the Day of the Lord, and they needed to *pay attention* to that truth!

God, through the writings of many different men, has also given us today the knowledge we need to understand what is to come and how all of it will happen. Here is the order of events the Bible teaches will take place on that day.

First, we begin with the words of the angel in Acts 1:11, *"Men of Galilee, why do you stand looking into the sky? This Jesus, who has been taken up from you into heaven, **will come in just the same way as you have watched Him go into heaven**."* From this, we are able to connect to the words of the apostle Paul in 1 Thessalonians 4:16, *"For the **Lord Himself will descend from heaven** with a shout, with the voice of the archangel and with the trumpet of God."* So, Jesus left mankind and went into the clouds and when He comes back to receive mankind it will be from the clouds.

Second, Paul says, *"The dead in Christ will rise first, then we who are alive and remain will be caught up together with them in the clouds to meet the Lord in the air"* (1 Thess. 4:16-17).

Third, the *"righteous judgment"* of God will take place, assuring a devastating penalty against the ungodly but also guarantees that the believers will be counted worthy of God's kingdom (1 Thess. 5:24; 2 Thess. 1:5), finding rest from hardships (2 Thess. 1:7) and experiencing salvation and glory in lieu of the terrible fate the unfaithful will experience.[2]

Fourth, at that point, when the sentencing has taken place, all of the faithful will reap the benefiting words of Paul at the end of 1 Thessalonians 4:17, *"And so we shall always be with the Lord."*

---

2 Denny Petrillo, et al., "Learning Section 1" *Excel Still More Bible Workshop 1 Thessalonians* (Nashville: Kaio Publications, 2020) 5.

Pay Attention to Where a Strong Faith Takes You!

It is at this point that we will be heading to what both Peter (2 Pet. 3:13) and John (Rev. 21:1) describe as the *"new heavens and new earth"*—the eternal resting place of God's people where we will dwell together with each other and with God (Rev. 21:3)!

What does He expect from me?

In other words, what am I required to do to receive an invitation to be home with Him? Again, regarding the statement made by the false teachers in 2 Peter 3:4, *"All continues just as it was from the beginning of creation."* To be honest, this is a statement I can appreciate, not in its context but in its most fundamental meaning. Just what has God expected from mankind since their creation?

According to Peter, there are a few things that the Holy Spirit has made him aware of as he wrote to those who had been *"scattered throughout"* (1 Pet. 1:1) the land.

1. **Faith**: πίστις, *pistis*, which can be translated as *believe* (1 Pet. 1:7, 21; 2:6, 7); faith (1 Pet. 1:5, 7, 9, 21; 5:9; 2 Pet. 1:1, 5), or faithful (1 Pet. 4:19; 5:12). It gives you protection (1 Pet. 1:5) from the wrath of God (Rom. 5:9), it brings you to a point or *"result in praise and glory and honor at the revelation of Jesus Christ"* (1 Pet. 1:7). Its outcome is salvation (1 Pet. 1:9). It allows for hope to be in your life (1 Pet. 1:21) and puts you in the same family as the apostle Peter himself (2 Pet. 1:1) which is of God. This faith is based not on feelings or tradition but rather on eyewitness accounts (2 Pet. 1:16-19) of those who lived long before us. There is no doubt that Peter concurs with the statement made in Hebrews 11:6 as the writer states, *"And without faith (πίστις) it is impossible to please Him, for he who comes to God must believe (πιστεύω) that He is and that He is a rewarder of those who seek Him."*

2. **Obedience**: ὑπακοή, *hypakoe*, although only used in the first letter, the message of both letters is filled with this concept. The word itself means to be "in a state of being in compliance,"[3] mainly compliance with the will of the Lord. Why were Adam and Eve cast out of the garden? Lack of obedience—in other words, they did not do as He said and therefore went against His will. Notice what Peter writes about this subject in his second letter. In chapter 1:5, Peter states, *"Now for this very reason also applying all,"* which is pointing them in the direction of something or some things they must do to live the Christian life. He follows up in verse 8 by saying, *"For if these qualities are yours and are increasing, they render you neither useless nor unfruitful in the true knowledge of our Lord Jesus Christ."* Essentially, what we can take from this is that one cannot become fruitful or useful to the Lord unless they have and are devoting themselves to His will. Therefore, the concept of obedience comes into play. The obedient are devoting themselves to complying with His will in their life to the fullest and live in a way that exemplifies *"faith, moral excellence, knowledge, self-control, perseverance, godliness, brotherly kindness, and love"* (1 Pet. 1:5-7).

3. **Baptism**: βάπτισμα, *baptisma*, used in 1 Peter 3:21, "the ceremonious use of water for the purpose of renewing or establishing a relationship."[4] Denny Petrillo said in his section regarding this passage, "If one is not baptized, then he will not be saved, just like those not in the ark were not *saved*. Baptism is an *appeal* to God. This is similar terminology to Acts 1:21; 22:16

---

3 William Arndt et al., *A Greek-English Lexicon of the New Testament and Other Early Christian Literature* (Chicago: University of Chicago Press, 2000), 1028.

4 Arndt et al., 165.

and Romans 10:13. One *"calls on the Lord"* only after having done what the Lord requires (cf. Matt. 7:21-23)." The command of baptism is something that Peter heard from Jesus (Matt. 28:19; Mark 16:16); preached to the people (Acts 2:38) and continued to teach as the only way to salvation (1 Pet. 1:3, 23; 3:21; 2 Pet. 1:9-11; cf. 2 Pet. 3:14). It is the connecting point to the blood of Christ (Gal. 3:27) which washes us clean (1 John 1:7) and places us into a relationship with God as we have reenacted the death, burial, and resurrection of Christ (Rom. 6:3-5). Accordingly it is this action that allows God to add you to His church (Acts 2:47) the body of Christ (Col. 1:18) where we *"in Christ"* are able to reap *"every spiritual blessing in the heavenly places"* (Eph. 1:3).

4. **Repentance**: μετάνοια, *metanoia*, in 2 Peter 3:9 meaning, "repentance, turning about, conversion; as a turning away."⁵ Peter states, *"The Lord is not slow about His promise, as some count slowness, but is patient toward you, not wishing for any to perish but for all to come to repentance."* Of course, this falls completely in line with the words of John the Baptizer, who began preaching, *"Repent for the Kingdom of Heaven is at hand"* (Matt. 3:2), only to be followed by Jesus Himself making this claim (Matt. 4:17). The apostle Paul would write in his letter to the Roman Church, *"Or do you think lightly of the riches of His kindness and tolerance and patience, not knowing that the kindness of God leads you to repentance?"* The call to follow the Lord is one that *"transfers"* you (Col. 1:13), one that *"transforms"* you (Rom. 12:2), one *"converts"* you (cf. Matt. 18:3), one that *"restores"* you (cf. Gal. 6:1), and one that allows you to be in right standing with God (cf. 2 Cor. 7:9-10). To turn from the ways of the world to the ways of God by stopping your ways and clinging to His is and can be the hardest set of choices you may ever make, but it is equally the greatest opportunity you could ever ask for. An about face in life!

While I know that there are many other things that could be in this list, all of these are connected to and under the umbrella of *obedience*. So to return to the question, "What does He expect from me?" It is simple. *He requires and/or expects your faithful obedience to Him.*

Jesus and others would put it in this way,

> You shall love the Lord your God with all your heart, and with all your soul, and with all your mind. (Matt. 22:37; Mark 12:30; Luke 10:27)

This is what He expects not only from me, but also from all people, which seems to be the reason that we find what I believe is the main point,

> *What sort of people ought you to be in holy conduct and godliness, looking for and hastening the coming of the day of God?* (2 Peter 3:11b-12a)

This provides us with our much-needed focus by the question, *"What sort of people ought you to be?"* First, we must be people of *holy conduct*, second, we must be a *godly people*, and thirdly, we must be a people who are *looking for and hastening* (lit. to be in a hurry) *the coming of the day of God*. So what does this mean? It means that all eyes should be focused on being ready for the Lord to come!

Our motivation for being in Heaven should be a simple answer: to be with Him. Our efforts should be a direct action—obedience. Our thought should be a moving force—our faith. Our goal

---

5 Arndt et al., 640.

Pay Attention to Where a Strong Faith Takes You!

of Heaven should be the driving point that takes us all the way to the parting of the clouds. So the foundation of our motivation should be in the wisdom that we have gained in the Gospel message. Therefore we ought to pay attention to the fact that if God raised Jesus from the dead and brought Him to His rightful place, then He will do the same to us. This is and should be motivating us to live righteously (2 Pet. 3:13).

Building on His Promise

God's promises are things that we can depend on with absolute confidence, as they are and have always been immovable and concrete. Not one of those promises that He has made has ever been broken or not kept by Him. This is something I can build on. Someone once said, "You cannot break God's promises by leaning on them," which I believe to be true. If God has said them, then I can hold Him to the promises made with an expectation that He will remain true to His Word. From the pages of the Bible, which have proven to be true over and again, God's track record in promise-keeping allows me to know I can cash in on His promises with confidence.

Let's think about a few of these promises…

- God promises His presence: Deut. 31:6, 8; Josh. 1:5; cf. Matt. 18:20; 28:20.
- God promises His protection: Gen. 15:1; Deut. 33:29; Ps. 3:3; Prov. 30:5; cf. Eph. 6:16.
- God promises His power: Ex. 15:2; Ps. 43:2; 59:17; Isa. 12:2; 41:10; 1 Pet. 4:11.
- God promises provisions: Deut. 33:7; 1 Sam. 7:12; Ps. 27:9; 70:5; Isa. 41:10, 14; 44:2; 49:8; Acts 26:22; Rom. 8:26.
- God promises His position: Ex. 13:21; Job 12:23; Ps. 23:2; 31:3; Prov. 19:23; John 10:3-4; cf. Acts 11:18; Rom. 2:4.
- God promises His patience: Rom. 2:4; 1 Tim. 1:16; cf. 1 Pet. 3:20; 2 Pet. 3:9, 15.
- God promises His plan: Matt. 25:34; Luke 22:22; Acts 2:23; 3:18; 4:28; 1 Pet. 1:20.
- God promises His purification: Eze. 37:23; Tit. 2:14; Heb. 1:3; 9:14; 1 John 1:7, 9.
- God promises His place: Matt. 3:2; 5:3, 10, 12; 6:20; 19:14; John 14:1-6; 2 Cor. 5:2; Phil. 3:20; Col. 1:5; 1 Thess. 4:16-18; 2 Tim. 4:8; 1 Pet. 1:4; 2 Pet. 3:13; Rev. 21:1-3.

What do all of these mean? Simply put, God has always desired to dwell among His people. From the time of the garden until He brings us home, that has always been His desire. For us to reach the goal of His desire, He offers us His protection, which is given through His Word, thus offering us His power or strength to fight the good fight of faith. With His ability to carry out His part of the plan to bring all to salvation, He leads us home by the direction of His Word with patience, having a great desire for all to come to repentance. This allows all to follow the plan of salvation that was once set in place and carried out by His Son, bringing the ability and opportunity for one to have purification of all of their sins, bringing them to the point that they can come home to be in Heaven with Him.

These are God's promises, and every one of them has been kept! However, some remain, which is the emphasis of our lesson, "Pay attention to where a strong faith takes you." To accomplish our goal with this lesson or chapter, it is important that we put everything into a proper perspective. To look forward, we must look back, because looking back shows you how to look forward. The blessing in doing this is simple: It shows us how to live in the now.

Looking Back: 2 Peter 3:5-6

> *For when they maintain this, it escapes their notice that* **by the word of God** *the heavens existed long ago and the earth was formed out of water and by water, through which the world at that time was destroyed, being flooded with water.*

The first of the two examples concerns how the heavens and earth were created and formed (Gen. 1). We cannot let the fact escape us that it was by the *Word of God* that all of this happened (cf. "*Then God said….*" Gen. 1:3, 6, 9, 11, 14, 20, 24, 26, 29) and as He spoke, all things came into being (Gen. 1; John 1:1-3), and all was good which includes everything in the known universe from the galaxies to the grain of sand. It came into being by the *Word of God*.

In the second example, Peter looks once again (cf. 1 Pet. 3:20-21) at the flood account of Genesis 6-9; he emphasizes that the flood came by the *Word of God*, which is important here. It was God who told Noah the flood would come (Gen. 6:13-17). It was God who told Noah to build the ark and how (Gen. 6:14-16). It was God who told Noah to board the ark (Gen. 7:1). It was God who told Noah who and what all would be in the ark (Gen. 6:19-20; 7:2-3). It was God who closed the door (Gen. 7:16).

So, as we look back on these two events, it is clear to us through Peter's words through the Holy Spirit that God was in charge of all that happened, caused all of it to happen, and dictated when and how it all would happen. Why does that matter to us? It is simple. When God said something during the six days of creation, *it happened*! When God told Noah a flood was coming and that He would save him, his family, and all the animals, *He did*! Because I know what God has done in the past, it helps to build a faith in Him as a result of His actions.

Looking Forward: 2 Peter 3:7

> *But* **by His word** *the present heavens and earth are being reserved for fire, kept for the day of judgment and destruction of ungodly men.*

Two things are essentially at play here. First, Peter is contrasting his words with those of the mockers who have stated that "*all continues just as it was from the beginning of creation.*" Second, Peter is further proving that the things that God has done in the past show clearly what God is planning to do in the future. So to the future, Peter looks and states that the "universe" is now being reserved for fire, which is the way that God plans to destroy (lit. *annihilate*[6]) all creation in the "*day of the Lord*" (3:10).

---

6 "Annihilation Synonyms: 50 Similar and Opposite Words," *Merriam-Webster*, www.merriam-webster.com/thesaurus/annihilation.

Pay Attention to Where a Strong Faith Takes You!

It is because we know what God has done in the past that we can know what He can do in the future in regard to the destruction. As we look back, we know that God said He was going to destroy the world with the flood, and He did. As we look forward, we also know that because He has stated that He has reserved the world for fire and destruction, He will. So, in essence, the past is showing us by the words of Peter as the Holy Spirit guides him, the future as to what God intends to do when time is up.

God's promises of the future reflect God's promises of the past. This means that in your life today, as you sit reading this chapter, you have a choice. You can choose to live a repentant life full of "*faith, moral excellence, knowledge, self-control, perseverance, godliness, brotherly kindness, and love,*" or to live a life of lust as an unstable soul. I know what has been; therefore, I can know what is coming. Because of that, I need to think about how I can live right now.

Here is why this is important. Because we are still focusing on "*What sort of people ought you to be*" as you are "*looking for and hastening the coming of the day of God*" (vv. 11-12). If I know that God said to create something and He did (v. 5), and if God said He would destroy it by water, and He did (v. 6; cf. Gen. 6–9), and He is also saying that He will destroy (lit. *annihilate*) the heavens and earth (lit. *universe*), then will not the outcome of the godly and ungodly be founded upon the same principles? These principles that show us that God's words are certain and final.

Remember, these things "*escaped their notice*" (3:5, 8), because God is powerful enough to **create** and **destroy**, therefore He is also powerful enough to **save** and **condemn**. So, on the one hand, Peter is discussing the destruction of the heavens and earth from a physical standpoint, and on the other hand, he is telling us about the "*new heavens and earth*" we are waiting for from a spiritual standpoint. Why? Because where you are right now is not a permanent place, as all creation has an end date. The false teachers have overlooked this because it has "*escaped their notice.*"

Have you ever watched any of the *Titanic* footage—not the movie but the documentary-type footage that James Cameron has done a magnificent job with? If you were to watch any of his films about the actual boat *Titanic*, you would realize he has filmed hours of this vessel. In one second, they might show you what the boat looked like before its maiden voyage, and then in the other, they will show you what it looks like now. It is nothing more than a remnant of what it was, of course, as the saltwater from the ocean has caused great decay of the boat's materials. This very thing is a prime example of what has escaped their notice. Not necessarily the decay of the *Titanic*, but the decay of all things.

How often have you gone through the country to see an old schoolhouse or home that someone lived in or went to school in at one time? Many of them were made out of wood, and over time, that wood has gone untreated and, in many cases, left abandoned, has gotten old and began to rot, losing its strength and integrity as a building structure. In the case of my grandmother's old home she grew up in, at least the last time I saw it, it was leaning, had holes in the roof, no windows, the floor was almost gone, and had become an uninhabitable space.

Both the *Titanic* and my grandmother's old house have withered away over time, and nature has essentially eaten them up to become something that is nothing more than a memory. Both uninhabitable and both a memory. That is the future for this place that we live in and the bodies we currently reside in. You might think, what do you mean by the bodies we currently reside in? I mean this. You are a physically created being with a body that is made from the earth. We know this because it was from the ground that God created Adam (Gen. 2:7) and to the dirt where our bodies will return (Gen. 3:19). So, our physical bodies will remain here with the earth even in its times of destruction. However, you are also a spiritually created being, and upon conception, a soul was created and placed in a physical body as it grew in a mother's womb (cf. Luke 1:39-44). James, the brother of Jesus, would write regarding the soul of a person that God "*jealously desires the Spirit which He has made to dwell in us.*"

What Peter is focusing on is this: God's promise of a day of destruction is not only real but is concretely founded and proven by what He has already done in the past which equally pertains to those who are faithful and unfaithful. God's promises come true!

Notice Peter's words in verses 14-16:

> *Therefore, beloved, since you look for these things, be diligent to be found by Him in peace, spotless and blameless, and regard the patience of our Lord as salvation; just as also our beloved brother Paul, according to the wisdom given him, wrote to you, as also in all his letters, speaking in them of these things, in which are some things hard to understand, which the untaught and unstable distort, as they do also the rest of the Scriptures, to their own destruction.*

FAITH BUILDING

Pay attention to where a strong faith will take you!

1. Don't Confuse the Stability of Our World with the Patience of God

There is no doubt that Peter characterizes the *mockers* or false teachers as confused, lost, or blind. Most likely this is due to their sinful tendencies of lust, "*having a heart trained in greed*" (2:14). But they are right about the stability of the world, even Solomon would agree to that as he stated,

> *That which has been is that which will be, And that which has been done is that which will be done. So there is nothing new under the sun.* (Eccl. 1:9)

The difference between these people and Solomon is found in their understanding. You see while the false teacher may have had the right conclusion, they had the wrong context. Solomon understood better. Look at what he wrote:

> *He has made everything appropriate in its time. He has also set eternity in their heart, yet so that man will not find out the work which God has done from the beginning even to the end. I know that there is nothing better for them than to rejoice and to do good in one's lifetime; moreover, that every man who eats and drinks sees good in all his labor—it is the gift of God. I know that everything God does will remain forever; there is nothing to add to it and there is nothing to take from it, for God has so worked that men should fear Him. That which is has been already and that which will be has already been, for God seeks what has passed by. Furthermore, I have seen under the sun that in the place of justice there is wickedness and in the place of righteousness there is wickedness. I said to myself, "God will judge both the righteous man and the wicked man," for a*

Pay Attention to Where a Strong Faith Takes You!

time for every matter and for every deed is there. I said to myself concerning the sons of men, "God has surely tested them in order for them to see that they are but beasts." For the fate of the sons of men and the fate of beasts is the same. As one dies so dies the other; indeed, they all have the same breath and there is no advantage for man over beast, for all is vanity. All go to the same place. All came from the dust and all return to the dust. Who knows that the breath of man ascends upward and the breath of the beast descends downward to the earth? I have seen that nothing is better than that man should be happy in his activities, for that is his lot. For who will bring him to see what will occur after him? (Eccl. 3:11-22)

Understanding is everything! While the world continues to turn, time continues to grow closer for His coming. While all things have a beginning, all things also have an end. We should not get these confused. Rather, we should focus on the words of Jesus that thrust our minds to our future abode, *"The Kingdom of heaven is at hand!"*

Remember, there is a reason that the world has continued and is continuing to move, breathe, and exist, and that is because of God's patience!!! I am thankful for God's patience because it continues to allow me to *"repent and return"* (Acts 3:19) to Him when I fall away. He wants all to come to Him and is allowing time for that to happen. We should never be confused about this truth. His patience is not to build the prideful and sinful actions of men; it is to allow souls to come to repentance (3:9).

Keeping these things straight helps me understand profound truths.

1. God loves mankind to a degree that is beyond my comprehension and patiently waits for the lost to come to Him, even in great times of sin.

2. God is providing more than enough time for us to both seek out His truth and apply it to our lives so that we can focus on the type of people we need to be. …*Regard the patience of our Lord as salvation* (3:15).

2. Be Diligent and Pay Attention so that God's Truths Do Not "Escape Your Notice"

One of the top 15 things people say when they lose something is, "If I had a dollar for every time something vanished, I'd be rich in frustration."[7] Have you ever lost something or couldn't find something? Just this morning, I couldn't find my shoes, so I went and asked my wife if she had seen them or knew where they were. She told me they were in my room by the closet, so I went and looked, and nothing. They weren't there. So I told her I'd wear something else if they weren't there, and she said, "If I go in there and walk right to them, you're going to be in trouble!" as she smiled at me, to which I replied, "That's where I normally am—smiling back."

What happened!? She came back with my shoes! I said, "Where did you find them?" She said, "They were out in the open, in plain sight, and you looked right over them!" Which was true.

Then she said, "I know why boys can't ever find their stuff—they never seem to look!" To which we both giggled a little bit, knowing it was true.

---

7 Admin, "15 Funny Ways to Say Something Is Lost," *Responsefully*, 21 Aug. 2023, responsefully.com/funny-ways-to-say-something-is-lost/.

Here is the point: Like my shoes, it is easy for things to *"escape our notice"* for us to look over them. Even while preparing for my work in this book, I read and read over both 2 Peter and Jude and seemed to find something every time that I had overlooked somehow before.

This is another reason I am thankful for the patience of God. Because I overlook things. Sometimes it may be intentional; most of the time, it is not. Either way, something happens. This is where our diligence to *"accurately handle the word of truth"* (2 Tim. 2:15) must come into play. I may overlook my shoes on the floor or something on my schedule from time to time, but what I cannot overlook is the foundational truths of God's plan for salvation. I cannot overlook my ability and responsibility to apply the seven virtues mentioned in chapter 1. I cannot overlook the way that I have connections with others in Christ and my connection with God Himself through Christ. I cannot overlook the fact that Jesus is coming and that I must be ready!

Notice that Peter uses the phrase "*looking for:*"

> **Looking for** and hastening the coming of the day of God, because of which the heavens will be destroyed by burning, and the elements will melt with intense heat! But according to His promise we are **looking for** new heavens and a new earth, in which righteousness dwells. Therefore, beloved, since you **look for** these things, be diligent to be found by Him in peace, spotless and blameless. (2 Pet. 3:12-14, emp. added)

If you are *looking for* something, you are paying attention to that something, which in this case is the day that is to come. The idea that Peter presents to us in both letters is this: Be on high alert (1 Pet. 5:8; 2 Pet. 3:10), be prepared (2 Pet. 1:5-8; 2 Pet. 3:12, 14), be right in His eyes (2 Pet. 3:11), and be equipped with the right kind of knowledge (2 Pet. 3:16-17).

We cannot be caught off guard when Jesus comes; it should not be a day of terror and tears but praise and excitement. The only way this happens is to pay attention to His words so that nothing will have escaped our notice when the time comes.

3. The Importance of the Word *All*

Notice what Peter writes in verse 9,

> *The Lord is not slow about His promise, as some count slowness, but is patient toward you, not wishing for any to perish but for all to come to repentance.*

As Peter closes out his second letter, he discusses the apostle Paul and says these words:

> *...And regard the patience of our Lord as salvation; just as also our beloved brother Paul, according to the wisdom given him, wrote to you, as also in all his letters, speaking in them of these things, in which are some things hard to understand, which the untaught and unstable distort, as they do also the rest of the Scriptures, to their own destruction.* (2 Pet. 3:15-16)

There are a number of people out there today who believe that the Bible is too hard to understand and, therefore, essentially just wave it off or leave the "interpretation" up to some guy they don't know but has an official name like "pope" or "priest" or "pastor." This, I believe, is where you get the phrase "my preacher or pastor said" mostly. However, those who do this and have fallen into the

Pay Attention to Where a Strong Faith Takes You!

trap of "believing it's too hard" fall under the two categories that Peter identifies. First, you have the *ignorant* (lacking knowledge or comprehension of the thing specified[8]), and second, you have the *unstable* (not steady in action or movement[9]).

These are the people who are finding it hard to comprehend the writings of Paul. But why does this apply to us? Simple today we have 13 confirmed books or letter who were written by none other than the apostle Paul himself. So the letters that we have today are the letters that were circulating during that time. Could there be something he wrote that we don't have? I guess anything is possible, but when it comes to the written Word of God I believe that we have what we are supposed to have. Therefore if this is the case, then what applies to them applies to us.

Denny wrote in his notes on verse 16, "It is possible to understand the difficult writings of Paul." I agree. Are some writings harder than others to understand without study, yes; but it doesn't mean they are not understandable. Why do I say this? The reason is simple. When we look at the word *all* in context of the verse, Paul has much to say on the matter.

For instance, notice how he begins in the book of Romans,

> *For the wrath of God is revealed from heaven against **all** ungodliness and unrighteousness of men who suppress the truth in unrighteousness, because that which is known about God is evident within them; for God made it evident to them.* (Rom. 1:18-19)

How about,

> *But now apart from the Law the righteousness of God has been manifested, being witnessed by the Law and the Prophets, even the righteousness of God through faith in Jesus Christ for **all** those who believe; for there is no distinction; for all have sinned and fall short of the glory of God.* (Rom. 3:21-23)

Or lastly,

> *Now if we have died with Christ, we believe that we shall also live with Him, knowing that Christ, having been raised from the dead, is never to die again; death no longer is master over Him. For the death that He died, He died to sin once for **all**; but the life that He lives, He lives to God. Even so consider yourselves to be dead to sin, but alive to God in Christ Jesus.* (Rom. 6:8-11)

The New American Standard Bible translates the word *all* 60 times in the book of Romans alone, and in many cases, the word describes just who the Gospel message is for. Here, both Peter and Paul speak the same thing by telling those they are writing to, including us, that the Gospel is for all, as God has a great desire for **all** people to come to repentance. Therefore, God does not get involved in the world's thoughts and does not care who you are or where the world puts you. He sees a soul and desires to have it (James 4:5)!

Know that you are included in the word *all*, which means that God's patience is waiting for you, too!

---

8 "Ignorant," *Merriam-Webster*, https://www.merriam-webster.com/dictionary/ignorant.
9 "Unstable," *Merriam-Webster*, https://www.merriam-webster.com/dictionary/unstable.

4. God Is Looking for You, So Allow Yourself to Be Found by Him

Peter writes,

> *Therefore, beloved, since you look for these things, be diligent* **to be found by Him** *in peace, spotless and blameless.*

Note these words,

> *For the Son of Man has come to seek and to save that which was lost.* (Luke 19:10)

What exactly was the purpose of Christ here on earth? What was the purpose of God's plan for man? What is it that He is trying to accomplish? I believe that Jesus helps us to understand these parables.

Parable of the Lost Sheep

> *What man among you, if he has a hundred sheep and has lost one of them, does not leave the ninety-nine in the open pasture and go after the one which is lost until he finds it? When he has found it, he lays it on his shoulders, rejoicing. And when he comes home, he calls together his friends and his neighbors, saying to them, "Rejoice with me, for I have found my sheep which was lost!"* **I tell you that in the same way, there will be more joy in heaven over one sinner who repents than over ninety-nine righteous persons who need no repentance.** (Luke 15:4-7, emp. added)

Parable of the Lost Coin

> *Or what woman, if she has ten silver coins and loses one coin, does not light a lamp and sweep the house and search carefully until she finds it? When she has found it, she calls together her friends and neighbors, saying, "Rejoice with me, for I have found the coin which I had lost!"* **In the same way, I tell you, there is joy in the presence of the angels of God over one sinner who repents.** (Luke 15:8-10, emp. added)

Parable of the Lost Son

> *The younger of them said to his father, "Father, give me the share of the estate that falls to me." So he divided his wealth between them. And not many days later, the younger son gathered everything together and went on a journey into a distant country, and there he squandered his estate with loose living. Now when he had spent everything, a severe famine occurred in that country, and he began to be impoverished. So he went and hired himself out to one of the citizens of that country, and he sent him into his fields to feed swine. And he would have gladly filled his stomach with the pods that the swine were eating, and no one was giving anything to him. But when he came to his senses, he said, "How many of my father's hired men have more than enough bread, but I am dying here with hunger! I will get up and go to my father, and will say to him, 'Father, I have sinned against heaven, and in your sight; I am no longer worthy to be called your son; make me as one of your hired men.'" So he got up and came to his father. But while he was still a long way off, his father saw him and felt compassion for him, and ran and embraced him and kissed him.* (Luke 15:12-32)

Pay Attention to Where a Strong Faith Takes You!

For each of these what exactly do they mean and who are they talking about? The answer is simple. The lost! The shepherd left the entire flock of ninety-nine, meaning he left possible property, wealth, a food source, his livelihood—all for one single sheep. Why? Because the one that was lost at that point meant more to him that those who were with him. The woman with the coin tore her house apart just looking for one coin. The lost son is of great importance to many people as a son left to squander all that he had but came back and found his father waiting and ready to celebrate because he was home. Now while there is much more that we could dive into with each of these parables, let's note the most important part of each of these parables.

> *I tell you that in the same way, there will be more joy in heaven over one sinner who repents than over ninety-nine righteous persons who need no repentance.* (Luke 15:7)

> *In the same way, I tell you, there is joy in the presence of the angels of God over one sinner who repents.* (Luke 15:10)

> *But we had to celebrate and rejoice, for this brother of yours was dead and has begun to live, and was lost and has been found.* (Luke 15:32)

As we look to this phrase, *"be diligent to be found by Him,"* it must bring a great truth to your mind—He is looking for you! But we must pay attention to what comes after those words. Peter says, "… *To be found by Him in peace, spotless, and blameless."* This means that when He comes looking, we better be what He is looking for. The shepherd was looking for a sheep, not a goat. The woman was looking for a coin, not her purse. The father was looking for his son, not a slave. When we look at these three parables, here is what we find about the person He is looking for. To Him, a person or soul is important; we are valued and *worthy of saving*. That is how He feels about us. But only those who are obedient to His will are the ones who will be invited in the door. Let your faith be built on the fact that you matter, and He is looking!

CLOSING THOUGHTS

As Peter continues to tell us in his writings, strong faith is built by powerful knowledge. As we have looked at chapter 3 from a faith-building standpoint, we must remember our eternal goal and what it will take to get there. Don't let the doubters and the naysayers pull you away and make you feel bad for what you believe. Don't let the false teachings of those against the Gospel of Jesus pull you away. Believe in what the Bible tells you because that is what God tells you. If God says it and the world doesn't believe it, then honestly that is their problem and not ours. That may sound harsh and faint-hearted, but it is true. He who believes has the opportunity to be saved, but those who turn from the truth are turning from everlasting life.

Everyone has a choice, and we will all face the consequences of our decisions. So, pay attention to where a strong faith can take you. Believe in Him, and He will save you!

Building

PAY ATTENTION TO THE WORDS THAT SAVE YOU!

Jude

GARRETT BERNETHY

"But you, beloved, ought to remember the words that were spoken beforehand by the apostles of our Lord Jesus Christ."
- Jude 17 -

INTRODUCTION

There are two letters in the New Testament that particularly interest me, and those are the letters of James and Jude. It isn't necessarily because they offer more than others or are any more enlightening than the other letters, but rather, the reason for me is that these are the brothers of Jesus by physical nature. Does it matter that they were of the physical family of Jesus (Matt. 13:55; Mark 6:3)? No, it doesn't. However, it does present us with an interesting perspective, doesn't it?

If we think about the writers of the New Testament that were and are apostles, it presents one perspective. One from a friend (cf. Luke 12:4), a student (cf. Mark 11:21), an apostle (cf. Mark 6:30), and a servant (cf. 2 Pet. 1:1). The perspective that each of these men (Peter, Andrew, James, John, Philip, Bartholomew, Thomas, Matthew, James the son of Alphaeus, Thaddaeus, Simon the Zealot, and Judas Iscariot [Matt. 10:2-4]) had, was one of what they were to Jesus, a friend, a student, and an apostle. This isn't to say that their relationship wasn't meaningful; it was, and we would do well to think about their relationship and how it may influence their writing. Now, I'm not saying that their relationship with Jesus persuades them in one direction or the other, but instead influences the way they speak about Jesus, how they think about Jesus, and how they reflect upon Jesus.

For instance, if we read through the writings of the apostle Matthew, he was very focused on the particulars of Jesus, mainly on what He said. Being a detail type of guy, it seems his relationship with Jesus was important to him, and Matthew was significantly influenced and moved by all that Jesus had to say. Now, Matthew's audience, the Jews, needed to hear all He had to say, so he wrote about the royalty of Jesus, the prophecies that led to Him, and many teachings and encounters He had with the Pharisees over doctrinal matters. Without Matthew's attention to the words of Christ, we would not be able to read the greatest sermon ever preached. The writings of the apostle Matthew are essential for the Christian today and a blessing that allows us to hear Him in a way that no other writer presents Him.

The apostle John, on the other hand, writes about all that Jesus **was** as he filled in the gaps of the synoptics and presented Jesus as being glorified by the Father and seen by the people, showing all that He was indeed the answer. Jesus was also significant to John, but the relationship was different with John than with Matthew. Not that it was any less important or valued by Jesus, but just like you and me, we sometimes get closer to some people over others. John was in the "inner circle," which, as we know, is also made up of James and Peter. John was one of Jesus' closest friends, calling himself *"the disciple whom Jesus loved"* (John 21:7), one entrusted with His mother (John 19:26), and one who was focused on the deeper meanings of spiritual things giving us a glimpse of the deity of Christ. Like Matthew, John's writings are essential for the Christian today and a blessing that allows us to see Him in a way that no other writer presents Him.

I look at each of these men to show one thing. While each of them knew Jesus in the flesh, they were equally inspired by the Holy Spirit to write (2 Tim. 3:16-17; 2 Pet. 1:20-21). These men were *"eyewitnesses"* to the life of Christ; no one else could speak of the things they knew or share the things that they saw like them. Peter clarifies this in his second epistle by saying, *"We were eyewitnesses to His Majesty."* Which is clearly seen in the Gospel accounts. Now, while these men were both inspired to write, they could also write in their own style or by the influence of their personality; in other words, they could be themselves as they wrote.

A great example of this might be found by the apostle Paul as he states, *"This is the way I write"* (2 Thess. 3:17), which was partly out of frustration. In the Gospel accounts alone, we have four styles: Matthew focused on the details, Mark was straight to the point, Luke was very historical, and John was very deep and meaningful. Why does this matter since they all wrote from their own perspectives? Not on the doctrines of Christ, nor the things He did, or what they meant, but rather from their own eyes and experience.

Jude, like James, on the other hand, was not an apostle and was very careful about distinguishing himself from them as he called himself the *"brother of James"* (v. 1). Both Jude and James were the physical brothers of Christ[1] as listed in Matthew 13:55 and Mark 6:3. Now it is unclear if Jude was the youngest of the brothers or not, but like any younger sibling the oldest one matters in their eyes. Like James, there is a relationship unlike anyone else—one of brothers. This matters why? Because as Jude begins to write, he doesn't claim the physical relationship he has with Jesus, but rather the spiritual one he has in Christ.

All siblings indeed share something in common, even though they are all different. It could be their mannerisms, their looks or their build, their attitudes, or the way they think. Jude, like the rest of the family at one time, did not believe, but that doesn't mean that they were extremely different; it means that it could have been harder for them to come to believe (John 7:5). But when convinced, there was no turning back. So, as Jude begins his letter, here is what he says,

---

1 Garrett Bernethy, "Building, James 1, Faith Sees What God Sees," *Excel Still More Bible Workshop: James* (Nashville: Kaio Publications , 2022) 97–100.

Jude: Pay Attention to the Words That Save You!

Jude, a bond-servant of Jesus Christ, and brother of James, To those who are the called, beloved in God the Father, and kept for Jesus Christ. (Jude 1)

This mindset resulted from his conversion (Acts 1:14) as he had become convinced that Jesus truly was the Son of God (cf. Jude 1, 4, 25). Therefore, as a result of his conversion and newfound belief system, he looks at himself as a *"bond-servant"* of Jesus Christ and references a *"common salvation"* that he has with all, *"those who are the called, beloved in God the Father, and kept for Jesus Christ"* (v. 1).

As a result of this newfound conviction in Jesus and His teachings, two great connections are made between Jude and Jesus. First, we have a physical family connection. Second, we have a spiritual family connection. This means that Jude would see Jesus from two different vantage points while only one came to matter to him. So, like James, he does not use his "claim to fame," if you will, but rather sees himself for what he truly is to Jesus, His servant.

However, like Jesus and James, there are similarities in the way they speak. Jude is plain and to the point; he is certain with his words and understands the focus of his teaching. While I wish I could tell you more and give an analysis of their speaking similarities, we don't have enough here to do that. But what I do believe we can see is this: Jude connected himself with those closest to the brother he lost so that he could be closest to the work of his Lord (cf. Acts 1:14). With one mind, they were *"continually devoting themselves to prayer,"* Peter being one among them, and that may explain why there are many similarities in both of their letters. Did Jude and Peter spend a lot of time together? It certainly seems possible. If that is true, which is entirely possible, then why would it not be possible that they are dealing with some of the same things during the same time, even if just a few years apart (2 Peter 64-68 A.D.; Jude 68-70 A.D.)?

Jude's love for the Lord, His work, and souls led him to write a letter about equality of salvation, a calling out of those who have crept in, and a reminder of what once was and how it continues to be, a recount of historical facts and of those who disobeyed a certainty of judgment, and a reminder of God's grace. His words, which he wrote while only packed into twenty-five little verses, carry a powerful punch and a message that may change our lives.

Words

We have all heard it before, "Words are important!" I mean, it's pretty embarrassing to say the wrong word at the wrong time. I know a few preachers, including myself, who have done this from the pulpit. While embarrassing, it is pretty funny afterward. Nevertheless, knowing what to say and when to say it is important. I mean, after all, your words can ultimately lead a person in the right direction or the wrong direction.

The idea of the word *word* carries with it a heavy meaning. For instance, when Jesus quoted the words of Moses in Deuteronomy 8:3, we find the word ῥῆμα, *rhema*, which is something that is said, a word, a saying, an expression, or statement of any kind[2]. In Matthew 6:7 in His sermon on the Mount, Jesus discusses the idea of using many "words" in prayer, which comes from the word πολυλογία *polylogia*, which refers to much speaking, wordiness, and long-windedness.[3]

---

2 William Arndt et al., *A Greek-English Lexicon of the New Testament and Other Early Christian Literature* (Chicago: University of Chicago Press, 2000), 905.

3 Arndt et al., 847.

But also in Mark 4:13-25 we have the word, λόγος logos, a communication whereby the mind finds expression, a word[4] which is also defined biblically as Jesus Himself (John 1:1-4, 14).

However, in the letter of Jude, we aren't simply talking about "words" in and of themselves but rather the "message," "preaching," or "teachings" (v. 17). These words (ῥῆμα, *rhema*) are made up of sayings, expressions, and statements, which are the words of those who have come before teaching the great message of God regarding the *common salvation* that one may have in Christ Jesus.

Here, we find a great connecting point between Jude and 2 Peter.

Jude writes,

> *But you, beloved, ought to remember the words that were spoken beforehand by the apostles of our Lord Jesus Christ, that they were saying to you, "In the last time there will be mockers, following after their own ungodly lusts."* (Vv. 17-18)

While Peter writes,

> *…That you should remember the words spoken beforehand by the holy prophets and the commandment of the Lord and Savior spoken by your apostles. Know this first of all, that in the last days mockers will come with their mocking, following after their own lusts.* (2 Pet. 3:2-3)

Some have undertaken the idea that Jude is nothing more than a copy of 2 Peter, but upon comparison of both letters in taking a closer look, this is not the case at all. In Peter's second letter, he is writing about the **coming of the false teachers**, which he is in anticipation of. In Jude's letter, he is dealing with the **arrival of those false teachers** who are already here, which now begins to separate the two writings tremendously as we look at the context and purpose of each letter.

It isn't unusual for one letter to repeat something from another writing of the New Testament. We accept the synoptic Gospels, and many things are repeated within those writings. Why do we accept them? As we stated earlier, each is written for the same purpose but to a different audience, all the while showing us a different perspective of Jesus. So why is it hard for some people to believe these two letters are stand-alone letters and not copies? That's a good question.

As Jude begins to write, he is focused on none other than Jesus Christ, who he mentions six times, thus allowing us to know that He is the main point. As Jude writes, *his desire to remind* (v. 5) *the called* (v. 1) seems to be the target audience who are running into those who have *crept in unnoticed* (v. 4) teaching things that were contrary to the message of Jesus. It was these people who were "*marked out for this condemnation, ungodly persons who turn the grace of our God into licentiousness and deny our only Master and Lord, Jesus Christ.*"

However Jude's desire was for them to "*contend earnestly for the faith which was once for all handed down to the saints*" (v. 3) so that they would "*keep from stumbling and make a stand in the presence of His glory blameless with great joy*" (v. 24). So it seems that Jude, like Peter, and like Jesus are interested in the well-being of "*the called.*" But what does that mean? This is a phrase which describes those who have responded to the Lord's teaching and have now become Christians. How do we know this? Here is what Jude writes,

---

4 Arndt et al., 599.

Jude: Pay Attention to the Words That Save You!

> *But you, beloved, building yourselves up on your most holy faith, praying in the Holy Spirit, keep yourselves* **in the love of God**, *waiting anxiously for the* **mercy of our Lord Jesus Christ to eternal life.** (Jude 20-21, emp. added)

The called are the faithfully obedient (Rom. 1:5; 16:26) who are in the love of God awaiting eternal life. It is the baptized (Acts 2:38) born again (John 3:3, 7; 1 Pet. 1:3, 23) believer (Mark 16:16; Rom. 10:4; 1 John 5:1; cf. Jude 5) who has accepted the call of Christ. We are all "called" to pick up our cross and follow Him (Matt. 16:24). We are called to be children of light (Eph. 5:8), called to peace (1 Cor. 7:15), called to freedom (Gal. 5:13), and called into His Kingdom of glory (1 Thess. 2:12). Peter would say that we are *"called out of darkness into His marvelous light"* (1 Pet. 2:9). It is these same people to whom Jude says,

> *Jude, a bond-servant of Jesus Christ, and brother of James, To those who are the called, beloved in God the Father, and kept for Jesus Christ: May mercy and peace and love be multiplied to you.* (Jude 1-2)

These are ῥῆμα, *rhema*, **words** that Jude is speaking to encourage remembrance of the things once said by the apostles (v. 17) to encourage their faith to grow, to allow it to fight off all false teachings that may come their way as individuals.

So, for the rest of this chapter, we will be looking at the "words" (ῥῆμα, *rhema*, sayings, expressions, and statements) of Jude to help us grow to the point that our faith is one of strength and not unstable in its ways. To do this, we will separate the chapter into three sections from verses 3-25. In verses 3-16, we will look at Jude's "Words of Warning," in verses 17-19, the "Words of the Apostles," and in verses 20-25, Jude's "Words of Building."

Words of Warning

Within Jude's purpose statement (vv. 3-4) he begins to set the stage for his **words of warning** as he moves into reminding them of the unfaithfulness of those who have come before them. These examples consist of the nation of Israel and the wilderness wonderings (v. 5), angels who did not keep their domain (v. 6), Sodom and Gomorrah (v. 7), men who defile the flesh, reject authority, and revile angelic majesties (v. 8), the devil who was rebuked in the name of the Lord (v. 9), Cain who murdered his brother (v. 11), Balaam who trespassed against the Lord (v. 11), and Korah who rose up before Moses and against God (v. 11). These are eight examples of unfaithfulness which Jude is attaching to *"these men"* who have *"crept in unnoticed."*

Like Peter, Jude identifies them as *"unreasoning animals"* who *"are hidden reefs in your love feasts when they feast with you without fear, caring for themselves; clouds without water, carried along by winds; autumn trees without fruit, doubly dead, uprooted; wild waves of the sea, casting up their own shame like foam; wandering stars, for whom the black darkness has been reserved forever"* (vv. 12-13).

He says, *"These are grumblers, finding fault, following after their own lusts; they speak arrogantly, flattering people for the sake of gaining an advantage"* (v. 16). But why is he stating all of this? Why is he giving all of these examples? It is simple **because the unfaithful are the unhopeful!** Jude wrote of these things, these people, and these stories because they meant something to the people he was writing to. They understood the outcome of Cain, Korah, the angels who left Heaven, as well as the cities of Sodom and Gomorrah.

Excel Still More Bible Workshop

The real question here is this: Do you want to end up the same way? The reality is that none of these individuals, cities, or the devil himself prevailed because God *does not* clear the guilty (Nah. 1:3). The fact of the matter is that Jude wasn't the only one who was warning of these people. John did in 1 John 4:1, Peter did in 2 Peter 2:1, and Paul did the same thing in 1 Timothy 4:1, and with these, we learn some undeniable truths. 1.) Many false prophets were in the world. 2.) False teachers with evil motives abound. 3.) Some, departing from the faith, spoke for Satan.[5] Paul may have said it in the best way possible in 1 Thessalonians 5:21-22, *"But examine everything carefully; hold fast to that which is good; abstain from every form of evil."*

In looking at these examples, here is what we find.

Unfaithful Example	Punishment	References
People out of the land of Egypt	Destroyed for their unbelief	Jude 11; 1 Cor. 10:5-10; Heb. 3:16-17
Angels who did not keep their own domain or proper abode	Kept in eternal bonds under darkness for the judgment of the great day	Jude 6; 2 Pet. 2:4,9
Sodom and Gomorrah	An example in undergoing the punishment of eternal fire	Jude 7; Gen. 19:24-25; Deut. 29:23
"These men" who defile the flesh, reject authority, revile angelic majesties	Judgment and Conviction Executed	Jude 8; 2 Pet. 2:10; Mic. 2:1; cf. 1 Tim. 1:20
The devil	Rebuked	Jude 9
Way of Cain	Cursed from the ground… Genesis 4:11	Jude 11; Gen. 4:11; 1 John 3:12
Error of Balaam	Sin resulting in death	Jude 11; Num. 31:16; 2 Pet. 2:15; Rev. 2:14
Rebellion of Korah	Earth swallowed them up	Jude 11; Num. 16

---

5 Johnny Ramsey, *Cover to Cover: Bible Questions Answered* (Abilene: Quality Publications, 1981) 311.

Jude: Pay Attention to the Words That Save You!

These punishments were *final*! The older Israelites said no to the land so God said no to them; the angels left God so God left them; Sodom and Gomorrah turned from God so God turned from them; "*these men*" rejected authority so God rejected them; the devil argued and God rebuked; Cain murdered so God cursed; Balaam led the people astray so he received death; Korah led a rebellion and God allowed the earth to swallow them. Is there anything good that comes from unfaithfulness? According to both God and Jude, the answer is no!

Like Peter, Jude profiles the characteristics of the unfaithful by stating they are ungodly, morally perverted, denying Christ (v. 4). They defile the flesh, are rebellious, reviling angels (v. 8). Dreamers who are ignorant and corrupt (v. 10) They are grumblers, fault-finders, self-seeking arrogant speakers and flatterers (v. 16). They are mockers (v. 18), causing division as they are worldly-minded and devoid of the Spirit (v. 19).

Here is the Word of Warning: If you choose to be this way and fall into their teachings of error, this will be your outcome! You will be the same! You will die, you will be punished, you will be swallowed up, you will have judgment directed towards you, and you will be convicted. You will be kept in punishment and destroyed *for your lack of faithfulness to God.*

Jude says, let me remind you of the things that have already happened so that you will know what will happen if you fall into the same practices as all of these. Here is your word of warning! I think it would do us well to note the words of Jesus in John 15:6, "*If anyone does not abide in Me, he is thrown away as a branch and dries up; and they gather them, and cast them into the fire and they are burned.*"

Words of the Apostles

If we think back to the beginning of the chapter, one of the things that we mentioned was the time that Jude and his family spent with the apostles (Acts 1:14). Jesus was no longer here on earth as he ascended (Acts 1:9) and now those who had been with him for the past three years were left to do His work. As we stated before, it is believed that this was the time of conversion for Jude and his brothers. While James may have been converted before him (1 Cor. 15:7), all of the brothers who did not believe came to believe.

Now, it was the teaching of the apostles that mattered. They had been given the message from the Helper (John 16; Acts 2:2-4) as Jesus had promised them, and they began to preach the Gospel to all men so that they would fulfill the Great Commission given to them (Matt. 28:18-20; Mark 16:15-16) by our Lord.

It was these men that Jude put his trust in as they carried the message of Jesus. He knew that God was with them, as well as Matthias (Acts 1:26) and Paul (Acts 9). Their words were His words, and that mattered. But was he talking about all of the apostles, a few of them, or one in particular? That is unclear, but what is clear was the authority given to them as the source of Christian teaching.

So, what are some things that the apostles taught? For most of the 12, we know very little other than our understanding of the commission's fulfillment. Each of them, minus one, fulfilled his ministry. But for a few, we know about their ministry and are blessed by their words.

In the case of Matthew, we have a book that bears his name. Did he travel around like Paul? That question is left unanswered. Tradition says that he ministered to the Jews in Israel and abroad for many years and was martyred for his faith while proclaiming Jesus.[6] While we may not have any of the travels or teachings recorded after the death of Jesus as we do for others, we do know that he spoke the same things (cf. Matt.; Acts 2:5-12) preaching on the Day of Pentecost. Matthew, also present in Acts 1:14, wrote about the life of Jesus in great detail. We don't know if he was a well-known preacher and teacher like Peter or Paul; he was a significant writer, writing a masterpiece that allowed people for thousands of years to get to know His words and be blessed by them!

The apostle John equally did not travel around the world, although it doesn't seem that he stayed put in one place his entire life. No doubt a powerful personality and one of the most influential writers of the Bible, John exemplifies a true follower of Christ. He saw and wrote of His Lord in a very personal and meaningful way, exemplifying what Jesus was to the world. Both his preaching and his writing have changed the lives of many people; in fact, this is what put him on the island of Patmos, where he would again pen another letter entitled Revelation. By his writing, we have come to know the words of Jesus, *"I am the Way, and the Truth, and the Life, and no one comes to the Father but through Me"* (John 14:6). Because of John, we also know Jesus as the Shepherd and the Door that leads to eternal life and that He alone provides all of those who would obey His Gospel with the blessing of fellowship with God and others in Him. Jerome says in his commentary on Galatians about John that in his final days, he had to be carried into the church building where they met in Ephesus because his worn-out body couldn't handle life anymore.[7] There is no doubt that John went to his grave preaching about his Lord the only way he knew how with all of his heart.

Paul, while not one of the original 12, was the ultimate form or example of what an evangelist is and should be. Some might question if Paul should be in the discussion of the term *"apostles of our Lord Jesus Christ;"* in my estimation, he absolutely should be in the discussion. After all, Jesus called him in the same manner as the others. Didn't He? Of course, he was called by Jesus—the only difference was that Jesus was not in physical form. Jesus would say of Paul, *"But the Lord said to him, 'Go, for he is a chosen instrument of Mine, to bear My name before the Gentiles and kings and the sons of Israel'"* (Acts 9:15). I think this verse sums it up pretty well, showing us that Jesus called him to be an apostle of His (cf. 1 Cor. 1:1). Paul's letters seemed to have by this time circulated around (cf. 2 Pet. 3:15), thus allowing many to read the teachings that Paul was in discussion of in different areas. Equally so, Paul was a missionary to his core. In taking three tours (Acts 13–14; 16–18:23; 18:24–20:38) and a trip to Rome towards the end of his life, he preached to both Jews and Gentiles about the Savior who died for them. A writer of a majority of the New Testament, Paul helps us understand both doctrine and theology unlike anyone else.

Simon Peter, apostle to the Jews and pillar in the Church (Gal. 2:9), was very vocal about how he felt about Jesus, rebuking thousands on the Day of Pentecost. He was a man of strength and conviction who wasn't afraid to open his mouth, even if at the wrong time. Peter, being an eyewitness to the life of Christ as well as to His transfigured body (2 Peter 1:16-17), both preached and wrote about the "right way" to follow our Lord. From his perspective, as he watched the Lord in the courtyard being beaten, he understood, maybe more so than the others to a degree, just how much Jesus

---

6 John MacArthur, *Twelve Ordinary Men* (Nashville: Thomas Nelson, 2002) 157.
7 MacArthur, 117.

Jude: Pay Attention to the Words That Save You!

entrusted Himself to God (1 Pet. 2:23). While only being a writer of two letters, his words are powerful and straight to the point. However, something else that we are able to see with this man is that it is his words (with the help of the Helper) that were spoken on the Day of Pentecost (Acts 2) and he is seen by many as a leader and powerful preacher who proclaims the excellencies of Him who died for you. If it were not for Luke's account of Acts, we would never know the well-known words, *"Repent and each of you be baptized in the name of Jesus Christ for the forgiveness of your sins; and you will receive the gift of the Holy Spirit."*

Are there records of the other apostles working, preaching, and teaching? In Acts 14:14, we find that Barnabas, called an apostle, was working with Paul. Paul, would also refer to *"James the Lord's brother"* (Gal. 1:19) as an apostle in some way. Duane Warden in his commentary on 1 and 2 Peter and Jude also asks the question if, because of this, Jude would fit into that category as well.[8] Could that be the case? I am unsure, but I know that Jude carefully separates himself from that conversation.

Regarding the others, Andrew, Philip, Thomas, etc.…not much is known about their teachings other than their story of tradition and the fact that it is recorded they fulfilled their commission given to them by Christ beginning with the Day of Pentecost onward as they worked from Jerusalem to Judea to Samaria and to the remotest parts of the earth (Acts 1:8).

But the real question is, exactly what words is Jude referring to? We know they were *"spoken beforehand,"* which doesn't necessarily mean they were spoken back in Acts 1:14, the days after Pentecost, or even during the journeys of Paul. We know they were spoken *"by the apostles of our Lord Jesus Christ"* and that *"they were said to you"* about the people here, which seems significant. Was Jude acquainted with the apostles? Yes, it seems he spent a good amount of time with them, even though we may not know exactly how much. But the main emphasis here might not be in exactly who said it, but the fact that it was said by one or more apostles to them. You see, they were the authoritative source of Christian teaching. So what Jude is saying is there is and was an apostolic message that was preached to these people, and those who have "crept in" are and have been undermining the apostles' teaching. Because of this, the salvation of these believers was in jeopardy because what the Church believes matters, and doctrine is important![9]

So here is what the apostles said,

> *In the last time there will be mockers, following after their own ungodly lusts."* These are the ones who cause divisions, worldly-minded, devoid of the Spirit. (Vv. 18-19)

While Jude cited no specific warnings that were given to him by the apostles, there are a number that the New Testament does confirm. Paul warns of false teachers who will or would come in the *"last days"* (2 Tim. 3:1-5; cf. Acts 20:29, 30; 1 Tim. 4:1-3). Peter would also warn of *"mockers"* that would come and follow their own lusts (2 Pet. 3:3), to which Jude would utter the same sentiments. These words of warning that were spoken beforehand should have given them the power they needed to fend and fight off the evil teachings and destructive heresies that had secretly crept into the flock. To follow these teachings is to go against Christ, thus creating division over worldly-minded thoughts, making them devoid of the Spirit.

---

8 Duane Warden, PH.D., *1 & 2 Peter and Jude, Truth for Today Commentary* (Searcy: Resource Publications, 2009) 506.
9 Warden, 507.

In an effort to gear up for spiritual warfare, Paul would write to the Church in Ephesus, telling them that they must *"put on the full armor of God"* (Eph. 6:11, 13), which consisted of truth, righteousness, the Gospel of peace, faith, salvation, and the Word of God (Eph. 6:14-17). Why would he do this? Because *"flaming arrows of the evil one"* (Eph. 6:16) are coming, and we know that those who teach falsely against Jesus are working in accord with Satan himself (cf. 2 Thess. 2:9).

Were the apostles in the business of giving words of warning, words of teaching, words of corrections, and words of His powerful truth? The answer is yes! Even if it was not popular (cf. Gal. 4:16). To the apostles, souls mattered, which, in my estimation, is the same mindset of Jude. Why can I say that? First, you do not write a letter like this to people you do not care about. Second, he calls them *"beloved"* (ἀγαπητός) four times. This matters because these people were dear to him like souls were to the apostles. So now, as he moves to the end of his letter, he demonstrates something very simple yet faith-building.

Jesus, who is most definitely the main point of this letter, is our Lord. He left His chosen men the apostles to speak with the help of the Holy Spirit (John 16) about the things that pertain to eternal life. Jude, in his understanding of who his Lord is and who His chosen men were, put forth the effort to point the minds of the readers back to those who were inspired by God and gifted by the Holy Spirit so they would cling to the holy words of warning about those who would swoop in and try to pull them away. The faith-building aspect of it is this. God cared enough about us and those who may not have seen Jesus and prepared men who had to tell you of the better life that can be lived.

Words of Building

The ultimate goal in my mind for each writer of the New Testament is simple: to encourage growth and be edified. Think about it. The Gospels help us to grow with Jesus. The Pauline epistles help us grow in His teachings. The general epistles help us to grow in our faith. Revelation helps us to grow in our hope. Now is this all they do? No, they each do so much more and overlap in many ways as they all equally encourage us to be His people.

As the letter of Jude progresses, we go through stages. Each section has a purpose of building up the believer to be God's man and to cling to the knowledge they have been given to fight off the evil schemes of the devil carried out by the *"mockers"* of the day. Let's think of this letter in terms of building a house.

First Jude **lays a foundation** identifying those who have been *"called"* in the Father and kept for Christ. The very fact that each person who has obeyed the Gospel of Christ automatically opens you up to three great blessings of God. 1.) **Mercy**—(ἔλεος *eleos*) also translated as compassion expressed for someone in need.[10] If we really think about this blessing which comes to us *in Christ* we should be overwhelmed with joy as we are given something that we do not deserve from God (cf. Rom. 11:30-33). 2.) **Peace**—(εἰρήνη *eirene*) a state of concord, harmony.[11] From a spiritual standpoint (which is the view of this word as none have been promised physical peace from a spiritual perspective, cf. Matt. 10:34), the believer what all people are looking for. None want to be in discord or war in a physical or spiritual sense, rather all desire harmony and unity. This is only

---

10 Arndt et al., 316.
11 Arndt et al., 287.

Jude: Pay Attention to the Words That Save You!

something that is found *in Christ* (cf. Rom. 5:1). 3.) **Love**—(ἀγάπη agape) the quality of warm regard for and interest in another.[12] If we look carefully at the text, we will notice some form of this word is used three times in the first three verses. However in verse 2 the word is used in a vertical fashion. The love of God. God's love is for all, but only those who have obeyed the Gospel are able to truly receive that love. His love sent Jesus as a ransom for many (Matt. 20:28; Mark 10:45). His love offered Jesus on the cross as the sacrificial lamb (Rom. 5:8; Heb. 10:10). God's love has brought us into Christ and keeps us close to Him (1 John 4:7-10). Spiritually this is where we want to be, in the love of God. Per Jude, these three things *"be multiplied to you."* The word *multiply* (πληθύνω *plethyno*) simply means to increase. So mercy, peace, and love are increased and are given to the called as they walk in a manner worthy of Him. Jude's desire is for these things to be multiplied in them as they walk the Christian walk.

Second, Jude **builds four walls** identifying the dangers that are out in the world, which have existed for thousands of years that offer dangers from the outside. The first wall is to protect from those who *"creep in unnoticed,"* which are the ungodly (v. 4). These are the people who take and steal your faith and salvation turning *"grace into licentiousness and deny our only Master"*. The second wall is to protect you from destruction that comes to those who do not believe (v. 5). The unfaithful tend to spread unfaithfulness by both their teachings and actions. So to put up a wall that protects your faith and shields you from destruction is a wise thing for the called. The third wall is to protect you from all immorality (vv. 6-7). These actions lead to nothing but *"eternal fire."* Notice that word *eternal* (αἰώνιος *aionios*) refers to a period of time without beginning or end.[13] This is true destruction that reduces and does not build. It tears down but can never be reconstructed. With God comes edification, but without Him comes destruction. This is worthy of building a wall of protection! The fourth and final wall protects you from the devil's evil ways and those who walk in his way of error (vv. 9-11). These describe hidden and empty men with no fruit as they only care about themselves. Jude says regarding them,

> *These are the men who are hidden reefs in your love feasts when they feast with you without fear, caring for themselves; clouds without water, carried along by winds; autumn trees without fruit, doubly dead, uprooted; wild waves of the sea, casting up their own shame like foam; wandering stars, for whom the black darkness has been reserved forever.* (Vv. 12-13)

Having a wall that protects you from these types of people is necessary because without it, they will infiltrate your "house" and bring these harmful ways into your home.

Third, Jude **places a door** (vv. 17-19). I know you were expecting a roof next because the doors generally come after the roof, right?! Well, maybe Jude is a different kind of builder, haha! All joking aside, roll with me on this one. The door represents those that you let in and those that you keep out. It is a way of entry but also a way of protection. Unlike the walls that are specifically meant to keep all things out without the ability to let anything in, the door represents a choice. Jude is referring, as we looked at just a moment ago, to the words of the apostles that would be worthy of remembering, but also the words of the mockers, which are focused on the world and *"devoid of the Spirit."* These Christians and you, for that matter, have a choice about who to let in. Will you let in the apostles' words that bring godliness, unity, and righteousness? Or will you let the *"mockers"* in that bring division and worldly-minded things? It is your choice, but that is the beauty of a door.

---

13 Arndt et al., 33.

Fourth, Jude **places a roof** (vv. 20-25). I know—about time, right? When we think about the roof itself, what is the main point of it? A roof shields from that which falls from the sky, rain, snow, or ice if you are in the right part of the country for that. But it also helps to hold all four walls together and seals the house, offering complete protection from the elements. In this part of the text that completes our house, Jude seals our home and puts the final part of protection to our "spiritual house." From a sealing standpoint, Jude offers us these things. 1.) Holy faith, 2.) Praying in the Holy Spirit, 3.) Keep yourselves in the love of God, 4.) Waiting anxiously for the mercy of our Lord Jesus Christ, 5.) Have mercy on some, 6.) Save others. These actions seal a person's faith as they are focused on the vertical aspect of his Christian life. If we, as God's people, are not thinking about things with the vertical in mind, we are not doing ourselves any favors. From a protection standpoint, this "roof," which represents our godly focus, will help us to keep from stumbling and make us *stand in the presence of His glory blameless with great joy.* While a roof seals, it also protects, thus completing our house.

All of this stems from one thing. Building. The word *building* (ἐποικοδομέω *epoikodomeo*) means to edify. To edify is to build up. Jude is teaching us through his words that we are to be built up by the teachings of the apostles, as those teachings are from God Himself.

Let's notice again what Jude writes here,

> *But you, beloved, building yourselves up on your most holy faith, praying in the Holy Spirit, keep yourselves in the love of God, waiting anxiously for the mercy of our Lord Jesus Christ to eternal life.* (Vv. 20-21)

FAITH BUILDING

1. Realize the Efforts of Others in Christ Who Care About You

Jude writes, "*While I was making every effort to write to you about our common salvation*" (v. 3). What is this telling us? It tells us that his heart was with them in a way of concern, love, and remembrance. A person is only concerned about those that he loves or cares about, right? I guess you could think about this from two vantage points: concerns for others and concern about others. But here, Jude's concern is for these brethren who were called into a common faith just like he was. From afar, Jude looks to the reader, presumably a Jewish people,[14] and sees or hears about all of the problems that are occurring with the people, which have been brought to them by those who have crept in, "*grumbling, finding fault, following after their own lust, speaking arrogantly, flattering people for the sake of gaining an advantage*" (v. 16). Jude knows the dangers that can come with this and cannot stop himself from thinking (cf. v. 3), writing, and sharing his thoughts of the matters of these sinful people who live lives of unbelief. You see, Jude understands that those who are "*called*" are not to live the same life as those who have not accepted the call of God. This hurts his heart and moves him with compassion. Maybe his words towards these people describe his own feelings.

---

[14] Warden, 452. "He had a specific audience in mind. One indication of that is his citation of uninspired Jewish apocryphal works. Apparently, he expected his audience to be Jewish believers. Gentile believers would not likely have been acquainted with the Ethiopic Enoch or with the Assumption of Moses, apocryphal works that Jude may have cited."

Jude: Pay Attention to the Words That Save You!

Keep yourselves in the love of God, waiting anxiously for the mercy of our Lord Jesus Christ to eternal life. And have mercy on some, who are doubting; save others, snatching them out of the fire; and on some have mercy with fear, hating even the garment polluted by the flesh. (Vv. 21-23)

What a blessing it is to know that others care about us. This can be a true faith builder for this simple reason. Sometimes, when things get a little crazy, bad things begin to happen, or people begin to wander off in the way of error, people begin to leave. However, Jude is not that person, Paul is not that person, nor is Peter or any of the apostles (minus one) for that matter. As a good friend of mine John Moore once said about the Christian life, "As Christians, suffering can be our finest hour." While we may not discuss "suffering" in this book, we can substitute that word for another. Maybe the words, trials, struggles, or temptation? Can this time be our finest hour? Yes, and here is how during each of these times of life. Whether suffering, trial, struggle, or temptation, we can give in or walk away from it. If our choice is to give in, it can and will be our worst hour, but if we choose the godly route of righteousness, it will truly be our finest hour because we have chosen Him, which is what matters. For a person to see us going through these things to step up or stand up to and for us and say, "I'm with you!"—there is not much else that can give you more strength than that.

2. The Words of the Apostles Still Matter

When we read our Bible, do we think the apostles' words are for us? From a contextual standpoint, we have to say that they were not "to" us. Many were written to specific Churches (cf. Gal. 1:2; 1 Thess. 1:1), or individuals such as Timothy, Titus, and Philemon. However, these words have been kept intact so that all can see and read the magnificent story of Jesus and His apostles. While so many people have tried to destroy the words of the New Testament, God has ensured their safety throughout time so that they could reach both your hands and mine. What this means is simple. The words of the apostles mattered to both Jude and his readers; they matter to you and me. Have people "*crept in*" and brought in words that mock the truth of the Gospel? Yes. Are there people who "*follow after their own lust*" today? Yes. Do you know people who "*flatter for the sake of gaining and advantage*"? Yes. But also, can we equally say that Jesus still matters? Yes. Can we say that prayer and faith are still important? Yes. What about our "*waiting anxiously for the mercy of our Lord*"? The answer is still yes!

So many people today have tried to push the Bible away from their lives by saying, "There is nothing in there for me" or "This doesn't apply to real life or life today because the things that happened then do not apply to us today." Even if for only a minute or two, if these people would just read the book of Jude or even 2 Peter for that matter, they would see that everything they were dealing with then is what we are dealing with now. The Bible is a "timeless" book that has eternal meaning. It applies to all of life for all of life. There is no time that it cannot reach, no action it does not touch in some way, no matter of importance that it does not connect to when it comes to things that really matter.

The faith builder is simply this. God has provided us a message through the writing of the apostles that not only mattered back then but also matters right now! The words of the apostles still matter because they still apply. I can be built up in the fact that this message is timeless and that it is only something that can come from a higher power than me!

Building

3. God Is Able to Keep You from Stumbling

> *Now to Him who is able to keep you from stumbling, and to make you stand in the presence of His glory blameless with great joy, to the only God our Savior, through Jesus Christ our Lord, be glory, majesty, dominion and authority, before all time and now and forever. Amen.* (Vv. 24-25)

Two words in this text regarding this idea are "*stumbling*" and "stand." Note how Jude says this, "*keep you from stumbling and make you stand.*" Who can make you do this? God through Jesus Christ. We stumble when we give into temptation, false teaching, or trials, usually because we begin trying to figure out how to get out of the situation on our own. What we need to figure out in our lives is *we don't know best*! Our knowledge, ability, and know-how can only get us so far. Why do Churches get into so many problems with their leaders, ministers, or members? Why do we, as families, struggle so much in many areas of our relationships? Why do we, as individual Christians, do many of the things we do and feel many of the ways we feel? In many cases, it is because we are not relying on our God and not digging into His Words.

God can only help you when you go to Him for help! Many will pray, and that is essential for all things. But if we pray and then we do not listen, isn't that a problem? You might be thinking, what do you mean, listen? Do you think that God is speaking to us? Yes! From Genesis to Revelation. You see, prayer is us going to Him, while the Bible is Him coming to us. Through years and years of turmoil, God has given you His way to get through life, not in just any way, but in His way. That way matters.

Are you dealing with struggles in your marriage? Read Song of Solomon, Ephesians 5, or the Sermon on the Mount (Matt. 5–7). Having trouble getting through the different trials of life? Read James. Have a problem with a brother or sister in Christ? Read Matthew 18 or 1, 2, 3 John. These are only a few examples, and the list is continuous because the Bible touches on so many things that are involved in the life of a person. After all, God knows you better, maybe, than you know yourself.

The important thing here is to remember that God has provided a message that will take you from a point in life where you are stumbling (lit. from falling[15]) and hold you up so that you can stand because you have assurance in Christ! The assurance is that the one who will put his faith in Christ, who will keep looking to Him for guidance, who will repent and turn from sin—this one will stand. God will "make you stand in the presence of His glory blameless with great joy"![16]

We would do well to think about the words of Peter,

> *Whoever speaks, is to do so as one who is speaking the utterances of God; whoever serves is to do so as one who is serving by the strength which God supplies; so that in all things God may be glorified through Jesus Christ, to whom belongs the glory and dominion forever and ever. Amen.* (1 Pet. 4:11)

As Peter wonderfully states, God should be the center of all things to us. If we will make Him that in our life, then when we do stumble, He will lift us up so that we will stand! Firm in our faith in the power of His Word! My faith can be built in knowing that even if the world leaves my side

---

15 James Strong, *A Concise Dictionary of the Words in the Greek Testament and the Hebrew Bible* (Bellingham: Logos Bible Software, 2009), 15.
16 Warden, 512.

Jude: Pay Attention to the Words That Save You!

laying on the side of the road with nothing and no one, as I have stumbled to the point of what seems to be a point of no return. God is still there waiting for you, offering you the opportunity to follow Him and His will. Offering you the invitation to come home. If accepted, God will take you, mold you, strengthen you, and make you stand not as your own man but as a man of God.

CLOSING THOUGHTS

With so many distractions, people trying to persuade you, and emotional religion running rampant all over the world. We, as New Testament Christians, *must* pay attention to His Words that save us. His Words are the only words. Not a variation of them, not a condensed version, but all. If you don't like something He has to say, I don't know what to tell you. You don't like how He wants you to live? I'm not sure you can do anything about that.

Here is the problem. We, as people in our time in this world, have become so overwhelmed with technology, information, and immediacy that we have become people who know best. Think about it: When you go to the doctor with your family member who has cancer, you most likely do extensive research on the internet, reading from other people who have at least some knowledge of that kind of cancer. Some readings may be from actual cancer doctors, while others are from a naturalist or some other study that some may deem radical. When you walk in the door or when somebody that you know walks in that door with their relative, do they not, in many cases, think they know more than the doctor who has spent thousands of hours practicing, studying, preparing, teaching, and even experimenting with every viable option available? While I'm not advocating for any treatment option or saying that all doctors are perfect, the idea is this. We have become a people who believe we know it all.

Don't let this be you! Only His words will save you. Only His knowledge can guide you. Only His ways will perfect you. Rely on Him because His words alone will bring salvation to your life.

Excel Still More Bible Workshop

Building

PAY ATTENTION TO WHAT HE EXPECTS OF YOU!

2 Peter 3:11; Jude 21

GARRETT BERNETHY

"Since all these things are to be destroyed in this way, what sort of people ought you to be in holy conduct and godliness."
- 2 Peter 3:11 -

"keep yourselves in the love of God, waiting anxiously for the mercy of our Lord Jesus Christ to eternal life"
- Jude 21 -

INTRODUCTION

What a study this has been! While short, both the letters of Jude and 2 Peter are nothing less than powerful and amazing. Upon looking at the second letter of Peter, Johnny Ramsey wrote, "No book of the Bible sticks with its major subject so consistently and thoroughly as does the epistle of 2 Peter."[1] He would also say regarding the letter of Jude:

> There has not been a more exciting chapter in any book than the epistle of Jude. It is extremely fast-paced and directly to the point. It has everything. A claim of brotherhood, servanthood, equality of salvation, a calling out of those who have crept in, a reminder of what once was and how it continues to be, a recount of historical facts and those who did not obey, a certainty of judgment and a reminder of God's grace. You don't want to miss out on this short twenty-five-verse epistle![2]

---

1 Johnny Ramsey, *Cover to Cover: Bible Questions Answered* (Abilene: Quality Publications, 1981) 295.
2 Ramsey, 307.

The final chapter of this section serves two purposes. First, this serves as the last lesson for the workshop, and second, it serves as the closing chapter of our main study for the letters of 2 Peter and Jude. If you are reading this for yourself, there is more to come in the book as far as studies go, but this lesson will be directed towards the close of our study to encourage and challenge all to live the life He wants us to live for the right purpose and the right reason.

Remember, Jesus said, "*But seek first His kingdom and His righteousness*" (Matt. 6:33). On the other hand, Paul would write, "*Set your mind on the things above, not on the things that are on earth*" (Col. 3:2). With these things in mind, I believe it important to note what I see as the main point of not only both of these letters but the entirety of the New Testament and the Bible itself for that matter. Peter sums it up by saying, "*What sort of people ought you to be?*" With this thought, we will in this lesson work to be built up in our faith, encouraged to go through life, and challenged to be His man. So ask yourself, "*What sort of person am I to be?*"

As I contemplate this lesson, I cannot help but ask myself, who am I? In reality, I am nobody. I'm not known by anyone famous, nor am I a person who travels around the country or world regularly speaking and preaching with an extensive schedule as I have sought to be heard. In some circles, I am nobody because of the size of the congregation I labor with, while in others, I am nobody because I have no degree from a preaching school or Christian university. Yet, with others, I am nobody because of what I do until they need someone like me. So, who am I?

I am a son and grandson, a brother, a husband, a father, and now a grandfather. I am a man who has struggles in life; bad decisions have sometimes stopped me in my tracks. I am a person who has walked away from the Lord more times than I can remember or can count, and a person who is not worthy of what I have or what I am blessed to do. I am a man who struggles to share his feelings and tends to keep things on the inside. I am a man who has to work on being a better husband and father because I fall short many times. I am a person who can sometimes be overly motivated, but at other times, may have no motivation. I am a man who faces the desires of sin and struggles like all other people in this world. I am a Christian and a preacher, but I also have self-doubt and sometimes say things I shouldn't. So, who am I to write a lesson like this, and why have I been given the opportunity to share thoughts on this subject? I believe it is because although I may be nobody to many people in many circles and fall short in many areas of life, I will always be somebody to God, and He will always be there to lift me back up when I fall.

Many people—maybe even you!—have a story much like mine. To some, you are everything; yet to others, you might mean nothing. You may have good days and bad days. You may struggle with sin. You may stand in strength. You might be a person who struggles as a parent, as a husband or wife, and as a Christian. You may even think from time to time, "Who am I?" as you struggle through the daily schedule of life, but we must never forget that we are somebody to God.

Understanding Who I Am

Now, I know that you who are going through this study may or may not be a Christian. If you are not, then I pray you will become one by following the teachings of the Gospel of Jesus

2 Peter 3:11; Jude 21: Pay Attention to What He Expects of You!

Christ.[3] If you are, then keep fighting the good fight and allow this study to bless you. Either way, whether you are a Christian or not, this applies to you!

From the perspective of a New Testament Christian (which is what we will mainly be focused on here), no matter your status or chapter of life, we must remember who we are to our heavenly Father. This is the relationship in our lives that truly matters!

In the writings of Peter alone, we can find many things that show us who we are as he writes to the New Testament Christians. According to Peter, here is the picture of who he says "I am."

I am:
- "*Born again to a living hope*" (1 Pet. 1:3; 23)
- Protected as a result of my faith (1 Pet. 1:5)
- Destined for salvation (1 Pet. 1:9)
- Redeemed (1 Pet. 1:18)
- Both faithful and hopeful (1 Pet. 1:21)
- Purified (1 Pet. 1:22)
- A "*living stone*" (1 Pet. 2:4-5
- Part of a "*chosen race, a royal priesthood, a holy nation, a people of God's own possession*" (1 Pet. 2:9)
- A proclaimer of "*Him who called me*" (1 Pet. 2:9)
- Part of the "*people of God*" (1 Pet. 2:10)
- A "*free man*" (1 Pet. 2:16)
- In submission (1 Pet. 2:13, 18; 3:1)
- "*Called*" (1 Pet. 2:21; 5:10)
- Respectful in my behavior (1 Pet. 3:2)
- Doing right even if I suffer for it (1 Pet. 3:17)
- Fervent in my love towards other Christians (1 Pet. 4:8)
- A servant of others (1 Pet. 4:10-11)
- Rejoicing (1 Pet. 4:13)
- "*Not to be ashamed of being a Christian*" (1 Pet. 4:16)
- Entrusting my soul to my faithful Creator (1 Pet. 4:19)
- A "*partaker of the glory to be revealed*" (1 Pet. 2:1)
- A volunteer (1 Pet. 5:2)

---

3 The "Gospel Call" is the call from God to be obedient children of the faith. One that convicts (cf. John 16:8) and converts (cf. Matt. 18:3) the heart and mind of an individual, transforming him into something that lives for eternal life and not destruction (Rom. 12:1-2). To become a Christian, you must hear the Word of God (Rom. 10:17; Matt. 7:24-25); believe (lit. active form of having faith) that He is the Son of God (Matt. 16:16; Mark 16:16; John. 3:16; 8:24; Heb. 11:1, 6), repent of your sins (Luke 13:3; Acts 17:30), confess Jesus as the Son of the living God (Matt. 10:32-33; Rom. 10:9-10), be baptized (lit. immersed in water) for the purpose of your sins being washed away so that God may add you to the Lord's body, the Church (Acts 2:38; Mark 16:16; cf. Col. 1:18), live an obediently faithful life to God (Rev. 2:10; Matt. 10:22; 1 Cor. 15:58). The only way to have "soul-cleansing blood" is to touch it, we do this when we are baptized "*into Christ*" (Gal. 3:26-27; 1 John 1:5, 7). This is what saves you (1 Pet. 3:21) from the wrath of God (Rom. 5:9)—the memorialization and reenactment of the death, burial, and resurrection (Rom. 6:3-5), to die to your old self and to be raised in newness of life (Rom. 6:4). In doing so, "*we are saved by His life*" (Rom. 5:10). We must never forget the words of the apostle Paul in Acts 22:16, "*Now why do you delay? Get up and be baptized, and wash away your sins, calling on His name.*"

- An example to others (1 Pet. 5:3)
- Part of the "*flock of God*" (1 Pet. 5:2)
- Humble and exalted (1 Pet. 5:6)
- A person who gives my anxieties to Him (1 Pet. 5:7)
- Resistant and accomplished (1 Pet. 5:9)
- The suffering (1 Pet. 5:9)
- Standing firm (1 Pet. 5:12)
- Able to have a faith like Peter (2 Pet. 1:1)
- "*Granted everything pertaining to life and godliness*" (2 Pet. 1:3)
- Called by "*His glory and excellence*" (2 Pet. 1:3)
- A partaker of divine nature (2 Pet. 1:4)
- Escaped from the "*corruption of the world*" (2 Pet. 1:4)
- Purified from my former sins (2 Pet. 1:9)
- Supplied the "*way of entrance into the eternal kingdom of our Lord*" (2 Pet. 1:11)
- "*Established in the truth*" (2 Pet. 1:12)
- A receiver of the eye-witness accounts of the apostles (2 Pet. 1:16-17)
- Paying attention to His Word (2 Pet. 1:19)
- A historian (2 Pet. 2)
- Thankful for the "*patience of God*" (2 Pet. 3:9, 15)
- Waiting for the Day of the Lord (2 Pet. 3:9-12)
- Looking for the place where "*righteousness dwells*" (2 Pet. 3:13)
- Striving to be "*spotless and blameless*" in His sight (2 Pet. 3:14)
- A student of Paul's letters so that I may understand them (2 Pet. 3:15-16)
- "*On my guard*" (2 Pet. 3:17)
- "*Growing in grace and knowledge of our Lord and Savior Jesus Christ*" (2 Pet. 3:18)
- A child of God (1 Pet. 1:14).

According to Peter, this is who I am.

By understanding the picture Peter is painting here, we can truly know how God sees us and **what He expects us to be**. His expectations of us were put together or formulated in His mind before the foundation of the world. These expectations were not just put together out of nowhere; rather, they were connected to who God is. Just as we were "*made in His image*" (Gen. 1:27), we are also to be conformed "*to the image of His Son*" (Rom. 8:29-30); this is by way of who we are spiritually and what we are physically. So when we look at a phrase Peter used in 2 Peter 3:11, "*What sort of people ought you to be?*" we know that who we are and who we should be are about our connection to God Himself.

Here is what I mean. If I am going through life with not a care in the world about who I am spiritually. I may have been "*made in His image*," but I am certainly *not conforming* to it. Thus, I am

2 Peter 3:11; Jude 21: Pay Attention to What He Expects of You!

"physically being," but not spiritually connected. Remember, God only looks to the faithful as His children (Rom. 8:16-21). This matters to me because His expectation of all people is to be faithful in His ways. This is how we show our love to Him (1 John 5:2-4). This is not something that applies to only one person or one group of people but to all people. So, maybe this is how I should think about myself to begin my journey towards faithfulness. I am His creation (Gen. 1:26-27; 2:7, 20-24). I am the object of His love and the one He desires (John 3:16; 1 John 3:16; cf. Rom. 6:10; 1 Pet. 3:18). Therefore, I am the person He is looking for because I matter to Him. I am as an individual one who matters to God.

What Type of Faith Is Expected of Me?

In my studies that I have done in both the Old and New Testament, I have come to a simple yet powerful conclusion. While it may not seem like much, I can assure you it is a powerful reality of truth. The relationship between God and a believer is based on two things: your obedience to Him and His acceptance of you. The relationship for every person is completely and utterly on an individual basis and nothing more. It is the connection between your heart and His heart. A connection through the Son and sustained by your obedience to His Word. It is not a connection built with a group, even the Church. It is built individually, and we cannot escape this ultimate truth.

Why is this important? God has expectations, which are directed toward the individual specifically, even though He has expectations of the group (the Church). Has God called upon all to follow Him? Yes! However, He has called on everyone individually, and that bit of knowledge matters. For the collective to be pleasing in His sight, the individual must do his part in the body of Christ. Suppose we are to be a people of love. In that case, should I not be a person of love (1 John 4:7)? If we are to be a people of forgiveness, then should I be a person of forgiveness (Eph. 4:32; Col. 3:13)? If we are to be a people of kindness, then should I be kind (2 Pet. 1:7)? If we are to be a people of faith, then should I be faithful (James 2:18-26)?

Maybe that is why the apostle Paul said,

> For just as we have **many members in one body** and all the members do not have the same function, so we, who are many, are **one body** in Christ, and **individually members** one of another. (Rom. 12:4-5)

Notice the term *individually* (εἷς *heis*, a single person, in contrast to more than one).[4] Paul would also state in 1 Corinthians 12:20, "*But now there are **many members**, but one body,*" then just a few short verses later in verse 27, "*Now you are Christ's body, and **individually members** of it.*" Much like a wall made out of brick, we are each added to the body of Christ one by one (Acts 2:47). We are individually faithful and individually responsible for who we are and how we act. This is a powerful truth. When each person does his part, the collective body glorifies our Father together as His people.

But why start with this? Why concentrate on something that we most likely all know very well? The answer, in my mind, is simple. There are too many people in the "religious world" who are reliant

---

4 William Arndt et al., *A Greek-English Lexicon of the New Testament and Other Early Christian Literature* (Chicago: University of Chicago Press, 2000), 291.

upon their connections and/or groups that they are a part of to fulfill their spiritual lives. Their fellowship with God is based on their connection with the "church" they are a part of, and this is an entirely wrong concept of how our fellowship works. Our fellowship is not with God through the brethren; it is with God through Christ. Only when I have established that relationship between myself and the Father can I have a genuine eternal relationship with the family of God.

So, when I think about what sort of people we ought to be, the Bible answers this question. We are to be a people of individual, undivided faith who are focused upon who He makes us due to His everlasting love through our Lord, Jesus Christ. The type of faith that is expected out of me is to be a reliable, functioning trust that opens itself up entirely to what He means by His words. It is a belief that is active in our day-to-day walk. A faith that is open to the possibility that I may not be right on everything but is continuously searching to understand. A faith that connects to His purposes for me as an individual and the Church as a whole. It focuses my mind on humility and not pride or power. It is something that pulls me away from the lustful practices of the world and into the righteousness of our Father. It looks to the point and does not get distracted by the particulars. It intensely focuses on God's picture of a Christian, not our own. It focuses on the prize and not the position. True faith looks for the city made without hands (Heb. 11:10, 13-16) and does not argue over where it is or what it looks like. In the words of Paul, it is a walk (2 Cor. 5:7), yet in the direction of Jesus, it is a decision (Matt. 4:17).

So the question is, what type of faith is expected of me? Here is the answer, according to Peter. It is one that stands and is not "*unstable*" (2 Pet. 2:14; 3:16). One that aligns itself with godly living (1 Pet. 2:12; 3:8-12; 2 Pet. 1:5-8). One that looks to God and entrusts him/herself to Him who judges righteously (1 Pet. 4:19; cf. 2:23) and focuses on how he/she may walk through the entrance of the "*eternal kingdom*" (2 Pet. 1:11).

It is the mindset of Paul,

> *For our citizenship is in heaven, from which also we eagerly wait for a Savior, the Lord Jesus Christ; who will transform the body of our humble state into conformity with the body of His glory, by the exertion of the power that He has even to subject all things to Himself.* (Phil. 3:20-21)

If we work just like Peter and Paul to conform ourselves to Him, we will fit this mold and be seen in the *righteous* column (2 Pet. 3:13) as we '*eagerly wait for*' our Savior. So, to answer the question of this section, we are to have faith that is, according to Paul, "eagerly waiting." According to Peter, "*looking for and hasting the coming of the day of God*" (2 Pet. 3:12). It is a faith that seeks, one that binds, something that conforms, an understanding that knows, and the patience that waits. This is the type of faith that He expects from us.

What Sort of People Ought You to Be?

Now to the main discussion. Have you given real thought to what God thinks when He looks at you? Now, let's clarify what I mean by this based on the foundation that we have laid. When He looks at you, it is a Biblical fact that you matter to Him (cf. 1 John 3:16). So, while there is a possibility that He may look upon you with disappointment or joy, either way His patience is waiting for you to come to repentance (2 Pet. 3:9) or supplying you with the strength needed daily to continue in your walk with Him (1 Pet. 4:11).

2 Peter 3:11; Jude 21: Pay Attention to What He Expects of You!

When He looks at you, does He recognize your faith? Is it faith based on feelings? Is it a faith full of prejudice? Is it a pharisaical type of faith? Or is it a focused faith? Let's define each one of these for us.

An **unrecognizable faith** is most likely nonexistent, one that believes in something contrary to Scripture or a belief that is founded upon false or corrupt narratives and perceptions. It doesn't act Christian and certainly does not reflect the principles of God. When He looks down, He does not recognize what He sees as it is not something that He desires.

A **faith based on feelings** is essentially a faith based on nothing. It attaches itself to a concept, the sound of music, an idea, a crowd, or a movement. As we, in some way or another state each year, this is a system of belief that, as Peter would say, *"are springs without water," "mist driven by a storm,"* or as Jude would put it, a *"cloud without water,"* an *"autumn tree without fruit."* Now, please understand I am using these phrases for a connection due to their general meaning. The context of these phrases are directed at the false teachers and their destructive ways. However, this same idea applies to their faith type as well. This type of "faith" is imaginary, but unfortunately, it seems it is there.

A **faith full of prejudice** belongs to an individual or group that often forces their preconceived judgments or opinions on others based on their traditional ideologies or practices. Regarding many subjects, they are right down the line, but with other things that are more traditional they seem to close themselves off to any possibility that they might be wrong on a subject, or, if it is against their traditional teachings, they are automatically against it and show prejudice against a person in particular, a group, congregation, and or belief.

A **pharisaical faith** is based more on power and following but is also highly focused on "law keeping." While keeping the laws of God is a good thing, they can become highly binding where God has not bound, forgetting that love, kindness, mercy, and grace are also a part of our belief system, as we find it in the New Testament.

A **focused faith** is concerned with being a "truth seeker." It is open to learning from the text, as it strives to see God's viewpoint in every word. It reminds us that while we are working to keep all of God's commands to the fullest, which also means correcting and rebuking, It also means loving and caring. It is open to all logical possibilities regarding Biblical things and is not afraid to be wrong, as it constantly strives to be correct. With every step, this type of faith focuses on one thing: obeying Him.

Which one of these "faith types" does He see in you? Honesty is the best policy here. So, while we think about that, are there Biblical examples of each? Yes, there are.

- **Unrecognizable**—In the case of King Saul and Judas Iscariot, each started at one place and finished at another. Saul, chosen by the people to be their king, began doing things in his way instead of obeying God (1 Sam. 15:11), and Judas sold out His Lord for very little money (Matt. 26:15; 27:3, 9). In the end, neither one of their faiths was recognizable, as all things were misplaced. Did each one feel remorse, or were they sorry for where they ended up? I think the answer to that is yes. But by the time of that understanding, their lives were at their end.

- **Feelings**—A couple of examples come to mind with this. First might be the friends of Job. You know, those guys who blamed Job for all he was going through; somehow, his wrongdoings had brought all these things upon himself. A second person that comes to mind is Jonah. As

Jonah was told to go to Nineveh, he was overcome with his feelings. Feelings of fear, hatred, or dislike, and anxiety no doubt took over his mind. In both instances, instability overcame these men as they began to turn from one direction to another, as they were what Peter would call *"unstable"* as they produced their perceptions and created their outcomes, not based on His will, but their own.

- **Prejudice**—The apostles James and John, unfortunately, at one point in their lives, exemplify this the best as they looked upon the Samaritans, a people they did not get along with and desired to command fire to come down and consume these people. Their lack of understanding, traditional thoughts, and calloused upbringing towards these people caused them to curse, condemn, and consume them before any unifying act or discussion—just pure and simple condemnation (John 9:51-56).

- **Pharisaical**—With so many examples of all that the Pharisees did during the days of Jesus, we will not name them all; Jesus sums up their terrible ways in Matthew 23:13-30 with His "eight woes," which He prescribed to them. His main terminology for each was *"hypocrites,"* as they taught one thing but lived and practiced another. While focused on "law-keeping," they forgot what it all meant. Many of these men, if not all, had studied the prophets and were looking for Jesus, but when He came, He was not the man they were looking for.

- **Focused**—Of course, examples would be Jesus, Paul, Peter, Barnabas, James, Abraham, Noah, and a whole host of other names listed in Hebrews 11 and throughout the rest of the Bible. Noah was found faithful in the eyes of God, which saved him and his family (Gen. 6–9); Jesus was an absolute example of what a focused faith looked like as He withstood the tempter (Matt. 4:1-11), felt compassion for people (Matt. 20:34), yet stood for truth because He knew it was the only thing that would lead to salvation (John 8:32; 17:17). Focused faith conforms and transforms to the image of how He desires to see you.

When we begin to think about the main thought here, "*What sort of people ought you to be,*" we also need to connect ourselves to the main point of the verse, "*Since all these things are to be destroyed in this way*" (2 Pet. 3:11). What does this mean? Well, it is simple. Something is coming. Something big! What is it? It is the end of time, well, the time of creation. In Genesis, we are told, "*In the beginning, God created the heavens and the earth*" (Gen. 1:1), which means that this was when time began for creation, not for God. Now, the apostle Peter is discussing not the beginning but the end of all things; something is coming. But what is it? Peter says, "*The day of the Lord*" (2 Pet. 3:10).

What exactly is the "*Day of the Lord*," you might ask? Well, that is a good question. It is the day that we are waiting for. A day that we can go Home. A day when God will wipe away every tear and all pain will cease to exist, at least for those who go to be with the Lord (1 Thess. 4:17). It is the end of time for creation as all things will be *annihilated* from existence in complete destruction as the heavens and earth will be reduced to nothing more than ash. It is a day filled with joy as the faithful in Christ will rise from the dead (1 Thess. 4:16), and all who are alive will be caught up with Him in the clouds. It is a day of sentencing, a day when your eternal destination will be fulfilled. A day when we all will finally see Jesus and hear either "*Well done*" or "*Depart from Me.*"

It is a day in which all things will end. There will be no second chance, as some doctrines teach, as this day marks the end of His patience. It will be the day that the Lord says it is time to send His

2 Peter 3:11; Jude 21: Pay Attention to What He Expects of You!

archangel to announce His coming (1 Thess. 4:16). A day when Jesus stands up from His throne and completes His work on the place that He is preparing (John 14:3) and a day when our rest will come from this life of weariness (Matt. 11:28; Heb. 4:9-10).

Why does this matter? It matters because Peter says the end is coming. Now, we can look at this in two ways. First, from a life-expectancy standpoint, our lives will end here on this earth as death will have its time in our lives. Because our physical bodies are not made to last forever, they will grow old and wear out from the lives that we live. From this perspective, the end is coming. Second, we can look at this from a spiritual standpoint. God is going to destroy (lit. *annihilate*) all of creation. From the Earth to the Milky Way galaxy. From our Sun to Pluto. From the farthest star that we can see to trillions of lightyears past that point and beyond, God will reclaim all of His words and take back everything that He has made.

This is important because our physical lives will have an end. Will it be that we see death in this life from growing old or perishing from something else? It is likely. Or will we be those who are going about our daily lives and out of nowhere hear an unrecognizable shout followed by a trumpet that will call all to attention and bring every person to their knees (Isa. 45:22-25; Rom. 14:11; Phil. 2:8). This is also possible. Either way, the end is coming, and we must be ready for it to come. That is why Paul said, "*We eagerly wait,*" and Peter wrote, "*We are looking for it*" because both of them knew that when it came, they had to be ready!

This is the whole point of Peter's argument,

> *Since all these things are to be destroyed in this way, what sort of people ought you to be in holy conduct and godliness, looking for and hastening the coming of the day of God, because of which the heavens will be destroyed by burning, and the elements will melt with intense heat!* (2 Pet. 3:11-12)

There will be no arguing with Jesus, God, or the Holy Spirit as to their decision on where you will be heading for all of eternity. There will be no appeals, no other lawyers that you can choose from, no letters you can write, and no law to find a loophole in. Because our judgment and sentencing will be so final, so right, so just, so concrete, and so undeniable that even you will have nothing to say about it, as you hear those words, "*Well done*" or "*Depart from Me,*" you will know that what you have received is what you deserve. Will someone try to argue on that day?

Jesus says regarding these words,

> *Not everyone who says to Me, "Lord, Lord," will enter the kingdom of heaven, but he who does the will of My Father who is in heaven will enter. Many will say to Me on that day, "Lord, Lord, did we not prophesy in Your name, and in Your name cast out demons, and in Your name perform many miracles?" And then I will declare to them, "I never knew you; depart from Me, you who practice lawlessness."* (Matt. 7:21-23)

However, we must notice that the argument will be nothing more than one-sided, with someone pleading their case and all that they have done "in the name of the Lord," but He will know the essence of their faith and the heart of their teaching. He will see the level of their obedience and the reason for their work. He will fully understand your true relationship with God with an understanding of whether or not you are in Him. You will be presented before God spotless or stained (2 Pet. 2:13; 3:14). Either way, there will be no doubt where you belong, either to Him or away from Him.

Have you ever had a deadline? You know, there is a project at work, or maybe at school, and the teacher or your boss says, "This is when these need to be in, and all needs to be done." In other words, when this date and time hit, there is nothing else you can do. What you have done is what you have done, or else. While this is a very mild example, the "Day of the Lord" is essentially the same. The only difference is you don't know what the Day of the Lord will be! If you are working toward a deadline at work, you have that date and time. Therefore, you do all of your work on that project in order that you may have done all that you can by way of study, preparation, papers, designs, etc., so that when the day comes, you will be completely and totally prepared to turn in your work and/or present it to your boss or a client.

While the Day of the Lord is slightly different, it is also the same thing. We don't know when the day will come (cf. 2 Pet. 3:10). However, we must do our due diligence to study His Word to know all we must do to be saved and remain who He wants us to be. Prepare ourselves to live and apply His Word to our lives to act in the ways He expects from us. Work in the Church and out in the world. This may include many projects, public speaking, one-on-one studies, raising and instructing our families, traveling the globe, publishing videos, helping others through problems, praying—you name it, the work of the Lord includes it. The ultimate reality of both Peter's and Paul's discussion when it comes to the end of time is this: When it comes, I must be ready!

In understanding the point that time will run out at some point, Peter's words should mean a whole lot more than they did before this study. The "What sort of people ought you to be?" phrase and question is about being ready as God's man when He comes! Because when time runs out, time is out!

So, What Sort of Person Ought You to Be?

First, I must be a person who belongs to God. Remember, I am not saved because of anyone else decisions or choices; I am saved by the things that I do and what I believe. Nothing else. To belong to God, we must obey His will. According to the New Testament, the only way one may become a child of God is to be baptized (βαπτίζω, baptize: lit. to put or go under water, to plunge, dip;[5] to immerse) into Christ (Rom. 6:3), according to Mark 16:16 and Galatians 3:27. In Christ is where all spiritual blessings are received (Eph. 1:3). It is how one is placed in the Church (Acts 2:47) and where one is placed in fellowship with God. In Paul's words, as a result of our being baptized into Christ, he states, *"For He rescued us from the domain of darkness, and transferred us to the kingdom of His beloved Son, in whom we have redemption, the forgiveness of sins"* (Col. 1:13-14).

Second, I must be a person of faith. The Hebrew writer very clearly states, *"And without faith it is impossible to please Him, for he who comes to God must believe that He is and that He is a rewarder of those who seek Him"* (Heb. 11:6). It is and was by faith that men gained approval (cf. Heb. 11:1). It was a point of rebuke from Jesus when it was not present (cf. Matt. 16:8) and is the manner for which one may hear the words, *"Well done"* (Matt. 25:31; Luke 19:17) and be *"well pleasing"* when found worthy in His sight (Col. 3:20; cf. Matt. 3:17; 2 Pet. 1:17). It both allows and drives you to

---

[5] William Arndt et al., *A Greek-English Lexicon of the New Testament and Other Early Christian Literature* (Chicago: University of Chicago Press, 2000), 164.

2 Peter 3:11; Jude 21: Pay Attention to What He Expects of You!

live for something greater than yourself. It helps you look for things you cannot see (cf. Heb. 11:10) and await the blessings of what is to come. Faith moves you through the point of fear in life yet holds you back when things aren't right. It allows you to take steps in life while keeping your heart and mind focused on His Word that will guide you through it. A person's faith pushes him to obey, and that is all God is asking for. When it comes to the person I ought to be, it should be the person that God is looking for: faithful to Him.

Third, I must be a person of obedience. Upon looking to history for those with whom God was not pleased, we find one common denominator with each one—a lack of obedience. An obvious illustration of this is found in the nation of Israel. They were a nation brought out of Egypt with the help of God just like they were brought into it. A people who walked through the sea, a people who were brought to the edge of the land they had heard about their entire life. A people who understood the power of God like no one else. A people who had all they needed with God on their side and at their lead, but also a people who lost their faith in His power and deliverance. Because of this, they were now a people who stood at the edge of a land promised only to look at a land they could no longer have. These actions would replay themselves throughout the history of the people, from the introduction of King Saul to the split of the Kingdom. From their idolatrous practices, which would lead to their destruction, to their rejection of Jesus, the answer they had been waiting for. Once again, they had become a people who stood at the promise of old, only for them to reject the very thing they had looked for. Obedience isn't just found in doing something upon being told. It also accepts what has been said. Obedience is found in the heart, and rejection is produced in the mind. A person must obey from the heart in his belief of all that has been said, which leads to the actions that we find in the life of Jesus. When it comes to what a person ought to be, we should know that He is looking for the obedient as they follow His ways, trusting fully in His Word.

An excellent illustration can be shown like this.[6]

HOW DO I GET INTO CHRIST?

Only the blood of Christ is able to wash away our sins.

How can I touch the blood?

…Eph. 2:13; Heb. 9:14; Gal. 3:27; 1 John 1:7; Acts 22:16

"INTO CHRIST"

Baptized into Christ (Gal. 3:27)

Baptized into Christ (Rom. 6:3-4)

"IN CHRIST"

You become a new creature… 2 Cor. 5:17

You receive forgiveness of sins…Col. 1:14

Your sins are washed away… Acts 22:16; 1 John 1:7

You have salvation … 2 Tim. 2:10

You can receive eternal life… 1 John 5:11

You receive every spiritual blessing… Eph. 1:3

OUTSIDE OF CHRIST?

"Remember that you were at that time separate from Christ, excluded from the commonwealth of Israel, and strangers to the covenants of promise, having no hope and without God in the world. But now in Christ Jesus you who formerly were far off have been brought near by the blood of Christ"…
Eph. 2:12-13

---

6 Jay Lockhart and David L. Roper, *Ephesians and Philippians*, Truth for Today Commentary (Searcy: Resource Publications, 2009) 36.
   This visual originally came from Owen D. Olbricht's *Teacher's Guide for Successful Personal Work* (Delight: Gospel Light Publications Co., 1993) 22. I have added to this visual for our discussion on the topic of being in Christ Jesus.

Fourth, I must be a person of knowledge. Paul wrote, "*Be diligent to present yourself approved to God as a workman who does not need to be ashamed, accurately handling the word of truth*" (2 Tim. 2:15). Why did he say this? Because there are so many who are spreading words that are not true. Just like we find in 2 Peter and Jude, the knowledge of God prevents the lies of Satan. Are we a people who want to discern right from wrong? Are you a person who desires to know the way of God as He has set it to be in His mind? I think this is the point. Every person has the responsibility to align himself with His way of thinking and not his own. The only way this can be accomplished is to set your mind to learn His teachings found in His Bible—the set of documents preserved throughout time that have proven themselves to be correct. While many try to prove the Bible wrong from history, what we have found is that the influence and documentation of the Bible have supported history. God, through the writings of men, has given us His insight, His wisdom, His reflection, His processes, His influence, His mentoring, His truth, His ways, and His eternal view from His spiritual perspective. Why is that important? Because we only understand spiritual things from a physical perspective. We do not truly understand what the spiritual realm is like or what it expects. Do you understand the concept of eternity? Do you understand His perspective of separation? Do we know what that land or place will be like in eternity when we get there? If we are honest with ourselves, we have to say no. But I understand the definition of eternity! I would submit that our understanding of the definition of a word and its true meaning may be two different things. Only upon being in eternity will we truly understand it. However, God's knowledge through His Word has been shared with us, allowing us to understand all we can about spiritual things. His primary focus is: Follow My words, be faithful in My ways, be obedient to My Will, and seek out all knowledge that I have given you to live a life of fullness and purpose so when the time comes that you may finally understand all spiritual things, you will experience true life that has no end.

Fifth, I must be a person of perseverance. James the brother of Jesus wrote that a person who perseveres under trial is to be counted blessed. Do we want to be blessed? I would say that we do. Persevering or enduring things of life is brought about by the focus of the individual him/herself. This has to do with his faith, his hope, and his knowledge. You see if we do not have these things in our lives, then it becomes hard to endure the trials, temptations, and struggles of life. With no hope, we have nothing to look forward to. With no faith, we have nothing to believe in. With no knowledge, we cannot produce either one of these things. Paul wrote to the Corinthian brethren about power of faith, hope, and love as he directed the minds of the brethren to the true power that they held within themselves as a result of their relationship with God through Christ. The effectiveness of ministry was not founded upon miracles but upon faith, hope, and love (1 Cor. 13:13). The same can be said of our ability to overcome all that life throws our way. I don't need a miracle to happen in front of my eyes because I have faith that needs no miracles to verify Him. Peter says we are blessed because we have not seen and believe (1 Pet. 1:8). Therefore, the faith I possess as a result of all that I know allows me to have hope in what I believe, allowing me to persevere because of His love! This is who He expects me to be.

Sixth, I must be a person of godliness. Denny defines this word in his notes on chapter 1:3 as "a word that describes holy and righteous conduct, where one imitates the qualities of God" (cf. 1 Tim. 1:5; 1 Pet. 1:13-19). In other words, I need to act like God, not as God but like Him. I do this by following His commandments and His rule. God has standards, which are to be my life's standards. Peter wrote, "*Seeing that His divine power has granted to us everything pertaining to life and godliness, through the true knowledge of Him who called us by His own glory and excellence*" (2 Pet. 1:3).

2 Peter 3:11; Jude 21: Pay Attention to What He Expects of You!

As one might expect from Peter if you have ever done a study on him, that he would lead you to look at who Jesus was, the ultimate example. Emmanuel, God with us, showed us, if anyone ever has, how to be like God.

Seventh, I must be a person of self-control. Peter wrote, *"For you have been called for this purpose, since Christ also suffered for you, leaving you an example for you to follow in His steps, who committed no sin, nor was any deceit found in His mouth; and while being reviled, He did not revile in return; while suffering, He uttered no threats, but kept entrusting Himself to Him who judges righteously; and He Himself bore our sins in His body on the cross, so that we might die to sin and live to righteousness; for by His wounds you were healed"* (1 Pet. 2:21-24). This is self-control. But how? Jesus did this because of His trust in God! Self-control can pertain to any act. Anger, frustration, lust, and the list goes on. But how does one do this? To control your emotions, decisions, and actions. The answer is found in the knowledge that you possess. Your knowledge produces godliness, which is the understanding of what God would do and what God wants you to do in a particular situation. Jesus controlled Himself because of His trust and knowledge about the purpose of what He was there to do. We, too, are called to entrust ourselves to Him (1 Pet. 4:19), to trust in His words, plan, purpose, and way. His way produces true faith based on real knowledge, and when real knowledge takes root, you are no longer unstable in your ways. Rather, by both applying and adopting His wisdom and methods to your personal life, you are steadfast. This matters because a person with self-control acts like God, who is in control.

Eighth, I must be a person of brotherly kindness. One who puts his/her brothers and sisters in Christ before themselves (cf. Phil. 2:4). A person who reenacts the kindness God has shown you. Giving you a chance to redeem yourself of the sin in your life. To Peter, this is very real (1 Pet. 2:3). To Paul, this was a command (Eph. 4:32) but also what is produced by love (1 Cor. 13:4). Jesus spoke of the kindness and compassion of a Samaritan who cared for a man beaten and left on the side of the road (Luke 10:30-37) and showed this very thing while on the cross (cf. Luke 23:34, 43). Kindness is goodness, and this is what God has shown to man. He has not given us what we deserve; rather, He is patient with us (2 Pet. 3:9, 15) so that we may gain our eternal reward in Heaven, the gift of salvation. Who am I to be? I am to be, in His eyes, a person who is kind.

Ninth, I must be a person of love. Notice what John wrote, *"Beloved, let us love one another, for love is from God; and everyone who loves is born of God and knows God. The one who does not love does not know God, for God is love. By this the love of God was manifested in us, that God has sent His only begotten Son into the world so that we might live through Him. In this is love, not that we loved God, but that He loved us and sent His Son to be the propitiation for our sins. Beloved, if God so loved us, we also ought to love one another"* (1 John 4:7-11). Do you see the connection here? God's love and our love? Remember, godliness is about imitating the qualities of God. So if love is a quality of God and I do not represent nor apply that quality in my life, then I am neither of God nor connected to God in fellowship. As we know, it was by and because of God's love that He sent His Son to the world (John 3:16). Equally, the love of Jesus held Him to that cross. As a result of His love for us, we give our love to each other. This means that our love as Christians goes in two directions, much like our fellowship. Vertically to God— shown by our willingness to follow Him (1 John 5:1-3), and horizontally towards my brethren (John 13:34). In doing this, I am imitating the qualities of God and following the example of Jesus, allowing me individually to be seen by God as pleasing. In a world full of hate, there is nothing greater for us to do than to show the love of God.

219

Tenth, I must be a person who anticipates His coming! I am to prepare myself for the moment that my life is over, whether it be by physical death or trumpet sound, to meet my Maker. Will He come in the next moment? I don't know (Matt. 24:44; 2 Pet. 3:10). Only God does. Because of this, there is no better time to prepare for Him to come than now. Unfortunately, many of us have become procrastinators who wait until the last minute to do something. The problem with this is obvious. We don't know when it's coming, so we don't know when we are to be ready. So the right time is now! What sort of person am I to be? Peter writes you are to be ready to go with God. So we wait, look, and anticipate our Lord's coming so that we can go home with Him (1 Thess. 4:17).

FAITH BUILDING

1. Pay Attention to the Fact that the God of the Beginning Is the God of the End

Notice that Peter discusses "*His coming*" (2 Pet. 3:4), the "*day of God*" (3:12), and that we are to be "*found by Him*" (3:14). What we can take from this is simple: the God that created the universe and all things that accompany it, which includes you and me, is the same God that will destroy the universe. The beauty of this is understanding that He is the same, He has not changed, and His expectation perfectly aligns with what they were back in the garden. He is unchangeable (Heb. 6:16-20) as He is always the same (Mal. 3:6; cf. Heb. 13:8). This is truly a faith builder because this shows us we can build trust in His unchangeable Word. So what He has promised is promised. What He has prophesied is prophesied. What is going to be is what will come to be! I can expect what He has said to come. Therefore, I can look to the end because I know that He is also the God of the beginning!

2. Pay Attention to the Fact that Jesus Is the Christ

Jude writes that we are "*kept for Jesus Christ*" (Jude 1), that He is our "*Master*" (Jude 4), which the apostles spoke about (Jude 17). He is the One we anxiously await who will extend mercy and give eternal life (Jude 21). He is our Lord who leads us to God our Savior (Jude 25). Not only did Jude come to know this (Acts 1:14), but Peter was the first to confess it (Matt. 16:16). He was and is the One we all are waiting for! Isaiah prophesied about His life (Isa. 7:14; 53). John the Immerser proclaimed Him (Matt. 3:9-11). The apostles wrote about Him (Matthew, John, Paul, Peter), and His brothers followed in their steps (James and Jude). However, it might be the words of Martha that may be most convicting. Not that her words are more important than any others. It is that she was not an apostle, not a prominent figure, a priest, or a person of any stature. But a woman who believed!

> *Martha then said to Jesus, "Lord, if You had been here, my brother would not have died. E v e n now I know that whatever You ask of God, God will give You." Jesus said to her, "Your brother will rise again." Martha said to Him, "I know that he will rise again in the resurrection on the last day." Jesus said to her, "I am the resurrection and the life; he who believes in Me will live even if he dies, and everyone who lives and believes in Me will never die. Do you believe this?" She said to Him,* **"Yes, Lord; I have believed that You are the Christ, the Son of God, even He who comes into the world."** *(John 11:21- 27, emp.added)*

2 Peter 3:11; Jude 21: Pay Attention to What He Expects of You!

Faith is essential, and we must internalize the words of the Hebrew writer, *"For he who comes to God must believe that He is and that He is a rewarder of those who seek Him"* (Heb. 11:6). Understand that the Bible centers around one event in which we have one Savior. The cross of Christ allowed God to save all of mankind from their sins! By the conviction and proclamation made by those before, let us build our faith in the fact that Jesus was who the Bible says that He is!

3. Pay Attention to the Consistency of His Teaching

I don't know of a better way to say it than the closing words of Jude.

> *But you, beloved, ought to remember the words that were spoken beforehand by the apostles of our Lord Jesus Christ, that they were saying to you, "In the last time there will be mockers, following after their own ungodly lusts." These are the ones who cause divisions, worldly-minded, devoid of the Spirit. But you, beloved, building yourselves up on your most holy faith, praying in the Holy Spirit, keep yourselves in the love of God, waiting anxiously for the mercy of our Lord Jesus Christ to eternal life. And have mercy on some, who are doubting; save others, snatching them out of the fire; and on some have mercy with fear, hating even the garment polluted by the flesh. Now to Him who is able to keep you from stumbling, and to make you stand in the presence of His glory blameless with great joy, to the only God our Savior, through Jesus Christ our Lord, be glory, majesty, dominion and authority, before all time and now and forever. Amen.* (Jude 17-25)

CLOSING THOUGHTS

As you leave this workshop or finish your study, pay attention to what He expects from you, as that is the only thing that matters! When He looks at you, does He see a person of faith, moral excellence, knowledge, self-control, perseverance, godliness, brotherly kindness, and love? If He doesn't, then now is the time to change that. To change your life from conforming to the world to being transformed into His children.

Our focus must be centered on what He expects us to be. While many argue over the location and look of eternity, we should diligently seek to be the righteous people who will, by God's grace, fill the halls of the Kingdom and walk the grounds with God. If we can be people who focus on the journey while maintaining the hope and goal of Heaven, then we will be rewarded in the end. We must be the people who anxiously wait and look for His coming instead of dreading the day it happens.

Individually, be a person of faith so we can collectively be a people of faith. Be a person of love so we can be a people of love. Be a person of knowledge so we can be a people of wisdom. Be a person who is saved so that we can be a people of salvation. Be a person who looks intently at the Word of God so that we will be a people of the Book, built on knowledge that produces a faith foundational in His truth that produces emotions that are a result of all that we know He has done.

And know this,

> *For we did not follow cleverly devised tales when we made known to you the power and coming of our Lord Jesus Christ, but we were eyewitnesses of His majesty. For when He received honor and glory from God the Father, such an utterance as this was made to Him by the Majestic Glory, "This is My beloved Son with whom I am well-pleased"—and we ourselves heard this utterance made from heaven when we were with Him on the holy mountain. So we have the prophetic word made more sure, to which you do well to pay attention as to a lamp shining in a dark place, until the day dawns and the morning star arises in your hearts. But know this first of all, that no prophecy of Scripture is a matter of one's own interpretation, for no prophecy was ever made by an act of human will, but men moved by the Holy Spirit spoke from God. (2 Pet. 1:16-21)*

Special Study

ARE WE LOOKING FOR A NEW HEAVENS AND A NEW EARTH?

2 Peter 3:3-18

J. MICHAEL HITE

AUTHOR'S NOTE - *As you endeavor to read this article, let me be clear from the beginning that I do not believe or teach a "renovated earth" from this text. I will show quite clearly from an exposition of the text that I believe Peter is saying that on the day of the Lord the present heavens and earth will cease to exist entirely.*

The apostle Peter writes that we, as Christians according to the promise of God Himself, "*look for a new heavens and a new earth*" (2 Pet. 3:13). That we look for these things is really not in question in most circles. The struggle occurs when we seek to understand what Peter meant when he said we look for "*a new heavens and a new earth.*" In order to reach a fair and accurate interpretation of this text, we must look at the context of Peter's statement and closely examine his letter as a whole. We have to ask a number of questions and seek the answers in the text. In what context did he make this statement? What has he already said about this idea if anything? What promise is he referring to? What do the words mean and how has Peter been using them? There certainly is much to consider, so let's dive into the text of 2 Peter and look for some of the answers.

CONTEXT—THE PURPOSE OF 2 PETER

The primary focus for Peter's second letter to the early church is to warn them regarding false teachers that will come among them (2:1). He begins the letter by assuring his readers that through a "*true knowledge*" (ἐπίγνωσις, *epignosis*) of God and Jesus one finds grace and peace (1:2) and through that same true knowledge "*we have been given everything pertaining to life and godliness*" (1:3). The word translated "*know*" or "*knowledge*" (γινωσκω) is a keyword in the letter appearing 15 times in the text (1:2, 3, 5, 6, 8, 16, 20; 2:12, 20, 21; 3:3, 17, 18). He writes to remind his readers to develop the qualities of faith, moral excellence, knowledge, self-control, perseverance, godliness, brotherly kindness, and love because "these things" are vital to their "*true knowledge*" of our Lord

Jesus Christ (1:8). He writes to remind them of *"these things"* (1:12) and to encourage them to *"remember the words spoken beforehand by the holy prophets* [the Old Testament writings] *and the commandment of the Lord and Savior spoken by your apostles* [the teachings of the New Testament]" (3:2). Peter assures his readers that they can trust the source of this prophetic and apostolic message because it was confirmed to them at the Transfiguration (1:16-18) and its source is the Holy Spirit not men (1:19-21). It is this *"true knowledge,"* that has been given through the Old Testament prophets and New Testament apostles, that is the foundational defense against the *"destructive heresies"* that the false teachers will introduce among them (2:1).

In the second chapter of the letter, Peter details the character and tactics of the false teachers in vivid detail. They are liars and cannot be trusted. They *"revel in their deceptions"* (2:14) and seek to *"exploit"* Christians with *"false words"* (2:3). They are worldly and are driven by greed (2:3, 14) and fleshly desires (2:10, 14, 18). But most importantly they reject being reigned over by God and Jesus. They *"deny the Master who bought them"* (2:1) because they *"despise authority"* (2:10). The word for *authority* here is κυριότης (*kuriotes*) which means "lordship or dominion" (Bauer, "κυριότης," 579). These false teacher simply refuse to allow the Lord to rule over them and they seek to convince others to do the same. Sadly, their tactics will work and many will *"follow their sensuality"* and even sadder, because people will listen to them, *"the way of truth will be maligned"* (2:20).

But Peter assures his readers that punishment will come upon these men and those who follow them. Two verses become key in understanding this entire discussion, and even the rest of Peter's letter. He states plainly that ***"their judgment from long ago is not idle, and their destruction is not asleep"*** (2:3). How are Peter's readers to know that? Because ***"the Lord knows how to rescue the godly from temptation, and to keep the unrighteous under punishment for the day of judgment"*** (2:9). The truth and certainty of these two statements is found in three examples Peter cites from the Old Testament to prove that God has always punished the unrighteous and ungodly and that He knows how to rescue the righteous and godly. The first example is that God *"did not spare"* the angels when they sinned (2:4), and second, He *"did not spare"* the ancient world (the world of the **ungodly**). But He *"preserved Noah, a preacher of **righteousness**"* with seven others when He brought a flood (2:5). Third, He *"condemned the cities of Sodom and Gomorrah to destruction"* as *"an example of those who would **live ungodly lives** thereafter"* (2:6). But He *"rescued righteous Lot"* (2:7). This idea—that *"God knows how to rescue the godly and to keep the unrighteous under punishment for the day of judgment"* becomes the key though of the entire letter.

The Immediate Context: 2 Peter 3:3-18

While the verse we are concerned with is 2 Peter 3:13 where he mentions the *"new heavens and the new earth,"* the context for that discussion begins much earlier in 3:3-4. Here, Peter reveals that one of the *"destructive heresies"* that these false teachers will introduce is about the return of Christ. *"In the last days, mockers will come with their mocking, following after their own lusts, and saying, 'Where is the promise of His coming? For since the fathers fell asleep, all continues just as it was from the beginning of creation'"* (3:3-4). Jesus clearly promised the disciples that He would return (John 14:3). But by the time of Peter's writing (mid 60s A.D.), it has now been over 30 years since that promise was made, and these false teachers, mocking that promise, seek to teach that if He has not come back by now, He is not coming. Do not forget these men *"deny the Master who bought them"* (2:1).

Are We Looking for a New Heavens and a New Earth? 2 Peter 3:3-18

They do not believe Jesus is coming back at all and they argue that *"all continues just as it was from the beginning of creation"* (3:4).

Peter responds to this mocking rejection of the return of the Lord by showing two things that have happened since the beginning that have *"escaped their notice"* (3:5-6):

1. God spoke **the heavens and earth** into existence (3:5).

2. God destroyed the world (mankind) with water in the Flood because of their ungodliness (3:6).

Then, having shown what these false teachers not been mindful of the power of God in creating the heavens and the earth and the judgment he brought on the ungodly with the Flood, Peter points to the two future events that should be looked for with certainty:

3. God has reserved *"**present heavens and earth**"* for fire and its complete destruction (3:7-12).

4. *"According to His promise"* we look for a *"**new heavens and earth**"* (3:13).

God spoke the heavens and the earth into existence (3:5)

Peter's refutation of their mocking begins by showing that *"it has escaped their notice"* that all is not as it was *"from the beginning."* In the beginning was God Himself and then God created the heavens and the earth (3:5). This is clearly a reference back to Genesis 1 and God's work in the creation of the universe. The word used here translated "heavens" is the Greek word οὐρανοὶ (*ouranoi*). This word describes "the portion or portions of the universe generally distinguished from planet Earth" (Bauer 737) (see also Matt. 3:16; Heb. 1:10; Rev. 12:12). To the Greek mind, Homer and others used this word to describe the firmament, or the vault of heaven. This was the place of the gods. To Plato, "heaven" or "the heavens" was equated with all of the cosmos—the universe that contained the sun, moon, and stars. Everything that existed above the earth was seen as the "heavens" (Beitenhard 188). To the Jewish mind, there were many levels of "heaven" but by the time of the first century, rabbinic teaching held that there were three "heavens." The first heaven was the space immediately enveloping the earth—the atmosphere around us that produces rain (Gen. 8:2), snow (Isa. 55:9f), thunder (1 Sam. 2:10) and clouds (Ps. 147:8). The second "heaven" describes outer space where the lights (Gen. 1:14) and the stars (Deut. 4:19) are found. Constellations like Orion, the Bear, and the Pleiades are mentioned (Job 9:9; 38:31) and to the Jewish way of thinking, everything that filled the universe above the physical earth was described as "the heavens." The third heaven described the dwelling place of God Himself (Acts 7:55f; Eph. 6:9; Col. 4:1, etc.). Paul references this idea in 2 Corinthians 12:2 (Shoonhoven 654).

When Peter uses the Greek word οὐρανοὶ (*ouranoi*), which is translated "heavens," it seems clear that has reference to the universe above the earth in mind rather than the dwelling place of God. We understand that because he will mention the destruction of the **heavens** in 3:10. It is not that God is going to cause His dwelling place to *"pass away with a roar"* but rather everything above the earth—space, the stars, the sun, the moon, the planets—the entirety of the universe will be destroyed in that moment. So from the beginning God spoke the heavens (the universe) into existence.

He also formed the earth. The word here translated "earth" is the Greek word γῆ (ge) which refers to the planet itself, the physical globe (Luke 21:35; Acts 10:12; 11:16; 17:26, etc....). The word occurs 250 times in the New Testament, and in every instance it is in reference to the physical planet. There are a few verses where some suggest that the word γῆ (ge) refers to mankind or humanity rather than the planet itself (Matt. 5:13; 10:34; Luke 12:49, 51). But even in these passages the word describes the *place or location* of humanity rather than the people themselves. Peter will use a different word (κόσμος, kosmos) when he writes about mankind.

It should also be noted that nowhere in the text of the New Testament is this word used figuratively or symbolically. Those who argue that the term "the new earth" (γῆ, ge) is figurative must concede that its use in 3:13 is the *only figurative use* of the 250 occurrences of the word in the New Testament.

Throughout this letter, Peter makes a distinction between the "*world*" (κόσμος, kosmos) and the "*earth*" (γῆ, ge). The word κόσμος emphasizes the inhabitants of the world more than the location or planet they live on. For example, John writes, "*For God so loved the world* (κόσμος, kosmos) *that He gave His only begotten Son...*" (John 3:16). It is certainly not the planet that God loves, but rather humanity. The vast majority of uses of this word in the New Testament use it in a similar way and Peter is no exception. Peter only uses the word κόσμος four times in the letter (1:4; 2:5, 20; 3:6). He notes that through the promise of God that we can "*escape the corruption that is in the world* (κόσμος—*humanity*) *by lust*" (1:4). He writes that God brought the flood "*on the world* (κόσμος—humanity, mankind) *of the ungodly*" (2:5) and again mentions escaping "*the defilements of the world*" (κόσμος—humanity, mankind) through the true knowledge of Jesus as Lord and Savior (2:20). Finally, he writes here in chapter 3 that "*the world* (κόσμος—humanity, mankind) *at that time was destroyed being flooded by water*" (3:6). The planet, the earth (γῆ, ge) was not destroyed (ruined) in the flood, but humanity, mankind, "the world" certainly was.

Understanding "Destroyed" and "Destruction" in 2 Peter

It is important at this point to clarify Peter's use of the word *destroy* or *destruction*. It is a critical key concept in the book, and we must understand it clearly in order to reach the proper conclusions. English readers will encounter the words *destruction* or *destroyed* a total of 12 times in Peter's text, specifically in 2 Peter 2:1, 3, 6, 12; 3:6, 7, 10, 11, 12, and 16. What is not seen in the English text is that Peter is actually using six different Greek words each being translated by either "destroyed" or "destruction." He uses ἀπώλεια (5x), ἀπόλλυμι (1x), λύω (3x), φθορά (1x), φθείρω (1x) and καταστροφή (1x). We will examine each of these to seek a better understanding the differences in their meaning and what Peter is saying when using them.

Peter uses the Greek word ἀπώλεια (*apoleia*) the most in his letter (2:1--twice, 2:3; 3:7, 16). This word carries the meaning of loss, perdition, or ruin. When used of people, it describes "the state after death wherein exclusion from salvation is a realized fact, wherein man, instead of becoming what he might have been, *is lost and ruined*" (Zodhiates 246). Peter never uses this word to describe physical objects or things, but in each case uses it with reference to people. Throughout this letter Peter expresses the punishment that will come upon the ungodly or unrighteous with ἀπώλεια (*apoleia*). These people with be eternally ruined or lost for all time if they refuse to repent. Peter states that the false teachers introduce **destructive** heresies—teachings that will

Are We Looking for a New Heavens and a New Earth? 2 Peter 3:3-18

bring spiritual ruin and cause to those who follow them to be lost. In doing this these men bring swift **destruction** (ruin—cause to be lost) upon themselves (2:1). The judgment of these false teachers is not idle and their **destruction** (ruin) is not asleep (2:3). God brought the flood and "*the world (kosmos*—mankind, humanity) *was destroyed*" (brought to eternal ruin) (3:6). The day of judgment will bring the "***destruction*** (eternal ruin) of *ungodly men*" (3:7) and those who twist and distort Scripture do so "*to their own destruction*" (eternal ruin) (3:16). Each instance of this term is discussing the eternal fate of people—they will be ruined or lost. The word ἀπόλλυμι (*apollumi*) is from the same root family as ἀπώλεια (*apoleia*) and also means to be lost or to be ruined. Peter writes that "*the world (kosmos*—humanity)...*was destroyed being flooded by water*" (3:6). It is not the earth that was eternally ruined or lost but man.

When Peter talks about physical things (not people), he uses four additional Greek terms to describe their **destruction**. Two of these words, φθορά (noun—*phthora*) and φθείρω (verb—*phtheiro*) are from the same family and carry the same basic meaning. These two words are only found in 2:12 where Peter compares the false teachers to "unreasoning animals." He states that in "*the destruction* (φθορά, *phthora*) *of those creatures [unreasoning animals]," the false teachers will also be destroyed* (φθείρω, *phtheiro*) (2:12). These creatures will undergo destruction (φθορά, *phthora*), which describes "the breakdown of organic matter; deterioration, corruption" (Bauer, "φθορά," 1054)—in other words the animal will ultimately rot or deteriorate. Much like these animals who will rot, the false teachers will also be **destroyed** (φθείρω, *phtheiro*) a verb meaning "to cause deterioration of the inner life, ruin or corruption" (Bauer, "φθείρω," 1054). In other words, the false teachers will rot and deteriorate just like an animal rots when it dies. It is a graphic description of the ultimate outcome of the teachings and lifestyle of these ungodly people.

When proving that God has always punished the ungodly, Peter states that God "*condemned the cities of Sodom and Gomorrah to destruction by reducing them to ashes*" (2:6). The Greek term used here is yet another word translated destruction—καταστροφή (*katastrophe*). It is the word we get our modern English word *catastrophe* from, and it means a "condition of total destruction, with the implication that nothing is in its customary place or position; ruin" (Bauer, "καταστροφή," 528). Because of their ungodliness God brought those physical cities to *catastrophe* by reducing them to ashes. It is a fitting word to describe what God did to Sodom and Gomorrah because of their sin—nothing in those cities was left it its original place, only ashes remained. No doubt they were brought to *catastrophe*.

But the last word used by Peter becomes the most significant to our understanding of the destruction he describes on the day of the Lord in chapter 3. It is the word λύω (*luō*) and it is only used three times in the letter, but all of those uses are found in 3:10-12. The word λύω (*luō*) is very different from these other Greek terms. Where all of the other words used carry more of the idea "to bring to ruin," λύω (*luō*) means "to reduce something by violence into its component parts" (Bauer 607). It is a word that means "to loose" and it has reference to the "loosing" of an object's very atoms being torn apart and scattered. This is a word that describes complete and total destruction—a cessation of existence. Peter makes it clear that the current heaven and earth will be **destroyed** (λύω, *luō*) (3:10-12). This is not a word that describes a "renovation" of the earth as some suggest. This word is a word that describes a **complete destruction**, a cessation of existence. We will examine the implications of this word more as we move through the text here.

God destroyed the world (mankind) with water in the Flood because of their ungodliness (3:6).

The next thing that *"escaped the notice"* of these false teachers was not only did God create the physical heavens (universe) and earth (planet) from the beginning but that He punished "t*he world of the ungodly with the flood*" (2:15). Peter had just made the point that God formed the earth (γῆ, *ge*) "out of water and by/through (διά) water" (3:5). It was then water "through which the world (κόσμος, *kosmos*—humanity) at that time was **destroyed**" (ἀπόλλυμι, *apollumi*—brought to eternal ruin) being flooded with water (3:6).

Again the false teachers had forgotten that "*the Lord knows how…to keep the unrighteous under punishment for the day of judgment*" (2:9). The Flood should tell them that their judgment was not idle and their **destruction** (ruin) was not asleep (2:3). God has never and will never allow unrighteousness and the ungodly to go unpunished.

Peter's point is that since the beginning of time a great deal has changed—God created the universe and the earth beneath it. He also punished humanity because of their ungodliness. Certainly all things are not just as they were from the beginning as the false teachers suggest.

God Has Reserved "Present Heavens and Earth" for Fire and Its Complete Destruction (3:7-10)

Peter now turns his discussion to future events. The same power of God that created the heavens (universe) and the earth in the beginning and brought a flood as punishment on the ungodly in the Old Testament is the same power that allows the "*present heavens and earth*" to continue until the day the Lord returns and all face judgment. God has both the heavens and the earth as they exist now "*reserved for fire, kept for the day of judgment*" (3:7). The word *reserved* means "to keep something safe by storing it" (Bauer 456) and the word *kept* is the word τηρέω (*tereō*) which means "to cause to continue, keep, hold, preserve" (Bauer, "τηρέω," 1002). Peter's point is that it has "*escaped the notice*" of these mocking false teachers that it is God that allows the present heavens and earth to continue at all. He is "keeping them safe" and "causing them to continue" until the day of judgment. But Peter is clear that fire is coming for the present heavens and earth and with the fire will come the **destruction** (ἀπώλεια, *apoleia*—ruin) of ungodly men (3:7).

While the certainty of these things may have escaped the notice of these false teachers, Peter wants to ensure that it doesn't "*escape your* [his readers] *notice*" that the Lord will come (3:8). Peter explains to them that Lord is not slow about His promise to return as these false teachers suggest, but rather He is being patient "*not wanting for any to perish.*" The word perish here is the word (ἀπόλλυμι, *apollumi*)—"ruined, lost") that has been translated **destroyed** previously. The Lord hasn't come back because He is given everyone, including these false teachers and their followers, time to "*come to repentance*" (3:9). The ungodly people should not be in a hurry for the Lord to return. If He does, they will be lost! It is God's patience with them and all those who live unrighteous lives that He has not come back yet—He does not want them to be ruined and eternally lost.

But the ungodly should make no mistake, even though it will happen at a time they least expect it ("*like a thief*"), "*the day of the Lord will come*" (3:10). When He does, the physical creation, the present heavens and earth, will be completely destroyed and driven from existence with "*intense

Are We Looking for a New Heavens and a New Earth? 2 Peter 3:3-18

heat" (3:10, 12) and "*by burning*" (3:12). He will use three phrases, each connected with the word καὶ (and) to describe the violent events involved in this destruction:

1) the heavens will pass away with a roar (v. 10) and be destroyed by burning (v. 12)

2) the elements will melt (v. 12) and be destroyed with intense heat (v. 10)

3) the earth and its works will be burned up (v. 10)

First, Peter states that on the day of the Lord "*the heavens* (the universe above the earth) *will pass away with a roar*" (3:10). There will be a roar (ῥοιζηδόν, *rhoidzedon*)—"a noise made be something passing by with great force and speed, a rushing noise" (Bauer 907) and the universe above the earth will "*pass away*." The word here rendered "*pass away*" is παρέρχομαι (*parerchomai*)—"to come to an end and so no longer be there, to pass away, disappear" (Bauer 775). With an incredible rushing sound the universe—every planet, star, and galaxy—the entire expanse above the earth will come to an end and disappear! Peter will go on to say that "*the heavens will be destroyed by burning*" (3:12). He previous wrote that the heavens and earth are reserved for fire (πῦρ, *pyr*), now he writes that the heavens will be destroyed by "*burning*" (πυρούμενοι from the verb πυρόω, *pyroō*). This is the root word from which we get our word *pyromanic*, and it simply means to burn.

Second, Peter states that on the day of the Lord "*the elements will be destroyed with intense heat*" (3:10). The word στοιχεῖον (*stoicheion*) translated here as "*elements*" (ASV, NASB, NKJV, KJV, NIV, NRSV, RSV) creates some discussion and debate. The word στοιχεῖον (*stoicheion*) describes the "basic components of something" and it is primarily used to describe "substances underlying the natural world, the basic **elements** from which everything in the world is made and of which it is composed" (Bauer 946). The word is used figuratively by the Hebrews writer where he mentions the "*elements*" or first principles of Christian doctrine (Heb. 5:12) and Paul uses it in Galatians 3:4 and Colossians 2:8, 20 figuratively as well. But it is evident from the context that Peter has something physical in mind because he states these "*elements*" will be **destroyed** (*luō*) with "*intense heat*" (3:10) and they will melt (3:12). The question becomes is Peter referring to "*the elements*" of the heavens (the planets, stars, and galaxies) or "*the elements*" of the earth (earth, air, fire, water)?

The ESV has chosen to render στοιχεῖον (*stoicheion*) as "*heavenly bodies.*" While this is a possible meaning of word, it is not used that way in Scripture and it is only used this way by a few extra-biblical writers—namely, Aristides, Justin Martyr, and Diogenes (Bauer 946). By choosing "*heavenly bodies*" to render the word in this context, it seems that the ESV translators are suggesting that "*the elements*" is a phrase connected to the heavens rather than the earth. It should be noted that the ESV is the only major translation to use that rendering. In essence, this translation of στοιχεῖον (*stoicheion*) suggests that Peter is saying that **the heavens** will suddenly cease to exist with a loud rushing sound and **the elements of the heavens** (sun, moon, stars, galaxies, etc....) will be destroyed with intense heat.

There are a few problems with this approach. First, the word στοιχεῖον as mentioned is primarily used to describe the elements (earth, air, fire, water) that make up the natural world. Jewish literature in the Intertestamental Period used the word exclusively in reference to the elements of the earth (Wisdom of Solomon 7:17; 19:18; 4 Macc. 12:13). Both the Jewish philosopher Philo and the Jewish historian Josephus also used the word exclusively to describe the elements of the earth—"Let us leave these merely particular buildings, and contemplate that greatest of houses or cities, this world. We shall see that its cause is God, by whom it has come into being, its material *the four elements*" (Philo 127). "The veils, too, which were composed of four things, they declared the four elements" which he then shows that these elements are a connection to the earth, sea, air, and water (Josephus 3.183). While "heavenly bodies" is a possible meaning, it is not the primary use of the term.

Second, if *"the elements"* (στοιχεῖον) here refers to the basic components that make up the heavens, what is Peter saying vanishes with a roar? Remember the first phrase states that *"the heavens"* pass away (παρέρχομαι, *parerchomai*—to no longer be, to disappear). But the elements (everything that makes up the heavens) are destroyed in a different way? This would have everything that makes up the heavens (the elements) and the heavens be two different things, and each is to be destroyed in a different way. But this separation does not fit either Greek or Jewish understanding of the "heavens" as we discussed previously. To the Greek and Jewish mind, everything above the earth was described with the word *heavens*. It is very unlikely that Peter would separate the two in this way.

It seems far more likely that when Peter talks about *"the elements"* he is referring to the elements that make up the earth. This connection to the "earth" rather than the "heavens seems to be clarified by a second use of the word στοιχεῖον (*stoicheion*) found in verse 12. There Peter writes, '*the elements will melt with intense heat.*' Both in verse 10 and verse 12 the elements are subject to 'intense heat' (καυσόω (*kausoō*) —'to be consumed by intense heat, to be burned up'" (Bauer 536). In verse 10, they are "*destroyed*" (λύω, *luō*) with this intense heat and in verse 12 they will "*melt*" with this same intense heat. The word translated "melt" is τήκω (*tēkō*) which means "to cause something to become liquid" (Bauer 1001). It seems clear by the use of this word that although "*the elements*" will ultimately be "*destroyed*" (reduced by violence into its component parts or atoms no longer to exist) (v.10), "*the elements*" will melt and become liquid (τήκω, *tēkō*) and then that liquid will be burned up (καυσόω (*kausoō*) and completely destroyed (λύω, *luō*).

This presents and interesting sequence of events given that earlier in the text Peter was very specific that the earth was formed out of and through liquid—water (3:5). Again, this is a direct reference to the creation account in Genesis 1 where God started with nothing. Out of that nothing God created the earth. The word created there is ארב (*bā-rā*), a verb that expresses the creation of something out of nothing (Vine 51). But that formless and void "earth" is described simply as water (Gen. 1:2). Then God caused land to appear and then the rest of the formation of the earth on subsequent days (Gen. 1:9f). Notice the sequence of events in the Genesis account— nothing, then water, then a fully formed earth. Peter, now in discussion about the destruction of the earth on the day of the Lord begins with the present earth (obviously fully formed—3:7), then states that it will melt (τήκω, *tēkō*—return to liquid, then be completely "burned up" (καυσόω, *kausoō*, and destroyed (λύω, *luō*) to complete nothing. Genesis: nothing => liquid => earth. Peter: earth => liquid => nothing. The sequence of events in Peter's description of the day of the Lord is the exact reverse of the Creation account in Genesis 1. All of these argument seem to indicate that Peter intends to connect *"the elements"* with the earth itself in 3:10 rather than with the heavens.

Third, Peter states that on the day of the Lord *"the earth and its works will be burned up"* (3:10). This is another challenging phrase whose text requires some deep diving and may be the most problematic text in the letter. The issue here is that there is a textual variant in the manuscript evidence with the phrase "*will be burned up.*" Manuscript evidence attests to two possible Greek words that should be used here at the end of verse 10. That *"intense heat"* (καυσόω (*kausoō*) will be the instrument through which the heavens and the elements of the earth will ultimately be consumed and completely destroyed is clear from the text (3:12). The phrase *"will be burned up"* (NASB) at the end of verse 10 however is in question. The word used here in the NASB is κατακαήσεται (*katakaēsetai*) which means "to burn, burn up, or consume by fire" (Zodhiates "κατακαήσεται," 830). This same Greek word and rending is found in the ASV, NKJV, as well as others. Yet the ESV, NRSV, HCSB, and even the newest version of the NAS2020 use the word εὑρεθήσεται (*heurethēsetai*) and it is rendered *"will be disclosed"* (NRSV, HCSB), *"will be exposed"* (ESV), or *"will be discovered"* (NAS2020). This word εὑρεθήσεται (*heurethēsetai*) means "to find out by inquiry, to discover" (Zodhiates, "εὑρίσκω," 682). The textual apparatus, a resource that rates the certainty of the various variants within the Greek text, gives this variant a "C" rating which means the committee had difficulty in deciding which variant to place in the text but gives εὑρεθήσεται (*heurethēsetai*) a slight edge (Aland 781). As more manuscript evidence comes to light, it appears that εὑρεθήσεται (*heurethēsetai*) is probably the correct word here. So, what Peter is saying is that "the earth and its works will be exposed or found out" rather than "burned up." The point is that nothing on the earth will be hidden from view. In the intense heat (καυσόω, *kausoō*)—to burn up) of destruction (λύω, *luō*), the earth and its elements will be completely torn down to their very atoms and no longer exist. In that process, everything will be exposed to examination.

Just to be clear, the word κατακαήσεται (*katakaēsetai*) at the end of verse 10 is not needed to prove that the earth will be "burned up." The words *"intense heat"* (καυσόω, *kausoō*) and *"destroyed"* (λύω, *luō*) are more than sufficient to prove the complete elimination of the earth. Peter will say in verse 12 that *"the heavens will be destroyed"* (λύω, *luō*) *"by burning"* (πυρόω, *pyroō*). Guy N. Woods summarized it this way, "The 'elements' are the rudimental portions of the earth system, the minute parts which comprise the whole. The heavens and the earth are to be dissolved; they are to lose their form and be returned to the original atoms from which they were constructed" (Woods 201-2). This planet will not be "renovated"—it will cease to exist completely. God has indeed reserved **"*present heavens and earth*"** for fire and its complete destruction.

"*Since all these things* [the present heavens and earth—3:7] *are to be destroyed* [completely eliminated from existence, torn down to atoms—3:10, 12] *in this way* [with intense heat and burning—3:10, 12], *what sort of people ought you be in holy conduct and godliness*" (3:11). Knowing beforehand of how the entirety of the Creation will be destroyed by burning and knowing that will this destruction of the physical universe will come judgment and the eternal ruin of ungodly men (3:7), should that not cause us to change how we live now? Notice the admonition to *"godliness"* (v. 11) in contrast with the fate of *"ungodly"* men (v. 7). All of this connects with the main point of Peter's letter that we mentioned earlier—"*their judgment from long ago is not idle and their destruction is not asleep*" (2:3). The coming judgment day, the day of the Lord, is a certainty regardless of the mocking these false teachers bring (3:3, 4). If you follow them your end will be the same as theirs. But **"*the Lord knows how to rescue the godly from temptation and keep the unrighteous under punishment for the day of judgment*"** (2:9). Let this knowledge of punishment drive you to holy behavior and godliness.

If we will allow this knowledge to change the way we live, then we should be *"looking for"* (προσδοκάω, *prosdokaō*—"to give thought to something that it yet in the future, to look of, expect" (Bauer 877)) and hastening ("to be in a hurry for") the coming of the day of God. Why? Because He knows how to rescue you! He knows how to save you! Yes—the ungodly will be punished, but if you seek godliness, if you seek holiness, God will rescue you! Isn't that a reason to be looking for and hastening the coming of the Lord?

According to His promise We Look for a "*New Heavens and Earth*" (3:13).

Peter has referred to the promises (ἐπάγγελμα, *epangelma*) of God from the beginning of the letter. God has granted to us "*His precious magnificent promises*" so that "*by them we could escape the corruption that is in the world by lust*" (1:4). His promise to come back is mentioned in 3:4 and 3:9. But there is no greater promise mentioned in 2 Peter than the "*promise*" of a "n*ew heavens and a new earth in which righteousness dwells*" (3:13).

So where did God "*promise*" there would be a "*new heavens and a new earth*"? The phrase "*new heaven(s) and new earth*" only appears four times in Scripture (Isa. 65:17; 66:22; Rev. 21:1; and here). It seems logical that Peter has the two prophetic statements in Isaiah in mind with this phrase. "*For behold, I create a **new heavens and a new earth**; and the former things will not be remembered or come to mind*" (Isa. 65:17). "'*Just as the **new heavens and the new earth** which I make will endure before Me,' declares the Lord*" (Isa. 66:22). While Isaiah had reference to the promise of freedom from Babylonian captivity when he wrote these two verses, Peter seems to be acquiring their same prophetic promise here in 3:13. He is showing that this promise will again be fulfilled on the day of the Lord (dual fulfillment). Note that Isaiah states that God will "*create*" (ארב, *bā-rā*—the same word from Genesis 1:1 which means "to create something out of nothing") a new heavens and a new earth (Isa. 65:17). Having just described the violent, total elimination of the "*present heavens and earth*," this prophecy of Isaiah fits Peter's context precisely.

In addition to describing our eternal adobe as a place "*where righteousness dwells,*" Peter also describes it as "*new.*" The word "*new*" here does not have reference to time as we might suppose. The Greek word used to describe "new in time" would be νέος (*neos*) (Bauer 669). The word Peter uses here is καινός (*kainos*), a word that focuses on the quality of something more than how long it has been in existence. It is a word which is means "new in nature with the implication of better" (Behm 389-90). Woods describes the difference between these two ideas when he writes:

> [Of the] two words translated "new" in the New Testament; one is prospective and indicates that which is young as opposed to old; the other is retrospective and points to that which is fresh in contrast to that which is worn out. It is the second of these (*kainos*) which is used here. The heavens and the earth which the apostle describes in this passage will be fresh and new, and not worn and old, as are the heavens and the earth which now exist (203).

In Peter's own words we are looking for a "*better*" heavens and a "*better*" earth. In context a "*better*" heavens than the "*present*" heavens and a "*better*" earth than the "*present*" earth (cf. 3:7, 13).

So What Does Peter Mean by a "*Better*" Heavens and Earth?

First some suggest that Scripture does not say and we cannot know what Peter means by "*a new heavens and a new earth.*" While it is true that Peter himself does not elaborate beyond what we have already discussed, he does point to another source in Scripture directly—the writings of Paul. Having said that "*we are looking for a new heavens and new earth*" (v. 13), Peter continues by writing,

Are We Looking for a New Heavens and a New Earth? 2 Peter 3:3-18

"*since you look for **these things**, be diligent to be found by Him in peace, spotless and blameless*" (3:14). The phrase "*these things*" connects to the new heavens and new earth as he continues in 3:15, 16. "*And regard the patience of our Lord* [mentioned in v. 9] *as salvation, just as our beloved brother Paul, according to the wisdom given to him, wrote to you, as in all his letters, speaking of **these things** in which some are hard to understand....*" If we follow the phrase "***these things***" through the context it seems to suggest that Paul has written about the same things Peter has been writing about "*in all his letters.*" While it is unnecessary to prove that all the topics appear is all of Paul's letters, it is clear that Paul has written about the same things that Peter has been discussing; the Judgment Day (1 Thess. 3:13; Rom. 14:10), the resurrection (1 Cor. 15), Heaven as the future abode of the righteous (2 Cor. 5:1-10), the end of the world and the destruction of the wicked (2 Thess. 1:7-10; 2:1-12) and even the regeneration of "*a new heavens and new earth*" (Rom. 8:18-23). In Romans 8:18-23, Paul describes that the physical creation as "*anxiously longing*" to be set free from "*its slavery to corruption*" (φθορά, *phthora*) (a word that Peter used four times in 2 Peter: 1:4; 2:12 (2x); 2:19). It was subjected to futility by God when man sinned in the Garden (Gen. 3:17-19). Paul goes on to say that the "*whole creation groans and suffers the pains of childbirth until now*" (8:22). So what is a pregnant "creation" (physical heavens and earth) going to give birth to? Could it be a "new heavens and new earth"? Both Roman 8 and 2 Peter 3 are talking about the end of time, the creation (present heavens and earth), being set free from corruption, and our resurrection to eternal life. Is it at least possible that Romans 8 is what Peter has in mind when he refers to Paul's writings about "***these things***"?

AUTHOR'S NOTE: *While space doesn't allow a complete exposition of Romans 8 in this article, I would refer you to Denny Petrillo's detailed discussion of Romans 8 in this same book.*

If so, Peter may be describing an eternal adobe for the righteous that is more "physical" than we often think. Peter discussed a physical, literal heavens and a physical, literal earth in 3:5, 7, 10; is it at least possible that he means a physical, literal "*better*" heavens and earth in verse 13? By "physical" we are not suggesting "just like" the heavens and the earth that we have now or "just like" the bodies we have now. But was the Garden of Eden not "physical"? Yet Adam and Eve were made by God to live in that Garden eternally. They had access to the tree of life (Gen. 2:9), and it was not until they ate of the tree of the knowledge of good and evil that they were changed and became subject to death (2:17). It was told to John in the Revelation, "*To him who overcomes, I will grant to eat of the tree of life which is in the Paradise of God*" (2:7). The word "*paradise*" is παράδεισος (*paradeisos*) which has a primary meaning of "garden" or "Garden of Eden" (Bauer 761). Is it so hard to think that God had a plan from the beginning to return mankind to that perfect Garden that He created for man in the beginning? Is it at least possible that these passages are connected and reveal more about our eternal, heavenly abode than we might have thought?

Is it possible that this view of a more "garden-like" eternal abode helps reconcile other difficult passages? What did Jesus mean when He said, "*The meek shall inherit the earth*" (Matt. 5:5). There is certainly never a promise in Scripture that God's people will inherit this present earth. Could He have been speaking of the "new earth" to come? What did Jesus mean when He spoke about the days when "*He will sit on His glorious throne*" that He referred to that time as the "regeneration"? The word He used, παλιγγενεσία (*palingenesia*), means "a state of being renewed with a focus on a cosmic experience" (Bauer 752). Zodhiates shows that the word is a compound word from *palin* (again) and genesis (generation). The word in its most literal sense describes an "again-genesis." He writes of this word that it "to the coming state of the whole creation, equivalent to the restoration of all things of Acts 3:21, which will occur when the Son of Man shall come in His glory" (1091). Certainly Peter is talking about those exact same events in describing our looking for a new heavens and a new earth. Is it possible they are describing the same regeneration?

Some Arguments Against this View

Some would suggest that it is not possible. They would argue that our eternal heavenly home is "spiritual" not physical, and any attempt to teach otherwise is borne out of a carnal and worldly heart. But there are times when the term *spiritual* refers to physical beings, not just spirits. Paul wrote to the physical Christians in Galatia, "*Brethren, even if anyone is caught in any trespass,* **you who are spiritual**, *restore such a one in a spirit of gentleness; each one looking to yourself, so that you too will not be tempted*" (Gal. 6:1, NASB95). Again, please understand. We are *not* arguing that our eternal existence will be physical like this current heavens and earth or like our current bodies are physical. Paul makes it clear that we will be changed (1 Cor. 15:52). But is it possible that that change will be much like the physical existence Adam and Eve had in the Garden before the Fall?

Still others would argue it's not possible because Peter is just using figurative language in 3:13 to describe Heaven. The question must be asked: Where in the text of 2 Peter 3 has he used figurative language? Again, he has been talking about a literal physical heavens in earth throughout the context. What in the text signals a shift from the literal to the figurative? As also mentioned earlier, the use of the word *earth* (γῆ, *ge*) does not has a single figurative use in the New Testament unless it is here in 3:13. Out of 250 uses, it would have to be argued that this is the one and only time it is used figuratively.

Others would argue it is not possible and would point to John's Gospel where Jesus Himself talks about *"His Father's house"* and its many dwelling places. In that text Jesus is clear, "*In My Father's house are many dwelling places; if it were not so, I would have told you; for* **I go to prepare a place** *for you. If I go and prepare a place for you, I will come again and receive you to Myself, that where I am,* **there you may be also**" (John 14:2, 3). The argument is that Jesus says, "*I go to prepare a place.*" The word here is ἑτοιμάζω (*hetoimadzo*) which means "to cause to be ready" (Bauer 400). It is obvious that He is *not* talking about preparing a place here on earth—He must go. And where He goes—they will go be with Him also. It is not here—it is in His Father's house.

There is no doubt that Jesus states that His Father's house is not on the earth. But there is one more mention of the *"new heavens and new earth"* that we haven't dealt with yet and it may certainly shed light on Jesus' statement in John 14:2-3. John is given the opportunity to glimpse that final day—Judgment Day and he writes, "*Then I saw* **a new heaven and a new earth**; *for the first heaven and the first earth passed away, and there is no longer any sea. And I saw the holy city, new [kainos—see previous discussion] Jerusalem, coming down out of heaven from God,* **made ready** *as a bride adorned for her husband*" (Rev. 21:1-2). John sees the *kainos* (better) Jerusalem coming down out of heaven from God. This "new" Jerusalem is described as the holy city (v. 1), the tabernacle (σκηνή, *skene*—a tent, a dwelling place) of God (v. 3), and when it comes down out of heaven from God to the new heavens and new earth (v. 2) a voice says "*Behold, the tabernacle of God is among men, and He will dwell among them, and they shall be His people, and God Himself will dwell among them*" (v. 3). Clearly John is seeing a time when and a place ("*the new heavens and new earth*") where God will dwell with His people. But notice the text also says that this new, better Jerusalem has been "*made ready as a bride adorned for her husband*" (v2). The verb used translated **made ready** here is the same one from John 14:2-3—ἑτοιμάζω (*hetoimadzo*). In John 14:2-3 it is an aorist active subjunctive—an uncompleted action. Here in Revelation 21:2 it is a perfect tense verb. The perfect tense describes an "action completed in the past, with implications in the present." Jesus did go "*to prepare*" a place for man to dwell with God in His house. John sees that dwelling place coming down out of Heaven from God to the "*new heavens and new earth*" prepared (completed action). It is a place for God and His people to dwell together—"*they shall be His people, and God Himself will dwell among them*" (21:3). What an incredible description! There is no doubt that at the time Jesus said it and even today, the present heavens and earth are still in existence and the heavenly realm of our Father and the faithful departed are where God is now. But John is clear that on the day of Judgment God's dwelling will come down out of Heaven—to the new heavens and new earth—and we will dwell together with God forever.

CONCLUSION

There is certainly a great deal to unpack here. In just a few verses, 2 Peter 3:5-14, Peter has dealt with some very deep ideas in describing the day of the Lord. At this point, we should all agree that if we know nothing else about this final place of rescue and rest for the righteous, His promise to provide it should be enough for us. We as faithful Christians seeking to live lives in holy conduct and righteousness should be looking with confidence for a "*new heavens and a new earth*"—that is what the inspired apostle has said without equivocation. We can be confident that:

1. The present heavens (universe) and present earth will come to a violent and total destruction (λύω, *luō*). They will not be "renovated" but will cease to exist entirely (3:10-12).

2. After this destruction "*according to the promise*" of God Himself there will be a new heavens and new earth (3:13).

3. This new earth will be the eternal dwelling place of the righteous (3:13).

Peter insists that armed with the knowledge of these future events we should change our current behavior and manner of living (3:11). We must remember that "*the Lord knows how to rescue the godly from temptation, and to keep the unrighteous under punishment for the day of judgment*" (2:9). These false teachers will be destroyed (eternally ruined) if they refuse to change and those who follow them will suffer the same end—"*their judgment from long ago is not idle and their destruction is not asleep*" (2:5). God will punish those who lead ungodly lives. But those who seek to live lives of godliness, seeking to be holy and righteous, can look to the return of the Lord with confidence and longing. Knowing that while God will destroy this current creation, we as His people look for a "*new heavens and a new earth where righteousness dwells.*" Regardless of your view of what those words describe, we all should be looking for and hastening that day. Because it is in that day that we will dwell with our Heavenly Father and our Lord Jesus Christ for all eternity. "*You therefore, beloved, knowing this beforehand, be on your guard so that you will not be carried away by the error of unprincipled men and fall from your own steadfastness, but grow in grace and knowledge of our Lord and Savior Jesus Christ. To Him be the glory, both now and to the day of eternity. Amen*" (3:17-18).

WORKS CITED

Aland, Barbara, et al., editors. *The Greek New Testament: Apparatus*. Fifth Revised Edition, Deutsche Bibelgesellschaft; American Bible Society; United Bible Societies, 2014.

Bauer, Walter. *A Greek-English Lexicon of the New Testament and Other Early Christian Literature*, 3rd ed., Edited by William Arndt, et al.. University of Chicago Press, 2000.

Behm, J. "kainós." *Theological Dictionary of the New Testament, Abridged in One Volume*, edited by Kittel, Gerhard, et al.. W.B. Eerdmans, 1985.

Bietenhard, H. "Οὐρανός." *New International Dictionary of New Testament Theology*, Vol. 2, edited by Lothar Coenen et al.. Zondervan Publishing House, 1986.

Josephus, Flavius. "*Antiquities of the Jews.*" *The Works of Josephus: Complete and Unabridged*. Peabody: Hendrickson, 1987.

Philo. "On the Cherubim, and the Flaming Sword, and Cain." *Philo*. Vol. I–X, Translated by F. H. Colson et al.. William Heinemann Ltd; Harvard University Press, 1929–1962.

Schoonhoven, C. R. "Heaven." *The International Standard Bible Encyclopedia*, Revised, Vol. 2, edited by Geoffrey W Bromiley. Wm. B. Eerdmans, 1979–1988.

Vine, W. E., et al. *Vine's Complete Expository Dictionary of Old and New Testament Words*, Vol. 1. T. Nelson, 1996.

Woods, Guy N. *A Commentary on the New Testament Epistles of Peter, John, and Jude*. Gospel Advocate Company, 1991.

Zodhiates, Spiros. *The Complete Word Study Dictionary: New Testament*. AMG Publishers, 2000.

Special Study

ROMANS 8 AND ESCHATOLOGY

DENNY PETRILLO

The study of last things ("eschatology") is one of the predominant topics in all of the New Testament. Obviously, God's people have an intense interest in what will take place at the end. Paul, in numerous places (cf. 1 Cor. 15:42-58; 2 Cor. 4:16-5:10; 1 Thess. 4:13-18; 2 Thess. 1:7-9; 2:1-10). The book of Romans is no exception. The section in chapter 8:18-25 is of special interest.

In 8:18 Paul sets the stage for a discussion of eschatology when he states, *"For I consider that the sufferings of this present time are not worthy to be compared with the glory that is to be revealed to us."* The phrase *"the glory that is to be revealed to us"* is the basis of what he says next. Using the word *glory*, he will make reference to the *"glory of the children of God"* (v. 21). Later he will say, *"...and whom He justified, these He also glorified"* (v. 30; see also 9:23).

What does Paul say about events on the last day?

First, he says that it will be that day that the sons of God will be **revealed** (v. 18). There have always been pretenders, those who through hypocrisy have led others to believe they are true Christians. God, however, is not deceived (cf. Gal. 6:7). The word **revealed** (ἀποκαλύπτω) means "to cause something to be fully known, reveal, disclose, bring to light, make fully known" (Bauer 112). In addition to the sons of God being *"revealed"* (v. 19), there will be other things that God will reveal. There are certainly things that God will show us, but there are other things that he will "make fully known." Part of what will be **revealed** is discussed in verses 19-25, including what Paul says about the creation. "Revealed in this context indicates something Christians will experience, not merely something they will see with their eyes" (Newman and Nida 157).

Second, he discusses the *"freedom of the glory of the children of God"* (v. 21). Our bodies, which are slaves to corruption, will be given life (v. 11). This ties back to the *"sufferings of this present time"* mentioned in verse 18, and then will be revisited in verses 35-38. The Christian will be set free from a body that is subject to pain and death.

Third, Paul says that "*we ourselves groan within ourselves, waiting eagerly for our adoption as sons, the redemption of our body*" (v. 23). He is going to say again that we "*wait eagerly*" in verse 25. As our bodies grow old and tired, we long for the renewed body—one that is immortal and imperishable (1 Cor. 15:53). Paul would say, "*For indeed in this house we groan, longing to be clothed with our dwelling from Heaven*" (2 Cor. 5:2).

> Paul suggests that these groans are not verbal utterances but inward, nonverbal "sighs," indicative of a certain attitude. This attitude does not involve anxiety about whether we will finally experience the deliverance God has promised—for Paul allows of no doubts on that score (cf. vv. 28–30)—but frustration at the remaining moral and physical infirmities that are inevitably a part of this period between justification and glorification (see 2 Cor. 5:2, 4) and longing for the end of this state of "weakness" (Moo 519).

Paul, however, spends considerable time talking about "*the creation*." The bulk of the discussion here is what is meant by the word *creation*. This word (κτίσις) is used to refer to the following in Scripture: people (Mark 16:16; 2 Cor. 5:17); food (1 Tim. 4:4); idols/animals (Rom. 1:25); sea creatures (Rev. 8:9); everything (Col. 1:16; 2 Pet. 3:4); the world (Rom. 1:20); created things (Rom. 8:39). While many propose that he is using the word to refer to humanity (as in Mark 16:16), it is clear that Paul is talking about the creation separate from humanity.

1. Note: "*The creation waits eagerly for the revealing of the sons of God*" (v. 19). It does not make sense to say that the sons of God wait eagerly for the revealing of the sons of God. Paul clearly has something in mind that is different than the sons of God.

2. Note the word *also* in verse 21: "*That the creation itself also will be set free.*" That is, the sons of God will be set free, and the creation also will be set free.

3. Note the words "*but also we ourselves*" in verse 23. This language clearly indicates that the creation is different than the sons of God.

4. Note the word *groan*. Paul says that the creation "*groans*" (v. 22), and "*even we ourselves groan*" (v. 23). Grammar and logic demand that there are separate groaners.

   > From verse 22 it appears at first sight that "the whole creation" includes man. But verse 23 alters this impression, for it sets the entire creation over against the whole body of the redeemed ("we ourselves") and therefore does not include in it the people of God. The groaning of the creation looks back to its subjection to frustration (v. 20), whereas the pangs of childbirth anticipate the age of renewal (Harrison 94).

5. It does not make sense to say that humanity was "*subjected to futility*" (v. 20).

It is clear Paul is not talking about humanity, but the material universe. "However widely encompassing was Paul's earlier use of κτίσις (see on 8:19), here certainly it is nonhuman, and, as we would say, inanimate creation which is primarily in view" (Dunn 472). Normally we would think of such as inanimate, but such is not the case here. Note all that Paul says about the creation: has anxious longing (v. 19); waits eagerly (v. 20); was subjected (v. 20); has will (v. 20); hopes (v. 20); groans (v. 22); suffers (v. 22). Since Paul is talking about the material universe, what does he say about it?

Romans 8 and Eschatology

A. She was originally created to easily produce fruit (Gen. 2:9-17).

B. She was forced, by God, to be *"cursed"* (Gen. 3:18) and to produce that which is worthless (Gen. 3:19) and to produce that which is valuable only with much effort (Gen. 3:19).

C. Paul says this subjection continues *"until now"* (8:22).

D. The creation will eventually be *"set free from its slavery to corruption"* (8:21). This is going to happen at the same time that the children of God receive glory (8:23). If we merge this thought with the teachings of Peter, the material universe will be burned up (2 Pet. 3:10-14). This is how and when the creation will be set free. It will no longer have to produce that which is worthless.

E. Paul says the creation *"groans and suffers the pains of childbirth together until now"* (8:22). That is, the creation is "pregnant" and is anticipating "childbirth" (v. 22).

It is that last point that gives us a glimpse into our eternal home. While some argue that this creation will be renewed, such does not fit the language here. If a human woman gives birth, what does she give birth to? A human child. Yet that child is not a "renovated" mother. The child is his own being. Equally, if the creation gives birth, what does it give birth to? A new creation. This creation is not a "renovated" earth but is new. Does Scripture teach anywhere else that we look for a new creation? Yes! Peter says, *"According to His promise, we look for a new heavens and new earth, where righteousness dwells"* (2 Pet. 3:13). John equally says, *"Then I saw a new heaven and a new earth; for the first heaven and the first earth passed away, and there is no longer any sea. And I saw the holy city, new Jerusalem, coming down out of heaven from God, made ready as a bride adorned for her husband"* (Rev. 21:1-2). The word translated "made ready" (ἑτοιμάζω) is the same word Jesus used in John 14:3, when He said, *"I go to prepare (ἑτοιμάζω) a place for you."*

> Currently, however, the entire universe is in travail as if it were giving birth. As in childbirth, the pain is not meaningless but "carries with it the hope of new life for all creation." Likewise, we ourselves are inwardly groaning as we await the final phase of our adoption—the redemption of our bodies (cf. Phil. 3:21) (Mounce 185).

It is clear that Paul's primary focus is on the redemption of the children of God. However, in the midst of this discussion, he provides valuable insight into the future of the material universe. This creation, subjected to futility, will find its release on the day of judgment. It will "give birth" to a new creation which will be the eternal home of the saved.

BIBLIOGRAPHY

Dunn, James D. G. *Romans 1–8, vol. 38A of Word Biblical Commentary.* Dallas: Word, Incorporated, 1988.

Harrison, Everett F., "Romans," in *The Expositor's Bible Commentary: Romans through Galatians*, ed. Frank E. Gaebelein (Grand Rapids, MI: Zondervan Publishing House, 1976), 94.

Moo, Douglas J. The Epistle to the Romans, *The New International Commentary on the New Testament.* Grand Rapids, MI: Wm. B. Eerdmans Publishing Co., 1996.

Mounce, Robert H. Romans, vol. 27 of *The New American Commentary.* Nashville: Broadman & Holman Publishers, 1995.

Newman, Barclay Moon and Eugene Albert Nida, *A Handbook on Paul's Letter to the Romans, UBS Handbook Series* (New York: United Bible Societies, 1973), 157.

Special Study

DUAL FULFILLMENT PROPHECIES

BILLY CLABAUGH

There is no question that prophecy was a very powerful and important way for God to convey His message to His people. As we study the prophets of the Old Testament, we learn a great deal about the character of God and His desire for His people. God used prophecy to encourage repentance, but He also used prophecy to offer hope for the future for the few who remained faithful or for those who repented and turned back to Him.

The fulfillment of prophecy is an important piece of evidence for the inspiration of Scripture. It reinforces to any student of the Bible that the Scriptures come from the mind of God. *Vine's Dictionary of Old and New Testament Words* says the word *prophecy* "signifies the speaking forth of the mind and counsel of God...it is the declaration of that which cannot be known by natural means."[1] The words of the prophets were the words from God that no man could have thought of or predicted on his own. Those words, time after time, have always proven trustworthy.

As we consider Old Testament prophecy, there are times when a prophecy might have a fulfillment that applies specifically to the nation of Israel. Then, later, an inspired New Testament writer uses that prophecy or similar wording from that prophecy to refer to a future event like the second coming of Christ. In an article titled "Principles of Biblical Prophecy," Wayne Jackson asks,

> Is it not possible that the omniscient Holy Spirit, who guided both the Old Testament prophets and the New Testament inspired writers, could have directed certain prophecies to ancient Israel, but also could have known that a future event would ultimately fulfill the meaning of his words? What is wrong with such a view? Absolutely nothing. It surely is possible and preserves the integrity of the New Testament writers.[2]

---

1. *Vine's Complete Expository Dictionary of Old and New Testament Words*, 492
2. Wayne Jackson, "Principles of Bible Prophecy," *Reason & Revelation*, 8:27-30, July, 1988.
3. Jackson.

Wayne Jackson goes on to refer to these prophecies as having an "immediate application" or "partial fulfillment" and then a more "remote fulfillment."[3] Another term that has been used to describe these prophecies is "dual fulfillment."

One example of this can be found in Isaiah 65:17 and Isaiah 66:22, where God through His prophet Isaiah promises to create *"new heavens and a new earth."* Then, the apostle Peter in 2 Peter 3:13 uses that same phrase, *"new heavens and a new earth,"* even though the prophecy in Isaiah had been likely fulfilled by the time Peter wrote his letter. Before we look at the context of what Peter wrote in 2 Peter 3, let's look at the context found in Isaiah.

New Heavens and New Earth in Isaiah

Isaiah, who prophesied to the southern kingdom of Judah during the days of kings Uzziah, Jotham, Ahaz, and Hezekiah (Isa. 1:1), made it clear that Judah, who did evil, was going to suffer great consequences. God would destine them for the sword. They would be put to shame, and Isaiah even says, *"The Lord God will slay you"* (Isa. 65:15). God then through Isaiah says, *"For behold, I create new heavens and a new earth; And the former things will not be remembered or come to mind"* (Isa. 65:17). In the next chapter of Isaiah, God says, *"'For just as the new heavens and the new earth which I make will endure before Me,' declares the Lord, 'so your offspring and your name will endure"* (Isa. 66:22). There is no question that Isaiah is referring to a better time, a time of great hope for God's people beyond their captivity, and a time where the former things will not be remembered. Although some believe Isaiah is referring to Jesus' return, the fact that Isaiah references death in Isaiah 65:20 seems to rule out that he is referring to the Lord's second coming.

A more likely possibility is that Isaiah is referring to a time before Christ's return. God is going to bring about great change by bringing an end to the nation of Israel as His people. They have rejected God, broken His covenant, and refused to repent. Because of Israel's complete unfaithfulness and, ultimately, the rejection of their own Messiah, God is going to create a new spiritual nation or kingdom through His Son, Jesus Christ. The apostle Paul wrote to the churches in Galatia in Galatians 3:24 and tells them, *"The law has become our tutor to lead us to Christ."* God used the old law and the nation of Israel to bring Jesus into this world to usher in a new and much greater kingdom. This will be a kingdom that all people, including Jews and Gentiles, can choose to be a part of through faith in Jesus Christ. This kingdom will never be destroyed; it will endure forever (Dan. 2:44), and it cannot be shaken (Heb. 12:28). This kingdom would be the church of Jesus Christ that He purchased with His own blood (Acts 20:28). Jesus brought about a renewal and a new kingdom on the Day of Pentecost in Jerusalem when about 3000 Jewish souls received Peter's teaching about Jesus. They obeyed and were baptized into the name of Jesus Christ. As they were being baptized, Luke records that they were also being added to those who were being saved (Acts 2:41, 47). The kingdom of Jesus, His church that began in Acts 2, was the fulfillment of prophecy, and there is a very strong case that can be made from Scripture that the new heavens and new earth that is predicted in Isaiah 65:17 and 66:22 was one of those prophecies.

New Heavens and New Earth in 2 Peter

As we mentioned earlier, the apostle Peter in 2 Peter 3:13 uses the same phrase Isaiah did, reminding his readers, *"We are looking for new heavens and new earth."* Denny in his section says

Dual Fulfillment Prophecies

this about Isaiah's prophecy and what Peter states in 2 Peter 3:13, "Whereas Isaiah is describing the future bliss after captivity, his promise can be reapplied by Peter (like a dual-fulfillment prophecy). The creation of the **new heavens and new earth** are exactly the words of God in the Isaiah texts." Peter uses the promise of a new heaven and new earth to direct the minds of his readers to Jesus' return.

Earlier in 2 Peter 3, Peter is clear about what is going to happen to the present heavens and earth and how Christians are to live in light of what is coming:

> *But the day of the Lord will come like a thief in which the heavens will pass away with a roar and the elements will be destroyed with intense heat, and the earth and its works will be burned up. Since all these things are to be destroyed in this way, what sort of people ought you to be in holy conduct and godliness, looking for and hastening the coming of the day of God, because of which the heavens will be destroyed by burning and the elements will melt with intense heat!* (2 Pet. 3:10-12)

Since the current heavens will pass away and the earth will be burned up without any warning, it's crucial that God's people live godly lives set apart from the ways of this earth. A person with wisdom from God and who trusts in the words of Scripture will look beyond this earth and its sinful temptations to the promised new heavens and a new earth, where righteousness dwells! In fact, Peter says you are looking for and hastening the coming day of the Lord. If we are living by faith in Christ, that coming day will be a glorious day, in which we will go to dwell with our Savior for all eternity. It will be a day of great joy where our faith in Christ will be rewarded, but it will also be a tragic day with great consequences for those who refused to live by faith in Christ on this earth.

The Hebrew writer says of those who died in faith that they hadn't received the promises but saw them and welcomed them from a distance (Heb. 11:13). They had lived their life on this earth by faith, looking to a heavenly country:

> *But as it is, they desire a better country, that is, a heavenly one. Therefore God is not ashamed to be called their God; for He has prepared a city for them.* (Heb. 11:16)

Faithful people like Noah, Abraham, and Sarah who lived before the prophecy of Isaiah 65 and 66 saw themselves as strangers and exiles on this earth and chose to put their faith in God, while trusting in His promises, and desiring a heavenly home! Peter is encouraging his readers to live in a similar way. Instead of focusing on the pleasures of this sinful, temporary earth that will be burned up, Peter wants them to live in holiness and godliness while focusing on their eternal home that is coming.

Conclusion

This earth is going to be destroyed because of sin and unrighteousness, and the new heavens and new earth will be a place where only righteousness dwells. It's a place prepared for those who have been counted righteous through their obedient faith in Jesus Christ. Regardless of the exact location of the new heavens and new earth, it will be an eternal place created by God. It will be a place for God to dwell with His people and for His people to dwell with Him! The hope of something better, something new and different than a sinful world destined for destruction, is what men and women of all ages need. We need to know that regardless of what is happening in the world around us, and regardless of our circumstances, God has created an eternal place where His faithful children can live in His presence forever!

God, through His prophet Isaiah, was offering hope to His people when He promised to create "*new heavens and a new earth*" (Isa. 65:17). In 2 Peter 3:13, Peter used "n*ew heavens and a new earth*" to motivate and encourage those reading his letter to live godly and holy lives as they looked forward to Christ's return and the blessed hope of living in the presence of their God and Savior for all eternity. May God's inspired words given to Isaiah and Peter motivate and encourage us to do the same. To God be the glory!

Special Study

WHAT DO WE KNOW ABOUT HEAVEN?

GARRETT BERNETHY

Introduction

Much controversy has existed and still does today regarding the topic of Heaven. From how we can get there to the location itself, conflicts of all kinds have risen over this place, which is unfortunate, seeing as this is the place of reward, an eternal home where the "*righteous will dwell*" (2 Pet. 3:13) for eternity. Many of these conflicts have come to be due to false doctrines taught throughout the years. Doctrines such as "Once saved, always saved" or any form of Premillennialism have clouded the minds of people who are searching for the truth of how to simply be God's people and go to heaven. This leads them astray into a belief that is nothing more than contrary to the New Testament teachings of salvation.

In this special study, we will examine a few things to gain a fuller understanding of this topic:

1. A Study of the Word Heaven in the Old and New Testaments
2. How One Can Get to Heaven
3. Those Who Will Be Present in Heaven
4. We Know When We Will Go to Heaven
5. The Characteristics of Heaven
6. The Location of Heaven
7. Overcoming the Divisions of Our Heavenly Home

But first, let's start on a positive note, which may bring us closer together as we begin this study of our heavenly home! Mrs. A.S. Bridgewater wrote these words to a song we often sing in our worship services entitled "How Beautiful Heaven Must Be." In it, we sing,

> We read of a place that's called Heaven,
> It's made for the pure and the free;
> These truths in God's Word He has given,
> How beautiful Heaven must be.
>
> How beautiful Heaven must be,
> Sweet home of the happy and free;
> Fair haven of rest for the weary,
> How beautiful Heaven must be. [1]

A Study of the Word Heaven in the Old and New Testament

The word מָׁיִמ (shâmayim)[2] is the most frequently used Hebrew word for Heaven in the Old Testament according to *Easton's Bible Dictionary*.[3] The word presents itself in three different ways according to the writers of the Old Testament, in our case, Moses. **First**, the home of the birds, i.e., the "*firmament*" or "*expanse*," meaning the sky (Gen. 1:6; 2:19; 7:23; Ps. 8:8). **Second**, the home of the sun, moon, and stars, i.e., "*the heavens*" (Gen. 1:1, 14, 15; Deut. 17:3; Jer. 8:2). **Third**, the home of God (Deut. 10:14; 1 Kings 8:27; Ps. 115:16; 148:4 cf. 2 Cor. 12:2; Heb. 12:22; Rev. 3:12).

Stafford North would affirm that not much is said in the Old Testament about the resurrection of the dead to go to a place where people would be eternally with God in the afterlife.[4] The apostle Paul would quote King David's words in Psalm 16:10 regarding the resurrection of Jesus in Acts 13:35. The psalmist would also write in Psalm 73:24, "*With Your counsel, You will guide me, And afterward receive me to glory.*" At the same time, the Hebrew writer about Abraham would state in chapter 11 that he was "*desiring a better country, that is, a heavenly one*," which, according to verse 10, was a "*city which has foundations*, whose architect and builder is God." While it is unclear what was understood about the afterlife with these people, it is believed they knew of something better that was not here on earth.

In the New Testament, we find the word οὐρανός, *ouranos*, the heaven: as later, Jewish cosmology conceived of a series of heavens one above the other (three), Heaven was conceived as the special realm and abode of Deity, hence the word is constantly used in connection with Him, and almost as equivalent to the divine name; cf. the practical equivalence of ἡ βασιλεία τῶν οὐρανῶν (*basileia ton ouranon*), the **kingdom (rule) of heaven**, a phrase which may be in origin, purely eschatological with ἡ βασιλεία τοῦ θεοῦ, God Himself being the ruler.[5]

---

1 A.S. Bridgewater and A. P. Bland, "How Beautiful Heaven Must Be," *Favorite Songs of the Church*, Taylor Publications, 2011, 194.

2 James Strong, *A Concise Dictionary of the Words in the Greek Testament and The Hebrew Bible* (Bellingham: Logos Bible Software, 2009), 118.

3 M. G. Easton, *Illustrated Bible Dictionary and Treasury of Biblical History, Biography, Geography, Doctrine, and Literature* (New York: Harper & Brothers, 1893), 318.

4 Stafford North, "Heaven," One Word Study Guide, Onewordstudy.com, 2016, 62.

5 Alexander Souter, A Pocket Lexicon to the Greek New Testament (Oxford: Clarendon Press, 1917), 183.

What Do We Know About Heaven?

According to Stafford North, it can be more literally interpreted as "the space above the earth" (Acts 1:10) or the abode of God, i.e., His dwelling place (Rev. 4:2). It is biblically defined, named, or referenced in many different ways, such as the place of the everlasting blessedness of the righteous; the abode of departed spirits. Jesus calls it His "*Father's house*" (John 14:2). John references it as the "*heavenly Jerusalem*" (Rev. 3:12; 21:2, 10; cf. Gal. 4:26; Heb. 13:14). Jesus and others refer to it as the "*kingdom of heaven*" (Matt. 13:4; 25:1; James 2:5; cf. Matt. 3:2; 4:17). Peter states it is the "*eternal kingdom*" (2 Pet. 1:11) as well as an "*eternal inheritance*" (1 Pet. 1:4; cf. Heb. 9:15). And as we have stated before according to the Hebrew writer for Abraham, it is a "*better country*" (Heb. 11:14, 16).

According to the New Testament, it is this place that all believers are striving to get to as a result of their faithfulness in Him who inhabits this place as this is the eternal dwelling place of God (Matt. 5:16; 12:50; Rev. 3:12; 11:13; 16:11; 20:9).

How Can One Get to Heaven?

The apostle Peter stated that Heaven is where "*righteousness dwells*." So, we have to figure out who the righteous are. The word righteous (δίκαιος, *dikaios*) is being in accordance with high standards of rectitude, upright, just, fair[7] (Matt. 10:41) or *righteousness* (δικαιοσύνη, *dikaiosyne*) the quality of being upright[8] (Matt. 21:32) is the standard which God has set. However, that standard is one that we, as human beings, have not lived up to and cannot live up to because we have fallen into condemnation due to our sins. All it takes is one sin.

As a result of Adam and Eve falling to sin in the garden, they were cast out of the garden, away from God and away from the Tree of Life (Gen. 3:24). This began the separation between God and man. At the point when man fell, God implemented a plan that had already been established to save man (Eph. 1:3-4; 3:9-12; 2 Tim. 1:8-10) from their sins. That plan was carried out on behalf of the whole world as "*all men have fallen short of the glory of God*" (Rom. 3:23).

John states, "*God is Light, and in Him there is no darkness at all*" (1 John 1:5). Therefore, darkness is the equivalent of sin which has separated man from God. To combat this problem, the Bible teaches us that God would initiate this plan through His Son due to His love (John 3:16; 1 John 3:16) to come and bear their iniquities (Isa. 53:11) on the cross at Calvary. Jesus died on that cross, "*entrusting Himself to Him who judges righteously*" (1 Pet. 2:23) so that the plan would be carried out as it was meant to be. Once dead, He would be placed in a tomb (Matt. 27:60; Mark 15:46; Luke 23:53) where His body would rest for three days.

During that time, it seemed that Jesus would remain in Paradise (cf. Luke 23:43) as He would tell the thief that Paradise was where He was heading, which He would also take him. On the third day, Jesus would rise from the dead, and the tomb would be empty because He had risen (Matt. 28:6; Mark 16:6; Luke 24:6; John 20:1-18). After Jesus ascended into Heaven (Acts 1:9), the apostles would begin preaching with the help of the Helper, the Holy Spirit, where they would preach the Gospel of Jesus Christ, which centered around the death, burial, and resurrection of Christ.

---

6 Strong, 53.

7 William Arndt et al., *A Greek-English Lexicon of the New Testament and Other Early Christian Literature* (Chicago: University of Chicago Press, 2000), 246.

8 Arndt et al., 247.

The Hebrew writer helps us to understand this act and what it did for the believer. Jesus became to the believer *"a mediator of a new covenant"* (Heb. 9:15), an eternal sacrifice (Heb. 10:10), and a High Priest forever (Heb. 7:24; 10:12). By this, we understand that He is and has brought a *"better"* covenant that allows the believer to have something more significant than God's people have ever had. Indeed, it is something that the angels long to look at (1 Pet. 1:12).

However, this does not change what God has always expected from those who believe in Him: obedience! The New Covenant is one to be obeyed. Thus, the apostle Paul writes in Romans 6:3-7,

> *Or do you not know that all of us who have been **baptized into Christ** Jesus have been **baptized into His death**? Therefore we have been **buried with Him through baptism** into death, so that as Christ was **raised from the dead** through the glory of the Father, so **we too might walk in newness of life**. For if we have **become united with Him in the likeness of His death**, certainly **we shall also be in the likeness of His resurrection, knowing this, that our old self was crucified with Him**, in order that our body of sin might be done away with, so that we would **no longer be slaves to sin**; for he who has died is freed from sin.* (emp. added)

When we are obedient to His will, which is in obedience to the Gospel call (Acts 16:10; cf. Rom. 1:1), being the *"power of God for salvation to **everyone who believes**"* (Rom. 1:16) only then can people receive the grace of God (Rom. 5:1-9; Eph. 2:8). This act of faith washes their sins away as they call on the name of the Lord (Acts 22:16), transfers them to the Kingdom of God (Col. 1:13) which is the Church (Acts 2:47) the body of Christ (Col. 1:18). This baptism for the purpose of their forgiveness and addition to the Church saves them (1 Pet. 3:21) thus clothing them with Christ (Gal. 3:27). For those baptized *"into Christ"* they are children of God (Rom. 8:16) who can receive *"every spiritual blessing in the heavenly places in Christ"* (Eph. 1:3). It is these people who will be called *"sons of God"* (Rom. 8:19; cf. Rev. 21:7) to whom God will dwell with in Heaven (Rev. 21:3) as they have heard as a result of their continued obedience *"well done"* (Matt. 25:21). Those who have had their sins washed away (Acts 22:16) and walk in the Light (1 John 1:7) will have continual cleansing which allows them to be presented without *"spot or blemish"* (Eph. 5:27; cf. 2 Pet. 3:14). These are the righteous who will get to Heaven.

Those Who Will Be Present in Heaven

To put it simply and to the point, here is who the Bible tells us will be in Heaven:

- God our Father (Deut. 26:15).
- Jesus our Savior (John 14:6).
- The Holy Spirit, our Guide (John 16:5-7; 1 Cor. 2:11-13).
- The angels of God (Heb. 12:22; Rev. 5:11),
- His Children (Matt. 19:13-14; 18:1-4; 16:18-19; Rom. 8:21; Heb. 12:23, 28).
- The patriarchs (Matt. 8:11).
- Those of the Mosaic Age (Heb. 11:17-40).
- Those in the Lamb's Book of Life (cf. Rev. 20:15; 21:27).

What Do We Know About Heaven?

Perry B. Cotham put it in this way,

> God, Christ, the Holy Spirit, the holy angels, the redeemed, and infants will be in heaven. Abraham, Isaac, Jacob, and others who lived in the Patriarchal age, which lasted from Adam to Moses, will be in heaven. Moses, the prophets, and the obedient ones who lived during the Jewish age will be there. Finally, Paul, Peter, John, and all the righteous who lived during the Christian age will be there. Jesus, at the judgment, will send all the righteous into eternal life (Matt. 25:34, 46).[9]

Again, as Peter stated, it will be the place where "*righteousness dwells.*" So all of those who are righteous will dwell and be present in Heaven as a result of their faithful obedience (cf. Heb. 11:1-2).

When Will We Go to Heaven?

First, we know that Heaven is a place where only the righteous will dwell (2 Pet. 3:13), which helps us rule out those who are not righteous as they will not "*inherit the Kingdom of Heaven*" (Gal. 5:21).

Second, because we know that the righteous will go to be with Jesus for eternity (1 Thess. 4:17) when He comes back, this tells us that there is a process for which all of this is to happen.

Each individual possesses a spirit ($\pi\nu\varepsilon\tilde{\upsilon}\mu\alpha$) or soul ($\psi\upsilon\chi\acute{\eta}$) (James 4:5), which has to do with the human personality or ego, the center of it being emotion, intellect, and will. Essentially, your spirit or soul is who you are. You see, God has placed our spirits within our physical bodies. That is who we are; we are not our bodies. Our bodies only house the spirit during our lives here on earth. But as the body will die the soul will not, as it is eternal in nature. We know this to be accurate as Solomon would write, "*Then the dust will return to the earth as it was, and the spirit will return to God who gave it*" (Eccl. 12:7).

Dave Miller wrote,

> God places within each prenatal person at conception a spirit that makes each individual a unique personality. Zechariah 12:1 observed that God "forms the spirit of man within him." Our spirits are what makes each one of us a distinct entity, a person that will survive physical death and live on immortally throughout eternity.[10]

So if we cannot dwell in the place prepared for us (John 14:3) until Jesus comes and receives us to Himself (John 14:3; 1 Thess. 4:17), what happens? Where do we go? Jesus answers this for us in Luke 16:19-31 in the story of the rich man and Lazarus. Now, while some take this as a parable, I disagree as this story's characteristics differ from parabolic form, which we will not get into mainly because you can come to the same conclusion either way you see this story.

Within the story, both men die. Lazarus is said to go to "*Abraham's bosom*" (Luke 16:22) while the rich man went on to "*torment*" (v. 23). Both of these places are said to be in "*hades*" (v. 23). The word *hades* ($\H{\alpha}\delta\eta\varsigma$) is the place or realm of the dead. This means it is where we go when we die *if* the Lord

---

[9] Perry B. Cotham, "What Is Heaven Like?" *Beyond the Sunset*, (Huntsville: Publishing Designs Inc., 2008), 359.
[10] Dave Miller, "One Second after Death," *Apologetics Press*, 26 Jan. 2024, apologeticspress.org/one-second-after-death-1188/.

has not returned. Because the soul/spirit continues to live on, it must have a place to go after it leaves here. This is why what Jesus said on the cross is so essential. Remember, He told the thief on the cross, "*Truly I say to you, today you shall be with Me in Paradise*" (Luke 23:43). Jesus did not go to Hell as some have come to believe[12] as a result of the mistranslation of the King James Version. The word for *Hell* is γέεννα (*gehenna*) and not ᾅδης (*hades*). So in ᾅδης, we know there are two places or parts that you will go to as a result of your faithfulness or lack thereof.

First, **the saved** will go to Paradise, also known as Abraham's bosom. Second, **the lost** will go to the lower realm of Hades known as ταρταρόω (*Tartaros*) (2 Pet. 2:4), also referred to as "*torment*" (Luke 16:23), a place where God cast the angels when they sinned. The saved enter into Paradise through the "*narrow gate*" (Matt. 7:13), which will ultimately lead to Heaven, and the lost will enter through the wide gate that leads to destruction. Between both is a "*great fixed chasm*" (NASB) or "*gulf*" (NKJV) (Luke 16:26), making it an impossibility to reach the other side.

Souls will remain in their respective locations until the day of sentencing, as they have already been judged at the time of their death. So while the Bible does call the *day of the Lord*, "Judgment Day," which is in discussion of judging the living who remain, it is equally a day of sentencing for those who have already perished from the earth.

Acts 1:11 states, "*This same Jesus, who was taken up from you into heaven, will so come in like manner as you saw Him go into heaven*," which connects us to the words of Paul in 1 Thessalonians 4:13-18. It is here that Paul tells us that Jesus will "*descend from Heaven with a shout*" and all will be called unto Him. For those who have heard "*well done*," they will "*always be with the Lord*" (v. 17). It is only at the time of His return that doors of the eternal Kingdom will be opened and ready for occupation.

The Characteristics of Heaven

A commonly asked question, or article title for that matter, about Heaven is, "What Is Heaven Like?" This is a great question to ask, but also one that we cannot know the complete answer to, and we must be accepting of the fact that we do not know all there is to know *and* because of our physical nature, we cannot truly comprehend our heavenly home as it is spiritual in nature.

For instance, the apostle John writes and paints a beautiful picture and scene of Heaven in Revelation 21 and 22, doesn't he?! It is something to think about and try to visualize. This scene discusses streets of gold, walls of jasper, foundation stones of many colors, pearls, transparent glass, and a city that does not need a sun or moon. He depicts the city of Heaven as a cube and a flowing river which contains the "*water of life*" to which on either side of it is the "*Tree of Life*," just like the one mankind was cast out of in Genesis 3. What a beautiful picture this is!

I want you to imagine something with me. You and a friend go to a beautiful place in the mountains of Montana. As you arrive, you both sit in a perfect place. As you look ahead, you notice a great mountain wonderfully shaped to the point where it contains a decent amount of snow, pure white as you gaze upon it. At the bottom of the mountain, you look upon a magnificent lake; the water is

---

11 Arndt et al., 19.

12 Kyle Butt, et al., "Did Jesus Go to Hell for Three Days?" *Apologetics Press*, 5 Sept. 2022, apologeticspress.org/video/did-jesus-go-to-hell-for-three-days/.

so still that it mirrors the picture you see before you, only upside down. On either side of this body of water, trees are beginning to change colors as you are there at the beginning of fall. Above all is a setting sun, creating an extensive range of beautiful colors in the sky. As you gaze at this incredible view, you see shades of blue, purple, pink, orange, yellow, and white in the sky and the trees. Wow, what a scene!

Now, as you are sitting there enjoying this breathtaking view, you feel a tug on your shirt, followed by a voice from your friend facing the scene you are looking at, who says, "Tell me what you see!" What I didn't tell you about your friend who is with you is that he has been blind from birth and is desperately desiring to know just how beautiful this picture is! Now let me ask you this: How can you describe the color purple to someone who has never seen color? How can you describe the beauty of the reflection if he cannot comprehend the image?

The reality is that we are the blind friends in the story, which helps us learn what John is trying to do: describe the beauty of a spiritual place in physical terms. So what can we gain from this? Heaven will be perfect in every way.

But what else do we know characteristically about Heaven? It is big, as Revelation 21:15-17 describes its dimensions. It is new (2 Pet. 3:13; Rev. 21:1- 5); as we know, the *first* things have passed away. It is pure (Rev. 21:8) and beautiful (Rev. 21:11), being designed by God (Heb. 11:10). It is a place and not a myth (John 14:2), which has been prepared for prepared people, resurrected in their eternal bodies (1 Cor. 15:53-54; 2 Cor. 5:1-5; 1 John 3:2). It is described as the "*tabernacle of God, with men*" (Rev. 21:3-5) and a "*great city*" (Rev. 21:9-27). Heaven is eternal, filled with the incorruptible (1 Cor. 15:51-53). A place of worship (Isa. 66:22-23), happiness (Isa. 65:7-9), that is occupied with the righteous (2 Pet. 3:13). It is where God will dwell with His people (Rev. 21:3) as He will "*wipe away every tear*" (Rev. 21:4). It is a place of life and no death (Rev. 21:4). It is a place of joy and peace (Rev. 21:4). It is the location of His throne (Rev. 21:5) and a place where the faithful will rest from their toils (Heb. 4:9). In Heaven we are brought back to the Tree of Life (Rev. 22:14) as the water of life surrounds us. It is the home of God and the home of His people.

Outside of these things, what do we know? The Bible claims it is above (Isa. 14:13; 40:22; Eph. 4:10; Heb. 7:26). He is its light (Rev. 21:23). It is the Christian's homeland (Phil. 3:20) where one will not age or die nor endure trial, temptation, or anything alike. It is secure and protected by its builder, a place where all who believe desire to be.

The Location of Heaven

God has not given us any information as to its physical location. However, it is the home of God (i.e., the third heavens; 2 Cor. 12:2; cf. Deut. 10:14; Ps. 148:4; Eph. 4:10), which is, as David Pharr put it, "The spiritual Kingdom of Christ, invisible, not physical (John 18:36, Luke 17:20)"[13] located at His throne (Heb. 12:2). Outside of this, because we know it is spiritual, it is clear that its location is in a realm unlike ours, and therefore we can say nothing more than wherever God is, so is this place.

---

13 David R Pharr, "Premillennialism," *The Spiritual Sword*, Vol. 44, No. 4, July 2013, 40.

Overcoming the Divisions of Our Heavenly Home

In one of my previous chapters, I stated that this place has become a point of contention. Satan has and is working very hard to divide us, even with a place that we are all striving to be. In a recent survey that the Jenkins Institute did entitled "A Survey on Heaven,"[14] here is what was found.

Questions and Answers:

1. I believe the question of where Heaven will be is solely a matter of opinion.
   - 61.3% No
   - 38.7% Yes

2. I believe...
   - The New Earth will be Heaven (or some version of that). 27.7%
   - Heaven is away from here (the earth will be no more) (or some version of that). 50.2%
   - I seriously don't have a view on this and am fine either way. 10.3%
   - I go back and forth on the question and see strengths on both sides. 11.8%

3. I believe... (Fellowship Question: New Heaven)
   - This is solely a matter of opinion. 26.9%
   - This is a matter of right or wrong, but I do not make it a matter of fellowship. 57.5%
   - This is a matter of faith, and I will draw fellowship lines over my belief on this. 15.7%

4. I believe... (Fellowship Questions: New Earth)
   - This is solely a matter of opinion. 44.6%
   - This is a matter of right or wrong, but I do not make it a matter of fellowship. 52.2%
   - This is a matter of faith, and I will draw fellowship lines over my belief on this. 3.3%

As we can see from this survey, in which 275 people responded, there are different ways of thinking regarding our understanding of Heaven and its surrounding topics. While these numbers do not tell us the mindset of every Christian, other things have projected lines of fellowship drawn by many through events, podcasts, articles, and TV. The problem with these lines that have been drawn is that we are pushing people to one side or the other based on what we think they believe about the location or look of Heaven!

---

14 Tji, "A Survey on Heaven," The Jenkins Institute, *The Jenkins Institute*, 6 Jan. 2024, www.thejenkinsinstitute.com/research/2024/1/a-survey-on-heaven.

What Do We Know About Heaven?

Do I agree that Heaven will be here on Earth? No, and we have extensively looked at why in our study of the book of 2 Peter. Do I believe that the world will be in "refurbished form" after the fire comes? No, again, we have established the Bible teaches it will be annihilated from existence. Do I believe there will be a **"new Heaven and new earth"** in a spiritual sense? Yes, I do; again, I believe there is enough evidence to prove that idea. Do I believe we will be in a spiritual place with harps in the clouds, worshiping every second of every day for eternity? No, I don't think that is what it will be like, so I'm afraid I must disagree with that idea as well.

But here is what we must know! While I may not agree with each line of thinking here, these *are not* lines of fellowship as there is *no eternal weight* connected to the location or look of Heaven! Because this is the truth, no lines of fellowship should be drawn on the matter! Suppose the discussion is outside the lines of Dispensational Premillennialism or any doctrine outside the realm of false teaching regarding our salvation and the Gospel call. What is the real problem that one would draw lines of fellowship based on location and look?

We often seem caught up in the particulars rather than the objective. I know this because I only hear anything about 2 Peter when the topic of "New Heavens, New Earth" comes up. However, Peter isn't fixated on this part of the teaching. It is the focus but not the point—the reason but not the way!

The real point is this,

> *Since all these things are to be destroyed in this way,* **what sort of people ought you to be in holy conduct and godliness, looking for and hastening the coming of the day of God**, *because of which the heavens will be destroyed by burning, and the elements will melt with intense heat!* (2 Pet. 3:11-12)

I truly appreciate the scholarship of many who are looking deeply at things like this to help others understand, but no lines of fellowship should be drawn when it comes to things that don't matter in connection to our salvation. Will Heaven be great? Absolutely, but my curiosity should not divide the brethren; it should unify them as we consider the greatness of our heavenly home.

I do not want to be, nor do I want you to be, a person who has the opportunity to walk in the gates—only to be like Israel who rejected the land as a result of their lack of faithfulness—by telling Jesus "This isn't what Heaven looks like!" Instead, we must be like Joshua, who, upon seeing the Promised Land, was ready to go in! Personally, I do not care where Heaven is or what it looks like. The truth is wherever it is and whatever it looks like, I want to be there!

Special Study

DOES A PHYSICAL "NEW EARTH" DEMAND A PHYSICAL "NEW BODY?"

JOE WELLS

It all began with me asking, "Will Porta Potties be in Heaven?"

Of course, I was joking, but as we discussed this section and the controversy surrounding this topic in many circles, I couldn't help myself. If, as some claim, there will be a material "new earth," as Peter refers to in 2 Peter 3:13, to what extent will we experience that "new earth?"

We understand on this earth the limitations of this flesh all too well. We get tired, hungry, thirsty, and have diseases, sickness, and death. However, we also experience pain when we kick the bedframe in the middle of the night with our little toe. We have headaches, a pain that is not like a broken bone but can be debilitating, especially for those who have migraines. As we age, the truth of entropy becomes all too real. Our skin changes as wrinkles begin to take over. Age spots decide to color our legs, knees start to give out, and backs begin to hurt for what seems to be no reason at all. Getting out of bed becomes a chore as we wake up sore, if we were even able to sleep at all!.

Our experience on this earth is not all bad news. We also enjoy the taste of food and the rejuvenation of rest. You know the refreshing feeling of playing in the water on a hot summer day, having your feet massaged, or someone scratching your scalp. We know of the blessing enjoyed between a husband and wife and the feeling of holding hands with someone who loves you. You also know that feeling of love when the baby in your arms looks up at you and smiles, or your child/grandchild climbs into your lap and asks you to read them a book. You know what joy, happiness, and satisfaction come from looking at a well-done job. In this experience, we know community, the blessing of burden sharing, and how praying for others and being prayed for by others comforts and encourages. We know what it is to be uplifted by worshipping God along with our brothers and sisters in Christ.

With this perspective of experiencing the environment we currently live in, the struggle to grasp the experience we will have concerning the *new earth* concept of 2 Peter 3:13 is difficult. As some have suggested, will it be an endless worship service in a celestial, floating cloud-like state? Does the Bible lead us to conclude there may be more to the eternal existence for the righteous in this life who die in the Lord?

I feel entirely underequipped to tackle this subject. So many questions circle in my mind, and I'm not sure I will have answers while in this body. When responding to questions pondering the depths of Heaven, I've often said, "I don't know because I've never been there." I believe God has revealed everything we need to know about Heaven while in this life. At times, we will ask the Scriptures for more detail. We will contemplate and discuss what could be as much as we can conclude.

I hope to accomplish that with this chapter in the special section. The question before us is regarding what kind of body we will have in eternity and whether a conclusion regarding a physical "*new earth*" from 2 Peter 3:13 requires one to believe that we must have physical new bodies to inhabit such. This is a similar question addressed by the apostle Paul in 1 Corinthians 15:35 when he said, "*But some will say, 'How are the dead raised? And with what kind of body do they come?'*" We're not the first to ask, nor will we be the last. Those interested in what happens after we die will always long to know more about the eternal. So, as much as my feeble mind can, I ask you to consider the following as you continue your studies on this matter.

1) The Relationship Between Environments and Inhabitants

In the first chapter of the book of Genesis, we read of the creative genius of God revealed in the creation of the heavens and the earth (Gen. 1:1). With a complete and perfect knowledge of the requirements for life to exist, He began with the environments. On Day One, we read of His separating light (day) from darkness (night) (Gen. 1:3-5). Day Two came the separation of the waters, the upper chamber from the lower, and the expanse called heaven (Gen. 1:6-8). Day Three saw the water below the expanse gathered into one place, and the dry land appeared (Gen. 1:9-13). Day Three also saw the earth (v. 11) sprout forth fruit and seed-bearing vegetation.

With the perfect environments now in place, God begins creating the inhabitants of each of these. On Day Four, we see the connection with the environment of Day One. The sun, moon, and stars were created and placed in the expanse of the heavens to separate the day from the night and to serve as signs for seasons, days, and years (Gen. 1:14-19). With Day Five came the inhabitants of the environment of Day Two. Living creatures for the waters and birds to fly in the expanse above the earth, in "*the open expanse of the heavens,*" were created (Gen. 1:20-23). Before resting on Day Seven, God created the inhabitants of the environment called Earth on Day Six. The beasts of the earth, cattle, and creeping things were all created. God also created humans on Day Six to inhabit and care for His creation (Genesis 1:23-31). The following chart may help see all of this.

Environment	Inhabitants
Day One: Heavens (Outer Space)	*Day Four:* Sun, Moon, Stars
Day Two: Waters and Heavens (Sky)	*Day Five:* Water Creatures, Birds
Day Three: Earth, Vegetation	*Day Six:* Land Creatures, Humans

Perhaps the most interesting observation regarding the relationship between these environments and inhabitants is that if you took an inhabitant out of the environment for which it was uniquely created and placed it in another, it would not live. We see this in simple ways, such as a fish that gets taken out of water and put on land. Eventually, the fish will die. Similarly, a land animal designed to live on land and not in water will perish if submerged. While this elementary observation may seem insignificant, a fact is revealed that will help us understand this entire discussion regarding

Does a Physical "New Earth" Demand a Physical "New Body?"

a "new earth" and what our existence in said earth would possibly be. Whatever our heavenly existence and what that environment will be, we will be uniquely and perfectly equipped for such according to the wisdom of God.

Taking that thought, in this study, I pondered whether I ever remember reading of a time in the Scriptures when one from the spiritual realm visited earth and didn't need a body or a host to be here. In other words, if spiritual beings are uniquely designed for a spiritual environment, when they came to earth—a material environment—what conclusions might we draw that might factor into this discussion concerning a "new earth" and a "physical, bodily" existence for us in eternity?

Except for God in the Garden of Eden, it appears that each time spiritual beings came to earth, they took on the form of a material person or thing. In other words, their form changed when the environment changed, while they were the same beings. Consider the following examples.

Scripture	Who Appeared	What Form
Genesis 18:1-33	The Lord and Two Angels	Men
Genesis 19:1-29	The Two Angels of Ch. 18	Men
Matthew 17:1-3	Moses and Elijah	Recognizable Beings
Matthew 17:14-23	Demon	Inhabited a Boy
Luke 8:26-39	Legion (Demons)	Inhabited a Man, Cast into Pigs
Luke 24:4; John 12:12	Two Angels	Men

This question is essential to consider because we seek a better understanding of what we have never seen. One way to explore such is to observe what the Bible has said, either explicitly or implicitly, regarding the necessity of the inhabitant to match the environment. When a celestial visits a new habitation for whatever reason or reasons, they take on the form of an earthy body or require a host, be it a human or even a pig. Of course, this applies every time a celestial being visits earth and reveals himself, except for Deity (Acts 9:3-4; 26:13; Exodus 34:5; etc.)

One can safely conclude a few critical concepts if the environment and the form match.

1. Whatever the "new earth" is, we will be ideally suited for such in eternity.
2. The current body was designed for this present earth.
3. As celestial beings remained the same in identity, we will still be us in eternity.

2) What Kind of Body Will We Have?

In 1 Corinthians 15:35, the apostle Paul addresses questions from skeptics and doubters regarding the resurrection of the dead, "*How are the dead raised? And **with what kind of body do they come?***" (emp. added). We know there was a belief in the resurrection that was accepted. When Jesus told Martha the sister of Lazarus that her brother would rise again, Martha replied, "*I know that he will rise again in the resurrection on the last day*" (John 11:24). However, there were those who denied the resurrection of the dead as stated in Acts 23:8, "*For the Sadducees say that there is no resurrection, nor* *an angel, nor a spirit, but the Pharisees acknowledge them all."* Along with an acceptance or denial of a resurrection, there was variation in thought regarding what the resurrected body would be like. Some held that the resurrected bodies would be just as they are now, only restored (Apocalypse of Baruch). Others claimed there would be no bodily resurrection at all because of a belief that the body was utterly evil, being the the extreme opposite to the goodness of the soul.

> *Greek thought, and in consequence many Hellenizing Jewish and Christian sages, regarded the body as a prison-house of the soul: sōma sēma 'the body is a tomb.' The aim of the sage was to achieve deliverance from all that is bodily and thus liberate the soul.*[1]

Thus, we can see why Paul would address these questions and begin with the exclamation, "You fool!" (1 Cor. 15:36). With this letter being written to a group of people who were steeped in Greek influence, Paul does not only set out to teach the truth but also confront erroneous teachings. I invite you to study what he says here very carefully, as the Holy Spirit inspired him to present four analogies to communicate effectively about the resurrection.

A. Your Current Body Must Die (vv. 36-38)

The sowing/reaping analogy is used in Scripture on several occasions (Gal. 6:7; 2 Cor. 9:6-8; Prov. 22:8), specifically by Jesus in John 12:23-26 when addressing a similar concept as Paul. This principle has substantial implications for spiritual truths, and in answering the questions before him, Paul returned to a critical point in this process.

> *You fool! That which you sow does not come to life unless it dies; and that which you sow, you do not sow the body which is to be, but a bare grain, perhaps of wheat or of something else. But God gives it a body just as He wished, and to each of the seeds a body of its own."* (1 Cor. 15:36-38)

You and I understand this principle best regarding an acorn and an oak tree. Within that acorn is everything genetically needed to grow an oak tree; however, unless the acorn is planted in the ground and "dies," allowing the sprout to come forth, never to be able to return to that same seed again, the tree won't grow. Paul is saying the very same thing. Our earthly bodies must "die" if a new one is going to come forth. God designed the "seed," our earthly bodies, and God is the architect of what will come. However, we must be careful not to forget that the acorn and the oak are connected in that they are the same life. They just have a different form. That's what Paul addresses next.

B. Your Heavenly Body Will Have a Unique Form (vv. 39-42)

It's evident that when God created everything, He did so in such a way and with such outcomes so that variation exists. We need to remember that these variations are according to the will and wisdom of God and that at the end of each creative day, God deemed it to be good. That entails how God, the author of good, wanted it to be.

This principle of variation by God's design and its being good is Paul's next point of emphasis in answering the question regarding the resurrected body.

---

1 M. H. Cressey, "Dualism," ed. D. R. W. Wood et al., *New Bible Dictionary* (Leicester, England; Downers Grove, IL: InterVarsity Press, 1996), 284.

Does a Physical "New Earth" Demand a Physical "New Body?"

All flesh is not the same flesh, but there is one flesh of men, and another flesh of beasts, and another flesh of birds, and another of fish. There are also heavenly bodies and earthly bodies, but the glory of the heavenly is one, and the glory of the earthly is another. There is one glory of the sun, and another glory of the moon, and another glory of the stars; for star differs from star in glory. So also is the resurrection of the dead. (1 Cor. 15:39-42a).

To better understand what we will be like in eternity and what experience we will have, especially concerning our question regarding the "new earth," the point of variation and uniqueness in this life is applied to our existence in eternity. We understand that all flesh is not the same and heavenly bodies such as the sun, moon, and stars differ from those on this earth. However, Paul's point is that all of them are the exact manifestation and are precisely made known as God desires. So it is with the resurrection of the dead.

C. There Is a Difference in Quality Between the Earthly and Heavenly Body (vv. 42b-44)

If you've ever experienced cancer, loss of limb, loss of function, diabetes, or any number of physical ailments our earthly bodies often fall victim to, you're going to like this point Paul makes. Your heavenly body will have some significant differences from the earthly one you inhabit now. God designs these differences and will ideally equip you to live in the new environment in eternity.

It is sown a perishable body, it is raised an imperishable body; it is sown in dishonor, it is raised in glory; it is sown in weakness, it is raised in power; it is sown a natural body, it is raised a spiritual body. If there is a natural body, there is also a spiritual body. (vv. 42b-44)

Consider this chart as a snapshot of the differences explained in this section.

Now	Then
Perishable	Imperishable
Dishonor	Glory
Weakness	Power
Natural	Spiritual

The most obvious observation, and I fully believe the one that is mainly intended, is that the body we will have in eternity is far better than the one we have now. That's not to say that God made a mistake or there was an imperfection in His creation. Keep in mind this is a section of comparison, and the point being relayed is that both bodies, the natural and the spiritual, are ideally suited for the environment for which they are designed. The negatives that are attached to the earthly body are tied to sin. Because of sin, there will be death and decay. Because of sin, there are lesser conditions and states we endure in this body that we will not experience after the resurrection. There's nothing to long for if there's no difference. The body we will have in eternity will far exceed this current earthly dwelling.

D. Your Earthly Body Will Be Raised and Changed (vs. 45-54)

For me, one of the most interesting facets of this study has been the concept that on numerous occasions, the Bible claims that our "earthy," "*made of earth/dust*"[2] bodies will be raised from the grave. Bodies that are made of dust and destined to decay and decompose (Eccl. 3:20; 12:7; Ps. 90:3) are going to be raised as Paul claims in 1 Corinthians 15:52 when he writes, "*Behold, I tell you a mystery; we will not all sleep, but we will all be changed, in a moment, in the twinkling of an eye, at the last trumpet; for the trumpet will sound, and* **the dead will be raised** *imperishable, and we will be changed*" (emp. added).

We not only find that concept here, but we also see it in other passages.

- Romans 8:11—"*But if the Spirit of Him who raised Jesus from the dead dwells in you, He who raised Christ Jesus from the dead* **will also give life to your mortal bodies** *through His Spirit who dwells in you.*"

- Romans 8:23—"*And not only this, but also we ourselves, having the first fruits of the Spirit, even we ourselves groan within ourselves, waiting eagerly for our adoption as sons,* **the redemption of our body**."

- 1 Thessalonians 4:16—"*For the Lord Himself will descend from heaven with a shout, with the voice of the archangel and with the trumpet of God, and the* **dead in Christ will rise** *first.*"

- John 5:28-29—"*Do not marvel at this; for an hour is coming, in which* **all who are in the tombs will hear His voice, and will come forth**; *those who did the good deeds to a resurrection of life, those who committed the evil deeds to a resurrection of judgment.*"

In 1 Corinthians 15:52, we see a few keywords that should not go unnoticed. The first is "*raised*," which means "to enter into or to be in a state of life as a result of being raised."[3] The second is "*changed*," meaning "to make something other or different, alter."[4] Both of these words are significant to our purpose because, on one hand, bodily resurrection is affirmed. On the other hand, we are to understand that something different will be. As Paul points out in this immediate section, the main difference is that our eternal bodies will not be perishable like our earthy or natural bodies. Instead, our spiritual bodies will be imperishable, never to decay and decompose. Just as we have born the image of the earthly in this life, we will bear the image of the heavenly in eternity (1 Cor. 15:49).

But what will that image be?

The apostle John speaks to this change when he writes in 1 John 3:2, "*Beloved, now we are children of God, and it has not appeared as yet what we will be. We know that when He appears,* **we will be like Him**, *because we will see Him just as He is*" (emp. added). Paul also offers insight when he writes to the church in Philippi, "*For our citizenship is in heaven, from which also we eagerly wait for a Savior, the Lord Jesus Christ;* **who will transform the body of our humble state into conformity with the body of His glory**, *by the exertion of the power that He has even to subject all things to Himself*" (vv. 3:20-21, emp. added).

---

[3] Arndt et al., 272.
[4] Arndt et al., 45.

Does a Physical "New Earth" Demand a Physical "New Body?"

Conclusion

Some have pointed to a study of the body of Jesus after His resurrection but before His ascension for clues as to what "***the body of His glory***" entails. I'm not sure we can with certainty do so because there was something unique and special in the body Jesus was occupying during that time, the most significant being that His body still bore the scars of crucifixion (John 1:27). There is nothing within Scripture that I am aware of that leads us to conclude that the physical scars we have in these earthly bodies will be present when we receive our spiritual bodies. Therefore, I believe a study of the body of the resurrected Jesus, while interesting and maybe somewhat helpful, is to be understood as something special and unique to Him and to the purpose He desired in showing Himself to so many during those 40 days (Acts 1:3).

Therefore, what can we conclude? Does a physical/material "new earth" demand a physical/material body in eternity?

In returning to the point made regarding the environment and the inhabitants of the environment, I will draw a conclusion working backward. There is a clear teaching that the tombs will give up the dead and that our bodies will be resurrected just as the body of Jesus was. While I do not entirely understand why bodily resurrection is necessary, I believe the Scripture clearly says it will happen. I conclude that a bodily resurrection will occur because our identity in this life will carry over into eternity. However, there will be a change to the body, a transformation or metamorphosis, that will put us in a perfect situation to inhabit the heavenly environment that has been prepared for us (John 14:2). Just as a caterpillar goes into a cocoon and comes out a butterfly, we will go into the grave and come out as something different. We will have the same form of the heavenly, just as we now have the earthly form (1 Cor. 15:49). Clearly, there is a difference between the two.

It stands to reason then that if our bodies change in all the ways as outlined throughout 1 Corinthians 15 and other Scriptures, the environment will also be different than what we currently have; thus, a study of Romans 8 where the creation groans is a beneficial study on this question (Rom. 8:19-22). The "new earth" will be suited for the imperishable, not the perishable. It will be prepared for the spiritual, not the natural. Thus, in working backward, since our new bodies will be much different, I conclude that the "new earth" must also be different from what we currently experience. That's not to say that we won't enjoy some of the things we now enjoy in eternity. However, I believe logic and Scripture lead us to conclude that eternity will be dramatically better than it is here on this earth.

To conclude, I'll simply say that I don't think there will be port-a-potties in Heaven. I feel like I should just get that out of the way first. It is my conclusion that we will each have a unique form and be individually known in eternity. I believe that in our spiritual bodies, we will not know pain, sickness, disease, or even tears or emotional distress. I believe the Scriptures teach our image will fit our environment and that the environment must be suited for the imperishable and immortal nature. As the apostle John stated in 1 John 3:2 regarding our bodies in Heaven, I also believe that "*it has not appeared as yet what we will be.*" I am entirely at peace with this statement. I don't know for certain what our bodies will be like in eternity. I know my spiritual body and experience in eternity will be far superior to what I now know.

Sermon Seeds

2 PETER 1

GRACE AND PEACE (2 PETER 1:2)

Intro: How might we survive in a world filled with corruption, lust and selfish desires (1:4; 2:2; 3:3)? Peter notes that these two great gifts of God are how we win the great battle. Notice the three observations he makes about grace and truth.

A. Can Be Multiplied

1. You can't have too much of a good thing, and spiritually speaking, what is better than grace and peace?

2. The word multiplied (πληθύνω) can mean to increase or grow. As Christians grow (see 1:8; 3:18), they become even more entrenched in God's gifts.

B. Is Founded in Knowledge

1. Their increased knowledge of God's grace disarms the false teachers and destroys their arguments designed to damage faith. Knowing God's forgiveness and grace is what firmly establishes them in peace. It is a peace that is so amazing that it defies a full understand (cf. Phil. 4:7).

2. Why do we study our Bibles? This verse provides the answer. Knowledge is our window into the truth of God. Through our study we know the truth about God's grace (a greatly misunderstood and applied concept today) and peace (which only comes from a relationship with Jesus—John 14:28).

C. Is Found Only with God and Jesus

1. The false teachers of 2 Peter "denied the Master" (2:1) and questioned the promises of God (3:3-4). Their flawed knowledge of God and Jesus has led them down a path of promoting "destructive heresies" that will prove to be their undoing (2:1).

2. While the recipients (and us) have not personally seen Jesus (cf. 1 Pet. 1:8), they know that He has chosen them (1:10) and have entrance into the wonderful eternal kingdom of Jesus (1:11).

Conclusion: What is the result of having this great faith? (1) Grace—God providing His unparalleled love and kindness; (2) Peace—not a shallow, temporary peace but one "in the fullest measure" (cf. 1 Pet. 1:2).

2 GOD—HIS WORD AND HIS CHARACTER (2 PETER 1:3)

Intro:

We say, "A man's word is his bond." Jesus said that a person's word reveals what is in his heart (Matt. 12:34). In this passage Peter is talking about what God has said, and how those words reveal who He is. God's call to salvation has revealed two amazing attributes:

A. His call reveals His glory

1. δόξα (doxa)—"the condition of being bright or shining, brightness, splendor, radiance" (Bauer 257).

2. "In other words, when Christ calls people to Himself, they perceive the beauty and loveliness of His moral character. His character becomes exceedingly attractive to them, and they trust God for their salvation" (Schreiner 293).

3. Pagan gods provided no genuine glory. Their flawed characters demonstrated weakness and fell far short of human praise. God, on the other hand, has proven Himself to be worthy of continued praise because of His splendor and perfect character.

B. His call reveals His excellence

1. ἀρετή (arete)—"a manifestation of power characterized by excellence—'wonderful act, powerful deed, wonderful deed.' ὅπως τὰς ἀρετὰς ἐξαγγείλητε 'so that you may proclaim the wonderful deeds (of God)' 1 Pet. 2:9" (Louw and Nida 681).

    a) Throughout history pagan gods have demonstrated uncontrolled power, used to satisfy their own evil desires.

    b) God's power is always used to accomplish a divine purpose. When such power is used appropriately, it brings attention to the God who wielded the power. This is what is unique about this word. It ends with God's excellence, but it began with a look at His actions.

2. In this passage Peter is considering how God's call to Him through His Word was a reflection on the excellence of God. He has not remained silent (cf. Heb. 1:1-3) but has provided a message of hope and salvation. How is that not proof of His excellence?

Conclusion:

"God has called believers 'by His own glory [doxa] and goodness [aretē]'—that is, God in salvation reveals His splendor (doxa) and His moral excellence (arete), and these are means He uses to effect conversions. In bringing people to the knowledge of Himself, God's divine power supplies them with everything they need for life and godliness" (Blum 267-8). "Power divine makes them what they are, which, according to the following verse, includes divine moral attributes. This transcendent and sovereign power of God, which He exercises on behalf of humans, is the foundation for honoring Him, in Peter's view" (Green 181).

3 ▸ EVERYTHING? (2 PETER 1:3)

Intro:

Catholics say we need the Catechism. Mormons say we need the Book of Mormon. Muslims say we need the Quran. Jehovah's Witnesses say we need the Watchtower. Many denominational groups argue for their own writings. However, Peter makes a claim that these Christians have been "granted…everything pertaining to life and godliness." Consider:

1) Everything—pertaining to life

    A. God has provided all that we need to know about living in a way that pleases Him (Rom. 12:1-2).

    B. John 10:10—Jesus taught how to have an abundant life.

    C. Do we need other writings to show us how to live so as to please God? Not according to the promise of this verse.

2) Everything—pertaining to godliness

    A. Godliness describes a lifestyle that is separate from the world; pure and holy. These Christians have been given divine instructions on what God desires.

    B. Paul defines godliness in 1 Timothy 1:5, and Peter calls Christians to a similar concept—holiness—in his first epistle (1 Pet. 1:13-18).

Conclusion:

These come through the "true knowledge of Him who called us." God's Word is all we need. Other writings, those authored by flawed (uninspired) men, should not be the foundation for what we believe and practice. If we need those other writings, then this verse is false. If this verse is true, then those other writings are unnecessary (and even dangerous).

4 ▸ VITAL CONTRASTS (2 PETER 1:3-4)

Intro: Sometimes we make things more complicated than necessary. Peter simplifies our walk with some powerful contrasts:

1)   Corruption vs. life and godliness

2)   Lust (evil desires) vs. a true knowledge of Him

Christianity has its challenges and enemies. Yet God's power has provided us the essential information we need to succeed.

5 ▶ KNOWLEDGE (2 PETER 1:5)

"And this is eternal life, that they may know thee
the only true God,
and Jesus Christ whom Thou hast sent."
John 17:3

To some, having knowledge is overrated. Maybe in some areas this is true. But when it comes to *Biblical* knowledge, it is far from being overrated. Rather, it is a vital link in the Christian's faith. It is what enables one to establish a faith upon a solid foundation. It is also that which permits one to venture beyond the scope of Christian infancy (Heb. 5:12-14).

The fact is, there are far too many today who make decisions (or make statements) based upon faulty information. This is true regarding business decisions (did we really understand that contract we signed?), and true regarding religion (does our religious teacher really know what he is talking about?).

Peter recognizes the struggles each Christian must face. He is keenly aware that ignorance might spell the destruction of his brethren (Hos. 4:6). He is therefore committed to the task of educating the brethren about those who would lead them astray. They must *know* about these men. They must be able to recognize their false teaching.

Yes, to Peter knowledge is essential. Even the casual reader of 2 Peter is struck by the obvious repetition of the "knowledge" theme. Various words for knowledge are found consistently throughout the letter (1:2, 3, 5, 6, 8, 12, 14, 16, 20; 2:9, 12, 20, 21; 3:3, 9, 15, 17, 18). There are over 20 occurrences regarding knowledge in this short three-chapter book!

When the context of 2 Peter is synthesized, the logic of the letter is revealed. For example, after reading the epistle, it is evident the writer is concerned about the false teachers and the influence their doctrine might have on the church. Therefore, he sets out to teach them and remind them about various doctrinal issues. Thus, the book might be divided:

Chapter 1—An attempt to establish the Christian in two vital areas: (a) their own spiritual strength—1:1-11; and (b) their confidence in the inspiration and authority of the Scriptures (1:12-21). No teacher would want a student to deal with false doctrine or a false teacher unless the student had been established in these vital areas. Any attempt to instruct concerning a false doctrine when the readers are shaky and unstable (cf. James 1:6-9) could result in a shipwreck of their faith. Paul maintains this same basic idea in Ephesians 4:11-14, where, after saying they are mature and equipped, argues, "As a result, we are no longer to be children, tossed here and there by waves, and carried about by every wind of doctrine, by the trickery of men, by craftiness in deceitful scheming...." 2 Peter's false teachers are scheming and deceitful (2:1, 3, 18, 19) and are untaught and unstable (3:16). Peter wants these Christians to be equipped spiritually to deal with them and their false doctrine. Having established the faith of the Christian, Peter is now ready to deal with the two major problems confronting them.

Chapter 2—Peter reminds them of the scope and power of the false teachers. They will introduce "destructive heresies" (2:1), heresies that wouldn't succeed if the hearers were grounded firmly in the Word. Because of the false teachers' work, and because of the ignorance of the hearers, the "truth will be maligned" and people will be exploited with "false words" (2:2, 3). How could Peter emphasize the importance of knowledge any more than this? The Christian must have good, sound information. They must be equipped with the truth. They need to know that God will judge the unrighteous and rescue the righteous (2:4-8), and they need to know the character and end of the false teachers (2:9-22).

Chapter 3—Christians who are ignorant of the Word (3:2) are going to fall prey to the doctrine of the false teachers regarding the end of time. Therefore, Peter admonishes them to "know this first of all" (3:3). These false teachers are basing their doctrine of the end-time upon a faulty premise regarding the work and operations of God (3:3-9). They should be convicted that the Lord will most certainly return, and when He does this earth will be annihilated (3:10-13). Those "in the know" are going to look for these things and live in a continual state of readiness (3:14). Meanwhile, the ignorant are going to twist the Scriptures "to their own destruction" (3:16). They know the truth (3:17) and need to grow in knowledge (3:18).

Now that we've seen what the apostle hopes to accomplish with this short epistle, the "Christian graces" of chapter 1 can be seen as an initial attempt to strengthen the brethren. These qualities will enable the Christian to be established on "true knowledge," not the erroneous, shaky knowledge of the false teachers. Note carefully 1:8: "For if these qualities are yours and are increasing, they render you neither useless nor unfruitful in the *true knowledge* of our Lord Jesus Christ."

In view of all this, it is not surprising that "knowledge" would be one of the first qualities mentioned in this section of Christian graces. The Greek word for "knowledge" in verse 5 (*gnosko*) is often considered a general word for "intelligent comprehension of an object or matter." However, in the Bible it is seen to mean something more specific. The Old Testament word akin to "knowledge" demonstrates an insight into the will of God and His commands and blessings. It is a working knowledge that should lead one to be obedient and gratefully submissive to God's word (cf. Isa. 58:2; Prov. 29:7; Jer. 22:16). The New Testament view of "knowledge" is strongly influenced by this Old Testament concept. The Christian considered knowledge a gift of God (2 Cor. 2:14; 4:6; 10:5). Indeed it was by His grace that the deeds and demands of God have become available for all to know. Jesus came to give us knowledge of salvation (Luke 1:77; John 17:3).

Once a person obtains this knowledge it should not be allowed to lie dormant but must demonstrate its presence by a life of lasting obedience and growth (Rom. 15:14; 2 Pet. 3:18). Notice what a knowledge of Christ led Paul to do: "More than that, I count all things to be loss in view of the surpassing value of knowing Christ Jesus my Lord, for whom I have suffered the loss of all things, and count them but rubbish in order that I may gain Christ" (Phil. 3:8). If a person's knowledge did not make him feel as Paul did, then it was not true Christian knowledge (cf. 1 Cor. 8:1-3).

Just as Paul emphasized the importance of knowledge, so also does Peter. Although knowledge was one of the favorite words of the false teacher, Peter was not afraid to use it. He knew that Jesus is truth, and a person needs to know this truth to be set free from the bondage of sin (John 8:32). But this knowledge comes only by study and careful investigation, then by living that truth in one's life. Some feel that an increase in knowledge might prove harmful; that "higher education" destroys. Peter, however, seems to think that the cure for false knowledge is not less knowledge, but more.

In conclusion, we can learn several truths by considering the word *knowledge* in 2 Peter 1:5:

1. Peter was convinced Christianity is not merely a matter of personal faith and practical goodness. One's knowledge has an important place.

2. The most important knowledge one can obtain is that which deals with God and His will.

3. This knowledge is gained by one's diligence in study and investigation into the truth.

4. Knowledge of the Word of God is a weapon to be used to fight and defeat false doctrine (Eph. 6:17).

5. This knowledge plays an important part in:

   a. Leading one to learn "everything that pertains to life and godliness" (2 Pet. 1:3).

   b. Securing the believer's salvation (2 Pet. 1:10)

   c. Making the Christian a fruit-bearing servant of Christ (2 Pet. 1:8).

This we can say that generally "knowledge" is the acquiring of information (dealing with spiritual truth). Along with this information comes the understanding and ability to apply this knowledge in the everyday affairs of life. When we learn more of God's Word, we can easily see how it speaks to us in our daily problems and concerns. It offers advice and encouragement when we are discouraged. It provides direction when we are lost (Ps. 119:105). It provides divine wisdom when confronted with spiritual questions.

Indeed, knowledge is a vital tool in building Christian character. May we all be devoted students of the most important writing of all time.

6. GOD'S GREAT PROMISES (A STUDY IN 2 PETER)

Intro:

The Bible teaches that God "cannot lie" (Tit. 1:2; Heb. 6:18). Therefore, His promises are sure and steadfast. Christians are wise to trust fully in God's promises. In 2 Peter, the apostle identifies several of God's "precious and magnificent promises" (1:4).

1. You Will Never Stumble (1:10)

    A. What Christian doesn't want the assurance that he or she will remain faithful?

    B. This promise is based on our "practicing" the attributes listed in verses 5-8.

2. Entrance into the Eternal Kingdom (1:11)

    A. The faithful are assured entrance.

    B. This entrance will be "abundantly supplied to you."

    C. Our future home is described with two terms:

        (a) *eternal*—The word guarantees that once we get there, it will never end—ever.

        (b) *kingdom*—The kingdom of Satan is gone. All that remains is the kingdom of God.

3. Prophetic Word Is Sure (1:19-21)

    A. The lies of the false teachers will be exposed (2:1-3).

    B. It is not a "cleverly devised tale" (1:16).

    C. Word comes directly from God through men inspired by the Holy Spirit (1:21).

4. The Wicked Will Be Punished (2:1-9)

    A. The false teachers' judgment "is not idle, and their destruction is not asleep" (2:3).

    B. The Lord knows how to "keep the unrighteous under punishment for the day of judgment" (2:9).

5. The Righteous Will Be Delivered (2:9)

    A. God proved this by delivering Noah and rescuing righteous Lot (2:5, 7).

    B. What God did in the past is proof of what He will do in the future. Those who are faithful will be preserved.

6. A Future Return (3:9)

    A. The false teachers are openly challenging this promise (3:4).

    B. God, however, is "not slow about His promise" (3:9). What may appear to be a delay to men is actually a demonstration of God's patience. He is giving men time to repent.

7. A New Heavens and a New Earth (3:13)

    A. This promise was first initiated by the prophet Isaiah (65:17; 66:22).

    B. This is connected with the "eternal kingdom" mentioned in 1:11.

Conclusion:

God is not the only one making promises in this book. The false teachers are "promising them freedom while they themselves are slaves of corruption" (2:19). Only God's promises are sure. The wise are able to discern the difference between divine promises and human ones.

7 ▶ THE CHRISTIAN GRACES (2 PETER 1:5-7)

Intro:

Perhaps one of the more famous sections in 2 Peter is this one. This list of eight qualities, often called "the Christian graces," describe goals for Christians who are confronted with immorality on one side and false teachers on the other. How can they survive? Peter provides the essential qualities that, if possessed and increasing, with assure one will have spiritual success (1:10-11). Let us briefly consider each of these eight qualities.

1. Faith—the foundation of the Christian walk. It is basic to Christianity. For Peter faith is the conviction that what Jesus says is true and that we can commit ourselves to His promises and act on His demands. It is the unquestioning certainty that the way to happiness, peace, and strength is to accept Jesus as His Word.

So let's put our faith to the test (2 Cor. 13:5). How often do we worry about things? How often do we pray, giving everything to God (1 Pet. 5:7)? Do we truly trust Him? Do we boldly and confidently let others see our faith? Do we move forward in faith and let our light shine—(Matt. 5:16)?

2. Moral Excellence (virtue)—a rare word in the NT. This is the word Greeks would use when they wanted to mention the highest quality of a person. It describes genuine excellence. An idea intimately connected with this word is courage. In a world dominated by corruption and lust (v. 4), it takes a special kind of courage to live a morally excellent life. Such a choice will be confronted with ridicule and even persecution. However a person with this trait has the "guts to do what is right—regardless." There are those who offer lip service to God and His Word. This person lives his confession.

If we are to imitate Jesus, there must be the highest moral standards. We must be people of purity, integrity, and selflessness. How are we progressing?

3. Knowledge—describes practical, experiential knowledge. It is that which is learned through study of God's Word and then applied on life's stage. It is knowledge which enables one to decide rightly and to act honorably from day to day. Peter wasn't afraid to use a favorite word of the false teachers. They claimed to have a higher/superior knowledge. Yet God alone provides a "true knowledge" (1:3, 8).

To truly be what God wants we need to *understand* what He wants. We study His Word, putting it in our minds and hearts (cf. Heb. 8:10). We then *apply* what His Word has taught us. If we don't, have we really learned?

4. Self-Control—describes one who has exercised power to discipline his mind and body. He controls it, not the other way around. Such a person is not free from desires and passions. However, they are under his control and so they become his servants, not his tyrants.

Our knowledge of God and His Word has taught us the importance of self-control. The self-discipline of the Christian must replace self-indulgence. Self-control is both the denial of fleshly lust, but also the practice of spiritual disciplines (like prayer, study, fasting). How are you doing?

5. Perseverance (steadfastness)—is a word often translated "patience." However, "patience" is too passive a word. This word does not mean to simply accept and endure. There is always a forward look that motivates one to be proactive in maintaining Christian faith. It is said of Jesus that He "endured" the cross. This word is the courageous acceptance of everything life can throw at us, and the transferring of even the worst event into another step toward Heaven.

God demands that we have a stick-to-it mentality. We are not wishy-washy, being strong one minute and weak the next. We have determined that we will endure. We will not give up—period.

6. Godliness (piety)—The godly person loves from a pure heart, has a sincere faith, and maintains a good conscience (1 Tim. 1:5). He has a dogged determination to "be conformed to the image of His Son (Rom. 8:29-30). He imitates Christ (1 Cor. 11:1), and demonstrates the holiness possessed by God (1 Pet. 1:13-18).

Godliness is a term that captures the essence of being a Christian. All that is good about Christianity is found in this word.

7. Brotherly Kindness—The city of Philadelphia gets its name from this Greek word. It means far more than "kindness" to others. It involves immersion into the fears, problems, and joys of our brethren. It includes "affection and compassion" (Phil. 2:1) and considering others more important than ourselves (Phil. 2:4-5).

This word requires each to exercise loving service to their brothers and sisters. It is an investment in their lives and cannot describe one who only sees a fellow Christian for a few hours every Sunday.

8. Love—*Agape* love is the highest form of love in the Greek NT. The one possessing this quality seeks the good and welfare of all—whether deserved or not. It includes all that we want God to be and to do for us: mercy, forgiving, caring, helping.

This word describes the most selfless kind of actions. It would describe a husband who stands between his wife and an attacker, a mother who reaches into a raging fire to rescue her child. It conquers fears to do the right thing.

▶8 ADVANTAGES & DISADVANTAGES: THE IMPORTANCE OF HAVING THE "CHRISTIAN GRACES" (2 PETER 1:8-9)

1. **Advantages (1:8)**
    - A. You are not useless
    - B. You are not unfruitful
    - C. You are demonstrating that you have the true knowledge of Jesus
2. **Disadvantages (1:9):**
    - A. You are blind
    - B. You are short-sighted
    - C. You have forgotten your purification from former sins

9 ▶ YOU WILL NEVER STUMBLE! CONSIDERING GOD'S DIVINE GUARANTEE (2 PETER 1:10)

A. Requires Diligence

1) The word describes concerted effort.

2) God does not force His desires on us. We can determine if we want it—or not.

B. Requires Making Certain About His Calling

1) In the Hebrew mind one who doesn't obey didn't really hear.

2) Equally those who do not obey the Gospel were not really called.

C. Requires Making Certain About His Choosing

1) God had predetermined to save anyone who would obey the Gospel (Rom. 8:29-30).

2) He did not determine one to be saved or lost but left that choice to each individual.

D. Requires Practicing These Things

1) The "these things" are the eight qualities listed in verses 5-7.

2) These eight are divine expectations. Every true Christian will have them; every true Christian will increase in them (v. 8).

Conclusion: When these four are applied, Peter says clearly: "You will never stumble." What Christian would not take advantage of this divine guarantee?

10 ▶ REVISITING THE TRANSFIGURATION OF JESUS (2 PETER 1:16-18)

Intro: The false teachers had worked hard to discredit Jesus ("denying the Master who bought them"—2:1) and His promise to come again (3:3-4). Peter intends to attack such falsehoods head on with his own experience—an experience that confirms beyond reasonable doubt the veracity of Jesus and His teachings. Note what Peter says about the Transfiguration:

1) What the Transfiguration Was Not

A) Cleverly devised (σοφίζω). This word means "to be skilled in formulating or creating something in an artful manner, frequently with implication of self-serving cleverness, reason out, concoct ingeniously/slyly or devise craftily" (Bauer 935).

B) Tales (μῦθος) means "tale, story, legend, myth" (Bauer 660).

C) Something "followed." This terminology is a slam on the false teachers, who are merely blind followers of earlier false teachers. The apostles were original in this experience. It wasn't created by someone else.

2) What the Transfiguration Was

A) A revealing of Jesus' "majesty" (μεγαλειότης). This word means "quality or state of being foremost in esteem, grandeur, sublimity, majesty" (Bauer 622).

B) An honoring of Jesus. Honor (τιμή) means "manifestation of esteem, honor, reverence" (Bauer 1005).

C) A glorifying of Jesus. Glory (δόξα) means "the condition of being bright or shining, brightness, splendor, radiance" (Bauer 257).

D) A confirming of Jesus. The voice from Heaven decreed that Jesus was God's Son.

3) What the Transfiguration Meant

A) Jesus has power (δύναμις), meaning that He has the "potential for functioning in some way, power, might, strength, force, capability" (Bauer 262).

B) Jesus is coming (παρουσία), which in this context means "of Christ, and nearly always of His Messianic Advent in glory to judge the world at the end of this age" (Bauer 781).

11 ▶ KNOW THIS ABOUT SCRIPTURE (2 PETER 1:19-21)

Intro: From the beginning Satan has worked to create doubt in God's Word. Since God's Word is truth (John 17:17), Satan is left with no other alternative but to foster lies (John 8:44). Sadly, the vehicle used by Satan are men. These men disguise themselves as "apostles of Christ" (2 Cor. 11:13-15). They claim to be speaking for God (Jer. 14:14) and to be inspired of the Holy Spirit (1 Tim. 4:1-2; 1 John 4:1).

1. It is deserving of special attention (v. 19)

A) It originates from the "Majestic Glory."

B) It stands in clear contrast to the destructive heresies of the false teachers.

C) It is the difference between light and darkness. When in a dark place, the one light that exists should receive welcome attention. So also in this world of darkness (ignorance) should men pay attention to the light (truth).

2. It is not from one's own interpretation (v. 20)

A) It was not originally from God but then twisted through the creative interpretations of man.

B) It is not something that is dependent upon the interpretative skills of man.

3. It was never made by an act of human will

A) Men have always longed to receive visions and to have dreams.

B) God's prophetic activity was not in response to what man desired.

4. Its origin was from men moved by the Holy Spirit

A) It was not men moving themselves, nor did they anticipate a divine message.

B) The Holy Spirit, the giver of truth (cf. John 15:26; 16:13) is the source (not man).

5. It's from God

A) When the Holy Spirit provides a message, it is ultimately from God Himself.

B) It must not be confused with, or compared to, human messages.

12. INTERPRETATIONS (1 PETER 1:19)

Intro: Peter claims that prophecy is not a matter of one's own interpretation. This statement has been interpreted as follows:

1. Catholic Interpretation

A) "Since every part of Scripture was written by the Holy Spirit inspiring men, and declared as such by the church, the church also is its interpreter in that God has promised to guide the church into all truth until the end of the world. Therefore…we submit to the judgment of the church and not depend on our own fallible and erroneous judgment" (Rheims-Douay comment on 1 Pet. 1:19).

B) The word church in Roman Catholic terminology does not here have reference to the members of that organization or even to the priests or bishops. It refers to the most holy see, the Pope himself. When he speaks "ex cathedra," he is speaking as if it were Christ Himself speaking.

C) Therefore, mankind should not trust the meaning they might place on Scripture.

2. Lutheran Interpretation

A) No one can explain prophecy by his own mental power, as it is not a matter of subjective interpretation. To explain it, one needs the same illumination of the Holy Spirit in which it originated.

B) The idea is that divine assistance is needed. Therefore, several translators have "that no prophecy of Scripture can be understood through one's own powers."

C) This is not talking about something miraculous happening when the Bible is read.

3. Logical Interpretation

A) No prophecy exists or came as a result of one's private or personal thinking. The purpose of the phrase (v. 20) is not primarily to the receiver of prophecy (you and me), but to the writer or speakers—the prophets themselves.

B) This then is explained by verse 21.

C) The prophets were conduits, not creators or filters.

2 PETER 2

13 ▸ THE FALSE TEACHERS OF 2 PETER

Intro: The early church faced numerous challenges. Foremost was the insidious influence of false teachers. This book provides a good look into the work, character, and doctrines of these false teachers.

1. They arose from among the people (2:1).
2. They were enticing many away from the faith (2:18-19; 3:17; cf. Jude 4, 12).
3. They denied the Lord who bought them (2:1; cf. Jude 4).
4. They discredited the Law of God (2:2, 10; cf. Jude 4, 12).
5. They were motivated by personal gain (2:3, 12, 14, 15, 18; cf. Jude 16).
6. They were not afraid to discredit others while lifting up themselves (2:1, 2, 10; cf. Jude 8, 19).
7. They scoffed at the Parousia (which was, in fact, the very basis of all their other sins—3:3-4).

Conclusion: Peter leaves no doubt how he feels about these false teachers: "But these, like unreasoning animals, born as creatures of instinct to be captured and killed, reviling where they have no knowledge, will in the destruction of those creatures also be destroyed" (2:12).

14 ▸ THE POSSIBILITY OF APOSTASY: A STUDY OF 2 PETER 2

Intro: There are numerous religious groups who promote the doctrine of "once saved, always saved." This doctrine cannot survive when compared to the clear teachings of this chapter. Consider the points that show that one can, in fact, be lost after previously being saved.

1. Had once been bought by the master (v. 1) but now face destruction (vv. 1, 3)
2. Had escaped the defilements of the world (v. 20)
3. Are "again" entangled (v. 20)
4. "Last state" worse for them than the first (v. 20)
5. Had known the way of righteousness but turned away from the holy commandment delivered to them (v. 21)
6. Are examples of the Proverb:
    = A dog returns to its own vomit
    = A sow, after washing, returns to walling in the mire
    *If he is not saying that they were once cleansed from something bad, what is he saying?

15. GOD KNOWS: A STUDY OF GOD'S PLANS FOR THE RIGHTEOUS AND WICKED (2 PETER 2:4-9)

Intro: The false teachers described in 2:1-3 might believe they escaped the punishment of God. Such foolishness will now be exposed in a carefully constructed section. Peter will provide three examples that all back up his major declaration in verse 9. Each of these examples are powerful proofs that support the claim of verse 3—"Their judgment from long ago is not idle and their destruction is not asleep." History proves Peter's point!

Event	Result	OT Text
#1—Angels who sinned (v. 4)	Cast into Hell	Genesis 6?
#2—Ancient world (v. 5a)	Not spared	Genesis 6 *Rescue #1—Noah (v. 5b)
#3—Sodom & Gomorrah (v. 6)	Condemned	Genesis 19 *Rescue #2—Lot (vv. 7-8)

Conclusion: These examples provide sufficient proof of verse 9: "Then the Lord knows how to rescue the godly from temptation, and to keep the unrighteous under punishment for the day of judgment."

16. GOD KNOWS—PART TWO: CLEAR PROOF OF THAT CLAIM (2 PETER 2:4-9).

Intro: Peter's thesis statement in 2:9 is that "God knows" how to rescue the godly…and how to keep the unrighteous under punishment." A look at the verbs used in this section clearly prove that claim! Most of these are participles, with a few aorist active verbs thrown in. All of them describe what God did:

1) Did not spare—angels (v. 4)
2) Cast them—into Hell
3) Handed over for judgment
4) Committed them—to pits of darkness
5) Did not spare—ancient world (v. 5)
6) Preserved (watched over) Noah (v. 5)
7) Brought—flood
8) Burned to ashes—condemned cities (v. 6)
9) Gave judgment against (v. 6)
10) Made example (v. 6)
11) Summary/Thesis Statement: **The Lord knows how to "rescue" (ῥύομαι) and to "keep" (τηρέω) and to "punish" (κολάζω).**

Conclusion: No man has either the knowledge or the power to do any of these. Only the omniscient and omnipotent God does!

17 NOAH AND LOT: RIGHTEOUS IN AN UNRIGHTEOUS WORLD. A STUDY OF 2 PETER 2:4-9

Intro: Consider for a moment what the Old Testament reveals about the wicked world during the times of Noah and Lot. With Noah, every thought of man was only on evil. It was so bad that God regretted making man (Gen. 6:5-6). Lot lived in one of the most evil cities in the history of mankind—Sodom. This city was so filled with immorality that when heavenly visitors stayed with Lot, men of the city from every quarter—both young and old—surrounded Lot's house and demanded Lot surrender his guests so that they might have sexual relations with them (Gen. 19:5). Because of this wickedness God "rained brimstone and fire" on it (and the other cities in the area), completely destroying everything. Yet Noah and Lot survived. How were they able to remain righteous during such wicked times? This text provides the answers.

1) Noah

A. Peter says that Noah was "righteous." As a matter of fact, he was a "preacher" (proclaimer of righteousness (2:5). This word describes one who determines to do what is right according to God's standards. They know God's law and are determined to follow it.

B. Genesis 6:9 says that "Noah was a righteous man, blameless in his time; Noah walked with God." This wasn't because Noah was better than everyone else. He simply made better choices.

Application:

We are called to be righteous and godly (1:3, 6; 3:11, 14). If such was unattainable, would God command it?

2) Lot

A. Peter also assigns the designation "righteous" to Lot (2:7, 8[2]).

B. He was "oppressed by the sensual conduct of unprincipled men" (2:7).

C. He was "tormented day after day with their lawless deeds."

Application:

Does our evil world bother us? Are we "tormented" when we see such open defiance of God and His Word, ridicule of Christians and of the church, and mockery of spiritual things?

Conclusion: Although Peter is focusing on the future blessedness that will result from godliness, he does not neglect its rewards in the present. When one remains true to God in this life, he will, like Lot and Noah, receive God's loving protection. This point would be comforting to the readers who are faced with the onslaught of the false teachers (2:1-3, 13, 18-22). Through the words of 2 Peter, they have the assurance that God is always mindful of their plight and has every intention of being a help in time of need (cf. 1:3-4; 2:9).

2 PETER 3

18. THE DELAY OF THE PAROUSIA: A STUDY OF 2 PETER 3

Intro: These early Christians were dealing with a serious threat from the false teachers. These false teachers, motivated by lust, had produced a convincing view that there was no judgment day. Jesus, they claimed, was not coming back. Therefore, why not party on and enjoy all of the pleasures of life? We will consider this in two parts: the claim of the false teachers and then the apostle's response.

1. Arguments of the False Teachers
    A. The long length of time since the promise was made
    B. The apparent stability of the universe

2. Peter's Response (vv. 4-9)
    A. Deals with 2nd argument first:
        It escapes their notice that…
        1) By the Word of God the universe was created
        2) By the Word of God the world was flooded
        3) That same Word has the present heavens and earth reserved for fire
    B. 2nd argument addressed (vv. 8-9)
        1) God does not operate in time, so it has not been long to Him
        2) There is a reason for the "delay"—God is giving men time to repent

19. THE DAY OF THE LORD (2 PETER 3:10)

Intro: The false teachers of 2 Peter have overtly denied that a day of judgment will occur. Their confidence in this has motivated them to a life of greed and sensuality. It might be said that now is "their day." However, there is coming another day, the "day of the Lord." This will be a day when all other days cease. It will be that which ushers in eternity, when time will be no more. Peter makes several important observations about that day:

1. It will come like a thief.

    A. Isn't it amazing that so many religious groups continue to make end-time predictions? Yet thieves do not announce their plans, neither does the God of the universe.

    B. Jesus taught clearly that no one—not even Him—knows when this day will be (Matt. 24:36). So why are there people today who assert they can figure it out when even Jesus Himself didn't know? Jesus even said that the Day would come like a thief! (Matt. 24:43-44).

    C. However, the Bible teaches that God has "fixed a day" (Acts 17:30, 31). God knows when that day will come; He set the time. It is assured!

2. The heavens will pass away with a roar.

    A. Ever heard the sound of a tornado? Some have described it as a train rushing past. Others have said it is a unique sound with horrific sounds of mighty winds.

    B. The word *roar* here is describing something that has swooshing sound that would indicate things falling apart—or being ripped apart.

3. The elements will be destroyed with intense heat.

    A. The word used here (*stoicheion*, στοιχεῖον) is a complex word that has a variety of meanings. However, its basic definition has to do with the principle parts of something.

    B. Whatever "principle parts" Peter has in mind is—in the long run—not significant. The overall truth remains the same. God is going to dismantle the universe piece by piece and then consume it all in a fiery conflagration.

    C. Intense heat describes a fire so powerful and strong that there are no elements that can withstand it. It will burn everything (literally!) up.

    D. Sort of puts things in perspective, doesn't it? My house? Car? Bank Account? Gone in flames—all of it. Maybe a better (wiser) plan would be to store up my treasure in heaven (cf. Matt. 6:19-21).

4. The earth and its works will be burned up.

    A. The better reading instead of "burned up" is "discovered."

    B. This word can be understood in a judicial sense. God, as the one and only Judge (cf. James 4:11), sees all and is in control of all.

    C. The Bible talks about nothing being hidden from God (cf. Heb. 4:13; cf. Ps. 33:13-15). God is well aware of everything that has ever been done, built, hidden, or said.

Conclusion: How can God say this more clearly? God will judge, and God will destroy. Therefore, to believe otherwise is foolishness! Our love, our hope, and our treasure must not be on this earth! What a great lesson on priorities!

20 ▶ THE NEW HEAVENS AND NEW EARTH (3:13): MOTIFS CONNECTED WITH THIS GREAT TEACHING

1. The present creation is ruled by the ungodly who are motivated by lust.
   1:4; 2:1-3, 10-12; 3:10-13, 16
2. Man alone is unable to correct the evil world and restore it to righteousness.
   1:4; 2:9; 3:5-7, 10-13, 15
3. The dominance of sin on the earth has led men to doubt the power and eventual Parousia of God.
   1:16; 2:9, 19; 3:3-5, 10-13, 16-17
4. God will punish the wicked at a designated time in the future. This event is called the Parousia, the "day of the Lord," and the "day of God."
   1:19; 2:3-9, 10, 12
5. Because of the wickedness of creation, it will be destroyed in a fiery cataclysm.
   3:7, 10-12
6. In the place of the old creation, God will create a "new heavens and a new earth."
   1:11; 3:13
7. The new abode for men, called the "new heavens and new earth," will only be for those who are righteous.
   1:4; 3:13-14

21 ▶ WHAT KIND OF PERSON ARE YOU? AN EXPOSITION OF 2 PETER 3:11-15

Intro: The false teachers made a serious doctrinal mistake (there will be no judgment day), that then leads to a serious moral mistake (live according to their lusts). Peter has corrected the doctrinal mistake (there will be a judgment day), and now makes a moral appeal. That moral appeal is a beautifully crafted exhortation for all Christians. It describes what kind of people we "ought" to be (v. 11).

1. **Christians have holy conduct (v. 11).**
   A. God calls us to separate ourselves from the world—from her morality (or lack thereof), her vain philosophies, etc. (cf. Rom. 12:1-2). This separation is the core of "holiness."
   B. To separate ourselves from the world also requires us to join ourselves to our Heavenly Father. We want to be holy like He is holy (1 Pet. 1:13-22).
   C. Holiness is not just a mental state; it is a lived state. Peter says we must have holy "conduct." This means more than Sunday only. The true Christian is holy 24/7.
   D. Conduct describes how we act, how we speak—our daily behavior. In view of the coming judgment, Christians are going to act appropriately and imitate their Savior (cf. Rom. 8:29-30).

Sermon Seeds

2. **Christians are godly (v. 11).**
   A. This amazing Bible word captures the desire of the Christian to be like the God they love and serve.
   B. In 1 Timothy, Paul emphasized this idea of godliness. In 1:5 he gives what could be described as the clearest, most concise definition of godliness. Any person who has those three attributes can accurately be called "godly."
   C. This attribute stands in stark contrast with the false teachers of 2 Peter. These men don't imitate Christ; they deny Him (2:1). They're not interested in being "pure" or having a "good conscience," but are characterized by sensuality and greed (2:2-3).

3. **Christians look for and desire the Second Coming (v. 12).**
   A. It is foolish to "look for" something that isn't going to come. It is wise to look for that which is guaranteed and assured!
      1. The idea of "looking for" doesn't mean that we're standing outside our houses looking at the sky…waiting.
      2. To "look for" something means that you are continually aware of its eventual coming. Christians are known to think "today could be the day!"
      3. To "look for" also includes the idea of preparation. The foolish slave conducted himself wickedly because he wasn't "looking for" his master's return.
   B. Christians also "desire" the Second Coming.
      1. One does not desire what he or she fears!
      2. When you live your life faithfully, you can't wait for Jesus to return. That day is what you've been excited about since you became a Christian.

4. **Christians look for the new heavens and new earth (v. 13).**
   A. The word "looking" is a present active participle (from προσδοκάω). This means that we continually look for and anticipate the coming of the new heavens and new earth.
   B. If we're looking for something, it means we think about it—a lot! And, if we think about it a lot, then it impacts who we are. It changes us and motivates us to be the kind of people that please God.

5. **Christians are diligent (v. 14).**
   A. Diligent to be found by Him in peace
      1. Based on God's justification, we have peace with God (Rom. 5:1-2).
      2. That peace only comes from Jesus (John 14:27).
   B. Diligent to be found by Him spotless
      1. Since all have sinned, the spotlessness can only come through the blood of Christ.
      2. Christ died for the church that she "have no spot or wrinkles" (Eph. 5:27).
   C. Diligent to be found by Him blameless
      1. Thanks to the sacrifice of Christ, the church can be blameless (Eph. 5:27).
      2. We are able to stand before God with no sins charged to our ledger.

6. **Christians regard His patience to be salvation (v. 15).**
   A. Peter had claimed in verse 9 that the reason for the delay in the Parousia was God's patience. He was giving men time to repent.
   B. If God had not waited, given you time to get your life right, would you have been lost? Such is true with many people. Therefore we should regard His patience as the only reason we have found "salvation."

22 ▶ THE FORMATION OF THE N.T. CANON (2 PETER 3:16)

Intro: How did the 27 books of the NT come together? Bible critics argue that this took place over a long period of time and was ultimately decided by 4th century Catholic councils. This passage, however, contributes much to this discussion. Note the following:

1. Paul is credited with being a writer, and even wrote "letters" (plural).

A. This shows that Paul's writings were known and recognized when 2 Peter was written.

B. If 2 Peter was written in 68 A.D., then Paul's writings were known early.

2. Paul is inspired ("wisdom given to him") and his writings were considered "Scripture."

A. This shows that Paul's writings were immediately recognized, because Paul was recognized as a genuine apostle of Christ.

B. "Scripture" (*graphe*) is a specific word that only applies to inspired writings (2 Tim. 3:16).

C. This shows that Paul's letters, written just a decade or less before 2 Peter, were already recognized as inspired writings and were already accepted by the church.

3. Peter refers to "the rest of the Scriptures."

A. This shows that at the time of 2 Peter, other NT books were circulating and recognized.

B. This adds more support to the argument that the NT books were recognized immediately.

C. This also shows that these books became a part of the canon well before there were any Catholic councils and votes.

Conclusion: The evidence supports that a majority of the NT canon was already collected and recognized by the end of the 1st century. This verse contributes considerably to our understanding of the process.

JUDE

23. MERCY, PEACE, AND LOVE (JUDE 2)

Intro: In a world filled with corruption and immorality, if you had to pick three gifts from God, what would it be? Perhaps this verse provides an answer.

A. Mercy
1. While this word can include forgiveness, it does not mean only forgiveness. Jesus talked about "giving alms" whereas the word *alms* is from the same root as *mercy*. The word can include any act of kindness, gift, or sacrifice made for another.
2. To receive God's mercy is to "catch a break." It involves receiving help in time of need; God's favor or blessings when we need them the most.

B. Peace
1. As Satan continues to infiltrate the world with evil men (cf. 1 John 5:19), Christian's righteous souls are tormented daily (cf. 2 Pet. 2:8). The wickedness makes it difficult to find "a state of well-being."
2. Jesus provides a peace that the world cannot (John 14:27). God gives us peace (Rom. 5:1-4), which surpasses all understanding (Phil. 4:6).

C. Love
1. This *agape* love describes the great extent God will go to be with us, bless us, and forgive us. The ultimate demonstration of His love is found in the sending of His Son (John 3:16). Paul says, "*But God demonstrates His own love toward us, in that while we were yet sinners, Christ died for us*" (Rom. 5:8).
2. It is important to see how God loves the unlovable. As we have defied Him, disobeyed Him, and ignored Him, His love remains steadfast. This is what encourages us to return to Him. We know that our Father will still be waiting to welcome us home, even when we were prodigal sons.

Conclusion: Jude wishes for these three gifts to "*be multiplied*." God who has an endless supply of all three is ready and willing to bestow them on His children.

24. IMPORTANT LESSONS ABOUT THE FAITH (JUDE 3)

Intro: Jude decided he needed to change course and write about something different than he had originally intended. Now his focus is on "the faith." There are several significant truths found in this important verse.

A. It Is All About "the Faith"

1. The Greek is interesting here. It literally reads: τῇ ἅπαξ παραδοθείσῃ τοῖς ἁγίοις πίστει– "the once for all time delivered to the saints faith." Or we might write it like this: "the once-for-all-time-delivered-to-the-saints faith." This curious structure adds extra emphasis to his point about the faith.
2. Most translations go ahead and bring the definite article with its noun: "the faith."
3. When Bible writers refer to "the" faith, they typically have in mind the body of doctrine. Such is the case here. This is a verse about the Bible and how God's people need to rise up and fight for the Bible.

B. We Must "Contend Earnestly" for the Faith

1. ἐπαγωνίζομαι (epagōnizomai)—a great struggle
    a) Not necessary if it is insignificant
    b) Not needed if the enemy is weak and easily defeated
2. It is not tomorrow's fight; it is not someone else's fight
3. The Gospel is being attacked, and it is God's plan that His people rise up to defend it
4. "The struggle Jude has in mind is the preservation of the received faith over against the theological/moral novelty of the heretics (v. 3b–4), the growth in that faith and the avoidance of error (vv. 20–21), and the rescue of those who have been drawn into the errorists' snare (vv. 22–23). Jude's call pertains to both the doctrinal and moral issues raised by the heretics" (Green 56).

C. The Faith Was "Once for All Delivered"

1. The Greek literally means "once for all time."
2. For 2,000 years men have ventured to add, adjust, and take away from God's holy Word. Such is against God's will and is an insult to Him.
3. We have all that we need in the Bible. Period. That automatically eliminates any other "holy" book (Quran, Book of Mormon, etc.). See 2 Peter 1:3—we have "everything" we need.
4. It was delivered (past tense). God did His part, and He isn't going to do it again.

D. The Faith Was Delivered "to the Saints"

1. "Saints" = Christians. Yet is used because it describes Christians who are separated from the world, holy, beloved in the eyes of God.

Sermon Seeds

   a) They became saints when they obeyed the Gospel (cf. Acts 2:40, 47).

   b) They remain saints by being faithful to the Gospel (cf. Gal. 1:6-9).

2. God delivered the message. He placed it in the hands of His children (saints). Will they be faithful to this divine trust and fight for it?

Conclusion: "Outsiders have come among the congregation, promoting an altered doctrine of grace that promotes sexual vice and that, in the end, is a denial of the authority of Christ. Jude urgently calls his readers to take action and enter into the struggle against their teaching, standing by the sacred tradition that was handed down to them and the rest of the people of God. Jude's disclosure of his intent identifies this as a paraenetic letter that calls for action. His goal is not merely to inform but also to exhort his readers to enter into the struggle for the faith against its detractors" (Green 52).

25 ONCE FOR ALL DELIVERED? (JUDE 3) THE RAMIFICATIONS OF THIS STATEMENT

Intro: Jude's statement that the faith (the Gospel) was *"once for all delivered"* is a powerful and relevant statement for today. Consider:

1) The Gospel was given once

   A. It is/was not something that was going to be given again.

   B. If men let it die, God will not send Jesus to preach it again.

2) The Gospel was given for all

   A. The Great Commission is to take it into "all" the world (Matt. 28:18-20) and give it to every person (Mark 16:15-16).

   B. God did not design a different message for different groups, nations, races. He didn't create a separate doctrine for Muslims, another for Jews, another for Mormons, etc.

3) The Gospel was given once for all time

   A. There was no plan, no thought of later revelations. No coming revisions, no new inspired messages (thus no need for modern day "apostles" and "prophets").

   B. The power of the Gospel is found in its timelessness. It is as powerful and as relevant today (2000 years later!) than it was on day one.

Conclusion: Our lives are centered around God and His one—and only one—revelation. It is our devotion to His Word that has saved us, defines us, and motivates us.

26. GOD'S GREAT LESSONS OF JUDGMENT (JUDE 5-7)

Intro: The Old Testament is filled with stories of God's judgment. Each of those provide valuable insight to how He judges, and why He judges. Among those many judgment texts, Jude finds three that especially fit his overall purpose—to show how the false teachers are on a dangerous path—one that will lead to God's condemnation and eternal punishment.

1. Example #1: The Rebellious Israelites (v. 5)

A. Much could (and should) be said about all of the blessings God bestowed on them. They were witnesses of His great power over Egypt and in many ways in the wilderness.

B. Despite those blessings, they "did not believe." God's promises to protect them and bring them into the Promised Land were rejected.

C. God "saved them out of the land of Egypt" but wasn't going to do it again. Their unbelieving heart—despite all that He did for them—was their undoing.

D. Result: God "subsequently destroyed those who did not believe."

2. Example #2: The Sinning Angels (v. 6)

A. Much could (and should) be said about the favored position given to angels. They were witnesses to God's creative acts. They did not have to operate by faith—they had sight. They had seen God with their own eyes; they had witnessed His mighty power.

B. Their favored position, however, was abused. God had entrusted them with a home and authority. They had a job to do, assigned by God Himself.

C. In sheer foolishness, they did not keep their own domain (their area of work) and abandoned their proper abode (where God assigned them to dwell).

D. Result: They are kept in "eternal bonds," "in darkness," and kept "for the judgment of the great day."

3. Example #3: Sodom and Gomorrah (v. 7)

A. These ancient cities were located in a beautiful part of Israel. They were the home of a righteous man named Lot (2 Pet. 2:6ff).

B. Their favored position, however, did not keep them faithful to God. Instead, they "indulged in gross immorality" and "went after strange flesh."

C. Result: They are "undergoing the punishment of eternal fire."

Conclusion: These three powerful examples should be for us—well—examples! They should teach us that defying God will bring His wrath. No one who lives in rebellion and sin will escape. That includes us, that includes all of humanity. Jude says these are "reminders." Indeed, good and valuable reminders—for them and for us.

27 ▶ KEEP YOURSELF! (JUDE 20-21)

Intro: While some in the religious world embrace the doctrine of "once saved, always saved," the New Testament is filled with admonitions for Christians to take steps that ensure they stay on the right path. Salvation is not assured; it can be lost (cf. Gal. 5:4). Jude is dealing with false teachers who are having a great (negative) impact on the church. Jude admonishes them to guard their own faith. We equally need this admonition! Notice the one command, followed by three present participles that describe how one can obey the command.

The Command: Keep Yourself!—Jude here provides a powerful imperative. It comes from the word τηρέω. It involves active, *dedicated involvement*. One does not stay strong or stay faithful accidentally. It happens by design! Each of us must ask ourselves, "What am I doing—right now and every day—to ensure that I grow and stay faithful?" Jesus told a parable about ten virgins, five of which didn't prepare themselves for the long haul. As a result, they were not ready when the bridegroom came (Matt. 25:1ff).

How one obeys the command:

A. Build yourselves up—The Second Law of Thermodynamics states that things left to themselves will go from order to disorder; from being valuable to being worthless. Christians must maintain an active lifestyle that builds, repairs and strengthens themselves. It isn't going to just happen. Only fools believe that. Faithful attendance, Christian deeds, Bible study, prayer, and being actively engaged in helping others is the pathway to faithfulness (cf. 2 Pet. 1:5-10). Work on the fruit of the Spirit (Gal. 5:22-23), put on the full armor of God (Eph. 6:10-18). Did you notice that "Bible study" was in that list? That is because Jude said to build yourself up in **the most holy faith.** That means the Bible. There is no encouragement greater than that which comes from the Bible. You cannot find a better way to encourage others then with the work of God.

B. Praying—I once had a very well-known preacher tell me, "My prayer life is non-existent." He devoted his life to preaching to others, but his personal relationship with God was bankrupt. If we are to successfully keep ourselves in the love of God, we are going to pray—short prayers like Nehemiah, long prayers like Jesus (John 17). If I never spoke to my wife, she would question my love and devotion to her. If I never spoke to my God, He would question my love and devotion to Him.

C. Anxious Awaiting—When you're excited about something, you can't wait for it to get here. Time can't pass fast enough. Christians are those who are excited about the certain return of Jesus. They think about it, dream about it, long for it to come. They are not so in love with this world and the things of the world that they have lost their focus and priorities (1 John 2:15-17). They're waiting for the mercy of Jesus. They know they don't deserve it (nobody does), but He is willing to give it to those who have denied ungodliness and worldly desires (Tit. 2:11-14; 3:4-7).

Conclusion: Jude wraps this up by saying it is *"to eternal life."* Our ultimate goal is to make it to heaven. These three admonitions are providing a way that we can do that and to hear the words of our Master say, "Well done, thou good and faithful servant!"

28. IMPACTING THE LIVES OF OTHERS CHRISTIANITY IN ACTION (JUDE 22-23)

Intro: The false teachers have had a powerful, but negative influence on the church. Some are hurting, some doubting. Souls are at stake, and God's children are called to action to impact the lives of those who have been damaged. Jude gives three commands to the Christian. All of these would be examples of "building up" that he told them to do earlier.

A. Be Merciful!

1. Life is tough, and people need help. They sometimes need someone to show some pity, some compassion, some understanding.
2. Mercy can be anything – providing some money or food. It could be giving them a break from their kids with a night out. It could be providing a shoulder to cry on.
3. Jude provides an example. To show mercy to those who are "doubting." There may be a time for reproving and rebuking, but there is also a time to "cut them a break" and show some mercy. Try to find out what are the sources of their doubt. Listen first.

B. Save!

1. Our ultimate goal, and the ultimate goal of the church is to save souls. We can be distracted with dozens of programs that have no direct or indirect bearing on the salvation of others.
2. Christians recognize that Satan is powerful and his temptations ensnaring. This is why they need to receive a break and obtain some loving compassion and understanding from other Christians.
3. They are "snatching them from the fire." What a vivid (and frightening) picture! They are on the brink of eternal condemnation, but God's people rescues them from this most terrible fate.
4. "The image suggests that some have nearly been seduced by the false teachers. And yet there is still hope that they can be reclaimed, rescued from the judgment to come and restored to a right relationship with God." (Schreiner 488).

C. Be Merciful! (repeated!)

1. There is another group that needs mercy: those deeply entrenched in sin. These are those who have their garments "polluted with sin." Christians can show them the wonderful forgiving nature of God, who is willing to save even the "chief of sinners" (1 Timothy 1:13-17).
2. Mercy does not here mean to forgive without repentance. It does, however, meaning a willingness to be kind and gentle to those who eventually repent. They need to feel the mercy of the Christian community.
3. Sometimes we have allowed the Catholic doctrine of penance creep into the church. When someone sins, they "need to pay." And sometimes, what they have done in repentance is not good enough. We want a 'pound of flesh.' When someone returns to God, the church should be welcoming and supportive (cf. 2 Corinthians 2:1-15).

Conclusion: When these three commands are applied, the church will grow in unity, and will move toward being the pure church that Jesus wants (Ephesians 5:25-27).

29 GOD'S POWER A CONSIDERATION OF WHAT GOD DOES FOR US (JUDE 24-25)

Intro: Christians have their work cut out for them. The forces of Satan are formidable (Eph. 6:11-12). The whole world lies in his power (1 John 5:19). How can we possibly succeed? The answer is found in great texts like this one. Jude intends to discuss not the power of Satan, but the power of God that is for us. Notice what that power does for us. These points are found in two aorist active infinitives.

A. God Is Able "To Keep"

1. He will not do this in a miraculous way and will not force His will over ours. He "keeps" us when we put forth the effort to put on His armor (Eph. 6:10-18).
2. The word keep is a word that describes God's protective care. Satan wants to destroy; God wants to protect (1 Cor. 10:13)
3. "In Jude, falling may have the general meaning of being defeated by any problem or difficulty, or of giving in to sin. But perhaps here it focuses on the particular meaning of a person losing faith and ceasing to be a follower of Christ, together with the consequences of receiving judgment. This of course happens if Jude's readers rely on their own strength in dealing with the godless. But in the end, it is God who will give them victory over these people and their false teachings" (Arichea and Hatton 59).

B. God Is Able "To Make You Stand"

1. When we live in sin, we have fallen and are not worthy to stand before the glorious presence of God (Isa. 59:1, 2).
2. We are going to stand "blameless." This word originally was applied to animals that had no defect and were therefore fit for sacrifice. It is the word that describes Jesus in 1 Peter 1:19.

30 KNOWING GOD: JUDE'S AMAZING DESCRIPTION OF GOD (JUDE 25)

1. He is the only God
2. He is our Savior
3. He is honored through Jesus Christ our Lord
4. He has glory
5. He has majesty
6. He has dominion
7. He has authority

These qualities are His. They have been (before all time), they are now (and now), and will be for time eternal in the future (and forever).

Authors

DENNY PETRILLO

Denny is married to the former Kathy Roberts. They have been married since January 1978. They have three children (Lance, Brett, and Laura), and six grandchildren (Chloe, Ashlyn, Sophie, Easton, Brelyn, and Kyson). He has served as the President of the Bear Valley Bible Institute since 2004 and has been a full-time instructor since 1985. He has preached in Mississippi, Arkansas, Nebraska, and Colorado. He has taught numerous classes for the World Video Bible School and has authored several books and commentaries. He graduated from the Bear Valley School of Preaching (now the Bear Valley Bible Institute), received an AA degree in Bible (York College), BA in Bible and Biblical Languages (Harding University), MA in Old and New Testaments (Harding Graduate School of Religion), and a Ph.D. in Religious Education (University of Nebraska).

JOE WELLS

Joe Wells holds an earned B.S. degree in Science along with a completion certificate from the Nashville School of Preaching and Biblical Studies and a Masters of Ministry degree from Freed Hardeman University. Joe travels the country as a frequent speaker for youth and family events, men's days, as well as Gospel meetings. He is the co-founder of Kaio Publications, publishers of the Family Devotional series as well as the Finer Grounds Bible Study series for women. Joe is also the author of the book Complete: Becoming the Man God Purposes You to Be and Game Plan: Developing a Spiritually Winning Strategy for Adults and Teens in Today's Culture. Along with this, he and Erin are the co-host of The Hey Joe Show, a podcast designed to challenge and strengthen families and teens across America. Joe has served God in a public way since 2000 in the capacity of youth minister and Gospel preacher, helping people make the connection with the Word of God and encouraging them to be transformed for Christ. He is blessed to the husband to the former Erin O'Hara, and they are the proud parents of four beautiful children: Colton, Michala, Camden, and Bennett.

GARRETT BERNETHY

Garrett married his wife, Cristen, in December of 2005, and they have four wonderful boys. Their son, Parker, is married to his beautiful wife, Claire, and they have a daughter, Taytum. Their other sons are Cohen, Ryder, and Kamden. Garrett has directed and participated in many camps, retreats, conferences, and workshops and serves on the national staff for Lads to Leaders. He is the president of Excel Still More and an annual writer and instructor for ESM. Garrett currently serves as the pulpit minister for the Hydro church of Christ in Hydro, Oklahoma, where he and his family reside.

BILLY CLABAUGH

Billy, his wife Shayla, and their son Caleb live in Sayre, Oklahoma, where he has been blessed to preach since 2012. He has a bachelor's degree in Math Education from Oklahoma Christian University and a master's degree in Sports Administration from Eastern New Mexico University. He enjoys reading, watching the Oklahoma Sooners, spending time with his family, and serving in the Kingdom of God. Billy also serves on the board of directors for Excel Still More and is a regular speaker and writer for the workshop and other publications.

MICHAEL HITE

Michael Hite joined the staff of the Bear Valley Bible Institute in 2002 where he now serves as a teacher and the Vice President of Operations. He currently teaches exegetical textual courses on the Gospel of Mark, the Gospel of Luke, and the General Epistles as well as specialized courses on research, teaching, and the use technology in ministry. Michael has particular expertise in exegesis and the use of Logos Bible Software. He has done short-term mission work and teaching in different countries around the world. He and his wife Lynn married in 1987 and they have two grown children—Melissa (who is married and living in Little Rock, AR), and Matthew (who is also married and a youth minister in Houston, TX). He and his wife Lynn are also the proud grandparents of Kaylynn Rey who was born to Matthew and his wife Haley in 2022.

www.ingramcontent.com/pod-product-compliance
Lightning Source LLC
Chambersburg PA
CBHW081441070526
44586CB00019B/2187